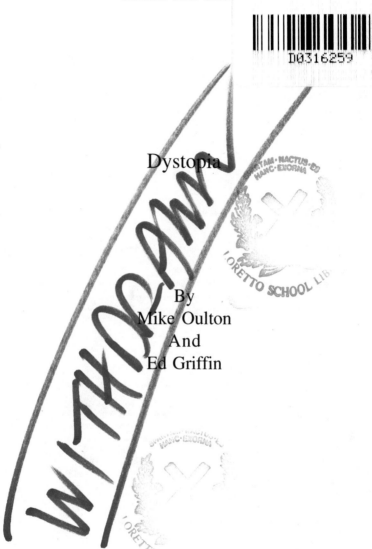

Dystopia

By
Mike Oulton
And
Ed Griffin

 www.trafford.com

North America & international
toll-free: 1 888 232 4444 (USA & Canada)
phone: 250 383 6864 ♦ fax: 250 383 6804 ♦ email: info@trafford.com

The United Kingdom & Europe
phone: +44 (0)1865 722 113 ♦ local rate: 0845 230 9601
facsimile: +44 (0)1865 722 868 ♦ email: info.uk@trafford.com

10 9 8 7 6 5 4 3 2 1

Dystopia is a society of human misery, squalor, disease, terror and overcrowding. It is the opposite of Utopia.

This book is dedicated
to the men and women who live in Dystopia

Acknowledgements:
Photograph of Ed Griffin by Brian Howell in Vancouver
Magazine
Cover Art by Vincent Bergeron
Copy edit by K. Bergeron

Dystopia

This is a book about going to prison. Mike Oulton went to prison for trying to smuggle fifteen kilos of cocaine into the United States. Ed Griffin went to prison to cause a revolution. He wanted men to write their stories and when the public discovered the horror of prison, the walls would come tumbling down.

Mike counts the years and the days until he can get back on the street; Ed numbers the converts to his revolution. One day they meet in a classroom and neither is the same again.

Book one introduces the main characters, Mike and Ed. Book Two reveals what happened to Mike after his arrest in Mexico. Book Three portrays Ed crusading against the massive prison system in the States. In Book Four the two men meet in a creative writing class in Canada. Book Five tells the story of challenge and change.

Dystopia

Book One

Chapter One
Ed
The Idealist

May 19, 1962.

Laying face down on the floor of St. John's Cathedral in Cleveland, Ohio, I waited to be ordained a Roman Catholic priest. Somewhere behind me in the big cathedral, my mother knelt in prayer. She was happy and proud – her son was becoming a priest.

I thought about my dad in heaven, dead six years. He was proud of me, too. He himself was in the seminary for a few years. I didn't think it then, but maybe I was fulfilling his life.

I was going to be a good priest to help people. My mom and dad had donated many hours to young people in the parish and I learned from them. I'd been a model seminarian, trusted by church authorities, conservative in my views. My mother made no secret of her desire that one day I would be a bishop.

We rose from the floor and one-by-one we approached the bishop. I knelt in front of him and he ordained me. "You are a priest forever," he said. I turned and faced the mass of people in the cathedral. This was my future, to serve these people and others like them.

1963. Holy Family Parish, Parma, Ohio, a Cleveland suburb. Priests' breakfast table in the rectory.

An older priest, Bob Knuff, walked in.
"Hey, kid, watcha reading?"
I picked up the booklet and showed him. "*Pacem in Terris*, John the 23rd's latest encyclical."

"Heavy stuff for the breakfast table. Gimme the sports page."

I passed him that section. "No, Bob, it's great stuff. All about world peace and poverty and racism. The Pope thinks democracy is a pretty good governmental structure and he thinks the UN's doing a good job."

"Yeah, well the people aren't interested in that stuff. They come to church to rest from a hectic week. A few minutes of peace with God. Where's the report of last night's game?"

At this point the other assistant priest, Vic, walked in. "Hi Bob, Hi kid. What are you reading?"

"*Pacem in Terris.*"

"Oh come on. That stuff's not religion. It's politics. Give it up, kid. Preach about the Blessed Mother. That's what the people want to hear."

The pastor, Father Benisek, shuffled in to breakfast, nursing his arthritic hip. He flicked on the TV to the morning show before he sat down.

Vic pointed to my book. "Hey, Bill, look what the kid's reading – an encyclical. Can you believe it?"

"Which one?"

"John the 23rd. The socialist."

Father Benisek snorted his disapproval and turned his attention to the TV where black people were picketing a Cleveland business. "Communists," he muttered. "Outside agitators," and he snorted more disapproval. Then, "Pass the toast, Vic."

1964. Parish Rectory

The pastor, Father Benisek, knocked on the door of my room.

"Father Griffin, I'd like you to take the housekeeper to the store. You know, her weekly shopping trip."

"Ah, Father, excuse me, but I was getting my sermon ready for Sunday. How about the janitor? Could he take her?"

"No, no, Father. I don't want to take the janitor away from anything important."

March, 1965. A plane bound for Atlanta, Georgia

I turned to my seat mate, Father Tom Gallagher. "Come on, Tom, let's go talk to him." I was referring to Martin Luther King who sat in the front of the plane. We were on our way to Selma to join his historic march to the state capitol in Montgomery, Alabama for voting rights. Doctor King was returning to his home in Atlanta after a speech in Cleveland.

"I don't know. He probably wants to rest."

"Ah, come on. Let's go."

Tom and I stood and walked to the front of the plane. "Doctor King," I said, "I just want to tell you that we really admire what you're doing in the South. We're on our way to join the march."

"Wonderful, wonderful, ah... Fathers, I presume. Catholic?"

Tom shook his hand and introduced himself and then me.

"How are you Fathers getting to the march?"

This surprised me. I expected a statement about the importance of his efforts, but instead, he asked about our travel plans. I explained how we were going from Atlanta to Selma by air, but we hadn't figured out how we'd get to the march.

"Here," he said, and wrote something on a piece of paper. "The white cab companies in Selma won't help you, but this company will. It's owned by blacks. Use my name."

We thanked him and wished him well.

"Well, God bless you, Fathers. I'm going to spend a little time with my family and I'll rejoin the march tomorrow."

We went back to our seats, impressed by a great man who bothered himself about our travel plans.

April, 1965. The bishop's office next to the cathedral

"I called you down here, Father, because you've raised a big storm out there in Parma. Your pastor is very upset. Some people said they're not going to contribute to the church as long as you're there."

I stood there, embarrassed. I shifted my feet. My face got red and I felt hot.

"Who went with you to Selma?"

"Father Tom Gallagher."

"Well, there's no trouble in his parish."

Could I argue with this man? I had always been taught that the bishop spoke for God. Could I tell him that Father Tom's pastor was one hundred percent behind him and had the people of the parish praying for his safety? My pastor listened to every racist who knocked on the door and soothed them with, "I know, I know. I'm going to get rid of him."

"Well?" the bishop demanded.

I took a deep breath. "I think we have to affirm the church's strong position against racism, Bishop."

The bishop picked up his pen and waved away my request for support. "I tell you, Father, normally I leave a new priest in a parish for five years, but I'm going to move you now into the inner city. You like working with the black people, don't you, Father?"

"Of course, but—"

"That's fine. At your own request, I'm moving you into St. Al's in the heart of the ghetto."

November, 1967. My brother-in-law, Tom Willmott, and I were hiking in a park outside Cleveland.

"It's all breaking apart, Tom."

"What is?"

I had to talk to somebody. I was going nuts inside. But I just couldn't come out with the problem. It was too shocking for a Catholic priest.

"Everything's messed up. You know the Pope threw open the windows of the church to get some fresh air in. But the trouble is, I can't get the windows closed. And those courses I took at the university – they have me questioning everything. I used to think the Catholic Church was the true church, now I think all churches are true. I used to support the Catholic idea on birth control. Now I think it's ridiculous."

Tom laughed. "Yeah, it *is* crazy."

"And I've been called downtown to the bishop so many times in the last few years I'm like a paddle ball that bounces back. Just this week I got called down for a sermon I gave."

"What did you do, promote heresy?"

"No. I was trying to explain the Incarnation, how God came down and became part of us. I started the sermon in that monster raised pulpit, far over the heads of the people and then at just the right moment, as I explained the Incarnation, I left the pulpit and went down into the middle aisle of the church and finished the sermon. It was really effective."

"So what was wrong with that?"

"The bishop said, 'Don't leave the pulpit again, Father.'"

"Cheez."

Tom was my friend and a mentor to me, but I wasn't getting to the heart of the problem.

"So here's my problem."

"Yeah?"

We walked through the leafless trees. I couldn't say anything. Tears came to my eyes. He looked at me and then threw his arm around my shoulder. "Come on, Ed."

"I'm in love," I said. There. It was out in the open. "It's a woman I work with in the parish. A youth worker. A beautiful black woman. I mean, I've never kissed her or hugged her or anything, but…"

"How does she feel about you?"

"It's mutual."

"So, you've talked about it with her?"

"Yeah." Happiness filled me as I remembered the long, long cup of coffee we had one night at a neighborhood restaurant.

"Talking about love is the first step to making love."

I stopped walking. "Hang on, Tom. I know some guys go with women and stay priests, but I can't do that. I'm either in or out. For one thing, it's not fair to the woman."

"Okay, okay, so you leave." Tom patted me on the back and we started walking again. He turned to me, "If you leave, what are you going to do?"

"Well, I..." I had no answer. I hadn't thought about it.

"Let's say you marry this woman and have a family. How are you going to support them?"

I just kept walking. I had no answer.

"See, that's the trouble. There aren't any businesses who need a post-grad scholar in theology. Get some training, then leave."

"I want to work with people."

"I repeat, get some training and then leave."

"But I'm in love now."

We talked for an hour. He felt I was just infatuated with this woman and it would pass. Of course he was right, but he missed the other love story.

My love affair with the Catholic Church was over.

January, 1968. The bishop's mansion on Lake Erie

"Good morning, Bishop."

He let me into an imposing entryway, marble floors, tapestries on the wall, stained glass windows and massive chairs with carved arms. This was the foyer – what did the rest of the place look like? I had left my parish where people lived in run-down apartment buildings owned by absentee landlords, apartments where rats frequently crawled into cribs, where lead paint coated the walls and where the repair man was a year away.

The bishop pointed to one of the big wooden chairs. I sat down but I didn't feel comfortable. The bishop sat opposite me and began by reminding me of the rules. "Father, I hope you know I only permit visits here for true emergencies. You left a message last night that this was an emergency."

"I'm leaving the priesthood today, Bishop. I wanted to be sure you had enough time to find a replacement."

"What's the trouble, Father. Is it a woman?"

"No, Bishop." I moved to the edge of the chair. "I've been trying to help people in the ghetto, but it seems the church just doesn't care. I mean, all the money is going to build new churches in the suburbs."

"That's where the Catholics are, Father. And we have a very strong inner city program, the Catholic Interracial Council."

A ray of early morning sun shot through the stained glass window and tinted the bishop's head with red. But I no longer believed that God spoke to me through this man.

"The Catholic Interracial Council does a few good things, Bishop, but it has no resources and it does nothing to feed the hungry and clothe the naked and house the homeless."

"I don't need a lecture from you, young man."

I stood up. "I'm leaving. I'm joining the many other young priests who are quitting the priesthood."

He got to his feet. "You're wrong again, Father. There is no mass movement of priests."

I put my hand on the doorknob. It was freezing cold. "Thank you for your time, Bishop."

"I'm going to pray for you, Father. Your immortal soul is in grave danger."

I muttered another thank you and opened the door to a blast of Lake Erie air. It was cold and wet and free.

Spring, 1968. Rockford, Illinois

She said her name was Amanda and I met her at the Quaker church. I was religion shopping and – looking at the women in the congregation.

"Hi, ah, ah, my name is Ed," I said as I pointed to my nametag at the social after church. I was super nervous, a thirty-two year old virgin attempting to make a date.

She pointed to her tag. "Amanda."

I had never done this before and I had never sat in on guys' bull sessions to learn the secrets. "I-I'm new here."

"I know. I've never seen you before."

"I got a job as the director of a youth center."

"That's nice."

"There's a beautiful park along the Rock River. I-I wonder if you'd like to take a walk with me later today."

God. That was terrible. How stupid. She will think I'm some sort of rapist or something, getting her alone in a park.

"That would be nice. About 3 PM?"

I could hardly believe it. I had just made a date. I was on the road.

Amanda gave me her address and promptly at 3 I knocked on her door. We walked to the park and strolled along the river, but a host of new questions came to me. Was I supposed to hold her hand? What should I do *after* the park? I was a total novice at this. I had never dated in high school and I frankly knew very little about women.

I asked Amanda about herself, her job as a social worker, her church and her family. She talked a lot about herself and seemed to enjoy talking. I told her that I used to be a Catholic priest, but she didn't seem too interested and the conversation reverted to her.

We didn't hold hands.

After an hour or two we started walking back As we neared her apartment, I got really nervous. What were the rules at the end of the date? In all the movies I'd seen the guy kisses the girl or tries to at her apartment door.

Into the building. Up the stairs. Down the hall. Her apartment. What was I supposed to do? Kiss her? Say I had a nice time? Make another date?

Hell with it, I thought. I wasn't going to follow any rules. I was going to follow my heart and do what I felt. Amanda was nice, but I didn't want to kiss her and I didn't want to date again.

"I had a nice time, Amanda. Thank you. Good evening."

"Thanks, Ed. Goodbye."

She went in, shut the door and I left, happy that I had discovered the rules of dating – there were no rules. I just had to follow my heart.

August, 1969. My mother's home in Boca Raton, Florida

I was sporting a beard – my very first – as I got off the plane for my annual visit to my mother. She complained about the beard immediately and kept it up the whole first day of our visit. When she attempted to hide me from the neighbors, I knew what was going on – she hadn't told them I'd left the priesthood. In those days, priests didn't have beards.

She had placed herself above her Catholic friends because she was the mother of a priest and I had severely disappointed her by leaving.

After supper on our first day, she said, "Please, Edward, I'm begging you. Shave that beard off."

I stroked my black beard. "I like it, Mom. Don't you think it makes me look mature?"

"It makes you look like a bum. Shave it off."

She began to cry. "You've broken my heart. First you leave the priesthood and break your vows to God and now you grow a beard and look like a hippie."

I didn't say anything.

"You've brought shame on our family. I hope God takes me soon. I can't stand this."

Fifteen more minutes of this and I stormed out of the house and walked through the streets of Boca Raton. A half hour later as I walked along, a car pulled up behind me. It was my mother. Suddenly the whole drama flashed into my mind. Here was the good mother rescuing her errant son from the devil streets of the city. Here was the good Catholic mother bringing her wandering child back to Mother Church.

In that instant, I grew up. I broke away from the concept of *son-hood* that my mother and the church had instilled. This woman was special for me, she had raised me, but she no longer had any say in my life. Polite conversation would replace honesty from then on..

I got in the car and she drove home. I shaved the beard – it wasn't important and I could grow another in a few days when I returned to my life.

June 1970. A four-student flat near the University of Wisconsin in Milwaukee.

"Hi, Mom," I said into the phone, my future wife, Kathy, standing right next to me. I met her one night in April when I went to her sister's house to apply for a job. As they say, it was love at first sight, or more correctly, it was love and friendship at first sight.

"I passed my exams, Mom. I've got a master's degree."

I could hear the distance in her voice. "I'm happy for you."

There was only one thing that would have made her happy – my return to the priesthood.

"Yeah, the exams were tough. Mom, I've got some news for you."

"Yes?"

I squeezed Kathy's hand hard. When Mom heard what I had to say, she would know that I would never return to the priesthood.

"I'm getting married, Mom. In August."

There was a long moment of silence and then a click. I turned to Kathy. "She hung up."

A few months later in a park outside Milwaukee Kathy and I were married in front of a hippie Catholic priest who left the priesthood himself a few months later. Kathy's niece gave out roses to everyone, including a park policeman.

March 2, 1973. St. Joseph's Hospital

I watched my son being born. I knew I could die then, because I would somehow go on, my genes, my legacy, something.

July 20, 1975. St. Joseph's Hospital

I took a break from the delivery room. In the waiting area was a city hall lobbyist and I was a city councilor. He tried to tell me about his building project and the zoning change he needed, but I hurried back into the delivery room. God and my wife gave me a warm and wonderful little girl that night.

April, 1983. Milwaukee, Wisconsin

In 1983, at the age of forty-seven, I discovered creative writing. It changed my life. I would sit down at the typewriter after supper and follow my creative muse. Whole worlds opened to me. I wrote about the space behind my childhood garage where I practiced pitching and dreamed of reaching the major leagues. I wrote a short story about a group of prisoners on an island. I wrote a poem about getting along with the Russians. Hours passed. Suddenly, as I wrote, an alarm would ring in the house. My wife and I owned a commercial greenhouse outside Milwaukee, Wisconsin, a ma-and-pa operation. The alarm meant I hadn't turned the heat on. I had to shut the door on the vibrant world that grew on the paper in front of me and hurry to the greenhouses to start the furnaces.

An hour later I'd be back at the typewriter. Type a sentence, stop, look at it, realize it wasn't quite true and then search deeper, ever deeper. Layers of middle-aged half-truths disappeared, the comfortable maxims I had surrounded myself with – "Business is good. Don't make any changes" and "Relax. You're getting older." The fires of my youth burned again – civil rights, world peace, a place in the sun for every person. I was a Catholic priest as a young man, filled with idealism. I marched in Selma with Doctor King, picketed local companies to give jobs to blacks, and confronted my own bishop over the church's institutional racism.

As I wrote, I dug, I searched, always deeper, ever more honest. It might be easy to speak a lie, but it wasn't easy to write one. I started to unravel the tangled skein that was me. These revelations came, not from writing philosophy or self-help dictums, but from writing fiction. Put a man and a woman in a fictional situation. What does the woman really think? What does the man think? Is this real? Is this how people are? Where do I get my ideas? What is human nature all about?

What a wonderful gift this was. How great it would be to give it to others. My creative writing instructor at Marquette University asked me to substitute for him one evening. My peers gave me positive feedback and I looked around for a place to teach. I had enough credentials to fill a wall, (a master's degree, five years as a Catholic priest, and four years as a city councilman) but no writing testimonials, such as a book or an article in a status magazine.

Who would have me as a writing instructor? I was just a beginner myself. Around this time the State of Wisconsin called for more volunteers to help reintegrate prisoners into society. Yes, that was it, I'd volunteer to teach in prison. I'd show the men that writing could melt the bars around their souls. Besides, prisons cried for reform. As a priest I'd visited a few penitentiaries and found them terribly inhumane – men locked in cages. In my opinion they were just warehouses. Men's lives were not changed. Instead they learned how to do crime better. I had read *Papillon*, the story of Henri Charriére's terrible experience in prison and his struggle to be true to himself. The book moved me deeply.

Perhaps I could teach the men to write like Papillon or the Russian, Solzhenitsyn. Then, like these mentors, they would tell the world about the dystopia they lived in. In a larger sense, the bars would melt away.

I told my wife, Kathy, about my plan. "Why prison?" she asked. "Why not help Jimmy Carter build houses for poor people?"

Good question. I didn't know the answer. I was silent.

She touched my arm. "I will worry about you."

"I know," I said and hugged her.

"We have it good now. Money, health, two great children."

"I know. I know, but ... I have to go."

My friends weren't impressed either. "Psychological need to help others." "Just going to get good stories." "They don't need creative writing – they need basic English and spelling." "Why waste your time on scumbags?"

I ignored everyone's advice and wrote to the warden of the toughest prison in Wisconsin, the maximum-security facility at Waupun. The prison's director of education approved my plan and I was slated to start that September.

This is the story of my prison journeys in the USA and in Canada. It's a record of success and failure, of finding myself as I helped others find themselves. I began like Joshua outside Jericho. All I had to do was sound the horn, the men would pick up their pens and the walls would come tumbling down.

That isn't what happened.

When I stopped blowing the horn, I heard words uttered in the stillness. They were words of power that demanded change of me. The words smolder in every corner of every prison, waiting to catch fire in the soul of every passing guard, official or convict.

I learned the words from the people you will meet in this book.

Mike
Welcome to the Jungle

1988, age thirteen, Victoria, British Columbia, Canada

I'd always dreamt of being a rock star. It seemed like the perfect life for me. Sleep in every morning and stay up all night. Who wouldn't love that sort of job?

I stood at the storefront window, staring in at the rock and roll display. My longhaired icons posed in sultry formations for the camera. They were my idols. I loved the music, and even though I already had one lucky *Guns and Roses* tee shirt, I wanted another.

On the walk back to my foster home, the wheels in my brain spun recklessly. I could break into a hundred cars before getting enough spare change together to buy the new album or a new tee shirt. I needed a bigger caper.

When I returned to the foster home, both my 'parents' were gone. I went directly to their bedroom, which they usually locked, but this time was open.

I searched their drawers and closet for money. They were keen to my little thieving problem, so they hid their stuff well.

Not that well.

I had never committed a cheque fraud before, but age thirteen seemed like a good time to start. In the top drawer, I found a cheque written out to my foster dad for two hundred dollars. I knew that I'd need identification in his name to cash it. After sifting through a small pile of I.D., I found his sailing club card tucked underneath a stack of boxer shorts.

I knew that I would have to be confident and assume the identity of my foster dad to pull it off. I remembered a cheque I received a year ago from an elderly lady for some lawn work. She had written *Good Job Mike!* on the face of the cheque. I'd cashed that cheque without any sort of I.D., so I wondered if that would work again.

In the bank, the teller smiled down at me from behind the counter. She scanned the cheque, then my innocent face. I made sure I bent my knees while standing at the counter so that I would appear smaller than I really was.

"What sort of work was this for, Ray?" she asked me in a proud motherly tone.

"Yard work," I said. "I want to buy my mom a birthday gift."

"Hold on a minute," she said and disappeared with my cheque.

That was the moment I learned something important about crime. There is no such thing as a halfway crook. If you embark on a criminal mission, you must stay to the end if you want to succeed. I felt like running out of that bank the minute she left to speak with her manager, but the thrill of succeeding at my first major crime kept me planted to the floor.

When she returned, the warm smile contained a touch of doubt. My heart pounded in my chest.

"Okay Ray, I can't cash this for you unless you have some sort of identification."

My criminal mind had not yet been groomed for any sort of fraud, so I can't explain how I understood my next move. I reached into my pocket and produced Ray's wallet. I removed the sailing club card and slid it across the counter to the woman. She picked up the I.D. and read the name.

"Is this all you have?" she asked.

"I'm only thirteen," I said. "I'm waiting for my driver's license. It should be here in a few years."

The woman laughed and slid my I.D. back to me.

"Well, that's definitely I.D.," she said with that warm smile. "How do you want the money?"

1989.

I've sat in a dozen principal's offices in my life. The sure events that got you a seat in the main man's office were fighting, yelling at teachers and acting the clown in class.

The chair next to the door in Mr. Macdonald's office was a familiar spot for me. I'd sat there at least ten times before the first break in the school year, probably a school record. His office was eerily similar to every other one I'd been in. Four white walls with little or no sign of creative inclination towards the decorating, the same school issue desk and chair, and a bookshelf filled with management guides and personal reading material. Principals were so boring. From my time spent in their offices, I'd have to say that they were all created from the same mold, and that was a shame, because the mold had gone out of style a long time ago.

I wasn't like most disciplinary cases. My mold had been broken the day I was born.

As I waited for Mr. Macdonald to return to his office, my mind began to wander. My criminal tendencies took over. Ten seconds to search his desk, five seconds in travel time from the chair to his chair. Twenty seconds in all it would take to find something to steal. The game was on. I noticed his jacket hanging from a hook on the back of the door. Later, in the playground across the street from my school – ex-school – I sat on the bottom part of the slide and removed the brown leather wallet from my crotch. Inside, I learned more about Mr. Macdonald's life. He had twenty dollars and a variety of food coupons in the money compartment and pictures of his family and his I.D. in another section.

I removed his credit card and smiled.

I'd never done credit card fraud, but at that moment in time, I had nothing else to do with my life. Since Mr. Macdonald felt the need to expel me from his school, he had a lesson of his own to learn, and I would be the teacher.

I felt comfortable with crime. The business of thieving had me hooked. Who needed school when there was so much more to learn on the streets?

I took the money and credit card and tossed the remainder of the wallet's contents into the garbage.

1990.

The yellow Datsun screeched around the corner, narrowly missing several parked cars. My foot was an extension of the accelerator. The automatic transmission of the stolen car ground away as I alternated from brake to gas.

"Slow down," screamed my friend Dallas from the passenger seat. He held on to the door as the car fishtailed around another corner.

"I can drive," I lied. "I got this."

Easter gifts for our girlfriends cluttered the back seat. Baskets of chocolate eggs and stuffed bunnies slid from side to side as the car recklessly spun its wheels around soft bends in the road.

Into a residential neighborhood we sped. Past manicured lawns and driveways with basketball hoops. These were the neighborhoods I targeted for my break-ins – the homes that I stole from to buy the goods in the back seat. This was the kind of neighborhood I had stolen the car from. The kind neighborhood that had unlocked back doors and open ground floor windows – all potential victims of my dishonest tirade.

The back end of the Datsun bumped a parked pickup truck.

Dallas's knuckles glowed white against the tan leather of the door inlay. "You should let me drive."

"One more turn," I said, and pressed down on the gas.

The hairpin turn came out of nowhere. I saw the oak tree on the front lawn, the elderly woman watering her flowers, the two young kids playing in a ditch across the street. I knew we were going too fast. I slammed my left foot down on the brake, at the same time pressing on the accelerator with my right.

"Look out!" yelled Dallas. His free hand gripped the dashboard in front of him.

I lost control of the car. The wheel jerked from my hand and the last thing I remember was how quickly the oak tree appeared in front of my face.

I crashed the car and made it out alive. That was my first trip to Juvenile Hall.

1990.

I removed the bottle of Ritalin from my pocket and showed it to Stevie. His eyes lit up with dollar signs and he snatched it from my hand.

"There's enough here to get at least a gram of weed," he said, and snapped the lid back on the bottle.

"Are you sure?" I asked.

Stevie tucked the bottle into his windbreaker pocket. "Trust me. Those guys eat these up like they're Smarties."

It seemed that whenever I moved to a new foster home, along with it came a new school and a new medication. I'd always thought the Ritalin was for kids who couldn't pay attention in class – at least that's what my foster mom told me. Ritalin was the latest attempt at settling me down in class, but it wasn't until I met Stevie that I realized what they were really good for. I listened to him because he was older than me, and had taken way more medication than I could ever imagine.

"You shouldn't take these," he said as we walked towards the high school. "They make you more stupid than they do smart."

Stevie told me three days ago that he had a guy in the high school that bought all of his Ritalin, and that it had been nearly two months since he had actually swallowed a pill. He'd perfected the art of concealing his morning application under his tongue, quickly expelling it behind his parent's back and saving them until he had enough to bring to his high school connection.

I had a better plan that would eliminate the wait. I stole my entire bottle.

When we arrived at the high school, three figures waited for us near the bike rack, just as Stevie had promised. The kids were much bigger than we were. When they saw us approaching, I noticed one search the area before taking any steps towards us. They acknowledged Stevie with a nod.

"You got the shit?" the biggest one asked.

Stevie produced the bottle of my Ritalin. "Fifty tablets. Two grams."

Stevie knew all the lingo when it came to dealing with drug dealers. I'd gone with him several times downtown to buy weed, which we'd smoke and ditch school in favor of doing break and enters in people's homes.

The big kid took the bottle. "Two grams. You're fucking stupid."

The other two kids laughed. One lit up a cigarette.

"I ain't giving you shit," the big one said. "You deserve less."

They walked away from us without another word. I stood staring at Stevie, shocked by what had just occurred. Stevie remained silent and his chin dipped into his chest.

"What just happened, Stevie?" I asked with a slight trace of panic.

"Forget about it," he said. "They're a bunch of dicks."

Stevie turned to walk away from the bike rack, but I didn't budge. They just took my entire supply of Ritalin and gave us nothing in return. Stevie promised that we would get something from these guys. That was the only reason why I had stolen the stuff in the first place. I watched Stevie walk one way, and the high schoolers the other. I was not about to get ripped off.

"Hey fuckers!" I screamed at the teens.

The three boys turned back to us. Stevie stopped and stared at me. His eyes wide with fear. I stood my ground, facing the three giants.

My face glowed red with fear and anger. "You owe me something."

The biggest boy laughed amongst his friends and walked slowly back to me. He tossed his cigarette to the ground and spat at my feet.

"What did you say?" he growled. I stood my ground.

"Those aren't free," I said, looking him straight in the eye. "You owe us some weed."

"Or what?" he said. "What are you going to do about it?"

I wasn't a small kid, just undersized compared to the teenager, but I had heart. Without another word I lunged out at the kid, punching him square in the nose. His face exploded, covering my shirt with his blood. As he fell to the ground, I continued to throw punches, hitting whatever I could in the process. His screams for help escaped from underneath me, but his friends stood by watching, shocked at my violent reaction.

The bottle of Ritalin fell from his pocket, and like a good sidekick, Stevie pounced on it and ran away.

After two minutes of fighting, I stood, his blood all over my hands and clothes. He whimpered on the ground as his friends came over to help him up. They ran off in the direction of the school, away from the crazy young drop-out with the unfortunate combination of attention deficit disorder and violent tendencies.

"You're fucking crazy," said Stevie. He slammed the bottle of Ritalin in my hand. "These are yours. We're dead once that guy gets better."

I looked at the bottle in my hand. The kid's blood stained everything from my coat sleeves to my pant cuffs. That was the first beating I'd ever been on the winning side of, and it felt good, even though my hand was swollen from punching the ground more times than his head.

I looked at Stevie and smiled. "I think he'll be back," I said. "But next time, we'll get the weed first."

1991.

Inside the basement suite of the old, two-story Victorian home, I noticed the wallpaper was made of bamboo. A throwback from the Eighties, the coarse overlay summed up the personality of my grade eleven teacher, Mr. Martz. Bad taste and out of touch.

I sat in his leather recliner across from my best friend Joey at the time. I twirled in the chair, watching the outdated living room spin around and around. The haunting memories of a generation past melded into one continuous blur, until finally a hairy hand on the headrest ended my ride. The cool eyes of our teacher warned me of unwanted horseplay in his home.

"This is not a toy," he said in the same levelheaded tone he used with his class.

Mr. Martz walked past me and sat on the couch beside Joey. Joey smiled and gave me a knowing look. I sat up in the chair and kept my mouth shut.

"You guys want a drink?" Mr. Martz joked.

I shook my head no.

"I'll have a tequila," said Joey and he winked at me.

I replied with a snicker.

Martz didn't laugh along with me. "You're too young to drink," he said and he got up and gave Joey a can of pop. Then he reached into a cabinet under the surface of the coffee table in front of him.

Martz lit a cigarette. "How much do you guys need to get started? Remember, you'll have to pay me later."

On the table in front of Martz was a ziplock bag filled with bright green marijuana. The two entities didn't match. My teacher and illegal weed. Just months before, I had been busted with weed in my locker. I was threatened with suspension if I didn't tell the police where I got my stuff. I kept my mouth shut, and the school had no choice but to suspend me for two days.

Now I was buying weed from them. That kind of stuff messed with a boy's mind.

"Two ounces," said Joey from the cabinet. He poured more alcohol into two low tumblers.

"Do that many kids smoke?" Martz asked. He opened the ziplock and pulled out a handful of the green bud.

"Not just at school," I said in the meekest of voices. "But downtown, too."

Martz looked up from his pot, and shook his head.

"You shouldn't go downtown," he scolded me as he dropped the handful of weed onto a set of scales. "There are some fucked up people downtown."

My pot-selling teacher was telling me about fucked up people. *There is no such thing as a halfway crook.*

Mr. Martz was led out of the school in handcuffs four days after we'd bought the weed from him. In front of the entire gym class, the police stuffed him into a squad car and we never saw him again. My final image of the *teacher* Mr. Martz was a wink in my direction.

His secret was safe with me. I wouldn't tell a soul about his dealings. He was a drug dealer, and from everything I'd learned about guys like him, it didn't matter what they did as their job, they would all mess you up if you even spoke their name in front of the police. I liked Mr. Martz, but it wasn't until I bought weed from him downtown years later that I realized he had become one of those fucked up people he warned me of.

After that gym class, I headed directly to my locker. My hands shook as I fumbled with the lock, opening it to find the two ounces of weed I'd bought from Martz still hidden in my jacket pocket. Since the teacher was gone, the weed was now free. Joey would be happy for the sudden boost in our economy. Because of Martz's carelessness, we were on the fast track to mini retirement. I grabbed my jacket and slammed my locker door closed. School had worn out its necessity.

1991.

We called it crack corner because it was the only place in the city you could find a real live crack-head. It was a grungy section of downtown, consumed by irregular traffic patterns and pedestrians seldom found in suburban areas of any city. Garbage and evidence of drug activity littered the sidewalks for more than two blocks, but the corner was the worst. It was a dangerous spot for anyone not involved somehow in the drug subculture, so few *normal* people ventured to that section of the downtown district.

But the description of normal changed drastically in that part of town.

A yellow line in the middle of the road separated the illegal merchants from the respectable ones. When a drug dealer conducted sales on that corner, the people across the street watched with disgust. It was as if a spotlight was shining directly down on the dealer from heaven, illuminating his evil plans to corrupt poor souls further into a life of despair. They watched with disdain as hobbled, broken down humans leeched their way to the corner, welfare money in their pockets, to buy small amounts of marked up drugs to satisfy the demons inside.

Many times I stood on that street corner wondering who looked worse – the addicts or the dealers. At any time of the day my mouth was filled with half-gram spitballs of cocaine. The spitballs consisted of the drug wrapped tightly in condoms, and were no bigger than a peanut. The latex prevented them from breaking open in case I had to swallow if an undercover decided to jump me. The packaging job was the most important part of the entire drug dealing operation.

At night, the wind chilled our bodies and the job froze our souls. The corner was an all around cold place to spend your time, and all forms of heat were the issue at any point of time. The night air lacked heat. The pressure to sell more than the other dealers made the competition hot. The cops who patrolled the corner were the hottest of all, so hot, we couldn't stand too close or we'd get burned.

When Joey arrived at the corner with a hot chocolate from Seven-Eleven for both of us, he had a crooked smile on his face, the kind he had any time he had just done something bad.

"Come on," he said walking away. "You gotta see this."

At two-thirty in the morning, there was a lot to see downtown. The corner became a main meeting place for dope fiends and dealers. Fights broke out. Pimps would drive by looking for their wayward girls. Patrol cars cruised the strip where the nightclubs were, up past the prostitutes on the stroll, ending at the corner, where they took notes and pictures of the who's who and what's what. At two-thirty, life forms were no more than immoral bags of skin drained of hope and direction.

Joey led me to a covered bus stop on the bar strip. He laughed out loud and pointed to a man on the ground, asleep and snoring as if he were drunk. In his hand was a single flower – carnation maybe.

A long thread of drool hung from the corner of his mouth, touching the dirty concrete. A drunken mess.

"Let's beat the shit out of him," said Joey. He tipped his cup and poured a portion of his hot chocolate on the drunk. "He deserves it anyway."

I stuffed my free hand in my pocket. It was too cold to do any sort of beating that night. We'd been on the street since seven that evening. I was hungry. My head hurt from carrying the spitballs in my cheeks the entire night. I was envious of the drunk's ability to just let go and fall asleep.

"Let's just leave him alone and go home," I said. "This place is dead anyway."

Joey poured the remainder of his chocolate on the man who didn't move. The steam from the drink fizzled in the air. Joey threw the cup at the drunk's head.

"We should at least rob him," Joey crouched down to search the guy. "Teach him a lesson for falling asleep in the street."

Joey unloaded each of the man's pockets. I stood over him, scanning the streets for witnesses to our unethical crime. He tossed a nylon wallet up at me. I held it in my hand for a few seconds, shocked that the guy still had some portion of his sober life attached.

"What's in the wallet?" Joey asked as he stood up. "He's got nothing else."

I looked in the wallet. "Fifteen bucks."

Joey smiled. "Cab fare." Spits on the guy. "Fucking bum."

We left the poor bastard in the bus stop and ventured back to the corner for one last attempt at relieving our jowls of the spits. As soon as we arrived, we were confronted by one of the most nervous junkies I'd ever seen. He stood in our spotlight, hopping from foot to foot to stay warm, scanning the corner for any sign of a dealer. When he saw us coming, his eyes lit up like a video poker machine. *Jackpot!*

"You guys holding?" he licked his lips repeatedly as he spoke.

Joey gave me a look, and nodded.

"Sure," I said. "What do you want?"

Rule number one was that you never made the transaction directly on the corner. There was always a back alley or a side street away from the corner in which I could conduct my deals. Joey remained behind on the corner as I followed the junkie about a block away into a small pedestrian alley between two business buildings.

"Let's make this quick," I said. "What do you want?"

The next moment caught me by surprise. I'd never been robbed before. I was always the quick one out of Joey and I. We were sixteen-year-old kids dealing with thirty-year-old druggies. Quick feet meant less trouble. Most of the time we never had a problem dealing to people, but we knew the danger involved with the game. I made the mistake of walking in a dark alley without Joey with me. It was too late at night. My brain wasn't functioning correctly. When the second junkie punched me from behind, I was lucky that I didn't lose my teeth along with the mouthful of spits. The thunderous punch disoriented me for a few minutes, just long enough for the fumbling junkies to pick up the spits as they rolled out of my bleeding mouth. They danced in silent confusion in front of my face. I tried to press my body up off the ground, but all my strength was gone. The long hours in the cold had paralyzed me. The urge to fight back was nowhere in my body. My head felt like a waterlogged blanket. The unseen junky picked my head up off the ground and squeezed my cheeks with his dirty hands. I couldn't see his face, the only thing I remembered was the smell of his body odor. I was completely vulnerable for the first time in my life.

After squeezing the remainder of the spits out of my mouth, he slammed my head down onto the cement. I lay helpless, listening to the two junkies talk between each other.

"Is that all of them?"

"I think so. What should we do with him?"

"Fuck him up. He'll come back to find me."

"He's just a kid. Fuck him. Let's go."

"I think we should do him. Crack his skull."

"I got the shit. Lets go."

I remember the sudden flow of warmth I felt inside when the footsteps of my assailants drifted off into the city night. The relief that I was still alive gave me the most comfort I'd felt in days, there on the dirty ground of what could have been my last stand.

The next night, I was back on the corner with a mouth full of spitballs, and a syringe filled with toilet bowl cleaner. I was going to find those junkies, and they were going to learn that they should never let a beaten man back up on his feet.

1992.

The most disturbing sight I've ever seen was the time I watched a junkie shoot cocaine into his eye. Louie, a strung-out fifty something junkie, gingerly pulled down the heavy black bag under his eye and inserted the tip of the needle into what looked to be a vein protruding from the eye ball. His hands were steady for a compulsive junkie. He'd done the operation a hundred – probably a thousand – times before, but this was the first time in my life I'd ever witnessed something like this. Every movement was methodical.

All I knew about Louis was that he bought at least a half-ounce of cocaine from me a day, he was going blind, and he didn't have a functional vein left in his body. He'd gone through the gambit of injections sites on his deteriorating body – arms, feet, penis – but just as quick as his time on earth was running out, so were his available points of entry. The eyeball was surely his *Hail Mary* of shooting spots.

He blinked his eye hard, once or ten times, before he looked at me again. He smiled in an attempt to hide his embarrassment. A tear crept out the side of his stoned eye and he swept it away as if it didn't exist.

"Promise me son not to do the things I've done," he sang. He tucked his syringe into a black needle case. A true professional. "You ever shoot?"

I shook my head. "Never had the inclination to. I'm in love with the money."

Louie chuckled and leaned back in his chair. "So was I, until I had too much of it. Guess every dealer has to spend it on something."

Louie had spent his money on nothing *but* drugs. His apartment left little to be desired with its holes in the wall and streams of garbage along the floor. The one bedroom cubicle reeked of sweat and moldy food, and his kitchen looked more like a laboratory than a place of food preparation. The building was a notorious drug complex in my city. Of the four hundred suites, dope friends, drug dealers and prostitutes, occupied at least half of them. I had set up shop in one of the apartments just down the hall from Louie. The apartment took me off the streets at night. It gave me somewhere to live besides hotels and other people's couches, but it mostly served as a convenient office space.

Louie was a harmless guy, until it came to dealing with drugs. He had a hunger for the stuff that I'd never seen before. Every time I arrived at his apartment, he always opened the door in complete silence, and not a word was spoken out of context. We had an understanding that there was no need for small talk. Strictly business. He wanted the stuff, I wanted the money.

Louie was a lonely guy; I could sense that every time I came over. There were no photos of family or friends hung on the wall or on a shelf. I wondered how a fifty-something man remained alive after years of shooting dope into his eye and living in filth and solitude. I spent a few minutes after every sale with him, talking about sports or, of all other things, the business of cocaine. I felt embarrassed coming over just to deliver drugs, contributing to his misery. Though we had little to talk about, we were sort of friends with literally nothing in common besides our individual fondness for dope.

Louie reached over and grabbed hold of my arm with old-man strength. With the stoned eye shut, he scanned the flesh between my biceps and forearm. He smiled and nodded his head.

"You got a nice one there." He traced a steady finger down the main vein in my arm. "God, I'd like to bang that when you're ready."

I yanked my arm away. "What the hell's wrong with you?"

Louie laughed and sat back in his rickety dining room chair. He closed his good eye and laughed to himself through his clenched jaw.

"I gotta go, Lou," I said and tucked the crumpled up bills into my pocket. "Call me later."

As soon as I made a move to the door, the entire apartment filled with an aggressive pounding from out in the hall. I froze, instantly thinking of the police. The bang sounded on the door. I glanced over at Louie, whose stoned eye was open now and aware.

"Who is it?" asked Louie, concealing his pathetic stoned voice.

"Open the fucking door, Lou." It was Mariano.

Mariano was a drug dealer's worst nightmare. He stood about six foot five and weighed no less than two hundred and fifty. How a cocaine addict managed to hold onto that sort of bodyweight always astounded me. Mariano liked his drugs as much as Louie, only he didn't like to pay for them. He was famous for beating the hell out of young dealers for small amounts of drugs. A week before, he had stabbed one of my friends in broad daylight on the corner for a spitball. The guy was insane, and I was in big trouble if he caught me in Louie's apartment.

I scrambled for a place to hide. "Louie," I pleaded. "Hide me."

Louie fumbled to his feet, tucking the leather case into the waistband of his pants.

"Hide in the shower." He pointed to a door next to the kitchen. "That fucker doesn't bath. He won't find you there."

I bolted into the washroom, quietly closing the door behind me. The room was cluttered with more garbage; used q-tips littered the counter. Empty bottles of over the counter medication and crumpled up balls of bloody toilet paper overflowed the garbage can in the corner. I peeled back the sticky black shower curtain and hid in the tub, popping the additional three grams of cocaine I stupidly brought with me into my mouth, ready to swallow to save my life from Mariano.

Everyone in the city knew that Mariano would kill you for drugs. Getting busted by the police was far better than having to deal with him. At least the police only took you to jail. This guy dragged you to hell, showed you the sights, then brought you back to Earth wishing you had jumped in the lake of fire instead.

From my hiding spot, I heard Louie open the door to the apartment. In a second, Mariano's voice filled the room.

"I'm gonna kill somebody if I don't get high!"

He was overly aggressive with people – which was one of the reasons no one wanted to be around him. He stole from anyone, and he had a reputation of ruining people's highs when he came around by beating them up. The worse thing about cocaine was that it made you paranoid. You thought about things that would be considered irrational. A cocaine junkie lived in an entirely different world than the rest of humanity. Everything focussed on getting drugs, doing drugs and living through the times when there weren't any drugs around. Mariano couldn't do either of those things without some sort of violence involved.

Louie squealed. "My guy just left. I'm out."

Mariano barked. "Bullshit. Empty your pockets."

I dug through my pockets for the money, stuffing it immediately into my underwear.

"I'm gonna kill somebody for sure tonight." A plate crashed to the floor. "Fucking drug dealers think they're special."

I prayed to the Lord I only visited in tight situations. For the first time, I was really scared for my life. I'd dealt with so many junkies, but none compared to Mariano. My entire professional career I'd avoided him. He knew who I was, and I sometimes wondered if he considered the fact that he had never gotten the chance to rob me. I understood that trouble had a way of eventually catching up to you in the seedy world of drug dealing. No dealer could ever go an entire career without having to deal with a psychopath customer. I hoped that day wasn't my turn.

"I gotta use your can," Mariano growled and the door to the washroom burst open.

I remained still behind the dark curtain. The spitballs in my mouth swelled to the size of Ping-Pong balls. I worried that I wouldn't be able to swallow if Mariano wrapped his massive hands around my throat.

Please don't let me die in a junkie's bathroom, Lord.

Cornered in that bathtub I realized that being the dealer wasn't exactly the strongest position to be in. We were really just pawns in the addict's game. The expendable energy source. If one of us dropped, another would take our place.

No one was perfect in the drug game. We all had to face our demons at some point of our lives. My demon stood four feet away, pissing all over the floor, on a manhunt for his perfect victim who looked just like me.

He flushed, I'm not sure why. When I heard him leave, I stepped out of the tub, trying to avoid his mess. I was glad it was his piss on the floor and not my broken body.

1994.

"God damn it, Rack."

For the first time in my life, I'd let my guard down when it came to dealing with a friend. Usually dealing with Rack was easy. He'd bring me the money, I'd give him the dope, and we'd do our separate business and meet up after for drinks.

Not this time.

He held the gun steady at his waist. Turned sideways in the passenger seat of my car, he watched my body language, ready for any move I'd make to disarm him.

"You don't have to do this," I said. "I thought we were friends."

We called him *Rack* because of his unbelievable talent to shoot pool. He could have made money on a pro-tour somewhere in the world, but he decided to waste his life dealing instead. Rack didn't look like a typical drug dealer. His curly blond hair and athletic good looks allowed him to fit in wherever he went. He seemed more like a college boy than a killer, but I knew he was no scholar. He had a twisted side to him that made him react differently to stressful situations. At that point in time, he was in the most stressful of situations. He'd robbed several dealers in the city, and foolish me, I thought I was different. I agreed to meet him to sell him a kilogram of cocaine. I didn't actually believe that he would rob me since we went back years, but as usual, the game always seemed to change when you least expected it.

"Sorry, Mike," he said and tucked the kilo package into his jacket. "If it makes you feel any better, I'm going to pay you back."

I shook my head and looked away from him. Getting robbed is the worst feeling in the world. It's not the robbery that makes a man feel like shit, but the degradation of the event and the loss of manhood that comes with swallowing your pride.

Rack left my car and left me thirty thousand dollars in debt to my guy. I was devastated, and I'd be a liar if the thought of killing Rack didn't cross my mind.

That's if I could find him.

Two weeks later I woke up to the ring of my building's intercom system. I had a snub nose .38 in my hand as I opened the door to find Rack's smiling mug. He had black bags under his eyes and looked as though he hadn't slept in days. With little emotion, he tossed a red backpack with a Spiderman emblem on the face onto the floor at my feet.

"Sorry about everything." His smile barely hung on his face. "There's the money I owe you."

I kicked the bag to the side. "What's wrong with you?"

Rack checked his watch. "You're a good guy, Mike. Not every nice guy has to finish last."

He left me that morning and I never saw him again.

1995

When my best friend at that time, Dwayne, showed up at my door with two brand new hundred-dollar bills, I should have sensed something was wrong. He'd owed me the money for cocaine for three weeks. He worked a straight job, and there was no chance in the foreseeable future in which he could pay me. His own words. We had been close friends since my days of juvenile hall, only he'd grown up and gotten away from crime.

There is no such thing as a halfway crook.

Where we completely went our separate ways was in our beliefs in drugs. He enjoyed dabbling every once and a while – the weekend warrior, I never touched a single drop of the stuff.

Dwayne handed me the crisp bills and I took a moment to inspect them. I was surprised at how new they were. "Are they fake?" I asked.

"Come on," he said, squirming in my patio chair.

I usually never took money, handed out drugs, or invited addicts upstairs in my apartment. Dwayne was a friend who was familiar with my lifestyle, so I felt comfortable enough to break that rule.

"Can you hook me up again?" he said. His eyes remained on the table.

I should have felt it. I should have seen his despair. His desperateness. The look of a desperate man is the same whether you know him or not. Dwayne had it, and I overlooked it.

I gave him three and a half grams of cocaine and he left, confessing that he had someone waiting for him around the corner of my building. We hugged, and I sent him on his way with his package – like a dad handing a bag lunch to his son in the morning before school.

Ten minutes later the drug squad kicked in my door. They stormed my apartment, searching for cocaine. Instantly I blamed Dwayne, and sure enough, when I spoke to the undercover cop later that evening, he confirmed my suspicion.

I remember that night in the holding cell, after the police had punched and kicked me into a state of silence, a cop came to the cell door. He smiled as he opened it, staring down at my beaten body on the cot. My eye was black and both sides of my ribs throbbed with pain.

"Seems you had an accident," he said in a cocky voice. "Too bad."

I turned away from him and spat in the corner of the cell.

"This is your first time," he said. "But it won't be your last."

I lay back down on the cot and turned away from the arrogant cop. He laughed and slammed the door; thus kick starting what would be the beginning of a long list of incarcerations with the drug task force.

1994.

Bang!

I kicked in the door of the house, instantly freezing the three occupants seated in the living room. My partner Morris, cloaked in the same black garb and ski mask as I was, flew into the house before me. I swept in behind him with a double barrel shotgun in my hands. The occupants of the house stared into my eyes, studying my concealed face as Morris escaped into the back rooms.

"Nobody move," I said. My hands shook with adrenaline and fear.

The occupants, two women and one man, lifted their hands into the air. I'd never done a robbery before, but Morris had convinced me to join him. Apparently the trio had been selling cheap cocaine to our customers, thus slowly taking our business out of the equation. Morris was never one to take undercutting lightly. We tried to sell out of it, but for some reason, these three were beating our prices at every turn.

Now it was time to show them the nasty side of drug dealing.

There is no such thing as a halfway crook.

I used powerful words to make my point. "If you move, I'll shoot you dead."

The guy stared narrow-eyed at me. I could tell he was getting restless. Maybe he thought he could overpower me, take the gun from my hands. Maybe he thought the gun wasn't loaded when he stood up and lowered his hands.

"Sit down!" I ordered.

"I don't think you'll do it," he said and took a step away from the couch.

"Sit down, Jason," yelled one of the women.

But he kept moving.

He inched closer to me; his eyes focussed on mine. I made the mistake of moving away from him. A sign of weakness. A sign that maybe I wouldn't shoot. He sensed it and leapt at me, grabbing hold of the gun with both hands.

The women screamed and bolted up from the couch. They remained out of the picture as we struggled in the doorway of the living room, then onto the floor. He managed to get on top of me. I sensed my defeat as I used all my strength to push him off me, but when I did, I monkey-kicked Jason across the floor. He slammed into a wall, then lay on the floor wincing in pain.

"Blast his ass!" yelled Morris from the hallway.

I pointed the gun at Jason. His eyes were red with anger as he breathed heavily from the fight. I could feel sweat drip down my back. I'd never shot anyone before in my life. This wasn't how things were supposed to end up. We were just supposed to take his dope and beat him and his crew. The idea of killing him never entered the picture.

Until that moment.

"Blast him!" screamed Morris.

I gripped the barrel of the shotgun with one hand and wrapped my finger around the trigger. "You got the stuff?" I yelled back at Morris.

"Yeah."

"Let's go then."

I aimed the gun at Jason. "Next time I pull the trigger. Stay the fuck away from our customers."

Morris and I never saw them again.

1998.

"There's got to be a better way to do this," I sighed as I opened the third package of cocaine.My new partner Marco and I had just mailed our latest shipment of cocaine to Canada from Belize. We'd been doing it for the past three months, never getting an entire shipment up in one piece, but it was an easy gig at that time. The plan was simple, we'd buy the cocaine in Belize, package it in air tight bundles so the dogs couldn't smell it, then package it once more in wooden carvings and send it to Canada marked *Fragile*.

When it arrived, I'd open the carvings with a chainsaw and remove the goods. Simple.

We sent it through one of the world's more famous courier companies, tracking its movement on the Internet. Whenever a package showed up in a city, the package handlers scanned it. The scan would appear on their system, which was available to the public via on-line. If at any time the package stopped for too long in one city, we would usually write it off, considering the fact that most prepaid *Fragile* packages were the fastest ones to clear customs. When the package arrived in Canada, the courier would call us on a dummy phone to notify us that we could pick it up. Even that was risky. If the cops knew that there were drugs in the carving, they could wait until the moment we came to get it before arresting us. It was a dangerous game, but very profitable.

"This is beginning to give me gray hair, Marco," I said as I counted the packages. "We sent eight packs, we have three left, we've lost five this time."

"What do you suggest?" he said. "This is paying pretty well."

I stood up and stretched. "Sure. But the amount of drugs we lose each time isn't worth the money. We need a big shipment. All at once."

"How the hell are we going to do that?" he asked, chuckling at me as he spoke.

The one thing I'd learned throughout my career of drug dealing was that if there was a desire to get this drug to people, there was always a way. All we needed was a grander mode of transportation.

"We'll find a way," I said. "For now, lets clean these wood shavings up before my girl gets home."

There is no such thing as a halfway crook.

Book Two

Chapter One
Mike
A Road to Nowhere

September, 1998. Sinola, Mexico

… senior! Alto!

… faceless gunmen behind killing machines…

…fear the trigger finger, not the trigger itself…

… Alto! Alto!

Somewhere in the back of my consciousness, I know the word stop in every language known to mankind. I don't need to be familiar with the language of that country; I just need to understand the tone of their voices. Every emotion carries a different level of arousal, which changes the tone, the delivery, and the result. Snippets of foreign barking behind machine guns and bulletproof vests must mean something is very, very…

Awake… What the hell just happened?

The first thing I noticed was the spot of sunlight in the center of the wide curtain across the room protecting me from the ultraviolet heat wave outside. The bad dream lingered around my head like a mist of fog sweeping inland off the shore. My senses hummed with a mixture of starvation and delusion. The message was strong. I didn't need to be fully awake to understand omens or premonitions.

I swung my feet over the side of the bed, still focused on the bright spot in the curtain. The only sound in the room was the snoring of my best friend Shelly in the twin bed beside mine. I tiptoed to the washroom, quiet not to wake him. He needed the sleep. He was the weak one.

The splash of cold water on my face lifted the fog and brought my awareness back to clearer skies. There was something deeply wrong with the way I though. I stared myself in the eyes in the bathroom mirror. They were the eyes of a liar. A good liar. One that could convince himself that the wrong thing to do was the right thing, and live with it, die with it, and bring others down with him. Why didn't these eyes care about themselves? Why put everything on the line for nothing? If the eyes were the windows to the soul, then this soul was destined for somewhere hot and tropical. A one way trip to hell.

Another cold splash of water. The bathroom was one of those hacienda style, modern faucets with old Mexican tile walls and floor. Cheap soap and towels made of some artificial Aztec cotton. The low ceilings drove me crazy. The first ray of sunshine in twenty-four hours touched my skin through the small window and it felt good. Alive. Real. I wanted more of it. I opened the window all the way allowing the sounds of the city to invade my wakeup routine. Culican, Sinaloa. The most beautiful women in all of Mexico. The streets are clean, safe for drug smugglers to relax and spend their money. The washroom filled with sensory overload... the air in a Mexican city carries with it the smell of the sun cooking the concrete with a splash of body odor... I should be on a beach somewhere...

In a bag next to the sink, marked by the brand name of the pharmacy down the street, I removed a razor and cream. My face was ready for the last part of my trip. The look... the surprise smile. I practiced every look that accommodated every emotion. I spent my entire life conning everyone I knew. Consciously, conscientiously. And because of it, my relationships suffered. No one really trusted me. Sure, I had a good name with petty thieves and high-ranking drug dealers, but they really didn't care about me. All they cared about was the money. If I had a good money making opportunity that they could cash in on, they liked me a whole lot better than if I came empty handed.

Funny thing, I felt the same way. Those eyes glaring back at me knew the truth. The truth about the truth. Selfish, uncaring, emotional to the point of having no real emotions. They knew about the manipulating, and the manipulating to cover up the manipulating. What was the point of telling the truth if the truth hurt so damn much? I liked me better when I had a great crime in mind or a ton of drugs to push on people. When I had money to waste and nothing to care about. That part of life was easy, fast and exciting. But now... I'm here. In the new reality. In a washroom in Mexico reading my own eyes, believing my own lies, inhaling sweat-saturated air and questioning every action I'd ever made...

Until now.

On the counter sat two razors. I bought two? One was for Shelly. If we had to wait for him to get the stuff, we would have been shaving from a bowl in the rearview as we drove the last stretch of highway. Like I did in Arizona on the way down.

I hated weak people. Having sensitive souls in your circle made the circle a square. Nothing kills a criminal operation quicker than a conscience. I set the razors apart from each other. Adjusted them so that the two heads were even on the counter... then adjusted mine so that it was higher on the counter than his... a little higher... the razorblade pecking order...

It took a lot of gusto to be a drug smuggler. A man didn't just fall into this profession. It took a lot of nerve and research, time and money, to get one simple package through. It took a degree of mental and physical fortitude presented to a man at birth. If you were weak or stupid, you were destined to fail in the seedy world of drug transportation.

Shelly was weak. If I told him about the dream, he'd lose his mind and want to stop. He wasn't a criminal anyway. Just a guy who got dealt a shitty hand and one of the cards was me. Shelly was a feeble minded person, easily influenced to get into trouble because he had a giant ball of acceptance that needed to be stroked. I met him when we were teenagers. I was the baddest kid in the school and he was the nerdiest. I liked him because all I ever saw him do was exercise to get rid of a piece of genealogy that hung over his belt line. Fat, neurotic, obsessive – perfect quality for a sidekick.

If we got caught, he'd break. They wouldn't even need to torture Shelly, he'd torture himself enough in the cell before they even got to him. Crying and snotting and babbling, praying to a God he didn't believe in, making promises to himself he'd never keep. When we decided five months ago to actually drive down to pick up our drugs, I knew we'd be put in a situation that would test our friendship. *What was the anger behind those eyes all about?*

I jammed his razor back in the bag and turned the water on super hot. Today was going to be the greatest day of my life. Guardian angels, bad dreams, guilty conscience – go to hell.

*   *   *

The entire operation was simple from the beginning, complicated only by the overpowering seduction of the nastiest of the seven sins – greed. If a conscience kills a crime, greed kills the criminal.

I was connected to the Belizian drug underworld through a friend of mine named Ryan. He had the look of a Wall Street hustler and the tongue of a stone cold pimp. He could talk a man out of his own identity and make him believe he was somebody else. I'd seen him do it.

We began by mailing the kilos of drugs from Belize to Mexico City, then up to the States, then to Canada. We'd pay the shipping and custom fees in Belize, then follow the package by Internet until it reached home. Every time the package stopped somewhere, they swiped it through customs. The information went to the mainframe, which could be accessed on the company website. It was a nerve racking operation. Five out of ten packages made it. We used replaceable cellular phones as contact numbers for the packages. If one took too long to reach Canada, or if it took an unusual route getting there, it became dead to us, along with the phone and the false identity that came with it. We must have killed a dozen fake personas that year.

No drug dealer in his right mind could ever pass up paying $1500 for a kilo of cocaine. Even if we lost every other one, the profit on just one of those packages would be enough to make a regular man live in comfort for a year. But greed had a vice grip on our egos, and we knew that if we were ever going to be really happy – happy meaning never having to consider money again –

we'd have to get bigger. To get that big, something would have to change in the way we shipped the stuff up.

Ryan came up with the idea to send the cocaine inside of furniture. He met an artist on the beach of some Central American country who could carve false centers in furniture. Soon, we were moving five kilos at a time inside of tables and statues. And as we tracked the packages through the mail, our losses grew. Now, we were losing five kilos at a time. Once, we stuffed five kilos into a three foot high wood dolphin riding a giant wave. The carving was so beautiful, that when we lost it somewhere in the Miami airport, I laughed at the thought of a rabid Miami Dolphin fan watching the Sunday games in his living room, rubbing our drug dolphin for good luck. That one cost us $250,000 in pure profit.

I got Shelly involved by sending him down to Mexico City on a commercial airline to pick up a piece of furniture. We abandoned the mail route in hopes to find a more secure way to get the drugs up here. He spent three days in Mexico waiting for the table to arrive by bus, and when it came, he packed it on the plane and walked right through customs. We were so worried for him that we never did it again. Later that summer, I came up with the plan to drive it back. Shelly knew better than to listen to me when it came to crime. He knew that I had a lack of respect for my own life. He knew, but his greed convinced him to go.

I remember those days before we drove down. I told my family that I had been left some money in a will. They believed me. Probably hoping it would be the one thing that settled me down in my life. I told them I was going to Belize to visit a friend. They had no idea that I was driving, just going. It never hurt to tell them lies. For some reason, I never had emotional reactions when it came to anyone in my family. The relationship was superficial and meaningless. Years of abandonment and mistrust had created a callused wall between us. I didn't care what they would have thought about the trip, all I worried about was the money.

I had a daughter back home who wondered who I was. How could I leave her behind without a father? That question never once entered my mind in preparing for my crime. She wasn't as important as getting rich. Besides, when I made the money, she would benefit. She could have anything she wanted when I got back.

The one thing that separated me from everyone I knew was my fearless nature. I wasn't shy, timid or scared, which usually meant I wasn't thinking, acting cautious or being rational. A ruthless fighter and a reckless man with my mind focused on getting rich any way possible. I knew it would eventually lead me to my death, or worse, poverty and imprisonment, but that was the chance a man took trying to fulfil an innate desire to live free.

* * *

As we packed that morning to go, the sun shining in from the hot Mexican street, I wrestled with the idea of sharing my dream with Shelly. I watched him across the room, packing his suitcase with shaking hands and that pathetic look on his face. He was scared today like he'd been every other day since we left Canada. He wanted an out, one that I could give him, but that he'd never ask for. Male egos hurt. We always have to save face somehow. Shelly couldn't stand that fact that I had his nuts in my fist. He needed the money just as much as I did, only I needed the thrill of the hunt more. I stopped packing and handed my friend an ultimatum.

"You can go if you want," I said plainly. "I won't cut you out."

Shelly stopped and gave me that hopeful look I've seen him use on women for sympathy. "No…" he managed. His word dribbled over his big bottom lip.

When a man is scared, truly scared, he reverts back to his childlike form. He remembers those school days when the older kids would pick on him and call him names. That feeling of helplessness becomes strong, and somewhere deep inside, he starts wishing his mommy were there to tell him things were going to be okay…

"This is the hardest part of the trip," I said. "You can fly home and leave me. I don't care. But your end will be smaller."

Just the thought of receiving a lesser cut of the profits would be enough to make Shelly pick his nuts up off the floor and stay on course. I knew he couldn't stand coming all this way for half of what he intended to get. I knew he hated me for convincing him to come, praying on his weakness to become my sidekick in a ludicrous drug smuggling operation. He once told me that I was the devil in disguise, sent to ruin his life. Little did he know that I was on a course to ruin my own life, and he was just an innocent passenger along for the ride.

A moment of bravado came to Shelly. "No. I'm in."

He would end up turning me into the biggest sucker in the world. His day to reverse the tables was near on the horizon, but as we packed in silence for the final leg of our journey. I felt superman feelings of complete control. He was under my spell... my self-enchanting spell of destruction.

I jammed one of the hotel pillows in my bag before leaving – *The Royal of Culican* emblem on the slip.

* * *

Packed in a car going 100 down a flat highway is the most relaxing feeling in the world. The freedom of feeling the world pass by your window at top speed was the exact metaphor for my life. With the music blasting and the wind pushing desert air through the vehicle, I felt more alive that any other time in my life. Still, I couldn't help but return to the images in my dream. Where on this familiar highway would they stop us... look in the car... in the secret compartment in the passenger side airbag? How would they figure out that to open the compartment you had to step on the brake, put the car in neutral and pop the trunk? I glanced over at Shelly - silent and feeling the pressure.

"What's the matter?" I asked him. I knew the answer and I bathed in the aura his fear created.

"Just nervous," he said. "That's all."

Like a crazed man I yanked the wheel to the right, slamming on the brakes and pulling the car to the side of the highway. A massive semi roared past us as I turned the music right down.

"I gave you the option to go home, but you said that you were ready. What the hell is it? One or the other? In or out?"

Shelly swallowed and turned up the air conditioner, forgetting that it didn't exist. "No. I'm okay. Just nervous."

"Well it's the nervousness that will get us busted. That stupid look you have on your face will tell them everything that they need to know. They'll jack our asses out of the car so fast you won't have time to wonder about your feelings."

My words hit him hard, they always did. Shelly looked up to me as the brother he never had. He came from a poor family with not much going on in regards to family lineage. His father was a sick diabetic and his mother a whore. He needed the money from this trip more than I did - that was his weakness. But more so, he needed the recognition that he was somebody. He wanted to feel alive almost as much as I wanted to die.

My self-destruction drove the car. And this car was on a highway to hell.

"Suck it up and stop worrying." My tone mellowed. "We're going to be fine. Just do what we planned."

I was under a false set of identification – James Baldwin. Our plan was to pretend to be two Christian missionaries on our way to Tijuana from Mexico City. We had bibles and a rosary hanging from the rearview as our ruse. If questioned, I had stories about my time spent in Mexico helping at the orphanage. They couldn't possibly stop two Christian men for a drug search. That was my plan. I thought it would work. It wasn't until we came across a car stop at two the next morning that I figured out we shouldn't have used God to provide us with cover. They say he works in mysterious ways, but that night, in the middle of absolutely nowhere, he taught us a very clear message.

We pulled up to the car inspection port in the middle of the Sinaloa desert. The cops welcomed us with badges and smiles. I tried to remain calm, but this surprise car inspection site was not on the map. Within mere minutes we were ushered out of the car and forced to our knees in the sand. The ground felt cool for being such a hot night.

I watched from my spot on the dirt ground as the soldier ripped open the airbag compartment and removed one of the fifteen kilos inside. With the machine guns pointed directly at our heads, all I could do was laugh. Shelly was in tears, the soldiers were hysterical with joy, and I was finally gifted the feeling of misery I'd been looking for the entire time.

Chapter 2
Mike
Nowhere

September, 1998. Police cells - Los Mochis, Sinola

An auburn skinned cockroach poked his head out in the hall from beneath the cell door. Glancing both ways before fully exposing his body to the open space of the human world, the cockroach scurried across the stone tile floor searching for a new dry spot to hide. I watched the bug move with precision – zig zagging across the floor – only to see the boot of the *policia* stomp it to death. I could relate to the bug. I myself felt like I'd just seen the underside of someone's foot. He stood at the door, hating me more every second he stared into my eyes.

The cell they put Shelly and I into was nothing short of an abandoned washroom on some rest stop in the middle of some god-forsaken hole in the ground. We were crammed in the cell with twenty other lawbreakers, all left with nothing but the clothes on our bodies and a keen sense of despondency. Besides two slabs of concrete in the shape of twin beds and a toilet in the corner that wouldn't flush if our sense of smell depended on it, the cell was cluttered with human bodies of all makes and shapes. Drug runners, speeders, murders – all gathered together in the cell awaiting some form of punishment, conclusion or reprieve.

A wide glassless window at the back of the cell allowed a breeze from the ocean to pass through every so often, chilling everything in the room for long stretches at a time. That first night in the cell, Shelly and I huddled close to complete strangers to keep warm, cringing at the putrid smells of body odor and bad gas that enveloped our cell mates.

After one night in the holding cell, I was ready to give them any information they needed to let me go. The pressure was hell on my brain. Mexican prison cells were worse than the ones I'd seen on TV. The grunge, the beatings, the rat infestation. At least the cells on TV gave you somewhere to sit. In this cell, I was fighting for a place to stand never mind sleep when night hit.

The staring contest with the jailer continued. He was a scammer, I could tell by the way he smiled sideways and volleyed the cigarette in between his lips. We didn't speak an iota of the same language, so our communication consisted of who could make the nastiest faces at each other and back them up by loud talking and a keen display of aggression. He won. He had the keys and with that came the power.

He blew a gust of cigarette smoke into my face. I flinched and looked away as he walked off laughing.

"What did he say?" asked Shelly from across the cell. He had taken up camp on one of the concrete slabs.

I turned back to the cell, looking over the mass of prisoners lying any which way on the cold floor.

"Nothing," I said, frustrated and angry. "This can't be happening."

But it was, and by the look of Shelly, he didn't have much fight left in him. In the past two days since our arrest, he had crumbled into a different sort of man. The law had a way of doing that to you. A man could be the bravest in the world, but stick him in a cell and throw away the key, you'll soon see what that brave man is really all about.

Shelly was a good kid. A handsome guy with tons of potential to do something with his life. The only problems he really had were his lack of confidence and me as his friend. I felt slightly guilty as I watched him hang his head and sulk on the concrete bed. I convinced him to come, but I didn't hold a gun to his head. We both knew the consequences for our actions, but as we sat in the cell, I realized that I was the only one who was prepared to deal with them.

That second night was the hardest of them all. As I huddled on the cold floor, spooning my best friend to keep warm, I closed my eyes and tried to think of my last great feeling. Driving free on a Mexican highway. The sun filled the car with its ultraviolet smile... the smell of freedom pushing through open windows. Stopping at a small store in the middle of nowhere to drink anything cold...

A stranger shifted behind me, jolting me awake. Shelly snored softly beside me. Probably cried himself to sleep. Instantly awake and aware my mind retraced my footsteps from this point. Back to the curb right beside the spot where they found our drugs...

I remembered sitting on a small block of cement, the car in full view, federal officers with machine guns and cheap *cigarillos* pointing away from their faces. A shudder of guilt passed through my body, but I smiled it away. Shelly was completely white. He turned to give me that look, but I couldn't face him. I knew what was going to happen. He needn't remind me.

The guard moved relentlessly through the car, pounding at the car doors with a rubber hammer, searching for trap doors. A trickle of sweat dribbled down my forehead. It irritated me like a fly on my face, but I refused to swipe it away in fear that it might show my guilt. Shelly's hands turned to fists. He was about to crack.

When the cries in Spanish erupted from the car, I knew we were done. Like anger, joy had it's own exclusive tone that carried all across the world. My entire body stiffened with fear. Inside my head I begged that they hadn't found the secret compartment. How could they? It was fool proof.

The officer in the car ripped the cover of the airbag off, immediately depreciating the value of the car and mine and Shelly's lives. He tossed one of the kilos onto the ground about ten feet away from us. A cloud of dirt rose into the air, covering the package with a light dust blanket.

An electric current of fear raced through my body. I wanted to stand up and scream at the top of my lungs. Flashes of my miserable and unstable life I had given up to be here, appeared and disappeared in front of my mind's eye. I felt sick. I wanted to throw up. I wanted to run and get shot by the Federalies. Anything to take me away from the drugs and the guns and the Spanish.

Shelly broke into tears immediately. His body shook as he tried to stand up and say something to the cops. As soon as he got to his feet, the cop standing over us knocked him back down with a simple nudge of his gun. There we were, two strong Canadian men – an athlete and a body builder – broken. The drugs sat piled on the side of the road one on top of the other. The cops screamed with elation as they counted all fifteen of the packages. All sounds around me died. Shelly's sobbing, the laughter of the cops, the echoing roars of tractor-trailers rushing down the freeway. Life gave way to a new silent reality. Nothing else mattered at that moment but to get through this wave of panic that consumed my body. Suddenly I wanted to live. Staying alive suddenly became important. I scrambled to ease the pain of a good decision gone badly.

I sprang to my feet, holding my hands in the air in surrender. The cop beside us nudged me with his gun, but I didn't fall. I turned to him, pleading with one word English pleas that I knew he didn't understand.

"I don't want trouble," I yelled at him.

The cop jammed the barrel of his gun in my side, pointing to the ground with his head. I didn't move. I turned to two other officers near the car, shaking my head as if to deny that the drugs were mine.

"Not mine," I said as serious as I could. "What's going on here?" I screamed...

When I jolted awake again, I was in that grungy cell and it was morning. As if life never stopped being glorious for the rest of the world, the birds sang a Mexican song of glee outside the window. The night chill was replaced by a scorching heat that wouldn't go away for the entire day.

On the third day a stout man, who was as tall as he was wide, appeared at the cell door. Weary and beaten, Shelly and I had given up trying to speak our cause to anyone who showed up at the door. I'd settled into the fact that we were in for some jail time, and with that came a renewed feeling of peace. Somehow, I'd managed to find some laughter in the miserable cell. We'd spent three days with twenty complete strangers, the only thing we had in common was the fact that we were all crappy criminals. I managed to lift everyone's spirits by performing a silent comedy act, tripping over my own feet and impersonating a routine similar to something out of a Charlie Chaplin movie. Tthe guys in the cell laughed and it loosened the tension in the room, but the guy standing at the door didn't dare smile.

He knocked on the steel door. "Hey, gringo!"

When I turned to him, his frown turned into a phony smile letting me know right off the bat that he was here for business.

"Do you speak English?" I asked.

"Si." He answered. "I'm a lawyer. I want to help you."

I leaned against the bars on the door. "How can we get out of here?"

The lawyer smiled and glanced at Shelly behind me in the cell. "Your friend looks tired."

"That's funny," I smirked. "He's the only one who's gotten any sleep around here. How can you help us?"

He told me that he had a way of getting us out of here without anyone knowing about our arrest. His friend was the captain of the police force, and for fifty thousand dollars he'd make sure that the front doors were left open and that we would have days to make it home before anyone knew we were gone. He told me that it took five days for the police to process us. The first three were used to interrogate the prisoners, the fourth day was spent on statements and writing the report, and on the fifth day, if deemed guilty, we would be taken to the main prison to await trial. I told him that I didn't want to wait for that fifth day and if he could get me a phone, I'd have his money in less than three hours.

I dialed the number of our partner Ryan in Mexico City on the lawyer's cellular phone.

Ryan sounded skeptical on the other end. "Where exactly are you?"

"Some small town named Los Mochis." I cupped the phone with both hands. "You've got to get us out of here, Ryan."

I should have known from the pause on the other end that Ryan intended to screw us. I know when a person doesn't feel comfortable. I have this ability to recognize emotion in people, and at that moment, I could sense that Ryan was considering abandoning us.

The deal was, if we got busted along the way, we had fifty thousand dollars on hold to bail us out. It was the only way I would have ever done the trip – as long as there was money ready to pay off the cops. Fifty thousand dollars wasn't a lot of money when you were smuggling drugs. Chump change that could be made in mere days in the underworld. Ryan knew the deal. He was fully aware of the situation. I still don't understand to this day how he could promise to help me, only to hightail it back to Canada a couple of hours later.

When I called Ryan ten hours later, wondering where the hell he was with our bail money, he was already in Vancouver. My heart broke into a million pieces as he gave me an excuse why he hadn't shown up to save us. He thought it was a trap. That Shelly and I may have given him up to save ourselves. A lowlife move made by the lowest human being possible. He was so consumed by his own greed that he left us to die in a Mexican prison.

That night, the guards showed up at the door ready to take our statements. Accompanied by a translator, the guard motioned for me to step forward. They were a little hesitant when dealing with me I noticed. I had scared them earlier by yelling and screaming into the phone at Ryan, threatening to kill him the next time I saw him. They pointed their guns at me as I walked down the hall toward the interview room.

My story was this. Shelly and I were on vacation in Mexico. We met a nice guy in Mexico City who wanted a ride from us to Tijuana. We told him no problem and drove to Culican. He told us that he lived in Culican and we stayed at his house for two days, partying and relaxing. He was well off, so we figured we could trust him. He borrowed our car for an afternoon to get it washed and detailed. When he got back, he told us that he would be going to LA and asked if we wanted to meet him and party for a few days. We agreed and said that we'd meet him there.

Shelly and I agreed that this was our story. We had no knowledge of the drugs. We were just visiting and someone duped us. The lawyer told us that our initial statement would be the one that we were prosecuted under. He told me that in Mexico, whatever excuse you give for the crime is the one that sticks with you. Unlike the rest of North America where you're presumed innocent until proven guilty, Mexico only cared about getting to the hypothetical truth rather than wasting time and money to find out otherwise. The lawyer said that it was a good story and apologized for the lack of respect from Ryan.

When I got back to the cell, I glanced in through the bars at Shelly. That feeling of guilt rushed through my body again. The entire time in that cell, we hardly spoke. Both of us were so rattled that we couldn't talk. He sat on the concrete slab, his knees up, head in his chest. A broken man in the worst scenario possible. I'd been to prison before. I knew what it took to survive the harsh environment. It took willpower and patience. Nothing was going to be solved in a moment. The process took days, months... years. Prison was a state of mind that required a man to turn his vision inward and determine how badly he wanted to live. By the look on Shelly's face, he didn't want to spend another second living the life he'd been given. As the guard opened the door to let me in, I realized what I had to do.

"You go home and I'll stay to take the charge."

Shelly couldn't believe what I was saying. "How is that possible?"

The lawyer told me one other thing. The police only wanted one of us to accept responsibility for the crime. He told me that the driver of the vehicle is the responsible one. At the time, Shelly was driving. But by now they had forgotten. Accepting the charge would be the boldest move I ever made.

We sat in tears on that concrete slab, sealing our friendship and making commitments to each other.

"All I want from you in return is that you go home and do something with your life," I said with sincere honesty. "Forget about this place, but don't forget about me."

"I promise to try and get you home," he said. And I believed him.

Shelly was my close friend and I loved him. That day back home when I convinced him to go on the trip with me, I promised that I'd never let anything happen to him. I was that big brother he never had, and that closeness was something I valued. When the time came for Shelly to make his statement, he smiled, gave me a big hug and walked out of that cell. When the door closed, my brain automatically switched into survival mode. I was now alone to deal with this mess, and somehow I felt stronger than I ever had before in my life.

When Shelly came back to the cell, he greeted me with apprehension. I thought maybe it was from the line of questioning he received. They were merciless on me, pushing me in the back of my head, yelling and trying to scare me. I knew sending Shelly in there with a trace of optimism would make the process smooth for him. I guess I was wrong.

Just as the lawyer said, a day later they came to take us to the prison, only Shelly wouldn't come with me. The court process in Mexico is fairly simplistic. They send the results to you in the prison via a member of the court. The attendee they sent was a petite woman with a small round face. Beautiful and harmless but packing a bundle of bad news in her file folder. Shelly was free to go because I had taken responsibility for the charge. In his moment of elation, Shelly reached out and hugged the woman, catching her and everyone in the room by surprise.

The moment passed by me in slow motion. I watched Shelly embrace the complete stranger much to the delight of the crowd around us. The police officers and no name hang-arounds laughed at Shelly's display of joy. He shook hands and broke into happy tears, then, he was whisked away from me, almost as if to make me believe that he never existed at all.

A cold shudder whipped through my body. I was instantly angry at the fact that I had taken the charge for both of us. Shelly had left me without a single goodbye or thank you. He just... left. I don't blame him for wanting to leave as quickly as he could. The last few days were soaked with misery. But as I watched him walk out on me, the once brave thought of getting through this alone finally hit me, and with it came intense fear. I gave my life for Shelly to get back home. I didn't regret it, but the way he left me made me feel like I had just made a big mistake. But I took a deep internal breath and buckled up for my part of the journey. My only concern was to one day make it home alive and stronger than ever before.

As I turned to head back to the cell, an officer stopped me, shaking his head. He pointed to a large set of doors, and I followed. Behind them was a massive vehicle that resembled a four-by-four truck with a huge cage on the back. He didn't need to speak a word for me to understand what was happening next.

It was time to see the battleground for my toughest fight ever.

* * *

I was a boxer in my previous life, and a good one at that. I'd never been beaten in the ring, nor had anyone ever gotten the best of me in a street fight. I was well known in my city for being a tough guy who never backed down from a fight. For some reason I spent the majority of my life backing up those claims. As a young fighter I relished the identification that followed me around, constantly proving people right. There was something about fighting that made me feel comfortable.

My entire life has been a fight. Abandoned by my family at an old enough age to actually feel some sort of emotion about it. Anger. Deceit. Embarrassment. I had such a grudge towards my family that I took it out on the very society that supported their decision to give me up. I had long stints in and out of detention centers, various foster homes and a psychiatric hospital, all fights that I survived, and won.

Boxing was a natural step for me. I had a lot of anger as a teenager and nowhere to unload it. I entered tough guy competitions against full-grown men and won. When I moved to fighting professionally, without a single match as an amateur, I won those too. A hard-headed, hard-hitting natural boxer who had the athleticism and discipline to go far in the sport. If it wasn't for the fact that I had a chip on my shoulder towards my family, my city and the world, I might have actually made it.

* * *

The back of the truck opened, instantly filling the cage with spots of light from police flashlights. The officers screamed at me in their language. Their beams of light poking me in the eye so I couldn't see. I held my hand up to shield my eyes, and when I did, the screaming increased. I edged my way to the cage door and managed to hop down on to solid ground.

Looking around, we were in a sally-port entrance. There were two massive doors about thirty feet high – the main gate to the outside. Those doors were locked tight and guarded by two prison officers with guns. In fact, as I looked around, I noticed more than ten prison guards with rifles standing over me. They screamed and yelled at me in Spanish, hoping that if I didn't understand them, I'd at least move out of fear. They were right. I moved.

They led me into a small office where they pushed me into a chair and forced a piece of paper into my hand. It looked like a contract, but I had no idea how to know. Spanish seemed even more confusing in writing. At the bottom, there was a space that looked like a signature line. The burly mustached guard slammed a pen in front of me and pointed to the line. I glanced up at him looking for some sort of reason for signing. He gave me nothing but another gesture towards the line. I swallowed and took my chances, signing the line with my fake name. My life was already gone. There was nothing else but my soul to sign away.

Before the ink was dry, they whisked me into another small room and told me by hand signs to remove my clothes. They strip searched me and took the clothes I was wearing away for a closer inspection.

How could I get out of this? With every minute that passed, my opportunity to manipulate my way out of this problem became less likely. As I sat naked in the room, waiting for my clothes to return, my demented thinking went back to Shelly and that time in the city cell where all he did was cry. I found solace in his momentary bout of pain. But now who was laughing? He was free to live again, whereas my death had just begun.

The only reason I made it this far was attributed to my ability to handle misery. I excelled when the chips were down, and floundered when I had it too good. All my life I'd been a loser - a sore one at that, never freely bowing to defeat, instead standing up and punching it right in its ugly face. My soul was encased in granite and my nerves were painstakingly calm. I knew I was stronger than anyone else in the world when it came to handling pressure situations. It was my job, my call to action I considered my life. From that moment on I vowed never to shed another tear for my sorry ass. I was going to fight to get back home even if it killed me, and if this place had plans on killing me, then they were in for the surprise of their lives.

When the door opened, a stout guard in a shirt that seemed to extenuate his large gut tossed me my clothing in a green garbage bag. He sneered at me, gesturing to the bag as if asking me to toss it into the bin outside. He watched me dress. Uncomfortable, even in a foreign language. When I was done, he nodded me out the door into a hallway that reeked of burnt toast and had walls that looked as if they hadn't been painted since the days of Poncho Villa. I walked a few steps ahead of him as if I knew where I was going. His heavy breathing increased as I quickened my pace, eager to get somewhere that I knew I was going to hate. When I took one too many steps, the rotund guard whistled at me as if I was a dog, and like man's best friend, I turned around to meet him.

Every door in the place was more like a cage door. They all groaned with age when opened, and the keys resembled something out of an old episode of the Munsters. The worst part of the doors were that you got a clear picture of where you were headed before you even got there, and what I saw behind those bars nearly made me break my promise to myself never to cry again.

Glancing through the cage door was like looking into a different world. I remembered a book I read as a child where the kids looked through the glass into a magical world filled with lions and witches.

The environment was stale, old and run down, like a back alley in some ghetto. The linoleum floor in the hallway converted to cobblestone and I noticed as soon as the cage door opened that the floor was as dirty as the rest of the place.

The "unit" was two tiers high. There were five rooms on the top floor and five on the bottom on both sides of the enclosure. Several ropes hung from the railing on both sides of the unit, and from them dangled wet clothing. The unit itself looked like a stage scene in a theatrical play. It had no real foundation being that the walls rose about thirty feet then just ended. There was no ceiling, just sky. It was like a dungeon stuck in a hole in the middle of nowhere.

The guard nudged me inside. I stepped in without knowing exactly what to do next. They hadn't given me a change of clothes, a bed or any soap or food. I couldn't ask for it because I didn't know how. As soon as I was past the threshold, the guard slammed the cage shut and disappeared back down the hallway leaving me in complete silence, alone and filled with questions I knew would only be answered over time and through experience.

I heard footsteps behind me!

When I turned around, three Mexican men stood there staring at me. They glanced me up and down a few times, and I returned the sentiment only because their appearances baffled me as much as mine did them. They were scantily dressed, draped in what looked like rags to me. They had no shoes and their hands and feet were black with the filth of the surroundings. I felt out of place in my "fashionable" clothing, almost embarrassed. I offered the men a smile, and one of them returned it with a smile of his own - but it was the other two I worried about. They didn't look happy to see me.

The darkness of the prison closed in on me in a heartbeat. The moon in the sky was the only light in the place, but it was strong, strong enough for me to make out that one of the men had something in his hand that he was trying to conceal from me. I shifted to the right, holding my hands slightly in the air in a sign of surrender. As I moved, I was able to see what was in his hand, and it scared the crap out of me.

A knife. I was about to die in a Mexican prison.

Chapter 3
Mike
Fast Talking and Flying Chicken

September, 1998. Cereso prison – Los Mochis, Sinaloa, Mexico

After some fancy footwork and fast-talking, that knife disappeared and was replaced with a deck of cards. After a few minutes of establishing who we were and what we were called, we settled on the floor of the grungy holding area for a game of blackjack for the only pesos I had to my name.

It wasn't as though I didn't see the card slide up his wrist and into his shirtsleeve. It was that I didn't care to say anything, or more so, didn't know how to accuse a man in a language I didn't understand. I had to admit though, he was quick. I'd been around hustlers and cheaters my entire life, so I knew the moves, perfecting many of them myself. On any other occasion I would have screamed and yelled and maybe even flipped the table while swearing and calling his mother names all the while stealing money right in front of his face – but this situation was different. I was on their home turf. My survival depended on my ability to blend in and go with the flow, and if that meant losing a few pesos to the cheater across the floor from me, I'd gladly let him have the measly pesos. Besides, I knew I'd catch him napping sooner or later and that's when I'd hit him with one of my own cheat moves.

He flopped down his ace and face card. Twenty-one. I smiled and pushed the pot towards him, shaking my head much to his delight. Funny thing prison is. One minute, I'm standing in the dark hall praying to god that this guy doesn't stab me, the next thing we're on the dirt floor playing blackjack for pesos I know he doesn't have. I lost the equivalent of two Canadian dollars late that night. A small price to pay for some breathing room.

The entire game all I could think about was where I was. The cards only satisfied my temporary need for distraction. I needed answers to questions that I wasn't ready to ask. My mind swirled with thoughts of back home and the people I called friends. Why had Ryan abandoned us? Would Shelly live up to his promise and try to get me out of here?

At what felt like the middle of the night, I retired to my cell – a small hole in the wall next to the entrance. It was meager by all means, resembling the smallest of small bachelor apartments. The cell was about ten feet by fifteen feet. It consisted of a short concrete slab about two feet off the ground (that was the bed) and a counter across the room (that was the kitchen area). There was a shower stall in the cell, but there was no running water. Along with the shower was a toilet and the entire area was separated from the bedroom by a wall in the middle of the cell. Cramped was a gross underestimation.

I huddled on the concrete slab, using my only shirt as a blanket and my right shoe as a pillow and I kept what little money I had in that shoe. I didn't sleep at all that first night. The cell nearly froze me to death. I never knew Mexico could be so cold. Sleeping in warm hotel beds never allowed me to experience the frigid nights and early mornings. When the sun finally rose, I didn't feel like a new man, I felt worse. I felt like a homeless man in search of his lost identity.

The sun pounded through the opening in the roof and filled the unit with light. Various inmates strolled out of their cells, all wandering down to my cell to see the gringo who lost all his money playing *cheatjack*. Mexicans of all shapes and sizes poked their heads into my cell to see what I looked like. I remained huddled on my slab of concrete, depressed like a caged animal that was used to running free in the wild.

I must have drifted off and woke up a dozen times before finally giving way to a full few hours of sleep. The air warmed up and the soft sounds of guitars and Mexican vocals on a nearby radio soothed my nerves to the point where I realized how exhausted I really was. When I woke, there was a Mexican guard standing over me.

The guard led me to the gate where a small-framed Mexican man with wide rim glasses awaited me. He smiled with honest sincerity. He was dressed in suit pants and an open collar shirt. He looked more like a teacher than a prisoner or prison staff.

The man's name was Jaime, pronounced *High-me*, and he was a teacher. He worked at the ESL school in Los Mochis teaching English. So when I heard my language spoken for the first time in days, I was stunned to the point of silence. For once in my life I was at a loss of words.

"I'm here to assist you in court." He spoke with a gentle tone.

"Where am I?" I asked.

"You're in seventy two hours. They will keep you here until they classify you for maximum or minimum security."

I leaned up against the bars and looked Jamie right in the eyes.

"Can you get me out of here?"

The question seemed to jolt him. He looked at his shoes then back up at me.

"No. I'm sorry."

Then what good was he?

"What is going to happen to me?" I asked him.

"Well, you'll be taken to court today, then brought back here. Tomorrow they'll send you to either maximum or minimum security where you'll be able to get some fresh air."

Still angry. "And my phone calls? Money? Food? How the hell can I get some food?"

Jaime turned immediately to a guard standing nearby trying to understand our conversation. He asked the guard something, then turned back to me.

"The officer said that I can leave and bring you back something to eat. Would that be okay?"

My mouth began to water. "That would be great."

I handed Jaime some bills through the gate. "Could you also make a phone call for me?" He handed me a pen and a piece of paper. "My friends will know what to do when you call them."

Jaime just smiled, took the money and walked away without another word. As I watched him disappear down the hallway and through the same door I entered, I wondered two things. Who was this guy and was he going to run away with my money?

*   *   *

Later that week in court, I broke down and cried. The *policia* threw me in another cage in a room that resembled a courtroom, and in front of a packed house I lost my cool and shed every bit of angst I had in me. For the first time since getting arrested, I actually cared about what was going to happen. I felt fear, regret and sorrow all at once, and as Jaime translated the words of the court, I couldn't help from falling apart.

They told me that I was remanded to the prison and that I would have my case heard before the court in six months. I learned of the court process. They only required this single court appearance from me. From then on the court would come to the prison to deal with me. This was the last vision of freedom I would have for the next year.

I sat on the floor of the cage screaming at no one and crying as if though begging for my life. The pain I felt at that moment was unlike anything in the past. Not only was I crying because of my situation, but also for the years of my life I'd wasted to this point, the grief regarding my family and the anger I felt inside against myself. I hated Mike Oulton. All those years of unresolved emotions came down to that moment. As far as I was concerned, this was the end of my life.

Jaime watched from across the courtroom. Empathy all over his face. When he walked up to the cage and touched my arm, I felt his concern through my skin. His job was to translate and nothing more, but he had a conscience, and with that came a desire to help. He told me that it was important that I calm down and relax, that nothing was going to be solved by crying. He was wrong. Crying felt good, and it wasn't about the court or the stenographers and how they felt, it was about me, and if I had to cry to get stronger, I would.

When I looked up at Jaime, I saw a tear roll down his cheek, then quickly get wiped away before he turned back to the court. I realized then and there that I had just made a friend.

* * *

September, 1998. Maximum Security Unity – Cereso

When the unit representative, Carlos, opened the door to my new home for the next year, I didn't know whether this was a bad joke or an insult because I wasn't one of them. My new cell was the old garbage cell, and it stank like a dead animal. I wouldn't stand for another *us or them* situation. I'd been to prison in three countries now and every joint was the same. In Canada, it's the convicts versus the guards and race versus race in America. If this was a sign of the torment that was to come, I'd better find out who *us* was and get with the program. I didn't want to be a *them*.

The maximum unit had the same makeup as the seventy-two hour dungeon. Everything was made of stone or cement. The only areas that actually had ceilings were the cells. Other than that, nothing but blue skies and hot sun baking anything exposed to it. There were two sides and two floors. The doors to the cells on the top floor opened to a walkway protected by a handrail. There were sets of stone tables in a common area, and next to that, an area with sinks and cement scrub pads for people to wash their clothes. The entire complex was surrounded by a twenty-foot wall creating a private compound for the maximum-security guys.

The men in the maximum unit were in transition. They had a number of inmates who'd been there for quite a number of years. They ran the unit like a real maximum-security jail, locking inmates in their cells at night. The unit representative – who had the only key to the doors – was the caretaker of the unit. There were no guards standing post or doing checkups. The security, and the discipline, was handled by the unit rep – *el cabello* – the horse.

At the moment, the representative Carlos standing side by side with me at the door of my new cell seemed like a pretty reasonable person. He didn't come on too strong with an attitude like most other Mexican men, but he did have that signature thick mustache under his nose. He was bow legged but moved with an aggressive ease, his shoulder blades open and his back as straight as a board. He carried himself with a lot of self-admiration. He gave me short sympathetic smiles which let me know that under that layer of show was a caring man.

My cell had a completely less admirable quality about it. In fact, there wasn't a single pleasant thing I could say about my new abode. The make up was exactly the same as the cell in the dungeon – a bed, bath and kitchen area. But the garbage! Beans and spilt Pepsi, rotten meat and old vegetables. When I turned on the light – a small bulb hanging from a chain in the middle of the ceiling – cockroaches hi-tailed it to the protection of darkness. I'd never lived with cockroaches before. I laughed to myself. Who was the invader in a dive like this, the cockroach or the Canadian?

The keys jingled in Carlos's hand. He laughed along with me as if reading my mind..

"You're going to have to clean it tomorrow!"

Those words came in English and were like a call from heaven. I spun around quickly, following the sweet sound to the bottom floor of the two-tier unit. There stood a man, brown but not Mexican, East Indian or Caribbean maybe. A dark black beard - thin and symmetrical - traced the lower outline of his face, around his mouth and up his jaw line to a tight knit mess of the same coarse hair on top of his head. He had a youthful glow to his face. His cheeks had a healthy rose hue to them, and because of his dark skin, his teeth shone brighter than the white snow on my own Canadian slopes.

I leaned over the railing and smiled down at my neighbor. "You speak English."

He laughed. "I certainly hope the hell I do!"

His name was Roger, and he was from Trinidad and Tobago. He and his wife Maria had been caught smuggling cocaine in his car up the Pacific coast. Maria was Mexican. She was in the prison on the woman's side. Roger was an American by citizenship and had only transported drugs once before. When they got caught, neither Maria or Roger took responsibility, which meant both of them were destined to spend their time together – rather than apart like in most countries – in a Mexican hell hole prison. They decided that fighting their case was in their best interest. When I showed up in maximum, they had just passed the fifth anniversary of their arrest and they were still waiting for the court to come to them.

"That is the garbage cell," he told me. I believed him. "If you like, I can help you sweep it all out into the bin."

It took us twenty minutes to sweep the cell clean, just in time to see the prison guards crash into the unit four strong and begin to check that people were locked down. Carlos escorted the officers to every cell, locking the doors behind him, his chest inflated with a pride that captured no admiration from me. I'd never seen a convict lock another convict up.

When they reached my cell and locked me in with snickers and rapid Spanish verbiage that I was sure never to understand, I felt for the first time what it would be like to get stranded on a deserted island. A cockroach scampered into a crack at the base of my bed. They were there, waiting for the light to go off so they could continue their scourge of the room. The garbage was gone but the smell remained. As I lie on my concrete slab - no mattress or blankets - I wondered if this was how POW's of world wars felt, huddling in a concrete catacomb wishing he'd taken a cozy job as a teacher instead of a soldier. The night hurled bolts of chill at me. I thought about the pool at the hotel I swam in just days ago. I knew it would be many, many more days before it ever happened again.

* * *

October, 1998 – Cereso

After a week in the new cell, things were beginning to work themselves out. I managed to buy a small mattress about an inch thick from a vender in the prison. It was more like a bed pad that I could roll up and sleep on. The bed was still hard, but at least I could begin to get some sleep at night.

Dystopia

Jaime had come in to visit the day after they moved me to the maximum. With him he brought some take out food (a hamburger and fries) a giant blanket and some sheets, and some groceries. Roger explained to me earlier that there were two ways to get food and water - take what they give you or buy your own. He told me how the food delivered to the units daily was cooked in dirty water. He bought his own water in the prison market. It came in big blue bottles and would become my most precious commodity.

What was the most unique about Cereso was that it was part of the community, unlike the prisons back home. They welcomed people into the jail any time they liked within hours of visitation which were from sun up to sun down. If families wanted to spend the night, they could, but they would have to stay for two days at a time with at least two weeks in between. Roger told me about the social events on the weekends where there were huge dances in the yard and every convict's family could be involved. Because the prison was a rehabilitation center, they considered the community important to the rehabilitation of the inmate.

The worst crime a person commits in Mexico is drug trafficking. The country was constantly hounded by the United States to patrol and control their side of the border in regards to the war on drugs. They are funded federally by the American government to train their police forces to catch drug runners. Mexico has the highest number of drug trafficking busts in all the Americas. Roger told me of a man who was arrested for killing his wife's lover. He walked in on them having sex in his bed and he shot the adulterer. The courts gave him sixty years, but because of Mexico's desire to rehabilitate their citizens, and because it wasn't a drug charge, the man was let out in less than two years citing his offense as a passionate crime and worthy of a second chance.

Being so close to the community would make my time much easier but who were these people I was living with? I'd met some of the guys on my unit. Most wouldn't dare attempt to break through the language barrier. From our brief conversations, I could tell that Carlos wished deep inside that he could speak English to me. His communication consisted of hand signs and bizarre sounds to go with them, which seemed traditional with foreigners. The Mexicans speak with great emotion, being passionate people with a flare for expressing how they truly feel. They shake their hands in the air with gusto; their faces light up like slot machines when they get into something personal and proud. Carlos was like a bandleader every time we stopped to speak. His chest majestically inflated and his prominent chin rose in the air, casting a small shadow on my foreigner brow. His hands moving and pointing... over there... this... that...

Sergio, a diminutive ex policeman in his forties was the first to get into a full blown conversation with me. Since it was one sided, completely to his favor, all I could do was nod my head and smile. When Roger came to translate, he told me that Sergio couldn't believe that I didn't speak Spanish. Roger told me to learn as quickly as possible because he hated translating.

The unit had it's own store where I could buy canned goods and cold drinks. Julio, the storekeeper on the unit had a refrigerator that he said I could use. *Muchos gracias*! Jaime brought me some canned fruit and fish, bread, peanut butter and frozen chicken. I left my frozen chicken in there along side other guy's food.

I was used to the crappy prisons in Canada – long boring days filled with loneliness and predictability. Well the Mexican prison was the same crappy prison only that it was taking place in paradise. The convicts were the same as in Canada. They minded their own business, looked at the ground when they walked by you, had the same bad attitude towards the guards. The only difference was that they never spoke back to an officer. They treated the guards like equals, in front of their faces. It would be hard to get used to that.

Another thing that was different was the way the Mexican people viewed crime and criminals. Everyone was equal in the sense that if you broke the law and got thrown in prison, you were the same as any other convict regardless of the crime. My cell was on the top row of eight cells. On one side was a cop caught for smuggling drugs, and on the other side a pedophile who raped and killed a young girl. Both were treated equally and fairly by the other cons. Talk about being stuck between a rock and a hard place. Back home, if I had two neighbors like that, it would usually mean that my life was in danger and I was in protective custody.

Everything seemed so primitive - the refrigerator, the small two burner stove, a radio I saw in someone's room. Everything was old and out dated, but in perfect working condition. I felt as if I was in old Mexico, before the touch of civilization and technical evolution. It made me realize how lucky - or perhaps how strained - we were to have the amenities we had back home. My chance to know what life was like without a microwave or television had finally arrived.

Later that night I went to get my chicken from the fridge and to my surprise it was gone. I double-checked, then asked Julio about it. He just shrugged and paid me no mind.

That little bit of ignorance set me off like a bottle rocket. A large-scale fit of rage had been building inside of me. Between the lack of communication and the numerous dirty looks I'd received since arriving, I was at the point of complete meltdown. I held my stare on Julio for a half minute more, then without thinking, walked back to the fridge and began tossing food everywhere, onto the floor and across the unit. Inmates came out of their cells to see what all the noise was about. Roger ran up to me pleading for me to calm down, but I was furious.

"You must stop!" said Roger. "They'll lock you up in the hole."

When I'd completely emptied the fridge, I stood up and glanced around the unit. Everyone was out of their cells, shocked at the mess of frozen and cooked food cast every which direction. Roger made an announcement to the unit. I watched Carlos, fuming, storm out of the front doors, his keys jingling at his side.

"What did you say?" I asked Roger.

"I told them that you're angry. Someone stole your food."

"All I want is my chicken back," I told him. "Or I want to guy who took it to tell me to my face why he stole it from me."

But there wouldn't be time for that. No sooner did I feel my arousal levels drop, a swarm of guards led by Carlos burst into the unit. The head guard, donning a classic pair of highway cop sunglasses and a ball cap raced over to me immediately. He grabbed my upper arm and pulled me to the stairwell, forcing me to my cell where Carlos locked me in.

The guard turned to Roger and spoke to him in Spanish. His tone was angry and determined. Through the small window adjacent to the door Roger told me what he had said.

"He's very angry with you."

"What's going on?" I asked. "How long am I locked down for?"

Roger ran his hands through his thinning hair. "There may be a problem." He said with a sigh. "They think you're going to kill someone. They want you locked up for good."

Chapter 4
Mike
A Hard Head Makes a Soft Ass

October, 1998. Cereso

Shithead. That was his name.

He wanted my money more than he wanted to help me, but I understood his intentions. Get the money from the helpless foreigner. There had probably been a few dozen other foreigners in my position – locked in a cell with the only hope of freedom lying in the hands of a guard who didn't give a damn whether I lived or died. The only thing was that I didn't care either. It was all the same. The only difference was living hurt more than death.

Shithead stood half my size and was ten times the asshole. He wore a prison emblem on his hat (the name of the prison written across the front) and a pair of sunglasses that hid his beady little eyes. He stood at the caged window to my cell staring in at me like I was some sort of mutant freak show, looking me up and down and spitting on the wall just under the window every few seconds. His inflated chest and the way he moved that toothpick from one side of his mouth to the other didn't give me the impression that he was in charge, just insane.

Roger sighed and ran his fingers through his hair

"He wants a hundred dollars to let you out," he said to me in English, offering a smile to Shithead who looked somewhat insulted that he couldn't understand a word we were saying.

"Tell him his head is too big for his body," I commented, offering Shithead a phony smile.

"I can't say that!" Roger suddenly stiffened. "He'll lock me up with you!"

I hate crooked cops. People in authority using their job to get one over on someone could go to hell. A hundred dollars was a lot of money to let me go and I wasn't about to pay him a dime. If he thought I was scared to spend a little time locked away from the rest of the world, he was thinking of some other sorry foreigner.

I leaned closer to the cage. "Tell him that if he lets me out, I won't knock those stupid sunglasses off his face."

Roger nearly fell on his ass. "No! I can't say that either. He'll throw you in the segregation unit."

The hole, my cell, back home – it was all the same. Shithead had no idea who he had locked up. I'd been in situations like this before – locked down with no hope of getting free. Every situation ended the same way – eventually I saw freedom again.

After speaking briefly in Spanish, Roger turned back to me, his face white with exasperation.

"He says that you won't like being locked up for a week. You should just pay the hundred and be free of this idiot."

An idiot he was, but I wasn't. The worst possible thing that could happen to me was death. The best, locked up away from everyone. I teased Shithead with a wave and walked back to my bed. Shithead stormed away, yelling out in Spanish to the entire unit. Roger told me that he warned everyone to stay away from my cell or they would all suffer the same punishment.

* * *

I thought I was tough enough to hold out for Shithead to return and show his cards. I thought that maybe there was someone higher than him who would force him to unlock me. Nothing doing. The relentless guards loved dishing out discipline. They only came to check on me at the counts. They didn't ask me if I was hungry or even let me out to get water for my shower. They just let me rot in the cell as if I didn't matter, and I quickly realized that I didn't.

The first day wasn't so bad. I slept most of the time, waking only to get a drink. All I had in my cell were canned fish and Pepsi I bought from the unit vender, six cans at a time. I could survive, but for how long I had no idea. From my bed, in the darkness of my room, I listened to the sounds of the Mexicans downstairs living their prison lives the best they knew how. In between short bursts of dozing, I heard children once and a while laughing and running up and down the walkway. At times, smells of food cooking on the stove wafted up to my cell and made me want to give in, but I refused to let Shithead get the better of me.

The second day really proved what I was made of. The unbearable heat sucked all the oxygen from my cell. I covered the window with a towel to keep the heat outside, but even in the darkness, the heat had a way of controlling my life. I lay in bed a restless man determined to fight the sun and get some sleep. I was covered in sweat, stinking from the lack of a bath, and angry that I couldn't do anything about it. But still, I was more determined not to let Shithead get me. He couldn't win. Never!

The third morning I woke up early. The unit was silent and impossibly cold. It was if I'd fallen asleep in a stove and woke up in a deep freeze. I put on every piece of clothing I had and huddled under my one blanket for protection. As I laid there under my sheets, I was reminded of my frozen homeland and how much I missed the Canadian weather.

As the morning progressed, the chill disappeared. For the second time that young day I awoke to a different temperature than when I'd fallen asleep. The scorching heat had returned. I stripped down to just shorts, gasping for breath and struggling to figure out where the hell I was. Finally, enough was enough.

* * *

Once again, I found myself at the caged window with Roger and Shithead standing in front of me. This time, Shithead wore a smile that said, "I knew you'd break". I hated every minute of our final negotiations, but I realized that locked up in Canada had nothing on locked up in Mexico.

"You're smart to pay him," said Roger. There was a sense of relief in his voice. "This guy can really make things difficult for you."

"How so?"

"He once charged me four hundred dollars just to let my wife stay over for the night," he said. "I paid him, but I didn't like it."

"Four hundred dollars," I looked Shithead right in his dark shades. "This guy's got a lot of nerve."

Roger offered Shithead a smile to ease his curiosity. "Well, he's got the keys."

He did have the keys, and that's what made it even worse. Charging for luxuries was normal around the prison. Everyone paid for special treatment. No one was exempt. He said that the guards hit up the drug dealers and smugglers more than anyone else. The belief was that they had the money to throw around, and they might as well throw it their way. The blackmailing was a prison tradition that Shithead believed I was going to conform to.

Think again. I was the one who made the hard deals, not a two-bit prison guard.

"Tell him to shove his freedom up his ass."

Roger flinched. "I can't say that!"

"I thought you were my translator."

Roger held his hands in the air in surrender. "You're going to get me in a lot of trouble. I quit."

And with that, Roger left. Shithead glared through the bars at me. I smiled and shrugged my shoulders. He knew that the money would never be produced. I was a tough nut to crack, but as he walked away, his chest still inflated and his sunglasses perched high on the bridge of his nose, I knew he still believed eventually I would pay.

Everyone paid. What made me so special?

* * *

For the second time in a week I stared through a cage at Jaime – only this time I wasn't in tears. He pulled up a chair and sat at the window. He passed me enough food to last another week in lock down and a jug of water to keep me alive for a month. I felt a surge of confidence surge through my body.

"Why are you doing this?" he asked me in his gentle way.

"There's a difference between me and any other foreigner that comes through here, Jaime. I don't give in that easily."

Jaime reflected on my comment for a second. "Why does that make you different?"

"Because I refuse to let these people get at me," I said. "All they want is my money and I'm not going to give it to them."

Jaime folded his hands on his lap.

"Is that what you think Mexicans want? Your money?"

"Yes," I said. "Ever since I was arrested, all anyone's tried to get from me is a statement and my cash. I'm not stupid you know. I'm not easily hustled."

A look of confusion swept over his face. "Hustle? What is that word?"

I shook my head. "Hustle. I don't know. Like a scam. Like someone's trying to steal my money."

"Oh," he said and looked down. "Like a con game."

"Exactly."

Jaime and I sat silent for a minute contemplating the conversation that had just passed between us. Finally, he spoke.

"There's an old story that was told to me by my father when I was young." His eyes darkened. "An old woman stood on the corner of the road looking for a ride from anyone passing by on coach. For a ride, instead of money, she'd offer them a piece of wisdom that might change their lives. Many coaches stopped, but none of the drivers would make the exchange. Finally one man stopped and took the deal, asking what the bit of wisdom was. The old woman smiled and said, 'Don't judge a person by what they don't have to give, but rather by what they have to offer'. And on her way from the coach, she gave him a bag full of gold pieces."

I thought about the story for a minute before shaking my head. "I don't get it."

Jaime smiled. "Not all Mexicans want your money. Even though their intentions seem bad, they're really just trying to find out what kind of person you are."

"So they take my money through blackmailing," I said. "Nice tactics."

"What I'm trying to tell you is that it may seem as though everyone is trying to take from you, but if you give them a chance, they will have something more valuable than money to offer."

Jaime looked at his watch and stood.

"I have to go." He reached into his pocket. "Your friends asked me to give this to you."

Through the bars he handed me an envelope. Inside, was two thousand dollars in cash and three phone cards.

"Please don't worry. It's all there," he said, offering me a simple smile filled with peace. "I'll come back to visit you in a week."

I watched him walk away until I couldn't see him any more. Sitting back on my bed with the envelope filled with cash I felt like a complete asshole for saying what I'd said.

I think the correct word I was looking for was *gringo*. At that moment, I felt like a total gringo.

I took out a hundred dollars and banged on the door for Shithead.

* * *

With all the dust and grime associated with Mexico, it's difficult to stay clean. The hardest thing to adapt to was the method I had to take to wash my clothes or my body.

Since there was no running water in the cells, getting water for a shower was no easy task. Upon entering the maximum, Carlos gave me a ten-gallon bucket. Roger said that the bucket was for water. At first I had no idea what he meant. The first time I turned on the faucet in the shower and nothing came out, I realized that the luxuries of my modern world were over a thousand miles away.

The process for fetching water took the phrase 'a quick shower' right out of the question. At the front gate of the maximum unit was a large cement lined hole in the ground about ten feet deep with a faucet near the opening. To get water, I had to hang the bucket under the faucet then carry it up two flights of stairs to my shower room. Since the water came old as cold as Canada, I was forced to buy a water heater constructed of two thick metal wires attached to a socket plug wrapped around a cylinder shaped piece of wood. When I plugged the device in and placed it in the bucket, I would wait fifteen minutes for the water to heat up so that I could take a very conservative shower. Ten gallons isn't a lot of water to complete a typical shower, but I made do. The first few times I ran out of water, leaving my cell to get a second bucket with a hair full of soap and dripping wet. It was a total inconvenience.

Washing my clothes wasn't any easier. Instead of machines, at the other end of the unit were cement sinks. Along side each sink was a pad of cement in the shape of one of those old washboards. Roger lent me his wash brush the first time I attempted to clean my gear and I almost scrubbed a hole right through my shirt.

"You need a gentle hand and a lot of soap," he said. "Eventually, you'll get good at it."

The maximum was the cleanest unit in the prison. Because it held some of the more respected members of the community, there was a focus on comfort and hygiene. Most of the men were lawyers, doctors or policemen. They came from nice homes with good families. They had money and education and there was no need to live in filth.

Every Friday was cleaning day. Carlos had a good grasp on that process that included four other guys, buckets of water, and about twenty bags of soap that everyone pitched in money to buy. The workers would fill the hole with water, which took about an hour. Then they would create a human line and pass the many buckets to and from the hole. Inside the unit, Carlos would spray bags of soap over everything, and using a large scrub brush on a pole, he'd lather everything up and scrub the hell out of it. The process took no less than two hours. It was an impressive show of cooperation and commitment.

* * *

I must have stood at the phone booth in the main yard for next to ten minutes summoning up the courage to call my family. They had to know about my situation by now, and if they didn't, they'd be wondering where the hell I was.

As I searched inside myself for the fortitude to dial those numbers, I glanced around the yard, watching the people only to find out that the majority of them were watching me. Scowls and inquisitive glances hurled at me through eyes of killers and sever drug addicts. One kid walked by me three times before stopping to speak to me in Spanish. I just smiled and it seemed to satisfy his curiosity.

The yard – *quadro* – was about the size of four professional football fields put together, massive in comparison to anything back home. A gigantic thirty-foot wall surrounded the entire prison, the gun towers loomed over the quadro like a row of soldiers on high alert. There were no guards in the yard, only in the towers. From where I was standing near the middle of the open space I could see the gleam off the glass of their rifle scopes.

Inside the walls, life thrived alongside misery. The inmates had it pretty easy for being in a bad situation. There were various venders peddling anything from ice cream to candy. At one end of the yard sat the restaurant court. There were chicken and hamburger stands, tacos and sandwiches – anything that you could buy on the street, you could buy in the prison. It felt more like a concession area at a ballpark than a prison.

The Mexican people loved their sports, so it was fitting that every sport was represented in the yard. There was a beautifully lined soccer field with green grass and stadium bleachers that had a game on at any time of the day. There was a baseball diamond and five basketball courts, and the venues were always in use. I loved sports, so passing time wouldn't be that bad once I got settled in.

But what about the dreaded phone call?

I picked up the receiver and held it in my hand for a moment. The plastic burned in my hand from the afternoon sun. A Spanish woman came on the line, speaking to me at a speed too fast to even try to understand. I hung up the phone in frustration, pocketing the phone card until I could get Roger to help me. A perfect timing excuse. I knew eventually I'd have to face the music.

On my way back to the max, I noticed a young Mexican with a pair of boxing gloves slung casually around his neck. He walked right past me, offering nothing as he danced towards a darker corner of the yard. With nothing else to do, I followed him. The boxer in me needed to know where he was going.

*   *   *

August, 1998 – A Texas Hotel

"What do you mean you can't make it?" screamed my boxing coach over my cellular phone.

We'd been planning for this fight for the past two months. It was supposed to be another opportunity to showcase my boxing skill to the city. The time to move up in the ranks was now. I was young and angry and fearless – a perfect fighter.

"I'm sorry Sean," I said with all sincerity. "I'm a little tied up right now."

"Well untie yourself and get back here!"

I couldn't do it. I was in Texas, stuck in a hotel during one of the nastiest rainstorms I'd ever seen. Outside, the rain pelted against the glass like little rocks thrown by mischievous kids. Two feet of water flooded the streets and a tornado warning was in effect. Moving was out of the question.

I didn't feel good about leaving Sean high and dry without a main event. He'd trained me from the beginning, when I was just seventeen, and there were huge expectations for a career in boxing. But at the moment, life had nothing to do with a potential career-making fight. It was all about the drugs that I needed to get home.

Boxing consumed my life. I ran every morning, sacrificed any youthful pleasure like going to bars, drinking, using drugs. My mission was to get a chance to fight for a world title. I focused on being in the best shape of my life, every day of my life. If it wasn't for being broke, I would have made the fight. But my lack of responsibility created poverty and desperation, and because I was a man of extreme pride, being broke hurt more than any punch in the head.

"I'll be back in less than a month," I told Sean. "We'll make it up then."

Before I could hear his response, the phone went dead. Then suddenly, the lights in the hotel went out. The loud beep of the generator in the hallway echoed throughout the entire hotel. I stood holding the phone in the dark.

Shelly burst into the room like a swat team on a surprise raid. He ran to the window and yanked open the curtains.

"Have you looked outside?"

We were on the seventeenth floor of the hotel, high enough to look over the entire city of Corpus Christi. When he opened the blinds, there was nothing but a veil of rain and wind, but through it all, near the edge of the city was a massive tornado almost as high as the hotel itself.

"Now that's something you don't see every day," I said.

We packed our things and headed the other direction by car. The storm blew us out of town, but sent with us a hurricane of trouble that I'd never get over.

That storm sent us to Mexico and we never looked back once.

* * *

October, 1998 – Cereso – boxing gym

I watched the black skinned Mexican kid bang on the tough-as-steel leather heavy bag with both hands, sweating hard from the sun overhead, gritting his teeth as it twirled in one direction hanging from the chain. His eyes focussed intently on the bag, his confidence increasing with every punch. He had to be no more than twenty years old, ripped muscles, with the only piece of hair on his body located right above his upper lip.

The small boxing gymnasium sat in the middle of the only corner with shade in the entire prison. Though cast in darkness for most of the day, the leather bags sizzled in the blazing heat. The gym floor was rugged cement and a steel chicken fence wrapped the enclosure up like a concrete burrito.

I sat on a bench far enough away from the gym not to be noticed. There were seven bags inside and all of them were being beat on by kids no more than twenty years old apiece. They pounded on those bags like their lives depended on it. Near an old wooden cracker barrel used for water, their coach stood with a timer barking out instructions and pointing out their weaknesses at random.

Those kids had what I once had. A dream of becoming a real fighter. That drive to get up every morning at three a.m. to run and train until the sun went down. I thought about all that time I sacrificed, believing that I was headed somewhere. I was. I was here. Somewhere in the middle of nowhere.

I don't know what caused me to go over to that gym that day. Maybe boxing still flowed through my veins and would never disappear like an incurable virus. But as soon as I stepped inside the coop, all those determined eyes turned from the bags to me. I felt as if though I'd just walked in on a crime in progress. The coach approached me, still yelling at his fighters. They all returned to their training.

He spoke in that damn language.

"No Spanish," I said. *Total gringo* had arrived.

The coach made a punching motion in the air with his hands. I nodded and threw a combination at him. Two heads looked away from their bags over to me. The coach smiled and blew his whistle. The entire group made their way over to us.

The coach gestured for me to throw the combination again, I did, and just like my trainer back home, he pointed out my good technique to the rest of the class.

Several of the fighters began hurling questions at me. I looked at the coach hoping he'd explain my lack of Spanish, and I think he did. Then they laughed after one boxer's comment behind me. I turned around. He was taller than me but significantly thinner.

Tattooes covered his body and his face was scarred from the middle of his forehead down the length of his nose. He had his gloves off and stood directly behind me, looking me up and down.

I smiled at Scarface, but he didn't smile back. The coach blew the whistle in seconds they were all back at their bags... except Scarface and two other fighters. I spun on my heels just in time to catch Scarface's head butt to the face. Instantly my head began to spin. I held my hands up to my face as I tried to regain my senses.

Scarface and his gang began hitting me from all angles laughing the entire time. I saw blood running down my shirt. I touched my eye. There was a bump the size of a golf ball and it was bleeding. The assailant to my right kicked me in the ass and that's when I got angry. I could accept a good unfair boxing match, but when people starting kicking, that was over the line.

The last thing I remember before completely fucking up all three Mexicans was my phone card falling to the ground and a dark skinned hand picking it up. It was never returned to me. The guy thought it was funny to rip me off, but little did he know stealing my card did me the biggest favour in the world.

Chapter 5
Mike
This Will Leave a Good Scar

I've had my fair share of stitches, but never have I had a doctor sew me up without a local anaesthetic. I flinched as the needle entered the skin just under the open wound beneath my right eye. The Mexican doctor smiled as he pushed the needle through, overlapping the corner of the cut, then pushing back through to seal the wound.

"This will leave a good scar," he said in English, broken but still recognizable.

Doctor Juan Martinez, or Doc Juan as I called him, was a gentle man, well educated and the steadiest hand I've ever allowed to stitch me up. He didn't speak much, but when he did, his voice carried with it a professionalism and concern that made people around him feel as though they were needed. He looked the role of a doctor. His hair was well groomed and his mustache small and unobtrusive. He had impeccable posture underneath his white doctor's coat. If he'd never told me that he murdered his wife, I'd never have guessed it.

"How did you end up the only doctor here?" I asked him between punctures.

In a roundabout way, Juan told me his story about when he walked in on his wife cheating with another man. He mentioned how he left their home a broken man, only to come back four days later to kill her while she slept. The courts gave him twenty years.

When he came to the prison, there was no doctor on staff. He volunteered to help out at the clinic only to find himself in a permanent position after the first week. He didn't mind the job. He studied for years at the University in Mexico City to be a doctor, his life ambition, so taking over the clinic was similar to him getting his own practice. The only drawback?

"They pay me ten pesos a day," he said with a trace of a brave smile.

Not a great doctor's fee. Ten pesos a day worked out to a dollar Canadian more or less.

When he finished stitching my face, he handed me a mirror. The work was primitive, a scar would be definite, but the wound was sealed. With all the dirt and disease floating around the prison, I needed to be safe.

"I'll get Nomi," said Juan as he dipped out of the room leaving me with my new disfiguration.

The examination room had all the qualities of a regular hospital room. There was one large shelf against the wall that contained jars of cotton swabs, bandages and surgical tools. The bed I sat on was multi purpose. They conducted emergency surgeries and routine check ups there. The floor was stained brown. Fresh drops of my own blood dried and turned the same color.

I touched my new scar again. My first Mexican prison souvenir. Getting out of the prison in one piece would prove difficult if I kept losing blood like this. I needed to learn Spanish quickly to verbally dissolve any problem the next time it came up.

When the door opened, it wasn't Don Juan. Instead, there stood a young woman about my age. Her skin was like dark milk chocolate, amplified by the clean white of her nurse's smock. She smiled at me, giving me eye contact for a brief second before scurrying to the shelf for gauze.

She had a primitive beauty about her. Her distinct Mexican features were attractive in a way that made me curious as to who she was. What was a woman so young doing in a place like this? When she approached me, her piercing blue eyes gave me a glimpse at her spirit. Nervous, shy, intimidated.

She pointed to herself. "Nomi."

I offered my hand, forgetting about the pain surging through my entire face. "Michael."

She shook with a shaking hand, trembling like a shy woman does when introduced to a man she doesn't know. Without another word, she went to work on my face, covering it with a small strip of white gauze, avoiding all eye contact as if I was an evil hypnotist after her soul.

"What kind of a name is Nomi," I asked as she taped the gauze.

She shook her head and finished her work as quick as she could. When she was done, she offered me a trembling smile then hurried out the door without another word or gesture.

"Wait!"

I jumped off the table and followed her. She moved quickly through the entranceway and out into the sun drenched courtyard, refusing to look back at me.

I stood at the entrance of the clinic watching her disappear back into the quadro wondering what the hell I did to make her so evasive. Doc Juan appeared from a back room to join me.

"She is a married woman," he said. "Her husband is here with her. It's not right for her to speak with another man."

"We didn't even speak," I mumbled, wincing as a shot of pain ripped through my face.

Doctor Juan placed a hand on my shoulder. "Do you want something for the pain?"

"What have you got?"

He just smiled and led me back into the building.

Behind the door from which he came was a long hallway with three metal doors on each side. As I followed, I noticed each of the doors had a small window. Like a cell or an observation chamber, each of the doors was locked tight, and as I passed the first door I caught movement out of the corner of my eye.

I peeked in the first door and nearly cried out in horror. Inside the room sat an older gentleman of about fifty years. His skin was white with evidence of a lack of sun and he sat in the chair hunched over as if waiting to wither away to death. His white skin was what shocked me. It looked like deep wrinkles. One flap of skin folded over another in thick chunks that reminded me of uncooked pizza dough. As if sensing my presence, his head snapped up and he caught me in the window. I jumped out of the way.

Juan waited for me at the end of the hall.

"Leprosy," he said plainly. "He can't come out of the room."

In the rooms were men and women who had no place in the prison community or couldn't interact because of their diseases. Leprosy, flesh-eating disease, open wounds that became infected with contagious viruses. In each of the quarantine rooms, inmates waited for their release from prison or their death – whichever came first. Juan informed me that the latter was more likely than going home.

Juan opened the door to the room but I wanted nothing to do with it. After seeing the poor men in the decompression chambers, my sad wound paled in comparison to their problems. I'd never been a whiner, and I wasn't about to start.

"I think I'll pass on the drugs," I told him. "It's not that important."

I realized that on any day I could find myself in one of those chambers if I didn't take drastic steps to keep my world clean and in order. Thoughts of my family entered my mind. Being that close to death put everything in perspective. I needed to call them before the chance wasn't there at all.

* * *

"You've really done it this time," said my mother. Her voice shook with anger and fear.

I remained silent and just let her speak. There wasn't a thing I could say to ease this situation. This was a time for me to just keep my mouth shut and let the emotions fly.

My mom's voice began to lose its strength.

"What about your daughter? Once again you've failed to realize how this will affect her." I could hear tears beginning to form on the other end.

"Mom, I'm sorry. I made a mistake."

My mom wasn't letting me off that easily.

"This is more than a mistake," she said. "Nobody trusts you any more. You've let us all down."

After that sentence, my mom let everything go. She burst into uncontrollable tears that made every word spoken sound like a woman begging for her life. I forced myself to stay on the line and listen. It was my punishment for being so stupid. I hated hearing my mother cry. It happened a lot in my short lifetime.

When I hung up the phone, the only word that came to mind was devastation. As humiliating as it was to tell them that once again I've landed myself in prison, the shame I felt after hearing my mother cry was punishment enough in itself. They could have released me that day from the jail and my life would have changed. In a matter of minutes on the line with her I must have dealt with a hundred different emotions, all making me feel like the biggest sucker in the world.

My head was in a cloud of gloom and confusion as I wandered aimlessly in the quadro, searching for nothing and wanting even less. I found a quiet spot on a random bench and sat down, staring into the sky as if searching for something to fall on top of me and put me out of my misery.

What good would calling home do me if it was going to be filled with tears and anger? I knew my family. They weren't impressed with me. I knew my father wanted to reach right through the phone and choke me out. But that was what love was all about. Angry love hurt more than sympathetic love because it had so much more value in life. With my friends, their sympathetic love would be easier to cope with in this time of immense stress. Real love, like that from my family, would weaken my defense and take my mind off of my main goal.

To stay alive and survive.

So many thoughts raced through my brain as I stared into the Mexican sky. The same sun that I had admired only days ago was now my worst enemy, shining down on me in a fit of rage hoping to break me down and drive me insane. I caught the eyes of Mexican inmates as they passed by me, ogling me as if I was a mutant. The cloud of gloom thickened as I tried to ignore their stares, hoping that they'd leave me alone in time, but relenting to the fact that I was the newest sideshow in town and the stares would become part of my new life. I always loved the center of attention. Now, I would get more than I could ever imagine.

Survival of the fittest, only the strong survive... Turn off all emotions and live day to day... Become a robot, void of feelings and thoughts... Ignore dreams and squash ambition... The only thing that matters is staying alive...

So many thoughts and so few answers.

* * *

I needed to learn Spanish in the quickest possible way. After a week in the prison, it became apparent that the only way I would survive was to communicate with the rest of the population. Roger wouldn't be there for me every time I needed to speak to someone. And what if I got into a conflict again? Hand gestures and animal noises would only get me so far before people either felt insulted or provoked. This was their world. It wasn't their job to relate to me – as much as they would have loved to speak English – it was my job to find their level.

When it came to ordering food, the only words I knew for sure were *atun* (tuna) and *huevos* (eggs). In my first few weeks it was all I ate, buying them religiously at the market in the quadro. They were so cheap, and always available. Roger taught me other food words, but after standing in the market line up for an hour, I'd forget them. When I got to the counter to order, I'd end up reciting the only two foods I knew at that point of my life – *atun* and *huevos*.

Scrambled eggs with tuna. Tuna and eggs in a tortilla shell. Fried eggs. Tuna from the can. There were only so many ways to eat the crap before it became the most boring food on earth. At one time, when I used to box, eggs and tuna were my favorite two foods on the planet. Now, every time I ate them, I thought of home.

After a while I became lazy, something Roger warned me about one morning as I prepared to eat the prison food.

"Whatever you do, don't get used to eating the food," he told me. "In fact, don't eat it at all."

Meal times were a great display of fortitude in the maximum. The meal cart came three times a day, and when it arrived, the men raced to it like a flock of angry gulls, fighting and clawing their way into a position of prosperity.

Meals were the same every day. For breakfast, eggs and hot dogs. Lunch, pork and vegetable soup. Dinner, rice milk with raisins and a bun. The meals came in the same twenty-gallon pot carried by two unknown Mexicans and placed on a table near the entrance of the unit. When the men entered, they would scream something out loud causing everyone to run at top speed, hooting and hollering, at the pot. They would dip their bowls or cups right into the meal, dirty hands and all. There was no such thing as an orderly fashion. It was every man for himself. The people at the front of the pack – usually the strongest and fastest – would walk away with the most food, their cups flowing over with food. The poor men at the back, sulked away with nothing but a half-filled container and the knowledge that they'd have to be quicker at the next meal if they wanted to eat.

Even though Roger warned me to stay away, there was something about the meals that drew me in. It wasn't some bizarre food that I'd never heard of. The meals were hot and had a flavor unique to Mexico that most tourists would actually pay for. I think what actually attracted me was the fight. The jostling for position. The aggression that was needed to stake your claim to a meal. At first I was timid to get in there with the men, but after a few times, I became the bull of the group using mind games and elbows to sternums to stop them in their tracks. I think I was just bored.

"You're going to get sick," warned Roger. "The food is cooked in tap water."

I didn't care. If the food didn't get me, the inmates would. If they didn't get me, the sun would, or a disease. There was always something to worry about. Eventually Roger got so sick of watching me fight for meals, he made me an offer. He told me to give his wife some money every week and she'd cook dinner every night for the both of us. I told him that as long as it didn't include tuna or eggs, he had himself a deal.

The next night, Maria came by the unit for her regular sleep over, and with her came a delicious meal of chicken enchiladas.

Twice a week she came to the maximum to stay the night. It was a regular occurrence in the prison for married couples or prostitutes.

There was one way to tell the hookers apart from the wives. Mostly, the hookers all wore high-end athletic gear. Nike, Adidas and Reebok. The wives wore Mexican clothing – plain and simple styles with no sexual appeal whatsoever. The sports gear was considered very fashionable. Only afforded by those with extra income. When the prostitutes wanted to spend the night with a customer, all they had to do was give the guards twenty pesos to pass through the gates to the men's side. The guards would pick them up before the first count in the morning and escort them back to their side. Maria told me that out of the two hundred women in her side, ten had husbands in the prison. One of the ten was Nomi.

"How does a woman as young as her end up in jail?" I asked.

Nomi was from a town on the eastern shores of Mexico called Vericruz. Her husband was a drug transporter, carrying packages all over Mexico for the cartel. On this particular trip, Nomi asked to go with him to the west. Her mother was sick and dying in the state of Sinaloa. In normal circumstances she would have taken a train, but because her husband was going there anyway, she hitched a ride.

Her husband screwed up by not paying off the police like he usually did. When he tried to sneak his car of drugs past the check stop, they busted him and put them both in prison. When given the chance to let his wife go, he refused to accept responsibility. They were both put in prison and given a ten-year sentence. Nomi had to leave behind her newborn son, but even worse, she missed seeing her mother before she died two days later.

"There are so many stories like that in Mexico," said Maria.

An awkward silence passed between us all in the room.

"Is that what happened to you two?" I asked, even though it felt inappropriate to ask.

"Yes," said Maria, casting Roger a stern glare. "The worst part is that we have two daughters in America. They were so young when we were first arrested. They didn't really know how to feel. Now they're almost teenagers and their anger shows."

I thought of my own daughter. How many times had I let her down in her life? I'd spent so many years in prison. She'd never gotten the chance to get to know me. When tears began to form in Maria's eyes, I felt the pain of my daughter at that moment in the cell. I'd been so focused on my own safety, I'd forgotten all about hers. How was she going to get through living without having her father around?

Survive ... turn off the thoughts...

"I'm sorry..." It was all I could say, but it was the truth.

"You're looking at the same crap," said Roger. "This court doesn't believe in due process."

"We've been fighting our case for five years and we're not even close," said Maria. "Sometimes I forget what our real life was like."

A lump appeared in my throat, but I refused to swallow. There was no way I was going to spend five years in this dungeon waiting for a guilty verdict. The thought of another few months was enough to make me lose my mind. They were stronger people than I could ever be.

"What are my options?" I asked.

Roger shook his head. "You can hire a lawyer like we did and fight your case, or you can plead guilty and take the ten years. Besides, there's always the treaty transfer once your case is completely finished."

Treaty transfer – spending the time you get in a foreign country in a prison in your own country. As long as the two countries have extradition laws, the transfer was easy. The paperwork was available through the consulate, which I could call anytime I wanted to from the new warden's office. Roger told me that the new warden was an easier man. He didn't believe in making things difficult for prisoners. The first thing he did upon starting his new job was take away the trusty positions. That was the reason why we stopped being locked up by Carlos at night. Roger said he would introduce me to him sometime soon.

After the dinner ended, I went back to my cell and huddled in the darkness like I did every night. The days ended the same way with me searching the unit for something to do only to find that boredom was my new best friend. No television, video games or even books to help pass the time. All I had were my thoughts and memories to flip through. As I lay on my concrete bed, I thought about the important decisions I'd have to make in the future. Fight or flight? Roger and Maria seemed determined to beat their case only because a transfer was out of the question for Maria, a native Mexican who didn't qualify to do her time elsewhere. There was no way Mexico would get five years out of me. I went to sleep that night convinced of my plan, and it would become either the smartest or the stupidest thing I'd ever do.

I was going to plead guilty and take the ten years.

Chapter 6
Mike
Viva La Canadiense

October, 1998. Maximum unit - Cereso

I opened the Spanish English dictionary to the one word I was completely sure of - *atun*. And there it was. The dictionary had the phonetic spelling of the word and the proper way to pronounce it. I was glad to know that I hadn't been completely butchering their language for the past few weeks.

Jaime sat across from me at the picnic table, smiling the proud way that he did whenever I did something "*angloish*" – as he put it.

"Now you can learn how to communicate," he told me over our lunch of hamburgers and fries that he brought with him.

"Sure. But does this book teach me the bad words?"

"Bad words?"

"Swear words. Cuss words. Words your mother told you never to say. The words every convict should know."

We both had a laugh, agreeing that those words would come to me after a little time in the prison. Jaime had no idea about my checkered past. For all he knew, I was a guy who made a stupid mistake and was living to regret it. I felt that there was no reason to tell him about my life back home – the stealing, drug dealing, and sinful living that I knew might change his opinion of me. Jaime was a good man. A Christian brought up by his family to see the good in everyone. Naïve by my standards, but I had a lot of respect for people like him. Finding good in assholes was a talent that I never gave much thought to.

Jaime handed me two notebooks filled with lined paper.

"These are for your studying. Writing your words will help you learn."

Jaime the teacher said that the best way to learn was by immersion. I would pick up Spanish quicker than a student in my own country because I would be forced to speak it twenty-four hours a day. I laughed and told him that I hoped I wouldn't be speaking twenty-four hours a day. A man needed to sleep too.

The best part about Jaime was that I could make him laugh like no one else I'd ever met. Those joy-filled interactions made me feel like I was somewhere other than prison. His kindness shone through every time we spoke. He got a kick out of my old jokes and lame impressions of celebrities and famous figures. When I used idioms that he didn't understand, I'd have to explain them to him. At times, I was more of a teacher than he was. When he got what I was saying, I felt a warm connection that made me even fonder of him. Keeping my past from him became harder the more we spent time together.

"Most of the people in Mexico would give anything to learn English," he said. "They all believe that English will give them a better life."

"How so?"

"Most Mexicans have family in America. They tell of great jobs and a life of freedom that is incomparable in Mexico."

"Why don't they learn English and cross the border?"

His face hardened with sadness. "My people are very poor. They don't have extra money for school or to start a new life even if they learned the language. Most Mexican people are so involved in taking care of their families here, crossing over to the *Estados Unitos* is just a dream."

"It takes a lot of initiative to learn a new language," I said.

He nodded, running the word over in his mental dictionary. "Initiative. That's another thing with a lot of Mexicans…" He hung his head. "I'm sorry to say that many of us lack a desire to change. We get so caught up in what we believe is the life God has given us that we don't make an effort to make that life better."

I nodded in agreement with his statement only to realize a second later that he'd just described my personality to a tee. I'd never taken any steps to make my life worth something. Here I was stuck in a country where people would give their lives to live where I came from, and I took it all for granted. Many times in my life I cursed my life, but the whole time, there were people way worse off than me. As Jaime spoke about the ignorance of his people, I realized that the most ignorant were the ones who willingly gave up life in paradise to live in hell. And if I thought that didn't apply to me—I came to a Spanish speaking country without knowing the language.

When he left, I wrote the first Spanish words in my new notebook: *estupido canadianence gringo* – stupid American Canadian.

* * *

November, 1998. Court cells - Cereso

The first time they called me down for court, a grumpy guard escorted me to a waiting cell near the front entrance of the prison. I walked cautiously down the same hall I saw on my first day in the prison, past the seventy-two hour lock up and into a reception area heavily surrounded by the thick steel chicken fence. There were twenty-five other Mexicans in the holding tank waiting for what I thought was a trip to a separate room for a talk with their lawyers. I was wrong. An inmate's right to privacy was gone the minute he stepped into prison.

There were two sides to the fence. The free side and my side. On the free side there was a long table and chairs set up facing the prisoner side. There was a door in the middle of the room, and when it opened, all convict eyes turned to see who was next to speak. When an inmate's name was called, he'd step close to the fence and speak to his lawyer in front of everyone in the room. A guard stood post near the door, and if anyone tried to whisper, he'd bang his rifle against the fence and tell them to speak up. There was no room for secrecy. Security held the floor every time.

Two men entered through the door and immediately their eyes locked on me. One man wore a police uniform that resembled the one I saw the night of my arrest. His eyes took on that look of a police officer preparing for an interrogation. He had a file folder in his hand that he opened and began to peruse, pretending as if I wasn't waiting anxiously to know if they were there for me or not.

The man beside him looked more like a librarian than a cop. His face was clean-shaven and he wore a pair of thin-rimmed glasses that couldn't seem to stay up on his nose. The only reason I knew that they were there for me was the fact that the shaven man kept looking at me through the fence, offering me a hint of a smile as the cop pushed papers towards him.

Finally, the librarian nodded to me. He stood from the table and approached me with the papers in hand. Something inside of me said this was nothing but bad news.

"My name is Guillermo," he said in broken English. "I represent the state."

"Is this about my case," I asked. Several Mexicans in the cage stopped to listen to the foreign language.

"No," Guillermo said. "My client is one of the arresting officers in your case. He has asked me to speak to you about selling the vehicle."

I'd completely forgotten about the car – a 1995 Mustang that was given to me specifically for this trip. When the police arrested us, the whereabouts of the car slipped my mind.

Guillermo held up the papers in his hand. They were contract papers written in Spanish.

"They will not release the car to you," he said. "My client is a captain and he wants to give you a choice."

I laughed lightly and glanced over at the cop. He remained seated, but the hard look on his face never changed.

"What's the choice?"

Guillermo's hands began to tremble. "He will either seize the car and they will auction it off, or you can sell it directly to him for $1000 American."

A thousand American was the most blatant rip off offer I'd ever been on the wrong side of. First they take my drugs, then my life, now my car.

"Those are some choices," I said. "What do you suggest?"

He was stunned by my question. Glancing back at the cop for a second, he leaned close to the fence and said to me in a whisper. "I don't think you have a choice."

So little choices, so few options. I told Guillermo to ask the cop to come to the fence. He signaled to the policeman, who stood abruptly and marched over to me. Like everyone else in the force, he had a thick mustache and stood no taller than five seven. His eyes connected with mine, and they didn't waver as he spoke in Spanish to Guillermo.

"Tell him I want one thing from him before I sign the papers." I met the cop's stare with an aggressive one of my own.

Guillermo told him. "What is your request?"

"I want all of my belongings from the car." I told him. "My clothes, books – everything."

The cop agreed and I signed the paper. He slid a thousand dollars under the window in an envelope, prepared as if he knew I wouldn't refuse the offer.

Two days later, I was called down to the same fenced in area to receive a large box from the local police. What I thought was my personal belongings turned out to be something else. Dirty laundry. It was all I could consider it to be. Cotton shirts and soiled pants stained with the remnants of a long day's work in some field. There were few of my personal items from the car – a skipping rope that I never left home without and a Nike gym bag with most of my personal grooming items in it minus my electric toothbrush, razor and water pick. The framed photograph of my daughter that I took everywhere was still in the bag. I touched her face. So young and delicate and I didn't care. I felt a surge of shame and regret that was well deserved.

At the bottom of the box, wrapped in the same lime colored slip, was the pillow I stole from the hotel the night before getting arrested. Never again would I use my shoe.

When I returned to my cell, the pillow was the newest, most welcome, addition to my sleeping arrangement. Jaime smiled when he saw my bed made up with a pillow at the end.

"I never thought I'd actually mean it when I said this pillow would come in handy," I told him.

We both had a laugh over the bizarre undersized clothing and my story of the good timing pillow. That afternoon, my daughter became the topic of discussion over fried chicken and salsa that Jamie bought at his favorite "Anglo" restaurant in town.

"I haven't been a good father," I confessed. Now that I'm as far as I can possibly be from her, I miss her more than ever."

Jaime looked away, giving me my moment of grief.

Lying awake in bed that night listening to the crickets outside, my thoughts couldn't help but wander to the beautiful face of my five-year-old little girl. She had no idea what her dad was going through. I had no idea what she was dealing with not having me around. She didn't deserve the emotions that came with not knowing her father, but I vowed to make it up to her one day… when I was free again…

For now, my life was being disassembled piece by piece. One memory at a time. Though I was down and out without a hope of seeing my home turf again, I refused to let things go. I would never lose touch of who I was. I'd been in charge of my city for years and I wasn't going to let some prison time take that away from me. All desires to accomplish something in the drug world remained fresh in my mind. Shelly and Ryan had screwed me over, but their time would come again. As I went to bed every night, my conscience wrestled with two scenarios concerning getting even. One with Shelly and Ryan, the other with my daughter.

For now, the car was gone. My clothes and personal items had been robbed from me. My own partners had denied me and left me to die. All I'd ever wanted from this life was to be accepted and successful. Now I was left with nothing more than my own guilty feelings and a cockroach infested cell. I was stripped of my dignity, pride and ego and left with my conscience to figure out how to manage the life I traded in for a one way ticket to misery.

When Jaime arrived again that weekend, he brought with him a book. Placing it on the table with the food, he was beaming with excitement.

I read the title. *A Man in Full,* by Tom Wolfe.

It would become the only book I read in English my entire time in Cereso. As soon as I finished it, I picked up my pen and began writing in the spare notebook.

* * *

November, 1998. Big yard pay phone – Cereso

I had only one real friend left in Canada. Angela had made me the promise to take care of me for as long as it took, and she was a woman of her word. Though my phone calls cost her a fortune, she stayed strong for me. If it wasn't for her, I might not have made it out of that prison alive. I owe her my life.

As for the rest of my so-called team, they proved what they were worth. For no reason at all, they had all disappeared off the face of the planet.

Angela would tell me about everything happening in our town. One day she told me about Shelly, and once again I hung up the pay phone in anger.

Not only was Shelly not living up to our agreement by adopting a positive life, he was running around our hometown spreading lies and rumors about me to our friends. He confessed secrets that I'd confided in him about and completely ruined what left I had of my good name. I was told that he had gone on a drug binge, smoking anything from weed to cocaine, probably in an attempt to get over the trauma of what had just happened to us.

When I picked up the phone again and tried to call one of Shelly's new partners, I heard him answer the phone only to have him deny the charges. The call left me boiling mad beyond words. But what was I angry about? Shelly being free or me being locked up? That question always seemed to arise in my mind.

Shelly was given money to help me out. Instead, he bought an expensive new watch. He'd been out every night, partying and smearing my name to those around him. *Anger!* He spread lies about girls I hadn't been with and made up rumors that eventually made their way back to me a thousand miles away. More anger.

I hung up the phone on Angela deciding that from then on, I would only call my family and her. Everyone else would get their chance to hate me, laugh at me and call me whatever names they wanted while I was gone. I probably deserved it all. I was an asshole and despicably proud of it. I agreed that I would forget all about those people and concentrate on survival and only survival. When I got home, they would all pay with their blood, and nothing or no one would talk me out of it.

That afternoon I wrote in my book: the Canadian has died. *Viva Mexican Mike.*

Chapter 7
Mike
Murly Kreezmas!

November, 1998. Warden's office – Cereso

The warden reminded me of a character out of an old western movie. He wore a cowboy hat low on his brow, just above a set of brown eyes that seemed to glance right through me and into my wallet. Like an old western Mexican, he had that signature mustache and leather boots on his feet that he crossed on his desktop. On a radio near his desk, low playing mariachi music hummed.

His intentions were clear from the moment I met him. What could I do for you to make you do something for me? He didn't beat around the bush when it came to making a point. I could respect that. He set me up by posing probing questions about my life, then not acting surprised when I disclosed to him a few of my guilty pleasures. I knew what he was after. He wanted what all the other guards wanted from me: a way to blackmail me for as much money as possible.

Roger sat in the chair next to me, his eyes wide with nervousness and anticipation. We watched as the warden poured us both an inch of tequila in a greasy shot glass. He sensed my hesitation. He winked and nodded at the glasses, tipping his hat back before downing his own shot directly from the bottle.

"He did this to me when I first got here," said Roger, taking his glass from the desktop.

I took mine as well. "What did he want?"

"Who knows with this guy," he said and tossed the entire drink in one gulp. "All I know is take the drinks while you can."

I agreed, downing the tequila in one shot. I held back that sour face that comes along with shooting tequila, knowing that the warden was watching, probably evaluating my toughness by the reaction of the booze. He seemed satisfied and poured us both another drink. This time, an inch and a half.

After three drinks and long bouts of bizarre silence, the warden finally spoke to Roger.

"He wants to know how you like the prison."

What could I say? There was plenty of sunshine and freedom. I had all the eggs and tuna I wanted. I had to say things were fine. The warden laughed and downed another shot from the bottle, urging us to hurry up and join him by finishing our third glass – now, two whole inches. I swallowed the drinks with a sour smile. What the hell was this guy's motive?

He spoke quickly and at length with Roger before stopping to allow him to translate.

"Now I understand," began Roger, turning to me with a sly smile. "You always have to remember that it's about money with these people."

"Is that what he wants from me?" I slurred. My head felt light as a biscuit.

"He said that if you'd like a bottle for Christmas, he will allow you to buy one."

I nodded and smiled at the warden. The man gave me another wink.

"He said that for every bottle you buy, you owe him a bottle of tequila," Roger looked over at the warden and smiled wanly. "That's a pretty good deal."

I didn't think so, but I kept my mouth shut. I wasn't that much of a drinker that I wanted to start haggling over the price of booze with the one man who determined how good my stay was going to be. I just nodded.

"Tell him that I'm very grateful and that I'd like to take him up on his offer."

Roger told him, beginning the fourth round of golden tequila shooters. The warden mumbled something to Roger as he poured again. My eyes glazed over as I tried to focus on the glass, measuring the amount of booze in each tumbler. The warden poured them deep now.

By the time I made it through that last drink, my head felt numb with the effects of good Mexican tequila, and my face hurt from over-smiling. My feet were up on the warden's desk as he suggested and we were laughing like old friends, neither of us understanding each other, getting by on animal noises and hand gestures only. Complete professionalism on both our parts.

The warden told Roger that I was free to use the phone any time I wanted to call the Canadian consulate. He told me that if I ever needed his help, just ask the secretary to come up and see him. As we stood to leave, I shook the warden's hand and thanked him in Spanish for his hospitality.

"Now that's a nice guy," I said to Roger as we wobbled out the door.

Roger laughed. "Yeah, that's what I thought after out first meeting too."

We stopped in the stairwell going back down to the prison. "What? You don't think so now?"

Roger's dark face turned pale. "Not since he tried to rape my wife in his office. I'm actually surprised that he allowed me in his office without a guard present."

My knees buckled slightly. "He tried to rape Maria?"

Roger waved it off. "I'm probably making it more than it is," he said. "He came on to her and she had to hit him to get away. A warden has a lot of pull around here. He has the power to get whatever he wants from whoever he wants."

We reached the bottom of the stairs safely. I knew the truth about our friendly warden. "The warden forces women inmates to have sex with him, huh?"

Roger chuckled and slapped his arm around my shoulders. "The warden forces nothing," he said with a smile. "If the women want a good life inside, they know how to get it."

We stumbled out of the warden's building and back towards the unit. I wasn't so drunk that I didn't notice Nomi as she slid out of the shadows and up to the warden's office. I saw her, even though she didn't think I did, or she didn't care if I did. If she was going up there to be with the warden to make her life easier, I didn't blame her. I might have done the same if I was a woman trapped in this heat.

*   *   *

December, 1998. Maximum unit – Cereso

I've never been a big fan of Christmas. Stress, depression and debt always seemed to find me at that time of the year. I always felt out of place, even with my own family. It wasn't until my first Christmas in Mexico that I realized the true importance the holiday played in life.

My family always believed in having strong, family-oriented Christmases filled with gifts and food. They worked hard to give the kids a good day. I remember my father telling me to wait until the day I had kids, then I would see how important this day was. I never thought I'd realize it in a sweatbox prison only two days from December twenty-fifth.

I'd developed a system to learn Spanish in the few months inside. The guys in the unit took the liberty to attach my dictionary to a rope and hang it around my neck. Whenever they wanted to communicate, they would open to the words in the dictionary and teach me how to say it. It started off as a gag, but after a while proved effective. The language came quickly to me. It became easier to understand those long sentences the more that people stopped to look up words, and with it came a chance to build relationships with everyone.

Still, I missed my home, my people, and my own miserable language.

When I called home, the resentful mood remained. I heard all about making this the worst Christmas ever. No one was happy with me. Only my mom would come to the phone and deal with me. I couldn't wait to get off that line. I wished them all a lackluster

Merry Christmas and hung up. Those seasonal salutations had absolutely no emotion behind them whatsoever.

On the day before Christmas Eve, Jaime came to visit and with him he brought his family. Mom, dad and sister greeted me with hugs and kisses. They instantly treated me as though I were one of their own. For complete strangers, they were generous and loving. His mother was a pillar of strength in their family. She took the lead and sat beside me the entire time. They laid out a wonderful meal of turkey and all the trimmings, firing questions at me about Canada as if I'd been on a long trip away from home for years. Jaime translated for me as best he could, deciphering my jokes the best way he knew how.

Their kindness overwhelmed me to the point of exhaustion. When the day had ended, I waved to them as they left from the front gate of the maximum like a child left behind waving to his parents from the orphanage door. In that short period, time enough to finish a meal and tell them all about my life back home, I was blessed with the addition of a new family. Their non-judging demeanor put a whole new perspective on my thoughts of the Mexican people. They didn't have to care about me, but they did it without a second thought. As I watched them disappear through the gate, I felt two emotions that I wish I didn't know – embarrassment for being in the prison, and shame for sitting through the entire meal and lying to them about who I really was.

* * *

The men of the maximum unit had a yearly tradition that dated back about fifteen years. Some inmate in the past had constructed a wrought iron frame in the shape of a Christmas tree. The frame was ten feet high, triangular in shape and could hold several hundred lights. Carlos came around the unit collecting ten pesos from everyone as a donation to the tree light fund.

The process would amaze anyone who hadn't seen it before. Fifteen men worked together to lift that tree high above the unit and into a slot on the roof. The move reminded me of the Egyptians building the pyramids and how they worked hard until the task as finished, defying physics and demonstrating human willingness to overcome obstacles. These men grunted and pulled ropes over balcony ledges to get that heavy metal frame onto the roof, and when it was finally inserted into the slot over two hours later, they stood back and admired their work.

That Christmas Eve, Maria and Roger asked me to join them for dinner. Throughout the dinner we talked about the things we enjoyed about the season and what we missed about spending the holiday in freedom. Maria missed her children and her family. She told me about Mexican Christmases where families would travel across the country to be with their clans. She spoke of the three-day parties filled with drinking and food and games. A tear came to her eye when she spoke about her family and how by now they were used to her being in prison this time of year.

"You're going to get through this," I said to her. "This time of year is always difficult."

She reached for my hand and squeezed it tight. "What about you? What do you miss?"

The question stumped me. I didn't have a great answer like hers. The truth was I didn't miss anything about this time of year. I'd spent so many Christmases in prison that I'd become desensitized to the whole ordeal. I never told her that for the past twenty-three years of my life, I'd only had twelve Christmases at home, and most of those were the first twelve of my life. Instead, I told her about the fictional family get-togethers and the snowball fights in the yard. I told her about all the years my daughter and I spent opening gifts and singing carols. All lies. I was on a roll.

"You must really miss your daughter," Roger chimed in.

"Sure," I said with conviction. "More than life itself."

That wasn't a lie. I hadn't been a good father or even close to a decent human being when it came to my little girl, but I did love her. The majority of my absence in her life was due to the fact that I didn't want to include her in my criminal lifestyle. I'd made a choice years ago never to give up being a criminal and with that pledge came a bit of selfishness and a ton of neglect towards my family.

Something about being in that prison during Christmas made that pledge seem more like a foolish schoolyard dare. As I lied to Roger and Maria about my life, shame reappeared. Every question they asked me was answered with a lie, a cover-up or a manipulative story. By the end of the dinner, I didn't even know who I was, but I wished I was that guy I'd been making myself out to be.

When Roger and Maria turned in for the night, I left feeling greasier than the leftover enchiladas they sent me home with. The unit basked in an aura of peaceful silence. The December sky, high above the prison, sparkled with stars – the North Star shining lower in the sky than at home.

I didn't go back to my cell. Instead, I stayed out in the unit watching the universe above, reminiscing about when I was a kid how I used to look out the window for Santa. The metal tree lights flickered on and off casting a signal of the holiday season back into space amongst the stars.

I didn't miss spending Christmas at home that year. I missed having the freedom to be at home and miss Christmas. Mixed feelings of loneliness and self-pity made that night one of the worst of my life. It wasn't fair that out of all my partners involved, I was the one left holding the bag and forced to do the time, suffer the consequences and deal with the let down. One thing was clear to me. They would be made to suffer one day, I would make sure of that. I glanced up at the North Star and made my Christmas wish – death upon every one of them.

* * *

On Christmas morning, I was awakened by Carlos standing over me. My first thought was that I needed to get a lock on the door. These Mexicans had the ability to sneak up on me while I slept and I didn't like it.

He took my dictionary from the desk and held it up as if to say, 'I'm going to borrow this.' I waved him off and tried to get back to sleep, but as always, mother nature struck and in ten minutes I'd gone from huddled in my bed to nearly naked and sweating. Imagine that, a sweltering hot Christmas morning.

The day passed and turned to night. The bottles of alcohol were handed out both to the inmates and the warden who by the look of how many bottles came in must have been up to his gills in golden tequila. The men cheered and opened their swag with gusto, drinking the first sip directly from the bottle before sealing it and tucking it away until after their Christmas feast.

Food, drink and sex were on every Mexican's wish list. The men were adrenaline-craved fiends, hunting for one of the three aforementioned items at all times of the day, holiday or not. Most of the inmates had family in that night. Visitors were allowed to stay over and party until all hours of the night. Mexican dreams would come true that night - sex, booze, food. What else could a man want in life?

I sat my bottle of tequila on my desk, waiting for it to jump up and do the Macarena for the price I paid for it. I'd been to Mexico many times before. I'd partied with Mr. Tequila on numerous occasions only to wake up in the morning with the worst frontal lobe pain anyone could imagine. As I watched the golden liquid shine in the sun, I didn't worry about the price I'd pay. I just needed something to take my mind off of the pain I had inside my heart. For the first time in my life, I was going to use a substance to mask over my feelings, fight my depression and quell my fears.

I twisted the plastic wrap off of the cap. I smelled the booze as soon as I lifted the top off. I lifted the bottle to my lips, inhaling its scent again before daring myself to take a long swig. It tasted like tree bark and had a bite worse than that. I must have swallowed a half-cup before ripping the bottle from my lips and slamming it back down on the desk. My face cringed with pain. I grit my teeth and tried to ingest some oxygen. The warming sensation that follows tequila is like a heat wave slowly consuming your entire body from the inside out, beginning in your stomach and working out, through your limbs and into your head. When the warmth reached my forehead, I knew that I was in for a hard drunken night.

Two hours later, I found myself in Julio the unit store keeper's cell, shirt off and drunk, sitting amongst fifteen other Mexicans singing Beetle's songs like "Let it be" and "Hey Jude" - one of their personal favorites. My golden tequila had turned to a stronger white version and I had a cigar in between my teeth as if I owned the store. To my surprise, I hadn't thrown up or gotten into a fight. It was a good night, considering the foul mood I was in.

Pecal - a skinny Mexican man with a long pointy head that resembled a traffic cone - called my name and whistled for me to pass the bottle. I removed the cigar and took a swig of the booze big enough to render me completely incapacitated then passed it to him. The Mexican convicts cheered me on as I forced the booze down my throat, holding back the pain and the puke, then pumping my fists in the air in victory and screaming *Viva la Mexcio!* to show that I had indeed sacrificed my dignity to the tequila gods.

Pecal took a sip of the booze and passed it down the line. Though blurred, I made out every one of the faces in the room. Lean, fat, bodies; beady, slanted eyes. They were all different but looked the same because of their mustaches. I touched the upper portion of my lip. A mustache? Wouldn't that be interesting?

A knock sounded at the door, and when it opened, there was Roger. With his hands in his sweatpants pockets, he stood over us all smiling like a father does when he walks in on his kids proudly doing their school homework. Roger nodded his head and looked right at me... at least I think he did...

"Mike, are you coming to eat with us?"

I couldn't even think of eating at a time like that, never mind be social.

"I don't think so," I slurred. Now my head spun out of control.

Pecal stood up and reached out for Roger's hand. Speaking to him in Spanish, all I could translate was that he wanted Roger to translate for him. Roger stepped into the room amongst the men and leaned down to Pecal.

Either someone turned up the radio or my hearing sense took over all portions of my consciousness, amplifying the beautiful sounds coming from the abyss. The guitar strummed in the

background as a sorrow-filled Mexican tenor belted out his pain
and heartbreak to the men in the room who listened. I felt the
cantador's sadness with every word he sang. For a moment I actually
understood the words. He wanted his love to come back to him...
he needed someone like her to love or no one at all...

As I listened, I glanced around the room at the other men. Some
of them sat with their eyes closed listening to the ballad, allowing
their souls to be captured by the tune of loneliness and despair.
Some smiled while others' faces took on a more profound passion.
More guitars and a stand-up bass echoed in the room. I scanned
from one convict to the other until finally resting on Roger.

His face looked pale and sick. A mood killer.

"What's wrong, Roger?" I tried to sound chipper and
encouraging. "It's Christmas."

Pecal squatted beside him, smiling ear-to-ear and poking at Roger
to speak for him. Roger gave him a wan smile then leaned in closer
to me. He hesitated.

"What is it?" I asked. The music. So beautiful...

"He wants me to tell you something."

The bottle arrived back to my left. I took it without consciously
knowing it. I held it in the air to Pecal, who smiled and nodded. My
friend. My friend Pecal...

Roger shook his head. "He wants you to know that he took
your chicken."

"My what?" I readied for a drink.

Roger spoke louder. "Your chicken. He took your chicken."

"What damn chicken?" I took a swig.

Then it hit me. I wasn't that drunk to forget such a short time
ago.

The thing about tequila is that it doesn't really get you drunk.
It's more of a body numbing high that enables you to drink a lot
before completely passing out. The other thing is that you can usually
remember what you did the night before when you wake up with a
nasty hangover. It doesn't make you blackout until you've gone
way past the recommended limit.

Dystopia

The last thing I remember is reaching out to strangle Pecal's pencil neck and everyone in the room standing to rip me away from him. Gone was the beautiful tenor and his song of regret, the passionate faces of the men, the good-natured pirate-style drink fest. All I saw was red, then white, then black.

* * *

When the light hit me in the morning it was from the door opening and a shitload of sunshine invading my cell. I was still dressed from the night before - pants and shoes only. As soon as my brain clued in that I was awake, it began to squeal with pain. I needed water.

I sat up to see Roger standing in the doorway with his arms folded across his chest and Carlos standing beside him juggling the keys. I groaned and glanced at my watch. It was way too early. That had to mean that something happened last night and I was in trouble. And why did Carlos have keys?

"He was ordered to lock you up last night," said Roger reading my mind. "Do you remember anything?"

"Murly kreezmas!" said Carlos before I could answer.

"What did he say?" I asked Roger. I was in no mood. I needed water badly.

Roger sighed and sat down in the only chair I had by the door.

"He said Merry Christmas. Don't tell me you've forgotten your own language already."

I swung my feet over the side of the bed. "What's going on?"

* * *

The one thing that did get my attention standing at Pecal's locked door was the simplistic design of his door lock. He'd constructed a hook and latch system out of wood, glued it to the wall beside the door and nailed it in with cement tacks. It was just what I needed to get a little privacy in the morning. I was going to have to ask him how he made it.

That is, after I convinced him that I wasn't going to kill him and that he could come out of his cell.

I pounded on the window while sipping from a water bottle. "Come on, Pecal." I thought of the Spanish words I'd been studying. "*Somos amigos*" - we are friends.

Roger stood against the wall with his arms folded across his chest. I shot him a glare for help.

"Can you translate for me here?"

He smiled smugly. "No. You're doing just fine."

Inside the cell, Pecal huddled in the corner of the room in a chair, listening to the radio and refusing to speak to me. I pounded on the window and I saw him flinch. He was scared all right.

I turned to Roger. "Can you please tell him to come to the window?"

Still smirking, Roger leaned into the window. "blah, blah... *vantana*... blah, blah..."

Vantana was window. I was getting better at understanding.

When Pecal came to the window, trembling slightly but putting up a good fight by smiling, I noticed a slight bump on his forehead. He shined away from looking me in the eyes, like a beaten dog does to his master when he knows he's done wrong.

"What happened to his head?" I clued in. "Did I do that?"

"You leaned over and head butted him after I told you he stole your chicken."

"Head butted him?"

Roger shrugged. "You scared him a little bit."

A little embarrassed and disappointed, I couldn't help but laugh out loud.

Standing in the window, Pecal's face contorted in disgust. He looked at Roger for help, but Roger was just as dumbfounded.

"What's so funny?" Roger asked me.

I shook my head and smiled through the window at Pecal. Without a warning, I thrust my head forward on the grate around the window, banging it hard enough to cause an instant bump in roughly the same spot as the one on Pecal's forehead. Both he and Roger were stunned silent.

I pointed to the bump and smiled in at Pecal. *"Somos amigos."*

It took him a minute to understand, but he did, and burst into laughter, making a motion with his finger at the side of his head as if to say I was crazy. He unlocked his door and allowed us to come in. Before going in, I turned to Roger.

"Can you ask him how he made the lock? I really need to get a peaceful night's sleep around here."

* * *

When Shithead the guard came into the unit, it was like a wave of fear enveloped the entire population. He strutted in as though he was the warden, his chest inflated, his eyes veiled by those ridiculous and cheap aviator glasses I'd never seen him without.

I watched him walk directly to Roger's cell as I scrubbed my clothes at the cement sink. He stayed for a moment, barking out a command before storming out. He was almost out the door before he noticed me by the sink with a handful of soapy laundry.

He must have sensed my scowl from across the unit, because when he turned to me he matched my look with one of his own. Chirping some insults in Spanish as he strode towards me, I dropped my laundry in the sink and rinsed my hands in the clean water. How badly I wanted to punch him. I knew that if I did that, I'd be fucked up and locked up until the Canadian consulate came to get me. And that was a while away.

Shithead stopped directly in front of me and made a sneering gesture towards my soapy clothing.

"Blah, blah… *puta*... blah blah…"

Puta - a whore. I'd learned all the bad words already.

I snickered with him at my own expense. My eyes never left contact with his.

When he sensed my unwillingness to crumble, he turned to my sink of water and spat into it, laughing as he wiped his face of over-spray. Now I really wanted to hit him. But my better judgment took control and all I did was smile.

At that time, the cut under my eye had begun healing closed. Shithead leaned in close to examine the scar, his face scrunching with the result of careful inspection. I leaned away from him not understanding what his fucking problem was with me. Like a disgusted kid he reached up to touch the scar, but I backed off. He held up a hand as if to tell me to relax. I did, like a moron. When I was still, Shithead touched the area around my eye with his slimy finger, then without out warning, karate chopped the wound with the side of his hand, backing up immediately out of my reach as I grabbed hold of my face in pain.

"You little fucking shit!" I screamed at him.

He didn't care. He stood back laughing at me, his chest puffed out and his hands on his hips.

"Blah, blah... *joto*... blah... blah..." Then he walked away.

Joto - homosexual. This guy was one insult away from the end of his career in prison reform. I sat on the bench nearby and checked my eye. It bled heavily and the cut had been reopened. As I wiped the blood from my face with an old shirt (or in my present situation, one of my only shirts) Roger sat down on the other side off the bench, his face white and sick looking again. I knew he had some bad news to tell me.

"Fucking shithead's gonna get it," I said to him. "What did he want with you?"

Roger sighed loudly. "He just told me that I was getting a new roommate."

"Oh yeah," I said. "Which one of these morons is it?"

Roger folded his hands on the bench table. "Actually, it's you."

"Well," I said as I bunched up the shirt and held it over the cut. "At least you got the best moron out of the bunch."

* * *

On New Year's Eve that year, I found myself alone in my bed, which at the time was the top portion of a wooden bunk bed above Roger that I'd made in the wood shop. The process to make a bed was more difficult than I'd imagined. The wood was cheap – a hundred Canadian dollars. It was the time and effort that nearly made me quit and relent to an eternity of sleeping on the cement floor.

Gustavo, the shopkeeper helped me construct the damn thing. In all honesty, he did most of the work because I was more in the way than anything. He was a genius with his hands, a true craftsman who took pride in building things with wood. He was the tallest Mexican I'd ever seen standing at least six four. A monster by Mexican standards.

When he'd completed my bed and nailed it to the wall of mine and Roger's new shared accommodation, he smiled widely under that thick mustache slamming his hand on the bed board as a sign of its sturdiness. Roger wasn't so convinced.

"I don't trust this guy's handiwork," he said eyeing the bed directly above him.

"Only one way to find out."

I hopped on the bed and began tossing and turning, testing the stability of the contraption. It held, but even more importantly, it soothed Roger's nerves enough that he was able to sleep the first night.

Two days later at the stroke of midnight, I was curled up in that bed, drunk from the remainder of my second bottle of gold tequila, wishing that I were somewhere else. You never realized how much you miss home until you're unable to spend New Years Eve with friends and family. But what did I miss really? The drinking that I didn't enjoy? Partying with people I hardly liked? Was it the feeling of invincibility that came with surviving another year in the drug game? Where were the feelings of mourning actually coming from?

As I lay there sulking, I thought about my family and how they were dealing with my absence during Christmas and New Year. I listened to the families downstairs in the unit celebrating and drinking to loud Mexican music. For a moment I hated how happy they were, almost as if they had no worries in the world. They didn't really. They had their families and friends there to celebrate with them. They had their language and their golden alcohol to help pass the night.

The door to my cell opened behind me and instantly the music and voices became louder. I didn't dare turn around to see Roger because I didn't want to explain my sudden departure from the party to be alone. I listened to him shuffle across the floor to the bed. I could feel his presence behind me, standing in the dark, watching me.

Finally when the pressure became too much to ignore, I turned over only to see Carlos standing there with a huge grin on his face.

"Happy New Years!" he said as clear as any English I'd ever heard.

I couldn't help but smile. I knew he'd been practicing that shit all day.

"*Feliz Anos Nuevo*," I told him.

He laughed and slapped me on the back before leaving just as quietly as he came in. These Mexicans were determined to make me as carefree as they were, but there would be no way I'd allow myself to relax until I got home.

As I turned back to the wall, the smile remained on my face. Damn those Mexicans. They sure had a way of ruining someone's night.

* * *

January, 1999. The Quadro – Cereso

The very day after New Year's Eve I found myself in the quadro enjoying the brightest sun I'd seen in the past year. The golden rays of the New Year's sun blasted my face, burning away all my negative thoughts from the previous night. There were some days in that prison when I felt good to be alive. I was young, strong and in full control of my survival plan. I'd managed to get away with limited calling back home during the holidays and it felt good, even though it probably made my family sick with worry. As I absorbed the beautiful sun that morning, I thought about them and how I would make it all up to them once I got home. Ten years and counting.

As I laid on the field in a remote corner of the yard, the bright sun became obstructed by a large shadow. When I opened my eyes, there stood a large round Mexican man dressed in denim pants, a collar shirt buttoned right to the top and a wide brim cowboy hat. He smiled down at me and offered his hand for a shake.

"My name is Juan Miguel," he said in English.

I sat up. "*Mucho gusto.*" Nice to meet you.

"I was wondering if you would like to have a drink with me," he said. "I have a deal for you that might change your life."

Chapter 8
Mike
Round One: The Win

January, 1999. Building Unit 4 – Cereso

The rest of the prison was nothing like the maximum. They were much filthier by comparison looking more like those seen in movies.

Juan Miguel's unit was like walking down a side street in Mexico City. The layout was the same as the max, but instead of a clear opening above, clothing lines filled with dripping wet laundry occupied any open space. Thirty or more sheets and blankets hung from the lines, blocking out any bit of sunshine in the sky above. The darkness made me nervous, so I followed him closely, through the glares and catcalls of *cholos* - gangmembers.

When we reached his cell, it wasn't the same cozy hole in the wall that I lived in. There were four beds stuffed into a cell that could possibly only house two comfortably. Juan Miguel's cell was clean and organized - like someone who gave a damn lived there. He had shelves against one wall and posters of Mexican soccer stars and starlets taped to the wall like the room of a Mexican teenager. He sat on his bed and kicked out a chair for me.

Juan Miguel had a look on his face like he was a little too eager to sell me his line of crap. Right away I picked up on his car salesman attitude that he seemed to carry with incredible ease. He was the Mexican version of me, and that made me nervous.

After some small talk about my country the real conversation began. I should have known why he'd asked me over. After all, what else were foreigners good for?

"I know how much you guys like cheap cocaine," he said with that ear-to-ear smile.

I shook my head. "I don't think I'm in any position to organize a drug shipment from inside prison," I told him honestly. "I can't even transport myself out of this shit hole."

He waved his hands in the air and reached behind him, shuffling around a few pillows and clothing only to come back with a leather belt. When he handed it to me, I realized it was something more than just a belt.

The belt was stiff in my hands. Thick and heavy. Made out of leather dyed purple, the designs on the belt were the most intricate I'd ever seen. Hand stitched with sinew, the designs were like ivy vines and flowers that consumed every inch of the belt. The pattern was consistent all the way up the belt, ending at the buckle. The buckle was another work of art. The same sinew pattern wrapped around what looked like a cow holding a small pistol.

"Why is this cow holding a gun?" I asked.

"In Mexico, the belt buckle represents the man who wears it."

Juan Miguel explained to me how each buckle design represented the "trade" that the barer was in. The cow - or *chiva* - represented heroine. The gun below meant that he was into selling guns as well. He told me that a shrimp equaled marijuana and a ram meant cocaine. Sometimes, one man would have a few different belts meaning that he was into everything. Juan Miguel was one of those men.

I handed him the belt. "What does this have to do with the cocaine?"

He handed me the belt back. "That is yours," ...car salesman all the way... "As a gift."

Juan Miguel removed another belt from under his bed. This belt was completely different from the gift. It was thicker and a bit wider than the other.

"This belt is the one I use," he said. "The trick is to make them wider so the customs don't notice the special lining."

I clued in right away. "The special cocaine lining."

He smiled. "I knew you were smart. We take the cocaine and put it into small bags, seal them with a vacuum press, then line the inside of the belts. There are thousands of belts sent from Mexican prisons every week into the *Estados Unitos*. The customs officers don't have time to check every parcel. They just use the dogs every once in a while."

"So let me get this straight," I said. "You smuggle cocaine into the prison, package it in small bags, line the belts and send them out of the prison into the States?"

He smiled and nodded in delight.

"How much cocaine per belt?" I asked.

"One ounce per belt," he leaned back on his bed. "One hundred and fifty belts per package."

One ounce per belt meant thirty-six belts per kilogram of cocaine which meant four kilograms per package. In 1998, four kilograms of cocaine in the States was worth approximately seventy thousand dollars. The numbers crunched in my brain almost by habit.

"And how much is each belt?" I was probing now.

"Cheap," he said with that Mexican snarl. His upper lip curled back as he shot me a look that said 'don't worry about a thing.' "We pay the men twenty pesos a day."

At that moment I knew I was addicted to drugs, not using them, but moving them from one place to another. All I could think about was the amazing turnover four kilos of cocaine would be worth back home. Four kilos in Canada were worth one hundred and sixty thousand dollars. Far more than in America. At twenty pesos a day for belts (two dollars Canadian) the deal was almost too hard to pass up.

Juan Miguel knew that. That's why his greedy little smile shone brighter than the sun outside.

"I'd have to think about it," I said.

And I would. There were too many unforeseen variables that could turn this deal into trouble. First I'd have to get the cocaine out of the prison in my name. Then there would be customs and the dogs. With my luck, they'd decide to thoroughly inspect my package and they'd find the drugs. Also, who would I send them to back home? Shelly? No chance. Ryan? I wasn't even sure if he was alive. Anything could happen when you weren't in control of the merchandise. How could I even trust the car dealer to sell me real cocaine, or keep his mouth shut about my shipment? There were too many risks involved, but unfortunately for me, taking risky chances was the story of my life.

"This deal will not last long," Juan Miguel grunted.

He was too anxious. I could feel it.

It was time to get out of there.

"I'll make a few calls and see what I can do."

We shook hands and I left with my gift belt slung over my shoulder. He allowed me to walk out alone, through the maze of dripping wet blankets and past the tattooed gangsters. On my way out, I heard some English words spoken, almost shouted into the air directed at me.

Kill the fucking gringo!

* * *

Roger couldn't believe that I'd ventured off into one of the worst gang infested units in the entire prison alone. He paced in front of the bed, frantic that I'd made such a stupid decision.

"You could have been killed!" he shouted. "Or worse. Raped!"

I waved him off. "No one is going to rape me. I outweigh every one of these guys."

His eyes widened with fear. "Sure, but they come in packs. Don't go back to that unit again." He stopped pacing. "What were you doing there anyway?"

Crime is secret. Always has, and always will be, or should I say, "should be". He didn't need to know about my conversation with Juan Miguel. In fact, no one would know. Lying there and watching Roger stress out about my safety helped me make up my mind. There he was, a complete stranger, wearing a path in our cement floor over my safety. He made me imagine what my family must have been going through, worrying about my well being almost a thousand miles from home. If my plan was to survive and get home,

I needed to stay focused on that and only that. Smuggling coke back home in cowboy belts seemed way too much like a Hollywood movie. I knew that dealing with these Mexicans in a criminal matter would only lead me to trouble, or worse, my death. I was the odd man out in that prison. Even though I was safe in the maximum, away from the gangsters and *cholos*, my life was in danger every moment I spent there. These drug dealers were nothing like the ones back home. In Mexico, they were ruthless thugs who would kill me for a hundred dollars never mind a thousand. I showed Roger the belt.

"I bought one of these from a guy," I said. "Nice dude. Juan Miguel."

Once again, Roger's eyes nearly popped out of his head.

"Stay away from him," he shook a long dark finger at me. "He's not a good one."

"He seemed harmless."

"Do you know what he's here for?" Roger panicked.

Roger told me that Juan Miguel's drug dealing was just the tip of the iceberg. He was a famous kidnapper in Mexico. He'd kidnapped seventy-five people – women, kids and grown men – and held them for ransom to their families. He'd demand anywhere from twenty-five thousand to one hundred thousand dollars, depending on the social status of the family. With every demand, he'd inform the family that their loved one would return in one piece. What he failed to mention was that the one piece would be dead. Of all the people he'd taken, not a single one had returned home alive.

He would have definitely taken my money and probably would have killed me. Juan Miguel was indeed a man who was into everything. I wonder what bizarre animal would be on the kidnapper's belt buckle?

* * *

February, 1999. Cereso.

Ever since I can remember I have been a great athlete. Growing up I played every sport. I wasn't born a natural at any one sport, but instead I was gifted with the ability to adapt to the level and intensity of anything I played. The only thing that prevented me from becoming a professional athlete was my lack of direction as a kid and a bad case of attention deficit disorder. I lacked focus.

Amazingly enough, I took to boxing like no other sport. At first, I fought for attention. I enjoyed the accolades and respect I received from the people who watched me. My body was made to fight. I had a low pain tolerance and a will to win that not many could match.

The Mexicans respected athletes more than any other figure in society. Soccer stars were gods. There wasn't a single Mexican boy who didn't dream of one day being a soccer professional. In the prison, there were soccer games every single day, all day. Their passion for the sport made the games highly competitive and entertaining to watch.

The mixture of confidence and boredom led me to the field one morning to play with the prison soccer team. The team consisted of ten inmates; their captain was Carlos who was also the star player. When he saw me warming up on the sideline, he called out to me and invited me to play with him.

I ran like I'd never run before, hurdling slide checks and spinning around defensemen. After the game, Carlos patted me on the back and gave me a thumbs up.

"Happy Valentine," he said to me, nodding in approval.

He had the holidays down to a tee.

The next week Carlos handed me a local newspaper sports section. I didn't fully read Spanish yet, but because I'd been writing my lessons in my notebook, I recognized some words. But that wasn't the reason he handed me the paper. There, on the second page, was a photo of me running down the field with the ball. The picture was taken from a distance, but it captured me perfectly.

I handed the paper to Roger for translation. "It says that you're the newest player for the prison team," he told me. "I didn't know you were on the soccer team."

"Neither did I," I admitted.

When Jaime came in that week, he had a copy of the newspaper with him. We shared a good chuckle over the fact that I had to go to a Mexican prison to become a celebrity.

"People are talking about you in the city," he said. "They are eager to come in and watch you play."

In Mexico, the Cereso prisons were considered part of the community. They encouraged families and citizens to get involved with prison activities. The sporting events were open for anyone in the public to see.

"What about security?" I asked. "Aren't the guards afraid of people smuggling things in?"

"They're more worried about people smuggling things out," Jaime said. "Besides, the prison collects ten pesos from anyone coming in. It's a very profitable business."

I asked Jaime to go and buy some soccer cleats for me and he did with enthusiasm. He was happy that I'd found a way to fit in with everyone in the prison. My safety was his biggest concern.

Later that weekend, Carlos invited me to the team's first practice. Everything went well and I made the team. I was the biggest player on the squad, but not the fastest. They put me on defense and told me to stop all balls coming down the pitch. I told them in so many words that it wouldn't be a problem.

On my way back to the maximum, I heard shouts of English coming from behind me. I turned in time to see a sickly thin man with glasses running after me, waving his hands in the air. I stopped to let him catch up.

"Hey," he said. He was breathing hard. "Damn you walk fast."

Chilangro looked like a character out of a zombie movie. His skin was weathered like leather on an old pair of cowboy boots. He spoke clear English that sounded like he was gargling gravel.

"Do you want to fight?" he asked.

"Excuse me."

"Box. Do you want to have a boxing match?"

"With you?" I sized him up.

"Hell no!" his eyes widened. "I may be Mexican, but I'm not stupid."

We both shared a laugh. Chilangro told me that he'd learned English by spending time in American prisons. They called him Chilangro because he came from Mexico City.

"The coach needs another fighter for the match next month. He has a heavyweight fighter, but no opponent."

"Sure," I said. I was in great physical shape. "No problem."

When I told Roger that night about the fight, he couldn't help but shake his head at me. "How can you concentrate on all these things while you have your case to worry about?"

I offered him a sympathetic smile. "This is how I deal with my case," I said. "I forget about it and go on with life."

"But you can't be that way," he pleaded. "This is a serious place. They want to lock you up for ten years. You need to be focused."

Focus? They didn't give me any other option but to wait. I couldn't call a lawyer every day or read over police reports and try to find a loophole. The truth of the matter was that they'd caught me cold nuts with the drugs in my car. I could shift the blame anywhere I wanted, but in the end, it would inevitably come back to me.

"I'm secure with the fact that I'm going to get the ten years and go home," I said. "I can't sit here and dwell on the fact that I'm locked up. I need to stay busy."

"I can't believe how well you handle prison," he told me.

He had no idea that he was dealing with a stone cold professional in the business of doing time.

* * *

March, 1999. Cereso Amateur Boxing Event – Cereso

I stood in the corner of the ring staring across at my opponent. The man was a giant. He had to be at least three hundred pounds of solid Mexican. He stood maybe six-foot-two and had on a pair of gloves that looked more like fingerless mittens at the end of his massive arms.

Men women and children surround the ring all with their eyes on me. It looked like the entire city of Los Mochis had shown up. At a table at ringside sat the warden with his cowboy hat and three judges. Behind them, a Mexican flag waved in the gentle breeze. As I scanned the crowd, I noticed people taking photos and holding video recorders. The sight of technology in the rustic jail threw me for a loop.

The monster at the other corner banged his gloves together and I thought I felt the entire ring shake. I looked back at my corner men, Carlos and Roger. They seemed more nervous than I was.

"What laboratory did they find this guy in?" I asked.

Roger swallowed. "Are you sure you want to do this?"

I wasn't.

"I can't back out now," I said. " These people either came to see me win or get killed." I banged my gloves. Either way, they're going to get a fight."

The referee called us both to the middle of the ring. The giant took two large steps and stood there waiting for me, growling in my direction.

Roger handed me my mouthpiece.

"If I don't make it back," I said with a sarcastic tone, "give my dictionary to Carlos."

Roger turned pale. "Oh my god. I can't do this."

"Relax," I told him. "I'm the one taking the shots to the head."

In the middle of the ring, I realized just what I was up against. The giant had at least three inches in height on me, and he was thick. As the ref gave me the rules that I didn't understand, I stared the big man in the eyes. Then he looked away. That's when I knew I had him.

Man has many unique ways of exposing his fear to the world. Sometimes it comes in the form of anger. Sometimes a man cries, showing that he's unable to deal with the pressure. In boxing, it's in the eyes. When a man looks you in the eyes in the middle of the ring then looks away before you do, it's a sure sign that he's a little nervous.

I stood in the corner waiting for the bell to ring, bouncing on the balls of my feet in anticipation. I felt a tug on my foot and looked down to see Carlos with his hands in the air in fists.

"Merry Christmas," he said sternly, throwing a few punches in the air.

"Carlos," I said and looked back across the ring. "Christmas is the least of this guy's concern."

As soon as that bell rang, I ran across the ring instantly jabbing at the giant. The crowd roared as I threw punch after punch at the big man. Shocked by my onslaught, he covered his face and backed up into his corner. I delivered a hook shot to his body, then to his head, waving my free hand in the air in mock wind up much to the delight of the kids at ringside, then delivering it to the giant's midsection. After the first round, we both went to our corners and sat on our stools. The crowd laughed and cheered for both of us.

Roger's face was red with life. "Oh my god! You really took it to him."

"What else did you expect?" I asked. "I'm not trying to let that guy hit me."

Carlos sprang into the ring and blasted me in the face with water.

"Bang, bang, bang," he said as he threw punches in the air.

Roger and I both laughed. Carlos had such a good heart. The best part about that minute in the corner was the connection that strengthened between us three. We were all on the same mission – a Canadian, an American and a Mexican. I knew I had to win that fight for all of us. If they were in any way like me, it had been a long time since they'd experienced success.

At the bell, I rushed the giant again, only this time, with the mentality to end the fight with a *bang, bang, bang.*

The next day in the newspaper I saw the knockout photo. That straight right punch to the giant's forehead sent him backwards into his corner, to the floor, and with a bad case of whiplash. The photo captured the punch on impact.

"What does the caption say?" I asked Roger.

He was so excited. "It says that you gave the crowd exactly what they came for, and that you beat the number one heavyweight in Los Mochis." He looked up at me like a surprised kid. "They're calling you the number one contender for the title."

It took a drug transporting charge in a foreign country to get a bit of acknowledgement for something good. That was just my luck. Finally I was worth something, and no one I knew was there to see it.

Chapter 9
Mike
Round Two: The Sell Out

April, 1999. Cereso

She had the most beautiful black eyes I'd ever seen. They complimented her straight black hair and pale skin that was flawless like that of a perfect angel. I sat on the upstairs walkway staring across the unit at her as she sat on a chair watching me with keen interest. I offered her a smile, but her courage wasn't there yet. After all, she was only eight years old.

So much sorrow in that little face, it made me want to cry for her. How hard was it for her to smile? She looked so detached from the world sitting outside her father's cell while he and her mother "spoke alone" in the cell during the visit. I knew that the "talk" didn't mean sex because her father was gay. All I thought about when I looked at her was pain. Mine, hers, my daughter's, my family's, my friend's. When our eyes met again, I reacted like the child, puffed out my cheeks and crossed my eyes. She didn't flinch. Not a single facial movement.

Her father, Jovan, was a nice man. He owned a hair salon on the street before being arrested for transporting drugs to America. His wife must have been the most understanding woman on the planet. She came in twice a week and each time they spent at least an hour talking while little Roxanna entertained herself.

That day, there were an unusual amount of kids in the maximum unit, and so few parents around to pay attention to them. As they ran around bored, I couldn't help but think about my daughter. I'd made a promise to myself not to think about her too much because it hurt. All those years choosing to stay away from her were beginning to take its toll on my conscience especially because now

I was forced to reevaluate who I was as a human being. In a way, I still didn't care too much about being a family member. They weren't helping me now in my desperate time of need. I owed them nothing and my daughter less. But something inside of me also wanted to go back in time and restart my life. I wanted to be a smart son and a good parent proving to everyone that they meant something to me. Roxanna's sad eyes reminded me of the good spirited little girl I'd been running from. I deserved to feel the pain.

Under the close scrutiny of Roxanna, I jumped off the top walkway right into the middle of a soccer game. The kids squealed with joy as I stole the ball and ran with it to the end of the unit to score. Instantly the kids took to me, jumping on my back, ganging up on me for the ball. It erased the negative thoughts instantly.

When I sat on the bench to catch my breath, the kids followed, starved for attention. They spoke to me in Spanish, and when I tried to answer them, they looked dumbfounded not understanding a word I spoke. Slightly embarrassing, but part of the journey into the world of learning a new language.

I wanted to connect with the kids, but more so with Roxanna. She remained seated upstairs, but couldn't help but watch me as I played with the dozen or so kids. I showed them card tricks with my own Canadian cards, juggled fruit to their enjoyment. Did one hand pushups – whatever it took to make them laugh and smile.

By the end of the day, when the mothers left with their children, I shook every kid's hand – except Roxanna's who wanted nothing to do with me. She averted her eyes as she walked past me. With Roger's help I had to ask Jovan about her.

"She hasn't spoke a word since I was arrested," he said to me. "I fear that I've broken her heart."

The way he said those words choked me up. He loved his family, it was obvious by the look on his face when he watched them leave and then spoke about them to me. I didn't have that connection with my own family, and it sucked. I had a daughter who hadn't spoken a single word to me her entire life, and that was entirely my fault.

"One day she'll speak," I told him. "Have faith."

* * *

Later that month, I came back to the unit from soccer practice to find a diminutive African American man in our cell. He sat in my chair eating my food, and when I walked in, he didn't say a word, just smiled with a mouthful of canned beans.

"How you doing?" I asked. "Please, help yourself."

"I'm really hungry," he stated in between swallows.

Andy stood about five seven and weighed no more than one hundred and fifty pounds. He told me that he'd been arrested in Mexico smuggling marijuana in his backpack. When he spoke, his words were long and drawn out with a slight drawl, as if he struggled to make his thoughts clear. Then he told me that he needed his medication.

Andy had a lot of problems, but his newest one was Roger. When Roger came back to find a new guy asleep on his bed, he nearly lost his mind.

"Who is this asshole on my bed?" he screamed.

I pushed Roger outside. "Quiet, he's sleeping."

Outside Roger was just as livid. "I don't care if he's dying! He can do it off of my bed."

"I guess we have a new roommate," I said. "He'll have to sleep on the floor."

Roger ran his hand through his hair. "Damn these people! What do they think, we're sardines?"

To me, it wasn't a big deal. I already hated my sleeping quarters. One more person wouldn't make it worse or better.

"Relax," I told him. "We'll speak to the warden about moving him to his own cell."

Roger couldn't help but relent a smile. "You may need to buy the whole fucking tequila factory for this one."

* * *

May, 1999. Boxing gym – Cereso

While training in the boxing gym one afternoon, I felt eyes watching me from the other side of the chicken fence. When I looked, I saw Juan Miguel and a friend dressed in similar attire. Immediately I noticed the cow on his belt buckle. I left the bag and greeted the two men..

"Hey," said Juan Miguel. His chest puffed outward as he spoke English to me. "How would you like to make two hundred American dollars?"

I remembered Roger's warning, but money was the bane of my existence.

"That all depends," I said and leaned on the fence.

Juan Miguel leaned closer. As did his friend. "We have a fight for you. All you have to do is show up and lose."

I laughed out loud. It made Juan Miguel and his friend shudder. I'd never lost a fight in my life, and needless to say, never thrown one for money. They were speaking to a respectable boxer who made it his mission to completely annihilate every one of his opponents.

"I don't think I can help you," I said. "It's not in my nature."

Juan Miguel waved off my comment. "Nature has nothing to do with money. I'll make it three hundred dollars and a rematch."

"You'll make it?" I shook my head. "Is there anything you're not into, Juan Miguel?"

He smiled. "A man has to make a living."

"No thank you," I said, nodding to his *amigo*. "I'm content just fighting for fun."

Juan Miguel turned to his friend and the two began talking. Their conversation became heated, Juan Miguel winning him over then turning back to me with a sick look on his face.

"I will let you think about this for a week." He held up five fingers. "Five hundred dollars American. My final offer."

I smiled and shook my head. "You don't give up, do you?"

"Five hundred will let you live well for a while here," he said walking away. "I'll see you next week."

* * *

Over a bowl of granola cereal with Andy, he revealed to me his secret plan. His eyes were wide with neurotic excitement.

"I'm going to escape," he said with intense determination.

The only thought that entered my mind was why I was wasting a bowl of hard-to-get granola on a man who was leaving.

"And how are you going to do this?" I asked.

He spoke with a mouthful of food. "I've got it all figured out."

And he did. He told me of the staircase he found beside the warden's building that went up one side of the wall and down the other. I asked him how he knew the stairs went down the other side.

"All stairs have to come down somewhere."

Made sense to me.

"I'll leave in the night, climb the fence around the unit and sneak over to the stairwell." His eyes filled with light. "Then I'll just run until I hit the border."

"That shouldn't take you more than ten days," I said.

"Ten days," he repeated. "I wonder if I should take some food with me."

I pulled the box of granola closer to me. "If you touch my cereal, I'll hunt you down myself."

* * *

Jaime and I sat at the picnic tables doing what we always did whenever he came in – eat. Over a lunch of Kentucky Fried Chicken the question about my life back home came up, much to my chagrin.

"What did you do for work?" he asked me.

"I was a professional fighter." It wasn't a complete lie. "I wanted to be a champion."

Jaime smiled. "You have the presence of a man who knows how to win."

"What does that mean?"

He leaned back. "You just have a good attitude. You love life and your family. Your daughter is a lucky girl to have you as her father."

From that point on the chicken tasted like shit. God, how I hated lying to him – or worse, not telling him the truth.

"I'm not that good of a father," I said. "Look at where I am."

"Yes, you made a mistake," he assured me. "But children are forgiving. One small amount of time away isn't that bad."

To any other person, his words made sense. My problem wasn't being away once, it was never being around once. A big difference.

Other families had visits that day. They sat around the unit in various spots, at tables spaced enough apart for privacy. One family caught my attention in particular.

The father of the family had only been on the unit for a week. He had a beautiful wife and daughter who sat close to him, crying and speaking low. His daughter caught me staring and offered me a warm smile. I returned mine to her. She had long brown hair and couldn't have been more than eighteen years old. She had flawless skin and a wide smile that exuded kindness. After I looked away, I noticed from the corner of my eye the occasional glance from her. As I visited with Jaime, I'd casually look over in time to catch her staring. We exchanged playful smiles until she left.

That next weekend I sat at the tables studying my Spanish when she visited with her father again. Out of nowhere, she came over and sat down across from me.

"My name is Lucinda," she said in English. "What are you reading?"

I peeked over at the father. He sat with his wife in deep conversation, glancing over at us periodically.

"What's your father in for?" I asked.

She hung her head. "He was a police officer. He was caught carrying a gun that was not registered. The gun was not police issue. They gave him one month in here."

This country really was crazy. They threw their own police in prison for that?

Her face was so beautiful, for a moment, I forgot about my plan to just do my time and delved deep into conversation with her, learning all about her life as a Mexican teenager.

She had just graduated from high school and was struggling to figure out what she wanted to do next. She told me about her difficult life now that her father was in prison. She had to work to help her mother pay bills because money was scarce. She said that she loved her father and missed him terribly. They traveled twenty kilometers to get to the prison from where they lived. The journey cost them more money than it did time.

After two hours I felt like I knew Lucinda inside and out. When I asked to see her next week, she told me that her father was leaving that week and she would not be back.

"But I will come back to see you," she said. "If you want me to."

She was smart, beautiful and kind. How could I say no?

That entire week I trained harder in the boxing gym than I'd ever trained since arriving in the country. Talking to a young woman rejuvenated me. I felt stronger than ever.

Juan Miguel trapped me in the *quadro* and warned me that the time to decide had arrived. When I told him that I wasn't interested, he simply smiled.

"You have one more week," said the Latino Don King.

That next weekend Lucinda came in alone and we spent the entire day in the *quadro,* eating at the restaurant and walking around the field. We shared stories about our lives at home. We came from such different places in life yet it was amazing how much we had in common. We were the foreign opposites of each other.

Our friendship was unique to me. I was so used to sharing my time with criminals and women with sharpened tongues. He soft spoken demeanor made moments of our courtship an awkward ordeal. There were long periods of time where we had nothing to say. We sat in silence, shy to speak to each other. After that one visit, I realized I had way more life experience than her, and that fact made our age difference seem so much more distant.

When she showed up the next weekend she had with her a small bag filled with personal things.

She smiled and gave me a hug, whispering softly in my ear. "I want to spend the night with you."

Any other man in my situation would have jumped at the opportunity. A beautiful, young, woman giving herself up to me. She waited for my answer. Her smile faded the longer I hesitated.

All I could think about was her father fifty miles away wondering where she was. Then another ethical consideration entered my brain. What kind of girl travels all this way to be with a complete stranger in a prison? Sex had its place in a relationship, but morals came first. The last thing Lucinda needed was a guy like me in her life. A life abuser, non-caring, criminal, liar, manipulator – everything she wasn't. Sleeping with her would make me the lowest person in the world because I didn't feel the intense emotions for her that she felt for me.

As we walked in the yard, contemplating wrong and right, rain began to fall. Our eyes locked on to the sky as we talked about all the reasons for her not to stay. I told her about my life back home, and how I wasn't such a good guy. I told her about my daughter and about how irresponsible I was as a father. She absorbed every word with a saddened look on her face.

As the rain soaked us from head to toe, we exposed every aspect of our lives to each other. She told me that she had no friends back home. She revealed to me how the kids in her school beat her up. She told me how her father was abusive and didn't really care about her. I listened to every word she said. As her tears mixed with the rain, I felt sympathy for her, which made my decision not to get intimate all the more wise.

I gave her the only money I had, enough for her to make it back home. We shared a passionate kiss and said our good-byes, knowing that she wouldn't be back that next weekend. It hurt to send her away with her heart broken the way it was. Her eye makeup smeared down her cheeks by the rain. That look of rejection and dismay was recognizable in any country. I told her that she was one of the most beautiful women I'd ever met, and that the kids would one day regret the fact that they picked on her. I promised her that she'd find a man who would love her the way that she needed.

I stood in the rain, watching her leave. She stopped at the front gate and turned back, waving slightly before disappearing for good. A touch of sadness fondled my heart. How much longer could I keep pushing people away from me before people stopped coming?

As I walked back to the maximum, I noticed a lone figure standing under the cover of the woodshop. It was Juan Miguel, and he was waiting for me.

"She's a beautiful girl," he said with his usual sneer. "Is she coming to the fight?"

I shook my head and laughed. "Okay. I'll take the fight..." I swallowed my pride. "And the deal."

His face lit up with excitement. "Spoken like a true *boxedor.*"

Suckered into a thrown fight by a broken heart. Since I'd given the rest of the money to Lucinda, I needed to make something quick. Juan Miguel gave me two hundred as a down payment and left smiling. At least one of us felt good about what we were doing.

With the *sell-out* money in my wet pocket I went back to my cell. The room was dark, but I could feel the presence of someone in there. When I turned on the light, there was Andy sitting on Roger's bed looking deep in thought.

"What are you doing?" I asked him.

He looked up at me. His face filled with intensity.

"I'm going over the wall," he said. "Tonight."

* * *

It must have been well past midnight when I woke up to movement in the cell. Roger slept soundly, snoring to himself. I turned over to see Andy stuffing items into a bag. I knew what he was doing and didn't say a word. The big escape was going down. I turned over and went back to sleep.

In the morning I woke again to find Andy's bed empty. Out in the unit, the regular activity played out. The men worked on their belts, the music played low on the radios. I leaned on the railing, absorbing the light of the morning sun.

Roger came up the stairs with a sly smirk on his face.

"That stupid bastard got caught escaping," he said.

I laughed. "Let me guess. There was no downside of the stairwell?"

Roger leaned on the railing beside me. "He didn't even make it to the stairs."

Andy made it over the wall of the maximum, to the parking lot where the stairwell was, but that was it. When he reached the parking lot, it was during the guard's shift change. Scrambling for cover, he scurried under a parked vehicle to wait until they left. One of the guards standing outside having a cigarette noticed a reflection coming from under one of the vehicles. Upon closer inspection, he found Andy hiding there, dressed in black with my backpack on. Unfortunately for Andy, my bag was equipped with light reflecting material used for night bike riding. He was arrested, beaten, then thrown in the hole.

He'd stolen more than just my bag. When I'd finished searching through what little clothes I had, I realized that Andy had taken a black shirt and a pair of black pants from me as well. I couldn't be mad. He'd attempted to do something that I felt like doing from the moment I got there. I admired him for being brave enough to try and faced the fact that I'd never see my clothes again.

My feelings for him soon changed when I checked the cupboard and realized that my new box of granola cereal was gone.

* * *

June, 1999. Cereso

The hype surrounding the fight was bigger than Hagler and Leonard or Tyson and Holyfield. Mexicans from all over the state piled through the Cereso doors to see the fight the papers called the true battle of power in the heavyweight division. Sinaloa never had a true heavyweight fighter, and even if they did, there was never anyone to pit against him. My fight against the giant months ago was a great spectacle for the people of the town. This one would prove to be even more interesting.

The newspapers sent reporters in to watch us train. My opponent was another inmate, Chapo something or rather. He was a tall kid with a face that looked like a chewed toffee. He must have taken many punches to the face in his career, and that made me worry just a bit. I agreed to throw the fight, but I didn't intend to get hurt in the process. Since my hands weren't going to be my main weapons, it would all come down to my feet. Because of that, my only training on that day that the reporters came in was dancing. That day, I was the Fred Astaire of boxing. As the reporters took photos of my opponent hitting the bag and sparring, I sat in the back eating chocolate bars and calling out any insult I could think of. When it came time to photograph my training, I surprised them by dancing to Mexican music, shuffling my feet, tapping, hopping from one foot to the other, all while stuffing my face with candy. The crowd worried that I wasn't taking the fight seriously. I wasn't. They asked me if I was worried about losing.

"I'm worried about losing weight," I said in between chocolate bars. "I don't want to be as skinny as Chapo."

They laughed. I was the Muhammad Ali of Mexico.

On the day of the fight, the crowd was thick with eager spectators all hoping for another dramatic knockout from *El Famouso Canadience*. The entire maximum came out to watch, cheering me on as I stood in my corner with Carlos and Roger.

Roger sprayed water into my mouth. "Is this going to be a quick fight?"

I spat the water into Carlos's bucket. "Nope. It's going to decision."

"You don't think you can beat this guy?" he asked.

I smiled. "Oh, I know I can beat him. It's just that I'm not going to." I winked at him. "I've been paid off."

Roger didn't quite catch my drift.

"The match has been fixed, duped, coerced." I told him with a sly smile. "They got to me, Rog."

Roger shook his head and handed me the mouthpiece. "Great. Then why the hell am I here?"

"You're my accomplice," I told him. "If I go down, so do you."

His face lit up with terror. "Don't be getting me involved in your shit," he yelled. "I'm no match fixer."

I had a good laugh at his fear, which allowed me to relax. I had to be honest, I wasn't too thrilled about the turn of events. I'd never thrown a fight before. In fact, I'd never lost a match in my life. I thought about my coach back home and how he'd lose his mind if he knew what I was doing. Things changed when the quality of life was on the line. Sometimes a man did things he wasn't so proud of just to stay alive.

As I waited for the bell to ring, I scanned the crowd. In the front row behind me sat the regular bunch of administration and reporters. Across the ring, near the judge's table I noticed Juan Miguel. We met eyes and he gave me a thumb up. I nodded, but before I could do anything else, I saw her – Nomi. She sat two seats down from Juan Miguel beside a stout man dressed similar to him. It must have been her husband. He stared directly at me as if in on the secret. As the bell rang I felt my heart sink into my stomach. Selling out suddenly seemed grimier than the crime that brought me there.

I must have given Chapo every opportunity to hit me in that first round. I danced around the ring, hands down, chin out – nothing. He hardly threw a punch and barely came within a foot of me for two whole rounds. The crowd jeered, the referee yawned, It was the worst display of pugilism I'd been a part of in my life.

Back in my corner between the second and third round, Roger splashed water on my face. Even his squirt lacked enthusiasm.

"I can't even throw the fight," I said. "This guy won't let me."

"The people think you're hurt," he said. "They're wondering why you're not beating on him."

That gave me an idea. "Tell them that I hurt my shoulder," I said. "I'll fight him with one hand until he makes his move."

And fight him with one hand I did. For the entire third round I did nothing but jab. Still, Chapo moved away from me. Every time he threw a punch, I leaned into it, taking the odd shot square in the forehead. I did everything to try and make the dive look real, but Chapo didn't have it in him.

I screamed at him in Spanish, calling his mother and sister names. Bad names. Names that would make a Mexican man stab me with anything he could get his hands on. The crowd laughed and cheered us both on. I thought for sure the insults would spark some sort of anger in him.

Nothing.

Back at the corner, I sat on the stool exhausted from talking while moving around the ring and leaning into Chapo's pathetic jabs. Across the ring, two women and a man approached Chapo and began yelling at him.;

"What's going on over there?" I asked Roger.

"That's his mother and sister," Roger told me. "They're a little angry."

I was frustrated and the extra weight I put on for the fight was beginning to take it's toll. "This is getting stupid. What's with this guy? He couldn't win a fight if it was handed to him on a silver platter."

As I caught my breath for the final round, I noticed Nomi get up and walk away from the ring. I followed her with my eyes all the way back to the gate. She stopped and turned back to the ring, holding my stare for a moment before disappearing.

"I gotta get out of prison," I told Roger as I stood up to begin the fourth and final round. "This place is going to get me killed."

Roger stuck the mouthpiece back in my mouth. "Just focus on losing this fight, okay?"

We both looked at each other.

"I can't believe I just said that," he remarked before leaping off the canvass.

I completely screwed up the entire fourth round. I didn't throw a single punch, make a single boxing move or even do a dance. The crowd actually booed us. I felt embarrassed for Chapo. He was going to win this fight on the fact that I completely sucked, not because of his talent.

I was so relieved when the final bell sounded and the fight ended. So was the crowd. Many spectators got up and left, angry that the fight had been a complete waste of their Sunday afternoon.

As predicted, Chapo's hand was raised in the end. A wave of confidence consumed his face as they handed him the first place trophy – a two foot gold marvel with a boxer figurine on top. The judge handed me the smallest trophy I'd ever seen. A perfect symbol for how I felt at that moment.

When Chapo and I met in the middle of the ring to shake hands, he had a smirk on his mashed up grill that made me want to beat the crap out of him. How good would that have looked? Beating a guy to pieces after losing to him in a four round fight.

"Good match," he said in Spanish. "Bad luck for you."

I glanced at Roger. "Bad luck, eh," I was boiling mad. "Tell him that I'm gonna beat the Mexican off of him next time."

Roger waved his hands. "I can't say that."

So I just smiled and shook Chapo's hand. "My day will come," I said in English.

Outside the ring, Juan Miguel met me and shook my hand. "You made a few good people happy."

"Yeah, well I'm not happy unless they're happy." There was only one thing I wanted to know from him. "That man who sat beside you. Is that Nomi's husband?"

"Ah, you like her?" he knew what I was getting at.

"No, I'm just asking..."

Juan Miguel winked at me. "Don't worry, I can keep a good secret."

Great. In one day I'd sold myself out, taken a bribe and revealed my interest in a gangster's wife to the biggest loud mouth in the prison. Shame, corruption and stupidity. I was on another serious roll.

* * *

June, 1999. Cereso

The toilets in the cells were like contraptions from a horror movie. Every time I went to use it, I heard that sinister music that played just before the character was killed. Rats and cockroaches liked to come up from the sewer through the toilet, so every time I used it, I rushed hoping to avoid any negative interaction with a dirty rodent.

There was no running water in the cells, so flushing toilets was out of the question. To "discard" waste down the toilet, I had to pour an entire ten-gallon bucket of water into the bowl when finished. It made running to the can for an emergency a big issue.

Early one morning I had one of those emergencies and found myself scrambling out of bed for relief. Roger was already up and excused himself from the room as I took care of business.

"I'll get you a bucket," he said. "You better hurry though. Count is in ten minutes."

The count occurred twice a day at five in the morning and five at night – every twelve hours. Inmates were required to stand outside in the maximum yard, in single file, and march past the guard announcing his personal number for his count. When I first arrived, they assigned me a spot in the line according to my alphabetical placement. My number was *ocho* - eight.

Number eight came quick, and so did five minutes. Before I knew it, the door to the cell was kicked in and the curtain to the washroom ripped completely down. I sat on the toilet with a look of fear. There in the doorway stood Shithead, his face red with anger. He held a clipboard in his hand and without warning began beating me over the head with it, screaming at the top of his lungs.

Roger raced into the room and explained to him that I'd lost track of time. Shithead didn't care. He grabbed me with both hands and ripped me off the toilet, pants down, and pushed me outside onto the walkway.

Other inmates watched as I scrambled to pull my pants up while defending myself from the clipboard. Shithead yelled at me the entire way down the stairs and out of the maximum unit. Two other guards joined him as he escorted me across the yard toward a small brick building standing alone in the corner of the quadro.

"Where am I going?" I asked in Spanish. Amazing how the words came to me in my moment of desperation.

"I'm locking you up," said Shithead. "I'll teach you for being late."

When he opened the door to the segregation unit, an odor of garbage and fecal matter wafted into my face. The building was cramped on the inside. Made of gray brick and sand floors, the place looked identical to the hospital corridor that contained the lepers and mentally ill. I nearly gagged to death as he shoved me towards the back of the building. My stomach gurgled with pain.

He opened the door at the very back of the building and forced me inside. The door was thick steel with a large barred window. He locked the door and walked away, offering nothing as an explanation.

The cell wasn't empty. Six men cramped inside the small room, and all of them were working on belts. Five o'clock in the morning and these guys were already hard at work on their cocaine belts. They all smiled at me and shifted to make room for me to sit down.

My head spun with anger, fear, frustration. I'd done nothing wrong but miss count. Shithead really had it out for me. He could have counted me there and given me a warning. This incident was exactly what he needed to mess with me, and I gave it to him.

I didn't know how long I would be there. The guys in the cell told me that missing count was worth a week. They told me to relax and get comfortable. There was nothing comfortable about the hole. The smell, the confinement – they were the worst things about being there. I could handle time alone, but cramped in that cell for a week with the smell and the company would put me over the edge of insanity.

I pressed my face against the bars and tried to look down the hall. The front door to the building was locked and the sun had begun to creep over the giant wall into the prison. In a matter of minutes, the entire cell became scorching hot and breathing became difficult. I closed my eyes and tried to focus on being calm.

Someone spoke to me in English. "If you stay low, you can breathe cool air from under the door."

I opened my eyes to see Andy across the hall at his window. He waved to me, offering a weak smile. The poor bastard looked beaten down.

"You've been here the whole time?" I asked him.

He shrugged. "They're afraid I'm going to run again."

When I focused on him more, I noticed that he had on my black tee shirt. By now, it was dirty and funkier than a dancer on Soul Train. We both leaned our faces against the dirty segregation bars.

"By the way," he said. "Sorry about stealing your shirt. I had nothing else to wear."

I banged my head against the bars and burst into laughter. If I made it out of that place in one piece with my mind completely intact it would be a miracle.

Chapter 10
Mike
Blood, Love and Gucci

I sat in the hole for two long days, breathing cool air from under the door. It felt as though my heart was melting in my chest and my head might implode due to the hot pressure. In the daytime, the cell heated up like a wood oven. There was a small skylight at the back of the small cell directly over a ten-gallon bucket that all six guys in the cell called the toilet. The sun blasted through the ceiling as though it were trying to kill us. The stench from the toilet bucket became a part of the environment. After the first day, I managed to stop breathing through my mouth.

At night, the cell turned into a great big dirty slumber party. Since the room had no bed, all six of us found a spot on the floor to sleep. It reminded me of my first three days in captivity back in the police station, curled up beside complete strangers to stay warm. The nights were deathly cold, and the cement floor was harder than my thick skull. I woke up continuously through the night cursing myself for being in this predicament.

On the morning of the second day, the door to the building opened and three sets of boots entered. I awoke to see Shithead standing at the door, peeking in at me through the barred window. His aviator shades sat high on his nose as usual. Behind him were two other guards looking equally as ugly.

"Get up," he said in Spanish.

I stood and faced him through the bars. I didn't understand why I took so much shit from this guy. In any other circumstance I would have punched his glasses into his face so they became a permanent accessory. He was half my size, half the man and half of my sentence away from finally finding out the difference between Canadians and other foreigners when it came to dishing out an ass whooping.

Shithead unlocked the door and told me to step out. I noticed the batons in the other guard's hands and hesitated. Across the hall, Andy watched, his arms hanging outside the door and his face pressed against the dirty bars. In the light from the sun I noticed for the first time that Andy had a black eye. He didn't smile when our eyes met. He had a look like he'd been in my impending position not to long ago. I didn't move.

"Let's go," said Shithead. He stepped aside to let me pass.

"No," I said. "What's going on?"

I could see Shithead begin to get angry. His lips pursed tight and his posture straightened. He looked straight ahead, away from me, as he barked out his order again. The two guards twirled their batons, waiting for the moment to pounce on me.

"Where am I going?" I asked.

Nothing. Just that military style stare that was seriously freaking me out.

By now, the other occupants of the cell had woken up. They were watching the interaction from the floor, probably saying to themselves how stupid the Canadian was for not listening to the guards. I didn't care. I knew well enough by this time in my life that three men with batons and bad attitudes meant trouble. I wasn't about to just bend over and let them take a piece of me without a fight, or at least without an argument.

They couldn't just beat me, could they? There had to be some law that prevented them from beating foreigners. I didn't do anything that required any form of punishment, at least not in my eyes. I caught Andy staring at me for a second more before dropping out of sight back into his cell.

He didn't want to see what was going to happen next.

"Move," said Shithead. "Or we'll move you."

That split second decision probably saved me a humiliating beat down in front of everyone. I took a step out of the cell with the thought that if I was going to be beaten with sticks, it would be where no one else could see, and if they thought I was going to just take it like a man, they were wrong.

One of the guards led me out of the segregation unit. Shithead and the other followed close behind. The silence was painful enough. As they led me outside into the early morning, I wondered if this was the end. The dawn had just arrived. The sun hadn't yet found it's way over the giant wall and all that alerted the prison that a new day was on the horizon was the frigid morning temperature. My skin broke out into cold bumps as I walked barefoot around the building to the back.

"Stop here," shouted Shithead.

The grass out back was a brilliant green. Surrounded by trashcans and work tools - shovels and wheelbarrows - the small section was completely sheltered from the rest of the prison. A perfect niche for a good old fashioned ass kicking.

I turned to Shithead with the bravest face. He stood five feet away from me with a stone face, the other two guards not to far behind me. I could feel his beady little eyes scanning me up and down. Make your move, I thought. I wanted nothing more than for him to throw the first punch. I knew I'd only get one or two on him before the batons got me, but that would be all I needed.

"Put your hands in the air," he commanded.

I did so slowly, keeping my attention on him. No sooner did my hands reach high, Shithead took two large steps to the side out of my range. Suddenly my already freezing body was blasted with a stream of frigid water from a garden hose. I screamed out in pain as the shower soaked me from head to toe. I felt my hair stick out on end and my genitals crawl back into my body. For a moment I couldn't breathe. The water wanted to kill me.

"Take off your clothes," Shithead yelled.

He was crazy. I slowly stripped down to nothing and twirled to let the water blast me in the chest as directed. I swiped my hands over my body in a washing motion. When the water stopped, I stood there like a drowned rat in a state of shock.

A towel appeared in Shithead's hand. I reached for it but he held it back, slinging it over his shoulder as a taunt. Shivering cold,

I stood face to face with him as he looked me up and down. Completely humiliated and angry I waited for him to let me go back to the segregation cell. How sick was that? I wanted to go back to the worst place I'd ever spent the night in just to get away from the biggest asshole I'd never had the opportunity to beat the crap out of.

As though he were sick of me, he tossed me the towel and walked away. Humiliated and disgraced I began drying off with the quickest hands I'd ever had. The towel wasn't nearly enough to get me warm and dry, but it helped.

I picked up my wet clothing and turned to go back inside, but one of the guards with the baton stood in my way.

"You're going back to the maximum," he said, poking his baton into my chest. "If you ever tell anyone about this, we'll be seeing you again."

* * *

I woke up one morning with a sharp pain in my stomach. It hurt so bad, I didn't even get out of bed until later that afternoon. Whenever I tried to eat, I would immediately feel nauseous and lose my desire to finish the food. The pain came in short bursts, almost like someone was jabbing a thin knife into my gut every twenty minutes.

When I told Roger, all he did was shake his head. "I told you about the food," he said. "You've probably got a virus."

Because the health care was non-existent, catching a virus was a potential death sentence. I immediately stopped eating the prison food and spent at least a hundred dollars on canned items and eggs. But I had one weakness - chilies.

Chilies in Mexico were a main staple with every meal. They ate them with everything. I learned in my short time there that chilies went well with all meals. The Mexicans would roast them lightly on the open burner then take periodic bites straight from the chili every few bites of the meal. I picked up on this habit, not being able to withstand the heat for the first while, but then as time went on, I became Mexican by way of the chili.

The prison basketball league began one weekend, and every unit participated. The maximum unit had the dominating team and I was the starting point guard. We played every four days and dominated – most teams crumbled and gave up whenever they played us.

On the day of our fourth game, I woke up screaming in pain. My stomach felt like it was about to explode. I rolled out of my bed and walked hunched over down to the health care.

Don Juan made me lie on the table as he asked me questions, feeling for lumps in my stomach.

"You have gastritis," he told me.

"What the hell is that?" I asked.

Gastritis was a stomach condition caused not by dirty food, but from eating too many chilies. The spice from the food had turned my stomach into a volcano of acid, and I was ready to erupt.

He told me to rest and that it would eventually go away. He wrote me a prescription for medication that I would have to get filled from a pharmacy on the street. I thought that would be it. With medication, I would heal and my trouble would be over.

I was wrong.

For the next six months, my time was spent fighting for my life. Roger reluctantly gave me the bottom bunk because I was continuously running to the washroom to throw up or other, and other was just as unpleasant. Jaime filled my prescription every month. Each time cost me a bottle of tequila to the warden. The guy was ruthless, even on my deathbed.

The worst part about gastritis was it inconsistency. The pain came in waves. One day up and about would cost me three days in pain. I fell for it every time. When I thought I was healed, I'd be up and playing soccer or basketball. Then the next day, I'd be crying in my bed, wishing to die. The virus played more with my mind than it did with my body.

Roger didn't make things any easier. I listened to him grumble every time he had to climb up on to the bed. Whenever he came down, I was helpless, listening to him scold me about eating the soup.

"It's the chili," I'd manage to squeak out in between painful tremors. "You bastard."

I tried to keep my sense of humor about the entire ordeal. When there were days of intense diarrhea, I'd ask Roger to run and get me a chili.

"You can't eat a chili at a time like this," he'd say.

"I don't want to eat it," I'd say with a wan grin. "I want to plug up my ass."

Sometimes the jokes were more serious than he knew.

One morning I woke up with a new pain. It began with an itchy sensation inside my ass, then it turned into a burning sensation that felt like a gerbil trying to gnaw his way out of my colon. I limped down to the health care, hoping it was just a side effect of the gastritis. After a close inspection, Don Juan had a chuckle at my expense.

"You have a bad case of hemorrhoids," he said. "This isn't your month."

He gave me two large pills wrapped in plastic sheaths.

"Take these rectally," he told me.

When I got back to the cell and showed Roger the pills, he set me straight.

"I don't like anything I have to shove up my ass," he waved his fingers at the capsules.

"Great Roger, thanks for the support."

"It's your ass, not mine?" he said with a chuckle. "I'll leave you three alone."

I sat there in the washroom staring at the capsules. Inside the plastic sheath, the pills were about the same texture as a soft chocolate. The coating was liquid smooth and left a greasy film on my fingers. They were the shape of a football and the size of my thumb. I'd never actually put my thumb up my ass before, but I knew it wasn't something I thought would feel good.

It felt like a lightening storm in my stomach, and a wild fire in my ass. As I stared at the pill, I lost my nerve more every second. Finally, after much self-talk, I stood and unwrapped the capsule.

The difficult part was that every time a sharp pain occurred in my gut, my entire body tensed. My muscles contracted and I felt like throwing up. I fondled the pill between my fingers and went for the insertion.

As soon as the cold capsule touched the outside of my anus, my body seized up. The lightening storm inside was the guardian, and it wasn't allowing me to relax. I spread my cheeks wide and tried to force my asshole open, but it was locked tighter than a bank vault. With two fingers I forced the pill against my sphincter only to have it crumble in my hand.

Sweat beads formed on my brow. The washroom became a sauna as I stood with one leg on the toilet, bent over and grunting from the stomach pain. I pushed again, but there was no way I was getting it in. the longer it took, the hotter the small room became. After five minutes of agonizing pressure, the once solid capsule turned into a mushy glob. I began to panic, smearing the slimy depository around the opening of my anus in a desperate move to gain some sort of satisfaction. When I was finished, my ass still hurt, my stomach continued to fuck with me and my ass was covered in greasy white hemorrhoid cream that was about as useless as a set of tits on a bull.

I sat on the toilet depressed and wondering if my life was ever going to be back to the way it was before all this pain. I stared at the second capsule knowing that it too would have its chance. I felt disgusted with myself. The white goo all over my hand and ass and no water to wash it off. At once, I hated everything. No fucking running water. Fucking chilies. Shelly, that asshole. Roger the whiner. I became angry to the point that I wanted to break everything in that washroom, but when I looked around, the only thing there was the damn depository.

Finally, after ten minutes of cursing and complaining, I'd had enough. I forgot about the pain in my stomach and stood back up. I breathed deeply two or three times, unwrapped the capsule and tried again. It was the same thing. My ass would not open.

"Relax," I told myself. "Just open the door. Open the door."

I felt my bowels relax. My muscles calmed and my breathing slowed.

"Open the door…" I said. My new mantra.

I felt my sphincter quiver, then loosen. With little excitement, I lowered the pill, which was already beginning to melt, down to my ass and right to the doorstep. With just a gentle push, I felt my ass swallow the pill in one gulp. No mess, no fuss, No nothing. All that drama for nothing. I thought maybe there would be a burning sensation, like the medication would go to work instantly and erase the hemorrhoids in one blast. Nope. Just silence.

When I let Roger back in, he came with a bucket of water for me to wash my hands. He asked me how it went. I spared him the greasy details.

"I just hope it works," I said as I scrubbed down with soap.

"After a few more times, they should be gone."

"A few more times?" I said. "What do you mean? I have to do this again?"

Roger laughed. "This is Mexico man," he said. "There ain't no miracle drugs here. You're going to need at least ten more of those little bastards before you're better."

The thought of attempting that process ten more times gave me a new pain, this time in the middle of my forehead. I walked to the bed and fell into my sheets. I closed my eyes and tried to think of something else besides the horrifying ordeal I'd just gone through.

Mexico had become an official pain in the ass.

* * *

Lying in my bed, dying, feeling an unbelievable pain that after two months had become part of my every day routine, nothing managed to cheer me up. The guys came in periodically to check on me, bringing with them food and drink, but most of it I had to send away. The doctor said no hot food or soda. And of course, that's all that people brought me. I knew I was becoming a true Mexican at heart because I still ate the food, even though it made me fell like that opening shot in Alien 2 when the creature came out of Sigourney Weaver's stomach.

One afternoon a tiny knock sounded on my door. When it opened, there stood Roger with a special guest. Little Roxanna stood rigid at the door, all four feet of her, staring inside through the dark, attempting to make out if I was there or not.

As the light entered the room, she was able to make me out. I sat up in my bed to give her more of an open invitation to come in. smiling so not to make her nervous, I waved her in. Roger held her hand as she took short steps into the room. Such a brave move for a shy little girl.

"Hola, Roxanna," I said as she stood at the end of my bed.

Silent as usual, she looked up at Roger who encouraged her to walk closer. She let go of his hand and walked over to me, keeping one eye on the door the entire time. She held out her other hand that was clenched shut into a fist. I held out my hand, palm up. With the gentleness of kiss, she dropped a wrapped candy onto my palm, then quickly retreated to the safety of the outside light.

"Muchos gracias," I said to her and glanced down at the candy. It was a hard candy. Chili flavored. My stomach turned.

Satisfied, she ran out of the room. I heard her footsteps disappear down the hall.

"She's such a sweetheart," I said to Roger. "Please thank Javon for me."

Roger shrugged. "Actually, I found her sitting outside the room by herself. I don't think he knows that she was here."

I looked down at the candy again and my heart melted. That sentiment alone made the pain in my stomach disappear for a split second. I smiled as I unwrapped the candy, then felt nauseous as I inhaled the chili flavored scent. Knowing that it was bad for me, I popped it into my mouth. I figured that if a shy little girl made such a brave move to give me a candy, I could be equally as brave and eat the damn thing.

* * *

On my good days, I wrote in my journal. I feared that the disease would one day catch me and that I would eventually die. Sure, I was being more dramatic than necessary. Something like ninety percent of people with gastritis fully recover, but I felt it mandatory to feel sorry for myself at all times since nobody else would.

I wrote about how I felt regarding my sickness. I appointed a single page to each of my family members, telling them things I would want them to know on my deathbed. Completely over-doing it, I wrote things that made it seem like I was on death row. But at the end of every page, as crazy as some of it was, I allowed myself to feel emotions that weren't part of my life in the past. I found an answer in my words to personal emotional issues that I'd refused to talk about to anyone. In my moment of illness, so close to my demise, the only thing that saved me were the inexperienced journal writings and confessions that no one would ever see.

On the good days, I played basketball. The bad days, I played coma. The in-between days, I played asshole. Roger began to feel guilty about my situation after the first month or so, and like the true professional prick that I am, I preyed on his weakness. He was too easy to order around. A moan here. A groan there. Eventually he'd ask what was wrong, and I'd tell him - or rather lie to him.

"I need some clean clothes," I'd tell him.

I had to contain my laughing when he left the room with my dirty laundry to wash, grumbling his displeasure over the fact that he couldn't say no to a dying man.

"I've got chills," I said one morning. "I think I'm going down to get some soup."

"What did I tell you about that shit," he yelled at me. "I'll make you some good soup."

I felt bad for playing with him that way, but he was a roommate, and roommates messed with roommates. That's the law. Roger was an uptight guy who needed to calm down and live life the best he could, even if it were in prison for the time being. Roger needed a guy like me to take the edge off his life, to help him relax.

After a week of waiting on me, he'd finally had enough.

"I'm sick now too," he said.

"What have you got?" I asked.

"I have my own hemorrhoid. And it's you."

We both laughed. Laughing felt good. It made my sickness feel like nothing more than a bad mood.

"I've got a surprise for you," he told me one morning before disappearing from the room.

Ten minutes later the door opened. I expected Roger to enter with some food or more clean clothes, but instead at the doorway stood something even more beautiful.

Nomi smiled in at me. In her hands, a large container of menudo soup.

She looked as radiant as ever, her long hair tied in a pony tail and her dark skin illuminated by the early sun. I felt a shiver of nervousness run through my body as she entered the cell and closed the door. It was as though she had trapped me in my own space. I watched her move around my cell without saying a single word to me. She dished out a bowl of menudo and brought it to me in my bed. I sat up and held the bowl in my hands.

"'It's good," I said in Spanish as I sipped the soup from the spoon. "'What's in it?"

"Cow feet and pig hooves," she said.

I nearly spat a mouthful of the green liquid all over my sheets. This made her laugh, and her laugh made me fall in love instantly.

That morning we spoke to each other for the first time. Really spoke. She'd been nervous to speak to me before because of the language barrier, and because of her husband. She told me how her husband was a jealous man, well connected with the Cartel, and if he ever caught her with me, we'd both be dead.

I wasn't sure what to think about Nomi's visit, as good as it made me feel. It wasn't my place in this country, a country where the men were so protective of their wives, to mingle secretly with her. The words "dead" and "Cartel" were two aspects of life I didn't want to fuck with. But as dangerous as our relationship was, her presence gave me new hope that I would one day be strong again. I needed her more than I needed the medication or the sticky ass pills.

When she left that day, my strength returned. She promised that she would be back. I asked her how she could slip away and not be reported on to her husband. With a smile, she told me that the other women covered for her. They thought it was cute that she had a thing for the Canadian.

"So you have a thing for me?" I asked.

Shy Nomi returned, realizing the error of her words. Worried that she might say something else to expose herself, she left me in my bed happy as a teenager with a schoolyard crush.

*   *   *

The explosion in the unit closest to the field rattled the ground on the soccer field causing all the players to stop running and look towards the massive puff of smoke emanating from the roof.

The next series of events occurred at lighting fast speed. From the center of the pitch, I heard screams. Angry, blood curdling, panic filled. I stood with Carlos watching several inmates scramble from the unit entrance on to the field. Some were bleeding; some fell to the ground in shock.

I heard the guard's boots stomping on the cement across the quadro. When they became visible, all twenty of them, they were dressed in riot gear - shields and helmets - and instead of making their way to the smoky unit, they marched their way on to the field. They were coming for me.

Without a word of explanation, a small pack of guards surrounded me and forced me towards the maximum. Another explosion rocked the unit, this one louder than the last. I ducked on instinct, turning enough to see that a second wave of smoke had made its way into the sky. A guard shoved me from behind and forced me to walk. They were serious. Something was wrong in the prison.

The guards escorted me directly to my cell, and when I got there I was surprised to find Roger standing on a chair looking towards the quadro from the only window in our cell.

"What's going on?" I asked.

"There's a riot happening," said Roger. "Some violent shit is going down."

For the first time since arriving, I could honestly say I was terrified. Why would the guards lock us in the cell unless our lives were in extreme danger? Roger seemed panicked as he hopped down from the chair and sat on his bed. I saw the stress on his face. He was worried about Maria.

"'She'll be okay," I told him. He could only nod.

I stood up on the chair and looked out at the scene in the yard. The window had a clear view of the soccer field and the basketball court where we played. I'd never seen a prison riot before, and what I witnessed was something I'd never forget for the rest of my life.

The fight was between two rival gangs. Apparently, one side gang raped a member of the other side and from that came a bloodbath. The explosion occurred when one of the gangs ignited a propane tank in the other's unit. The explosion rocked the entire bottom floor of the unit, seriously hurting cholos and innocent bystanders.

What I saw through the window was a battlefield. Mexican youths of all sizes fought hand to hand, hand to knife, machete to hand. They stabbed and beat on each other, sometimes two on one, other times five on one.

At one end of the basketball court, I saw five Mexicans beat a kid to death with baseball bats and gruesome handmade clubs with nails sticking on the end. They smashed him in the head, the body and broke both his legs. When they were sure he was gone, they propped him up against the pole and kicked him in the face enough times until his entire jaw collapsed. When they were done, they moved on to someone else.

In the field, there were twenty or so cholos fighting to the death. They punched and kicked and stabbed each other as if nothing else mattered in their lives. One half of the field got the better of the other, and soon the morale of the defeated team failed them. I watched one kid take a swipe at another with a long machete. The sliced kid stopped moving, took a look down at his body, then probably watched in immense pain as his shirt nearly fell off his body as his insides exploded onto the ground. I heard his scream from my window, then, I watched him fall dead.

The entire scene horrified me. I wanted to step down from the chair, but I couldn't help but watch. It was like a scene from a movie. The blood, the screaming, the violence. No wonder Roger worried about Maria. What man wouldn't want to run out and rescue his wife from this?

When I looked back at the dead man propped up against the basketball pole, my own humanity came into question. That could be me at any time. I thought back to the threats I'd heard in the unit that day. Kill the gringo. They weren't just talking shit. They meant it. Killing was no big deal to these guys. One swipe of the machete or a hundred swings of a bat didn't faze them one bit. If they wanted to kill, they would.

Out of nowhere, a young Mexican kid, screaming at the top of his lungs at no one in particular ran by the dead guy against the pole. He waved a knife in the air, his pants and shirt covered in blood, I assumed wasn't his. When he noticed the man with the caved in face just sitting there either dead or trying to die, he ran up to him, drop kicked his head, then repeatedly stabbed him in the chest, over and over until more blood sprayed from his chest onto the ground and over him. He beat his chest like a wild gorilla and ran away.

I watched a large pool of blood slowly spread across the court from the dead man's corpse. As it consumed the cement, the fighting and screaming subsided. The sounds of the guards and their riot gear batons banging against their shields took precedence. As the blood spilled into the cracks in the cement, I watched as the guards inflicted their punishment on the remaining cholos who weren't hurt or near death. They beat them with batons, cracking open skulls and breaking their arms with single swings. If a cholo fought back, he got beat bad. The guards spared no one. They paralyzed a kid, beat another comatose, and ganged up on one until he was nothing more than a limp piece of human that they dragged to a pile of dead inmates for removal.

It wasn't a movie, it was real life. That day twenty people died as a result of the fighting and the explosion. When the guards let Roger and I out, I couldn't believe how quickly the prison returned to normal. The Mexican music played on transistor radios. The belt makers went back to their early morning labor. The soccer teams continued their daily games. Business as usual.

I asked one of the guards about the incident. He told me that most of the dead cholos didn't have family, so their bodies were sent to a morgue where they were probably incinerated. The families of the rest had to come into the prison to identify their loved ones. For most, their demise was their destiny and their families accepted it as another sad part of Mexican life.

It took more than a week to clean up after the melee. The basketball court was stained red from one end to the other. Since it was the best court in the prison, the league games had to be played there. When the outside team came in to play us, I watched their faces as they warmed up on the blood drenched court. One of my teammates told them that the blood came from the last team we played. That didn't sit well with the outside guests. I laughed, even though it wasn't the classiest joke. We beat that team bad that day. They couldn't wait to get out of the prison with their lives intact.

*   *   *

Roger and I had just sat down to eat when there was a light rap on the door. We looked at each other and he stood to answer it. To my surprise, there was Nomi with an evening bag, looking guilty as if though she'd done something terribly wrong.

"There goes my comfortable sleep," said Roger. He quickly packed his sleeping gear and half the food, and left.

I didn't know what to say. Her appearance caught me completely off guard. Nomi sat on the bed, looking ashamed.

"What's wrong?" I asked her.

"I shouldn't be here," she said. "My husband will get angry."

"Then why are you here?" It was a fair question.

One of the prostitutes on the women's side had told Nomi that she'd slept with her husband. Nomi told me that it devastated her and that she was considering a divorce. She wasn't in my room for revenge or to spite her husband. She was there because she needed to be around someone completely neutral and non-judgmental. But I knew I was the revenge guy. What I wasn't sure of was if it would be smart for me to have her there. After all, her husband was connected.

It was difficult for me to relax that evening. Too many men saw her come in to the unit. If word ever got to her husband, he'd kill me. He'd have no other option. Sleeping with another man in Mexican culture is one of the worst marital crimes a woman could commit. The same couldn't be said for the husband. The men were allowed to cheat all they wanted. They were considered weak if they didn't.

We sat on the bed and talked for the next few hours. She told me about her life in Vera Cruz - on the other coastline of the country. Nomi came from a poor village where they still had to carry water from a well and had goats for milk.

"Have you ever been out of your village?" I asked.

"This is my first time anywhere," she admitted. "I wasn't allowed to leave the house."

Her husband sounded like a demanding bastard who didn't really give a damn about her or the rest of the family. The more we spoke, the more I realized just how inexperienced with life Nomi was. She'd never seen a TV until coming to Los Mochis. I didn't think that was possible.

"What about a Canadian?" I asked her.

She stifled a laugh. "I've never met a white person before."

"Never?" I said and grabbed her hand. "What do you think of me?"

I could tell the question would be difficult for her to answer. Her face blushed and she tried to pull her hand away, but I held it tight.

"Tell me," I said.

"You remind me of a man in a magazine," she said. "Like one in an advertisement."

"Wow," I said. "'That's a great compliment."

"What about me?" she said, looking directly into my eyes.

She had me on the spot.

"I think you're the most beautiful woman in this prison," I told her. "Not just your face, but your corazon" - her heart.

We sat in awkward silence again, but there was an urge pounding on my lips that I couldn't ignore.

"So then you've never kissed a Canadian before," I said with a sly smirk.

She shook her head. "No."

"Because you know," I said. "'It's how we keep warm in my country. We're probably the best in the world."

That made her giggle. Before she could say anything else, I leaned across the space between us and softly planted my lips on hers. She welcomed me and I could feel her entire face shake with nervousness. The kiss lasted seconds, but when I tried to pull away, her hands reached up and pulled me back. She pressed harder against me, forcing her tongue into my mouth like a first time kisser. There was no rhythm or delicate passion, just intensity, like a woman yearning for the sensation of love on her deathbed.

She finally let me go after a minute. Shocked beyond words, I knew that Nomi was in need of comfort and respect. I tried to talk myself out of what I knew was to come, but every feeling inside told me that this situation was far different than the one with Lucinda. We were both adults, lonely and looking for something to take our minds off of our miserable situations. Both of us had been duped by people we thought cared about us. At that moment in time, no one else mattered but those with the broken hearts.

"So then you've never seen a naked Canadian before either," I said with a silly grin.

We both burst into childish laughter as Nomi stood and removed her blouse revealing the rest of her Mexican beauty to me, and only me. Her husband was a fool.

*   *   *

I woke at three in the morning to Nomi asleep beside me. As I listened to the crickets sing their love song to me, I thought about how rapid my thoughts changed every minute I remained alive in the prison. One day, I turned down a woman because everything seemed wrong. The next day, I'm sleeping in a bed with someone else's wife. The one thing that had changed the most was that I actually gave a damn about these people, even though I didn't know them and would probably never see them again once I left back to Canada. Never before had other people's feelings ever become an issue in my life.

I lay there thinking about all the wrong that had been done to me in my life. How my family sent me to a mental hospital when I was just ten years old then abandoned me to foster care when the treatment ended. How I took Shelly under my wing in hopes I could make his life worthwhile, only to have him ditch me in the prison. I thought about the relationship I had with my daughter. How I abandoned her for a criminal lifestyle. All my thoughts came back to one thing - giving up.

I slipped out of the bed and walked over to the table. I opened my journal and began a list. At the top of the page, I wrote:

MOST IMPORTANT RELATIONSHIPS on one half of the page, LEAST IMPORTANT RELATIONSHIPS on the other.

I made a quick list of all the people I knew and how I felt about them. For the first time in my life, I was completely honest about my feelings. When I completed the list, I had more people on the least important side than on the other. The one name that stood out to me was at the top of the most important side. It was my daughter. Kelsey MacGregor. The person I knew the least.

Nomi stirred and sat up in the bed. A shard of moonlight from the front window fell on her body.

"Que haces?" she asked - what are you doing?

"Nothing," I told her. I stood to come back to bed.

Before I returned, I wrote her name on the important side. If things were really going to change, I had to start somewhere.

Before the first count in the morning, I walked Nomi out to the gate to meet the guard. We kissed once more before she was let out to go back to the woman's side. I stopped the guard and tried to hand him a folded one hundred peso bill, but he shook it off.

"That's against the rules," he said. He looked offended.

As they walked away, I had no idea that would be the last time I ever saw Nomi. I should have picked up on the guard's attitude, but I didn't. My head was clouded with the effects of an emotion I hadn't felt in a long time.

Four days later, the new warden declared the women's prison a separate facility, and the only people allowed to pass through were those with actual marriage certificates. And apparently, there was no amount of tequila to persuade him otherwise.

* * *

One week before Canada day, I heard my name being called to the front gate. A guard waited for me and escorted me to the warden's area for a meeting. When I got there, I couldn't believe the surprise.

Sitting behind a long foldout table were three women dressed in what looked to me like club clothes. High end, short skirts with six-inch heels and designer bags at their feet. At first, I thought it was some joke being played on me by the guards. I thought the women were hookers to be honest. The way they sized me up and down as the guard led me to the table. When he left, he closed the door, leaving me in the room alone with the three ladies.

I'm a natural charmer. I can't help myself when it comes to dealing with people, especially those of the opposite sex. I flashed a smile, spoke clear Spanish and made them laugh from the onset of the interview. It wasn't until the woman in the middle with the Gucci bag and pink heels told me that she was the judge on my case that my ego got up and left the room.

"Is there anything you'd like to say on your behalf?" she asked me.

For once in my life I was stunned silent. They caught me by surprise. I knew the day was coming, but I didn't expect it to be like this.

The judge had long brown hair, teased by blonde highlights and dazzled by a single diamond braid. The two women at either side of her dressed similar, flashing gold bracelets and necklaces at me as if it were part of their uniform. The woman to the right wrote on a pad as the judge spoke.

"I'll be giving you a decision in a week," she said. Her perfume became noticeable. "I would like to hear your explanation."

My mind was all fucked up. How could I take this woman seriously? She looked like someone I'd see dancing in the middle of a club with her girls on a Friday night rather than up at a bench deciding my future. Then that thought hit me. My life was in the hands of a Mexican Barbie doll. I was doomed.

I gave her the same spiel that I gave the police that night, hoping my story about lending the car to a stranger might alter her decision, and maybe she'd let me go. All three women listened with curiosity, nodding their heads as I finished up.

"Tell me something," said the judge. She leaned closer to me. I looked directly down her blouse by habit. "What is the shopping like in Canada?"

When I left that meeting, I felt so negative. Even though I knew I was going to get ten years, I felt somehow ripped off. Like this country wasn't taking my life seriously. From the very beginning of the ordeal the Mexican people took the crime as a joke. The cops stole half the drugs and charged me with the other half. The prison didn't care about my well being. And the judge looked like she just happened to stop by and do her job on the way to the club.

Fuck a duck. I was doomed.

When I got back to the maximum I was pissed off. I wanted to go to my room and sleep it off. I knew from that meeting that there was no chance I was going to get off the charge. At least I knew my decision to not fight the case was the smart one. By the looks of that judge, she would have had to fit my case in some time between the nail salon and the hairdressers.

When I walked into the unit, I noticed small groups of people chattering amongst each other. A buzz of excitement filled the air and people were laughing and joking. I didn't understand a lot of Mexican street slang, so the jokes slid right by me.

I went upstairs to the room just as the dinner cart came in. Roger sat on his bed reading, and smiled wide the second he saw me.

"You'll never guess what happened," he said.

I was still angry. "I'll bet it doesn't beat a judge with a boob job."

"What?" he said, confused. "Never mind. Follow me."

Roger lead me out to the walkway and pointed down towards the meal line. What I saw nearly made me crumble to the floor. There, standing at the back of the line with nothing to protect his beady little eyes from the sun, was Shithead.

"He was caught bringing in drugs," said Roger, the happiest I'd seen him in a long time. "I guess in Mexico, they get you when you come in and don't let you leave."

"I can't believe my eyes," I said.

I watched Shithead at the line, waiting his turn. When an opening in the pack came, he dipped his bowl in the pot only to come out with absolutely nothing. He walked away from the pot totally dejected. He must have sensed me on the upper tier. He glanced up and for the first time I noticed he had eyeballs in his socket. I gave him a smile and a salute and watched him sulk head down into a cell.

Barbie dolls and shitheads. This place never failed to surprise me.

Chapter 11
Mike
The Grim Road Back to Reality

July, 1999. Cereso

I watched Shithead mope around the unit every day. He paraded his self-pity door to door, looking for sympathy from anyone he thought might give it to him. After a while, made me literally sick to my stomach, begging for mercy from people he'd mistreated and battered. I knew I shouldn't have felt even a tiny bit of sorrow for the guy, after everything he'd done to me personally over the last year or so, but watching him skulk around in ragged clothing and without the shield of his sunglasses and guard uniform, I honestly felt bad for the little son of a bitch.

The only memento remaining from his prior life of authority was a single white tee shirt with the logo of the prison on the front right chest and the word officer on the left arm sleeve. It may have been his only piece of clothing because I saw him wear it every day. It was the one sign that Shithead had truly lowered his status to that of the rest of us. A commoner, with no hope and one change of clothing.

The day before Canada day, Jaime came to visit, and brought with him a small white cake.

"This is to celebrate your country's independence," he said and placed the cake on the table along with several paper plates.

I never cut a cake on my country's birthday before, but the Mexicans were different in that way, traditional and sentimental. They actually respected their heritage on their country's birthday. Canadians used the day as an excuse for getting drunk.

I invited Roger and Carlos to join me in a slice, and when I noticed one last piece remaining on the plate, an idea came to me.

"Hey puto!" I yelled out at Shithead sitting alone by the sinks, his chin in his chest like a disciplined child.

I waved him over, and with a sheepish grin, sat down and I slid the cake towards him. I knew at that moment that my enemy had felt humbleness for the first time in his life. We didn't speak. There was no need for words.

* * *

I stood in the reception area waiting for the news I'd been expecting for the past year. The news that I had been writing about in my journal since day one. I'd never been so excited about receiving prison time in my life, especially such a large amount. Ten years wasn't like a summer inside or a month long stint in a rehab center that would kick you out just as easily as it brought you in. The sentence I was about to receive would change my life forever. I was twenty-three, looking at getting out when I was thirty three, twenty eight if I was good.

The accumulation of wasted years was about to get bigger. All those years I'd spent apart from my family and friends. How could they love me, if they still did, after all the nasty things I'd done to them, leaving them crying on my expense, causing them to deny my name out of embarrassment. I'd suffered a lot in my short existence, but nothing like that of the ones who gave a damn about my life more than I did.

When I saw the court clerk arrive, the same women who gave Shelly his good news, my body tensed with anticipation. I shuddered as she smiled and made her way to the end of the cage where I stood. Moving in slow motion, she seemed hesitant. Her tiny smile seemed phony. She knew something. Something bad. A guilt-like nausea swept over me.

That feeling of guilt stayed with me even as she read my particulars, the case evidence, the prosecutor's statements and my court appointed lawyer's arguments that weren't exactly powerful. She mentioned how I accepted responsibility for the crime and let Shelly return home. The judge commended me for it, but none the less, chastised me for attempting to commit such a devious act in their country.

Her final statements hit me, then knocked me senseless... dumbfounded... speechless. The words, which I fully understood, didn't make sense to me as I listened. I watched her smile fade, then attempt to remain perky. I watched her fingers shake with uneasiness, turning the pages on my case, before finally closing the file and sliding the paperwork through the fence.

That same cute face that released my friend Shelly condemned me for my charge. I managed a brave smile, but she saw right through it, apologizing to me for the results. There was a hint of sympathy in her voice. I wished I could have stepped through the gate and hugged her like Shelly did, but the show of affection wouldn't have fit the mood. When Shelly left, there was salvation in the air, glee, and a renewed sense of hope that made the hug seem appropriate. In my dire moment, there was no hope or passion. As she walked away from me without a goodbye, I felt like a man whose heart had just been shattered by the love of his life, the massage of detachment his only explanation for the hurt inside of his soul.

I stood at the fence... the muted sounds of the Mexican slang around me... the anger and frustration and despair playing games with my mind. My family... my freedom... my life. I flipped through the pages of that document to the last page... the page that mattered... that contained those lines that made me want to vomit right there on that hot cement. They'd lied to me. I was a sucker to believe they wouldn't.

My sentence: twenty-four years in prison.

* * *

I didn't tell Roger about the sentence at the time. He didn't need to know. He had enough to worry about without feeling my pain as well. When I arrived back at the cell I smiled and waved the file in the air, minus the last page, and declared my ten-year sentence. He shook my hand with a genuine smile.

"Now you know where you're going," he said. "You're a lucky man."

Luck. Ha! I kept the smile and good attitude up until he left the room, then I collapsed on my bed and bawled my eyes out. The pain was different than anything I'd felt in my life. I thought that moment in the holding tank was hard, or even the time in the court. Nothing compared to the moment I found out that my life had just been stripped away.

I fell asleep, only to wake up in the dark gasping for air. I heard the song of the crickets outside and Roger fast asleep in the bed below. I opened a can of tuna on the picnic tables outside and ate it right from the can. I brought my journal with me, but couldn't think of a thing to write. My mind was blank all except for the number twenty-four. That was a life sentence in Canada. People received that for killing another human, not selling drugs. In my eyes, the crime wasn't that bad. I made some mistakes. I was an ambitious kid. Grew up hard, little support from family. Played sports, and could have been a professional until life got in the way and forced me to look out for myself. Drug dealing came out of necessity for survival, not because I was lazy or ignorant of the law. All I wanted was to live, to be someone, do something, anything that was even remotely important to someone, anyone. My decision to travel for drugs came out of anger. I was angry with the people I sold drugs for. I wanted to get my own connection, start my own empire. I was angry at the world for allowing me to get to this point. The point where my life took the worst turn possible.

Twenty-four years to a twenty three-year-old man was nothing short of a death sentence.

A burst of anger came over me and I opened the journal and began writing. I can't remember how I came to what I wrote, but it came out in radical spurts of aggression and surrender. I cursed my family, the people who took a vow to protect me and help me grow the moment I was born only to have them dump me when times got bad. Fuck Shelly. Fuck Ryan. Fuck Jaime, Roger, Carlos, and everyone else in that god-forsaken shithole prison. I wrote things that made no sense. As the night turned to early morning, I realized that I'd filled ten pages with absolute nonsense. My hand ached and my arm felt numb from gripping the pen so damn hard. As I looked upward to the heavens, the orange sky looked like a warning signal of a fire on the way. The burning, just a sign of the hellish days ahead of me. All eight thousand seven hundred and sixty worth.

*   *   *

I didn't call my family to let them know about my sentence. A week after receiving the news, I stood at the payphone summoning the courage I knew would never appear. Embarrassment mixed with shame caused me to push away from them, something I'd become good at after all these years. The news would devastate my mom and infuriate my dad. My close friends would promise never to forget me, but in time, they would. As I stood there with the phone receiver in hand, I came to the conclusion that never telling anyone the truth was better for them than having them live through it. Once again, a selfish self-pity had found its way into my life.

I strolled the quadro aimlessly, listening to the many sounds of the prison that had become familiar to me. In just ten short months, my face was a regular in the prison. People walked by me and knew my name. They spoke clear Spanish to me knowing that I'd studied and become eighty percent fluent in the process. The children of the inmates who lived there had grown, some becoming almost as much a part of the environment as the environment itself. I found the bench near the basketball court and sat down.

That brown patch of blood from the riot was now black from all the dirt and footprints layered over top. The memory of the horrific battle was long forgotten. I sat in silence, watching inmates walk by, on their way to the library or the market or the drug dealer's cell. Everyone involved in something important, relevant to their life, the prison life... my life. That familiar feeling of being locked up... safe... felt too good at times, and I consciously felt it, and I hated it.

I was at least a thousand miles away from my home by land or by sea and I didn't feel the strain or cabin fever that I was supposed to. I felt part of the Mexican people, and with every passing smile or wave from the inmates, that feeling grew stronger. Maybe, I thought, I'd make it through the twenty-four years. I'd eventually forget about home and my family, my friends and my daughter, and I'd just live. If they wanted to see me, they'd have to come down here... work it into a vacation. I thought about the long beard I'd grow and the weight I'd lose before they came, just to show them that I was dying and happy about it. If I was going to suffer, so would they. I'd send them home with a postcard memory of the man I'd become not the man I used to be.

A well-dressed Mexican man approached me from one of the units. His black pants and open collar dress shirt stood out in the prison, and when I met his eyes I noticed his watch and gold necklace. He wasn't an inmate. Those possessions would have been ripped from his dead body a long time ago.

He stood in the sun for a moment. I squinted as I reached for his outstretched hand.

"Where are you from?" he asked me in clear English.

"Canada," I told him. "Home of the moron."

His name was Ernesto Gonzales. He'd studied law at the University of Guadalajara before returning home to Los Mochis to visit his cousin. Ernesto was clean cut and had that lawyer sense of style. My impression of lawyers and the Mexican legal system at that time wasn't so high.

"How are you feeling?" he said as he sat beside me.

"I'm fine," I lied. "Just a little beat up. I received my sentence a week ago."

He seemed concerned. "Really. How did it turn out?"

I told him my story, the true version since I had nothing else to hide. I told him about the trip, Shelly, the story I told the police. Everything. When I mentioned the twenty-four years, he shuddered and became anxious.

"That isn't normal," he said. "Would you mind if I took a look at your file?"

Ernsesto followed me to the maximum, and on the way, shared with me his own story. He'd grown up in Los Mochis but moved to live with his uncle and Aunt in Los Angeles when he was thirteen. He learned enough English to get himself a job transporting drugs over the border posing as a student on his way to visit family. It wasn't until his best friend was murdered in Mexico for drugs that he decided to give it all up and remain in Mexico to go back to school. He told me that education was cheap for most students, and because he taught English in his free time, it was even cheaper. He worked hard and received his law degree in four years.

"I know what it's like to take chances," he said. "If my friend hadn't died, I might have been next. Sadly enough, his death was the best thing that ever happened to me."

We sat at the picnic table looking over my file. He read it quickly, marking pages with a pen, and keeping me out of the loop. I anxiously waited for his response, and when he got to the recently attached last page, all he could do is shake his head. He looked me straight in the eye and gave me the truth.

"You've been screwed."

I chuckled at my own expense. "Tell me something I don't know."

"All right," he said and opened the file. "Have you read this entire document?"

I shook my head.

"Well, there is a missing report that you're entitled to, and apparently it's the main reason you got what you got."

Before Ernesto left that day, he made me a promise to get that document from the police. I signed a contract written on paper naming him as my attorney and thanked him for his help.

"I couldn't leave you looking as sad as you were on that bench," he said. "My mother would have killed me herself."

Ernesto exemplified the true kindness and consideration that enveloped all the Mexican people. For the first time in a long week I felt as though I had something good coming to me, I just didn't know what it would be.

* * *

When I finished reading the document I nearly lost my mind.

Alone in my room was where Ernesto told me to read Shelly's statement. So I did, and he was right. I was angry and it was best that no one was around to share that moment.

I stood and paced the room. My anger higher than it had ever been before. I wanted to punch the wall, rip down the shelves, tear up my books and journals, anything that would calm me down.

The statement stared up at me from the table. Shelly's harmful words... death blows... sucker punches aimed at making me look worse than I already was. I remembered that night in the police cells where I vowed my life to him. My friend. That night where we went over our statement together – how we leant the car to a stranger... he filled it with drugs... set us up. I fumed when I thought about his promise to start his life over and do something with himself, his pledge of allegiance to our friendship. His face. His tears. My guilt. My charity.

Now all I could think about was his death and how I would do it.

I imagined him sitting in that small interrogation room, the smoke filled air that he loathed, the aggressive police standing over him, pressuring him to tell all. Our made-up statement on his mind, the words slipping away from him with every second of pressure he endured. I saw the tears reappear from his eyes, stream down his face as he told them the horrible truth. The truth about my plan to smuggle drugs to Canada from Central America, and how I was a habitual criminal, an old hat to the game of dealing. A merciless mercenary of cocaine distribution in my community. I pictured him blabbering my story to the eager swarm of police, then begging them not to mention a word to me that he'd broken our sacred oath, and the police agreeing, smiling under their thick moustaches that they'd broken one of the gringos and set the other on fire.

The statement had it all, my life, the truth, the revelation of the lie. Shelly gave them what they really wanted, walked back to the cell and hugged me like my friend, allowed me to drown the day I stood up for him and let him walk home. He did it like a professional. I never thought he had it in him, but he did, and the more I stood there hating him and wishing his death, the more I came to realize that I deserved every ounce of what I got.

I wasn't a fool to actually think that I was in the right. I'd sat in the prison for almost a year stewing on the fact that no one was responsible for being in that prison more than me. In fact, as I calmed down, I told myself that it was I who convinced Shelly to come to Central America with me. I told him that day we left that I'd never let him get hurt, and I followed through with my promise. Even though he'd taken the easy way out and ratted me to the Mexican police, left me to die with twenty-four years, he wasn't to blame. I should've known that he was weak. I should've seen that he that he wasn't like me as much as I wanted him to be. Then again, why would I want that? I wasn't anybody special. I wasn't a good son, brother, father, friend. I chose to make people promises who ended up screwing me in the end, meanwhile leaving the people who truly cared about me hanging. The more I thought about the entire situation, the more I commended Shelly for finally standing up to me and making a decision for himself. It was the smartest thing he'd ever done in his life.

When Ernseto returned the next day, he came with a gift.

"How do you feel?" he asked me.

"I was angry, but I'm better now."

He leaned across the table to speak with me in private. There were visitors everywhere that afternoon.

"I have a connection that may be able to help you."

I was interested in any sort of help.

"In Mexico, most files are kept strictly on paper until they're sent to Mexico City for documentation. Usually that takes a month, sometimes more."

"How does that affect me?" I asked.

"Since this country is behind the times, not technologically advanced like your country, sentences aren't finalized until documented in the District Federal. Even this prison won't know your sentence until next month. This means we have a chance to change your sentence."

His words created a rush of excitement inside of me.

"I have a friend, for five thousand dollars, can make that change," he whispered. His voice shook with caution. "Your twenty-four can turn to ten,."

I was desperate, and desperate men made desperate decisions. I didn't want to seem too eager.

"I know you have a difficult time trusting me because you don't know me," he said. "So what I will do is pay for this myself, and you can owe me."

"Are you sure?" I said. "You'd trust me like that?"

"Shouldn't I?" he said. "Are you a dishonest man?"

"Actually," I said with a smile. "I am, but one thing I'm not is a back-stabber. I'll get you your money."

We shook hands, sealing our deal and reawakening a new sense of hope that I'd been missing.

* * *

I had only one problem: where the hell was I going to get five thousand dollars? My finances were short. I had four thousand dollars from the sale of the car and friends tucked away in my cell in case of emergency. Because I'd learned how to budget my money, I'd spent next to nothing of it. So I had about four thousand dollars miraculously available.

When I counted the dough, I felt an attachment to it like it was a piece of my body. If I let this cash go, and the deal didn't work out, I'd be crippled not to mention humiliated. Four stacks of thousands pleaded with me not to let it go, but my future was on the line. Not to mention the future of my sanity. I had a small window in which to work and two options. I could call home and ask for another loan or I could do the first thing that popped into my mind, the one thing I knew I would end up resorting to and would feel like crap after it was all said and done.

* * *

August, 1999. Juan Miguel's cell – Cereso

Juan Miguel's three young boys sat on the edge of their father's bed staring at me as though I was *Jesus de Christo* himself. I smiled, wanly but sincerely, their stone faces just watched my act... the gringo clown. The youngest of the bunch, a thin boy, barefoot and dressed in cut off shorts, had enough and got up to leave. He didn't make it to the door before his father returned with a large bag of nacho chips and salsa. The kids recognized feeding time and scrambled for the snack.

Juan Miguel laughed as he released the bag to his oldest boy, who immediately took charge of the situation much to the chagrin of his two siblings. Juan Miguel sat on the bed where his boys just were and shook his head.

"I knew you'd come back," he said. "It's in your nature. Isn't it?"

My attention flickered from Juan Miguel to his swarm of kids with the open bag of nacho chips, ransacking the bag like wild dogs who hadn't eaten in a long time, the eldest now in control of the salsa, guarding the jar from the smallest brother, regulating every dip.

"They stay with me four times a week," Juan Miguel said, noticing my interest in his kids. "Their mother leaves to fuck someone else, I know it. I don't care. I have my own party when she's gone."

"Where do they sleep?" I asked.

Juan Miguel jerks a thumb behind him. "I rent the next cell. Give the guy some *chiva* – heroin. The kids stay there, and I sleep here with my wife. It works."

As soon as the bag was empty, the kids tossed it to the floor and walked away, like a crime that no one wanted to admit to. Juan Miguel burst into rapid fire Spanish that I couldn't decipher and the oldest returned to pick the bag up off the floor.

"They need to learn some manners," he said. "I think the oldest has been hanging around too many criminals."

"Four days a week," I said. "That's a lot of time to be spending in a prison."

Juan Miguel waved my comment off, grabbing hold of his youngest and sitting him on his knee. The reluctant child attempted to squirm away, but Juan Miguel held him steady.

"It's good for him," he tried to convince me. "They will one day take over the business. Maybe one day they will have to come to prison." He grabs his son with two hands on his shoulders and squeezes him tight. "This time will make them tough. They'll be strong if that day comes."

Watching Juan Miguel with his son caused the wheels in my head to spin. The father sat on the bed with a wide smile, that car salesman smile, not a care in the world. He had his money... his drugs. On his knee, the apple of his eye, the chip off the old block, the reluctant apprentice... no smile... no shiny eyes that spoke of a desire to be alive. Nothing. I couldn't help but stare at the kid. Nothing on his face resembled his father. Juan Miguel had a round face, plump and hearty, jolly almost, with a touch of color making his skin glow even though it was dark. But his son, his pride and joy, the next great *trafficante* of the family, the mule in training for something greater than even his own father's love for him, sat there stupefied, staring back at me as if to say "get me the hell out of here, please."

The look on the boy's face wasn't happiness. Even though he sat on his father's knee, a love grip holding him in place, he wasn't content. How could he be in a place like this? The rats and cockroaches muscling him for food, the older brother in charge of anything and everything, no chance for a kid to be a kid in here. I saw in his eyes the many nights he'd spent outside the cell, banging to get in, away from the hoard of strangers with tattoos and facial scars and drug problems, while his father, the boss, mercilessly fucked his wife inside the cell knowing that his youngest boy, a mere baby, skulked outside the door, right in the middle of the most dangerous place in his inexperienced life. I was scared to be there. He must have been terrified.

His saddened face haunted my soul, made me shiver and wonder what the hell I was doing in that cell with this greedy freak and his three kids that looked nothing alike. How could I even think about doing business with a man who entrapped his family in a prison just so they would suffer along with him because they were in training. No wonder his wife was out with another man, probably the real father for these kids. She wasn't stupid. She knew the game. The training session was never meant for her because a woman could never become a high-ranking drug dealer, but she was just as much to blame. What good parent let their kids go through an ordeal like this? Bad ones. Ones like Juan Miguel. And when I thought about it a little more, ones like me.

As the boy squirmed to get away from his dad, I thought of my own kid. My innocent daughter who couldn't seem to mind her own damned business and just let me do my time, let me survive without trying to fuck with my moral compass. What Juan Miguel was doing to his boys, the tormenting sacrifice he forced upon them, living in the prison like they'd done something wrong themselves, unable to speak their minds with the person who supposedly loved them the most, I was doing to my own kid. The littlest one fighting for nacho crumbs, just trying to get by with no help from his role model, his teacher, his own flesh and blood who cared about nothing but selling this gringo some of the dope his mother jammed into his pants just before entering the prison. What Juan Miguel did to his family, his boy, I was doing to my little girl. At least they got to see their father every other day.

Though it was my sorry ass in jail, far from home and trying to survive in my own fucked up way, what I didn't realise until that moment was that every minute I spent locked away, my family spent time in their own prison, the one I'd created for them. They were innocent people forced to suffer at my hand, like some sadistic mercenary who tortured his victims instead of putting them out of their misery. Juan Miguel made me sick, but in all honesty, I was no better than he was. In fact, I was worse.

And there I was ready to get involved doing the same shit that had brought me there in the first place. Gung-ho to smuggle drugs to solve my problems instead of swallowing my pride, what was left of it, and asking for help. If I got caught, it would be over for me for sure. The twenty-four would stick and I'd look like a fool.

"I'm sorry," I said, not sure if it was to Juan Miguel or his kids. "But I'll have to think about this some more."

I stood, not sure who I was any more. A man or less than that? I walked out of the room. No goodbyes to the family I felt sorry for. No special thanks or guarantees to Juan Miguel, there was no need, I wasn't buying or selling what he had. That afternoon I just walked out, promising that my days of dealing were done for good even though in the back of my mind, where I kept my confidence reserved for athletics and manipulation, I knew I could still do it.

* * *

When I hung up the phone on my last remaining friend from the unimportant side of my friend list, I breathed a sigh of relief, not because I felt good that he was sending me the money for my endeavour, but because it took all the nerve in my body to ask him for help. My hands shook with anxiety as I made my way back to the maximum, trembling like a mouse under the cat's paw. I didn't understand why it hurt so much to ask for things. Maybe because my entire life had been spent fending for myself, and if I needed something, I'd steal it or perform some other sort of crime to get it.

When the money came a week later, and Jaime handed it to me with suspicion, I put it in an envelope and sealed it, away from my pathological desire to spend needlessly.

"I hope you know what you're doing," Jaime said. He cared. Sometimes that caring bothered me.

"So do I," I told him.

I put the money away until I knew the job had been done. When Ernesto returned with news that he'd spoken to his friend and the paperwork was on its way to the *district federal*, I nearly hugged him. In fact, before he left that day, after telling me that he wasn't in a rush for the money, I did hug him. He'd become a friend, one who didn't need any sort of tangible repayment for his good deed. It was a trend I noticed rang true for everyone I'd met in the prison. Unsolicited kindness doled out just because they could. As my list of Canadian friends dwindled, my Mexican amigos flourished.

Ernesto told me that in a month, I'd be a new man with a new sentence and on my way back home.

* * *

September, 1999. Cereso

Now that I spoke clear Spanish, slang and all, the little subtleties of the language worked out, I felt comfortable enough to speak to the warden and other officials on my own. So when the new warden called me into his office, me being one of only two foreigners in the prison, I went without hesitation. Everyone knew that being on the warden's good side was worth almost as much as freedom itself.

The new warden had a completely different approach to his job than the tequila-wrangling warden he'd succeeded. Jose Morales stood no more than five feet tall, and that was with boots, but what he lacked in height, he made up for in stature. He stood erect, even when he sat, and when he spoke to me, he looked me straight in the eyes, looking through me, but not in a demeaning way, almost as though trying to get to the heart of my troubles. I liked him instantly, especially when I entered his office and he offered me a glass of mango juice instead of tequila.

"You are a special case," he told me, smoothing out his moustache with his fore finger and thumb. "The consulate would like to speak to you this afternoon."

He smiled and gave me a knowing nod. "We treat you well here."

Was that a question or an order? I simply nodded and gave him his moment.

"You have been very good. Better than other gringos we have had." His speech sounded educated. "How would you like a job in my office?"

I shrugged, pretending as though actually having something to do didn't really matter. My days were long from the onslaught of boredom, playing soccer and twiddling my thumbs. A job sounded like Christmas had come early.

"We could speak English," he said, then cut off his Spanish to show me what he knew. "Tank youb erry mazch!" he smiled, and it felt good, to him and me, but mainly himself.

The phone rang before I could answer, so I nodded and smiled like a good gringo, watched him pick up the phone, then hand it to me after a few moments of rapid Spanish.

"Hello," I said into the receiver. The warden watched me with a smile, drinking from his glass of mango then wiping his moustache off on his shirt.

"Hello, I am calling from the Canadian consulate," the voice had a trace of a French accent. Very direct. To the point. "Is this Mr. Oulton?"

The sound of my own name froze me to the chair. I glanced up at the warden worried as if he heard the woman say my real name instead of the phoney one I was registered under.

"Yes it is," I couldn't lie any more. "How do you know my name?"

The woman told me about the investigation into my past for reasons of security. They had to verify that I was a Canadian citizen before engaging in the process to bring me home. She told me that she knew about the fake name and the man I'd stole it from, and where he was and how upset he was that I'd stolen his identity, and how much trouble I'm in back home and how much trouble I'd be in if the Mexican government found out about my lie. After a few minutes of conversation, the woman told me everything about myself. More than I needed to know.

"Whatever you do," she said. "'Don't tell them your real name. We'll send you a transfer package in the mail. Just mail it back with your real name and information and we'll get the transfer underway."

I thanked her, but before I hung up she asked me, "How are they treating you there?"

"Fine," I said. "Fine."

She sighed. "Ten years is a long sentence. Don't worry. We'll get you back."

I couldn't help but smile myself. "Ten years is a long time."

I handed the phone back to the warden, who spoke to the woman for a moment, his face turned sour, his eyes darted over to me then back to the floor, then he hung up. He raised his glass in the air.

"Salut!"

I raised my own to meet his toast. "Go fuck yourself."

His first English lesson. Never trust a smiling Canadian. While he drank his nectar, I thought about money well spent.

*   *   *

The transfer package came a week later in a large envelope with the Canadian flag on the front. An impressive package, filled with application forms, identification forms, and a booklet listing the rules of the international transfer treaty program, which seemed more like a high school final exam, the questions demanding full-length sentences and near essay explanations.

After two days of tinkering around with the package, I sealed it in the provided blue envelope and whistled it down to the mail slot. When it disappeared into the mailbox, I felt a sense of renewed power come over me. The first step to going home was complete.

I'd already begun my new job in the warden's office, not only teaching the warden a word a day, but also taking out his trash and flirting with his secretaries. They were all nice women, middle age and well past their due date, but beautiful Mexican women none the less. I caught a few of their snide comments, their graphic mentions of what they'd do to me if they had a chance, and I let them go without comment, knowing that they were women with overactive imaginations.

A part of my job was to take the week's worth of garbage from the big bin out to the truck near the front gate. Bags upon bags of paper and food awaited me that Monday morning, and I hauled them by wheelbarrow to the awaiting truck.

As I tossed two bags at a time in the waiting cab, I noticed something in one of the bags that caused my heart to drop into my stomach. There amidst some other paperwork, was the blue envelope, my envelope of freedom. I saw my handwriting, my stamp that Jaime brought me. It was there on it's way to the Los Mochis dump, along with my dreams of going home and my damned twenty page essay I'd stressed over for two days.

Right in front of the guards I ripped open the bag and removed my envelope. The nearest guard grabbed my hand as it came out with the envelope, casting me a glare as if I'd just breached a major security rule. I held the envelope up to him to show him my name and he let go, knowing that I'd just stumbled onto a conspiracy he wanted no part of.

Steaming mad, I took the envelope back to the warden. His initial reaction told me that he'd done it. His face turned red and he was at a loss for words. For some reason he'd thrown away my transfer and with no words yet spoken about it, denied the act with raised eyebrows, menacing frown and a shaking head.

"We will find out who did this." He held his hand out. "Let me have that so I can question my office."

I gave the envelope to him knowing that I had a second one in my cell.

"I would like to call the consulate, *por favor.*" I said and sat in the visitor chair.

The warden's face whitened, then turned red again with either anger or embarrassment. Either one I wasn't buying. He knew what he'd done, I knew, I just didn't know why. He had no choice but to dial the number for the consulate, but before he handed me the phone he said, "We should keep this to ourselves until we find out who is to blame."

Sure, sure.

The woman from the consulate spilled the beans immediately.

"The Canadian government sends them money every month for your well being," she said. "The money goes to medication or hygienic items that you may need." She sounded angry now. "Have they been supplying you with these things?"

Sure, if tequila and mango juice counted as medicine. I lied to her and said that they had, only because I didn't want it coming back to me and potentially making my time any worse than it already was. I thought about the past couple years and how sick I'd been.

The gastritis and the stitches. The riot where I could have been killed. What would they have done for me then? I was thankful that I'd proven to be a survivor because there wouldn't have been any help if I wasn't.

"The warden's are known for pocketing the relief money, "she said. "'Don't worry, you should be out of there soon. If you can, courier me the package, but don't get caught smuggling it out of the prison. They don't take well to those things."

They don't take well to me wanting to get the hell out of Mexico. I was their cash cow, their meal ticket. I didn't take well to being buggered by a two-bit warden. I handed him the phone and he hung up without speaking to the woman this time.

I shook the man's hand and left the office knowing two things, he was a jerk off and I was done working for him.

The next day, I gave Jaime the blue envelope and asked him to mail it for me far from the prison.

"What's the problem?" he asked in a low whisper.

I told him about the other envelope.

"He did that to you?" his voice raised an octave. "This close to Christmas? How could he?"

I smirked. "This is a prison, Jaime. Usually the people who run these places don't care about us. We're cattle to them, and I'm the cash cow."

He looked confused. "Cash cow?"

I waved his question off. "'Don't worry about it. Just please make sure you get that in the mail. And don't let the guards see you take it out of here. The consulate says that they are allowed to shoot you on site."

Jaime's eyes widened. "You are joking?"

He knew me by now not to believe the first thing that came out of my mouth.

I watched him walk out of the prison, tucking the envelope under his shirt and walking wide-eyed out the gate, the guards watching him curiously as he stiffened as he passed them. Jaime would never make a good smuggler. But who was I to talk?

* * *

October, 1999. Middle of the night – Cereso

The sound of helicopter blades overhead woke me from a good night's sleep. Like thunder erupting from the sky, the noise was too loud to just roll over on and go back to sleep, which was what I tried to do, but couldn't because something in my head told me that something out of the ordinary was occurring.

I sat up in bed in time to see Roger stand and walk to the window. Squinting, he peeked up at the sky, then turned to me shaking his head.

"'What's going on?" I asked.

"Sounds like someone's escaping," he said. "I wish it was me."

I laughed and hopped down from the bed. As I did, the sounds of boots on concrete filled the maximum area, screams from baritone voice boxes echoed in the air as the chopper silenced. I reached for a pair of shorts, and just as I put them on, a knock sounded at our door. Roger froze, then scrambled for his pants. The door burst open and there in the doorway, the lights of the maximum hallway illuminating him from behind, stood a masked man, dressed in black clothing, aiming a machine gun directly at me. I couldn't see his eyes. I raised my hands because I knew nothing else to do.

In hard Spanish he spoke. "Both of you. Outside and face down on the floor!"

Chapter 12
Mike
El Paiaso

The man who rushed Roger and me out of the cell was an officer in the federal police. Besides the few words he yelled to us in the cell, he remained silent as he followed us down to the main area where the inmates of the maximum unit waited in small groups next to the sinks.

We were all moved outside into the courtyard, in silence, single file and in a speedy fashion. More masked gunmen jerked their weapons at us, their fingers loose around the triggers.

They pointed to the wall of the maximum enclosure. We all shuffled over like cattle and stood side by side, waiting for an answer or reason to this assault. I stood between Carlos and Roger. When the *federales* were out of range, I whispered to Carlos. "What are they doing?"

Carlos's eyes followed the officers. "They are here to search. They want to find contraband."

"You guys better cut it out," said Roger. "I'm not getting shot because of you two."

The military created task forces to swarm on prisons and complete full searches of the premises and the people. Even the guards were subjected to the search. Carlos told me that across the compound right now, the guards were being stripped down and their lockers ransacked for drugs and unregistered guns. The Mexican government did this to weed out corruption. Several prisons across the country were subject to this search every year. It was Los Mochis's turn.

When the guard came back down the line, Carlos shut up, staring straight ahead and his body was as stiff as a board. The guard pointed his gun down as he passed us, stopping at Roger, then backing up to me. He looked me up and down. I wasn't like Carlos. I looked him right in his eyes. He didn't scare me. I was a fool.

"Where are you from?" he asked me in English.

"Canada."

He smiled underneath his mask. "Nice country. We went to Montreal on a class trip once."

"You speak good English."

"I grew up in San Diego. I only came back to Mexico two years ago to become a *federale*. What did you do to get tossed in here?"

"Drugs," I said. "I'm going home soon."

The man laughed. "Will you ever come back to Mexico?"

I smiled. "We always come back to Mexico, right?"

He laughed again. "Just relax and this will be over soon."

I wondered if he referred to the search or my never-ending stay in Mexican captivity.

The soldiers' search lasted six hours. They swarmed the entire prison, searching everything from cells to vending carts and restaurants. Nothing was exempt. By the time they finished with the maximum, half the guys were asleep on the dirt floor, the other half frustrated. For some reason, the guns didn't seem to intimidate us as much as they did hours ago in the dead of night.

As the sun rose over the walls, the officers ordered us back into our unit. We shuffled back only to find that the officers had taken everything out of the cells and left it in one big pile in the middle of the unit. There was a pile of clothing, food and belt material stacked almost to the bottom of the second tier. We released a collective groan as we got to work sorting out everybody's things.

* * *

December, 1999 - Cereso

The Christmas raid didn't stop the festivities from going full steam ahead. The prison received a good rating from the *federales*, which meant the warden was given a commendation for running a smooth prison. This citation played out well for all the convicts. He declared that we could bring in twenty-four beers and a bottle of tequila each – free of charge. I bought the maximum number I could. After all, the turn of the millennium only came once in a lifetime.

Two days before Christmas I was called down to the reception area. A single guard led me to the fenced area in silence, walking close behind me. I asked him where we were headed, but he remained quiet. The hush-hush killed me.

When I reached the area, I noticed a single white woman sitting alone and she looked sick. Her hair was flat against her head, saturated with sweat and oil. She hunched over in her chair, rocking back and forth with her arms folded across her stomach. As the guard opened the cage door, her head jerked up and her eyes locked onto mine. She smiled when she recognized that I wasn't Mexican and sat up straight. I offered her a smile, but hesitated to go inside the cage, unsure why the hell I was there. The guard sensed my hesitation and finally spoke.

"She's sick. She needs someone to talk to."

He locked me in the cage and walked away. The girl stood and offered me her hand. She was young. Maybe twenty. When I looked at her hand, I saw open scabs, her nails were dirty and her whole body trembled, as if lifting her hand for that long hurt somehow.

"My name's Julie," she said, still waiting for me to shake her hand.

I didn't. I walked past her to get a chair and sat down next to her.

As soon as I sat down, Julie began talking, about her life back in Portland, her trip down to Mexico with her two Spanish boy friends, the drugs they'd done all the way down, the cops and the rape, the abandonment and the imprisonment. She talked for an hour straight, not allowing me to get a word in edgewise, and any time I tried, she'd talk over me until I relented the floor back to her. As she spoke, she scratched, she twitched on and off her chair, and she paced and danced on the spot. After an hour, I felt drained, my ass hurt from sitting and my eyes hurt from watching. I wondered how long the guards wanted me to be there.

"Watch the door for me," she said, and danced to a blind spot in the area.

I watched the door, but kept an eye on her as she pulled her pants down and squatted in the corner. I thought she was having herself a piss, but when she reached behind her and came out with a small bundle, I knew that this night was about to get crazy.

She stood and pulled her pants back up. Hobbling to the counter, I watched her unwrap the package and remove a small baggy of powder, dumping about a gram onto the table.

"Do you have any money on you?" she asked me.

"I don't use drugs," I told her.

She laughed, and for a second, she looked beautiful.

"I need it to snort," she held a finger to her nose. "The heroine helps me come down from the coke."

I told her no.

I'd never really seen a heroin junky before. Dealing with cocaine users is a completely different game. Cokeheads tend to be a lot more hectic, calling you up at any time of the day to get high. Since a cocaine high only lasted an hour tops, I could potentially speak with a coke head twenty four times a day. Heroine users only called you once a day, and that was because they were usually out cold after getting high.

Julie was on road to nowhere, snorting the line of coke using a dirty piece of someone's discarded court papers she found on the floor. As she scrambled to hide the package inside of her again, the moment became too surreal for me. I thought back to all those years I'd sold drugs without conscience, pedalling that shit to anyone, old or young, not caring about what they did after they left me, only caring about their money. As I watched Julie do her dance and talk out of the side of her mouth, twitching and fidgeting while confessing intimate moments about her boyfriends and her life as a prostitute on the run, I thought about the people back home I'd corrupted with my drug dealing. I wondered how many people had turned into Julie.

"Are you supposed to stay or are you going home?" I asked her.

She shrugged and did a little ditty. "They're letting me go in the morning."

There it was. The dealer stays and the junky goes home. At that moment I understood the game better than ever before. As long as I continued to deal, transport, import, export or push drugs, I'd be the one who went to prison. As long as I kept producing Julies, I'd never be a free man. I knew it, my country knew it, and the Mexicans knew it.

I told Julie to clean up and go home, then banged on the gate until the guard returned. I'd had enough "This is Your Life" for one night. It only took that hour for me to realize I was the biggest loser in the cage.

* * *

That New Year's Eve I got drunk, drunker than I'd ever been before in my life. I drank tequila after tequila, beer after beer, and stayed awake longer than anyone else in the unit. Only one man kept up to me - Francisco - and the only reason he could was because he snorted a line of cocaine every half hour. The music played all night, and it had me singing in Spanish even though I didn't understand a single word.

Francisco had a kind heart, a man made of gold. He had a family who travelled three hundred miles to visit him twice a year. He was a well of farmer from Juarez - a well known drug dealers paradise in northern Mexico. He was a weed grower, who loved his drugs and his family equally as much. Francisco told me about his life on the ranch, the ranch he bought by moving thousands of pounds of marijuana into the United States. It was always his passion to live there one day, but because of his recent charges, he knew it would never happen. I told him that the States weren't all that great. He laughed and told me that there was nothing greater than the American dollar.

"How is your country for marijuana?"

Now it was my turn to laugh. "Our country has the greatest weed on earth."

I told him about British Columbia, where I lived, and how the weed literally got people so high, it was almost like that white shit he kept stuffing up his nose. I told him about the prices, and his eyes widened with that ambitious awe that I was so familiar with. I could see the numbers crunching in his head, the dollar signs floating through his brain, hovering like a hummingbird suspended in mid air. All of a sudden, the American dollar didn't seem so great after all.

"One pound of weed is worth two thousand dollars," I teased him. "If it's good."

Francisco sat upright in his chair, tossed back a shooter of tequila, then another, then spoke.

"We should make a deal," he said. "I will give you a thousand pounds, delivered to your door, for five hundred dollars each."

The deal was tempting, but what Francisco didn't know was that the Mexican weed was so bad, if I ever tried to sell it in Canada, I'd have weed fanatics beating down my door wanting to kill me.

"I'll have to pass," I said. "We have too much there already."

"Four hundred," he shouted. "All you have to do is sell it and send me the money."

The song *Desperado* erupted from my lips. I was drunk and in a teasing mood. I loved these people, but their ambition was unlike anything I'd ever come across in my life. It wasn't the first time that this propositioned had been made to me, but it was the first time I didn't struggle with my answer. It seemed like every Mexican wanted that route to a better life, and most of them thought it was through drug trafficking. Funny thing, for most, it usually was.

I raised my glass in salute to Francisco. He smiled and joined me.

"Here's to your future book," he said.

"My book? What are you talking about?"

He shrugged. "I see you writing every day. If you're not writing a book, then you're not paying attention."

As we downed the booze, I thought about that statement. He was right. I wasn't paying attention.

* * *

Three days after New Years I started paying attention. As I wrote down notes, I began to see what Francisco was talking about. I knew nothing about writing a novel. The thought had never entered my mind. I was a career criminal - my career was crime, not autobiographies. As I wrote down what I saw, I began to see a story, much like Papillon, but without the revolution. I wrote down names and events that had happened to me. The soccer games and the stitches from fighting. The riot would make a good story. Who got to see real violence like that in their everyday lives?

I had enough material to make most writers' assholes pucker with joy. I had a dilemma, an ordeal, a bad choice, a life changing situation, a near death situation and a cast of characters right out of a Hollywood movie including a love interest and a sex scene. But how would it end? What would happen to me? Would I learn my lesson and never commit a crime again? Would the scars and despair cause me to change my life for good?

The answer, in my head, was no. Unfortunately, I still had thoughts of crime in my head, as thick as it was, and even though I'd survived two years of Mexican hell, I wanted revenge more than I wanted change. My partners had left me to die, alone and broke, wondering if I was ever going to see my home again. The only thing I positively knew how to do in life was a drug deal. Even as I wrote down the events of this time in prison, I knew in the back of my brain that it would somehow get lost in the shuffle, and I'd revert to my old life.

The photo of my daughter smiled across the table at me- her beautiful face that resembled mine. I had no emotional attachment to her, and I didn't know why. I thought that maybe this callous life of crime had stolen all emotion from me, caused me to be a hard man with no sense of family or honor. I'd committed to my criminal friends in the past, why couldn't I feel the same way towards her?

It wasn't until the afternoon of January 5, 2000 that everything changed.

* * *

As I sat in the barber's chair staring across at my painted face in Javon's little makeup mirror, I asked myself why the hell I agreed to be dressed up like a clown in the first place. Of course, when he came and asked me to be a clown – a *paiaso* – for his daughter's birthday, I couldn't say no. How could I say no to little Roxanna's special day? She was turning nine years old.

There was a hoard of children in the unit that day. Javon had asked the men to invite their families to the prison that day in hopes of giving Roxanna a party with more kids than convicts. He'd purchased a clown suit and a massive amount of decorations that the younger inmates were hanging up all over the unit. As Javon did my makeup, the crowd of children grew around us. I made faces to them as the colors went on, asking them if it looked good. As usual, the kids couldn't understand a word of my Spanish, and just cast each other quizzical glances whenever I spoke.

The language barrier was going to be a problem. If the kids couldn't understand me speaking normally, how were they going to understand me with a silly clown voice and makeup.

"Just be yourself," said Javon as he drew eyeliner on me.

"So I'm a damn *paiaso* to you, then?"

He smiled right at me. "Yeah. That's why I asked you."

When the makeup was done, I stood and showed the room. Smiles erupted on their dark faces, so I knew the job was up to their standards. Javon gave me the suit and told me I had five minutes until show time.

What got me the gig was my carefree attitude, and my ability to do card tricks, act the fool and make the kids laugh, and my uncanny ability to juggle. I could juggle anything, literally. I'd impressed the kids so many times over the past two years, that every time they came to visit their fathers, they'd run to me and hand me things to toss around. After a year it became tedious, but if it gave the men some alone time with their wives, I didn't mind playing with the kids.

As I changed into the fluffy white suit with green and red buttons, pink and yellow fluff balls on the collars and cuffs, and a green curly hair wig, I couldn't help but think about my own little girl. She was six years old. I knew these kids better than I knew her. I thought about all the years I'd wasted and all the birthdays I'd missed. What a lucky girl little Roxanna was to have a father put so much effort into a birthday from the confines of a maximum security prison.

My only problem was the language barrier, and for all the thinking I'd done, I couldn't figure out how to get over it. I searched through my stuff for props and items to juggle when I came across a referee's whistle I used during basketball matches. The idea hit me. I'd be the whistle clown. I remember seeing this clown on television who did that, whistling when he was happy and sad. The kids on TV liked it. It had to work, I had no other options.

The kids downstairs welcomed the mute clown with cheers and Mexican catcalls. I waved to the group of fifteen kids and families sitting at the benches. I danced in the big red shoes and whistled my happy tune. The kids were of all shapes and sizes, and in the front row, sat two mental handicapped children with wide smiles on their faces. I held out my hand to the biggest child in the group, a large headed child with two front teeth missing and a constant strand of drool hanging from the corner of his mouth. I soon regretted offering my hand when he stood and nearly yanked my entire body to the ground. I played like he'd tried to rip my arm off by stumbling and falling to the floor, much to the kid's delight, but in all truth, that kid was strong.

I led all the children in a congo line, using the whistle to mark the beat. The kids followed in single file, all holding on to each other's waists as we walked. I made a large turn at the back of the unit, and on my way back to the sitting area, I noticed that one kid wasn't joining us in line. The birthday girl sat huddled in her mother's arms at the back of the benches.

She seemed so sad. Always on the verge of tears. I saw the look on her mother's face as I turned the line around. Hopeful, optimistic. They wanted to give Roxanna the best birthday surprise they could, but unfortunately, all they had was an illiterate clown with very few tricks in his bag.

I stopped the line, pointed towards Roxanna, blew my whistle and commanded the line forward. I took one step before the meathead kid kicked me in the back of my leg, causing me to wince in pain and stop the line. I looked back at him with the inclination to feed him a combo, but he was just a kid, and I was just a clown, and I didn't know whose kid it was. As he kicked me again and giggled half humanly, I just smiled back at him, knowing his time was going to come if he kept it up – clown suit or no clown suit.

I led the line of party goers to the back of the room, one by one, walking past Roxanna and shaking her hand. The kids followed, and soon Roxanna had a smile on her face that I hadn't seen in either of the two years I'd been there. It was a good start.

The entertainment went on for an hour. I juggled, I did every magic trick I knew. I danced, pretended to get in shape by exercising and failing miserably, I played spin the meathead kid around in circles until he got dizzy and fell. He didn't like being made a fool of, and when his senses returned, he scowled up at me than delivered a punch right to the stomach area – more like the groin area – and because I knew he was a total bastard child, I figured his aim was right on target. Never the less, like a good *paiaso* I feigned like it hurt and crumbled to the ground. The kids laughed and cheered. The demon child leapt on me and began beating me with both fists. The kids had such a good time that afternoon.

Roxanna watched from a safe distance next to her mother. If I was a complete outsider, I'd never be able to figure out whose birthday it was. Every kid in the unit that day was on their feet, playing games and learning to juggle except for her. I tried to get her involved in the festivities, but she was so shy, every time I came to speak to her, she cowered away into her mother's safe arms. But that didn't deter me. I wanted Roxanna to know I cared for her, that I was only doing this for her.

At only one moment of that day did I actually feel a pang of sadness. When I used Javon's cell to take a break, I couldn't help but think about my daughter again. What did it take to be a good father? It took time, and commitment. Love and honesty. Javon had contracted me to be a clown for his kid's birthday, trying his best to do something nice for her with whatever he had available. I hadn't even tried to be a good dad. I'd abandoned my daughter in search of a better life, and basically left her to fend on her own. I was a terrible man and a poor excuse for a father.

How would I even know if she wanted me back home? We had no connection and there was bound to be some resentment towards me for being away so damn long. A loud pound sounded at the door followed by a primitive scream for me by my new name – *paiaso!* It was meathead. The entire cell rattled as he pounded away on the door. I glanced at my reflection in the mirror. My makeup was beginning to run. The show's almost over. That moment I was just a clown facing a reality that I might never be a good father. I had blown my opportunity to ever know if I was good enough for my own little girl.

At the end of the day, I handed out candy to the kids. Javon gave me little bags filled with evil chili candies and other crap that kids liked to eat. I was tired. My makeup felt heavy now. I'd scratched the wig because it was covered in sweat and I was ready for a nap. The sun mixed with the excitement of the day had worn me out to the point that I was I sitting duck for the wrath of meathead's unlimited energy which didn't care if I was in a clown suit or back to my regular self. He smacked me across the face and began stuffing more sugar into his body. If only he were ten years older.

At the back of the line, hand gripped tight to her mother's, was the girl of the hour. Her innocent face was as strong as a new day sun. The smile was there, wide and bright and she looked like a little angel. I offered her my warmest smile and she let go of her mother's hand and shuffled over to me. I could sense Javon's quickened breath behind me as I squatted down to be face to face with her.

As she stood in front of me, she seemed so small, so insignificant in this great big world. How easy it would be to just forget about her, leave her to figure things out on her own. At three feet tall, who could she hurt if her parents decided not to care about her? Her little hands reached out to me and I handed her a bag of candy. She opened the bag and peeked inside, smiling when her eyes retracted back up to mine.

Without prompting, Roxanna stepped closer to me and gently placed her arms around my neck. We all fell silent as she hugged me with all of her small body. I returned the thanks by giving her a squeeze, Her frail body melting in my arms. When she pushed away, she spoke.

"Paiaso," she sang. Her voice was like that lone oboe in an orchestra of violins. Special and distinct.

The moment was too surreal for me to grasp what feelings Roxanna's mother had at that moment. When she reached down to hug her daughter, she was nearly in tears. Javon pushed past me and joined his wife in a loving grasp of their once speechless child. I held my ground, in a squat, watching them tear their daughter apart with love. She'd spoken, for the first time in years, to me.

Javon turned to me and hugged me. "This is a miracle. *Gracias dios!*."

I didn't believe in miracles. What happened with Roxanna that day was nothing more than good timing. She'd been waiting to say something, but the moment hadn't been right for her. She was angry at her father for leaving them alone, and it wasn't until he'd done something so wonderful and loving for her that she decided to end her protest. Javon said it was my doing. He and his wife sobbed tears of joy as they thanked me, but I knew I'd done nothing. Roxanna speaking was her way of thanking them for loving her.

"Hold on a second," I said and rushed upstairs to my cell.

When I returned, I brought down my boxing trophy. Back in the clown persona, I blew the whistle, summoning the remainder of the kids to watch the official presentation of the birthday champion trophy to Roxanna. I had no connection to the damn thing. The female figurine on top was clearly not meant for me, and as I presented it to wide eyed Roxanna, I thought for an instance that maybe miracle was too strong a word. Fate might have been a better term.

Roxanna took the trophy and smiled. She spoke non stop to her mother and father as they whisked her over to the benches. I watched from a distance as the family reconnected with one another, talking and laughing and praising their daughter for winning such a beautiful trophy. I smiled to myself, but inside, I wanted my own daughter. I wanted Kelsey in my arms at that moment and I wanted to tell her how much I needed to hear her voice and listen to her laugh. I suddenly had a connection to her that I realised had always been there, just for some reason I'd never paid it any mind. I was so wrapped up in my own life, my own story, that I'd forgotten what it meant to love another person. It took time, and understanding, and commitment, but most of all, it took just being there so those things could immerge. As I watched Roxanna get love from both parents, I realized that fate had once again stepped in to teach me a valuable lesson in life.

"Paiaso!"

The scream came out of nowhere, and before I could react, I had eighty-five pounds of meathead on my back, yanking at my wig and drooling down my neck inside of the suit.

I turned to the kid. "You're a real fucking brat, aren't you?"

His face scrunched, attempting to understand what I was saying.

"That's right. No fucking brains to understand English, huh?"

In Spanish, the kid asked me what I'd just said. I just smiled and kept swearing at him. Sometimes revenge is a dish better served hot.

*   *   *

On the night of my last day in Mexico, I sat outside under the midnight stars, watching the sky move above me. Every night was clear in Mexico. No smog or clouds ever blocked out the universe from the earth below. I'd become used to spending quiet hours alone in the maximum in the middle of the night, without the music or the yelling, the religious zealots with their megaphones and soapboxes. No laundry or food to do. I thought about my life at that moment, the struggle I'd been through to survive. The near death riot and the unfair fights. I'd come a long way in two short years. I'd matured more than I could have ever imagined, and learned a lot in the process.

That night, I thought about what I was going to do once I got home. I was going to be a father, a family member. Spending time with the Mexicans stirred up a desire within me to be part of my family again. I didn't want to feel left out and scared to speak to my own blood. I wanted to have a relationship like Javon and his family, or Roger and his. This time in Mexico had taught me a lesson about my ability to adapt, survive and love.

I also thought about Shelly and Ryan, two people who I vowed my allegiance to only to have them screw me over in the end. As I considered all the love and changes I'd make in regards to my family, I thought about the death and misery I'd impose on my two enemies. My excitement for revenge mixed with my excitement to be a new family man, and the result confused me. Could I be both hate-filled and loving at the same time? If I couldn't, which one would take precedent? The sky offered me no answers.

Two nights later, in the dead of night, I woke up for the last time in Mexico with a gun pointed at my head.

"Get up," said the masked officer. "You're going home."

Book Three

Chapter 13
Ed
First Day

September, 1985. The small town of Waupun, Wisconsin

As I got out of my car, I looked up. Overhead a flock of Canada geese flew in a V formation in the same direction I was going – Waupun Prison, a maximum security facility. It was 8 AM on a Friday morning and I was going to prison, not as an inmate, but as a volunteer teacher of creative writing.

I had parked on a quiet side street in this small rural town seventy-five miles north of my home in Milwaukee. Waupun is known for two things: naturalists will tell you that Canada geese break up their flight south every fall by resting in a local marsh. Come spring, they stop again in the marsh. But poor people in Wisconsin's urban centers say something different about Waupun. "Waupun, man, that's where *The Walls* is."

I could see *The Walls* as I stood by my car. The prison sits right in the heart of the city, three streets from the center of town. It consumes an entire city block. Four towering yard lights, taller than any tree, taller than any church steeple, stand ready to change night into day. The lights God put in the sky, the sun and the moon and the stars, do not rule this city block. The State of Wisconsin does.

No Roman collar protected me now as on my previous visits to prison, twenty years earlier.

I took a deep breath, grabbed my briefcase and locked the car. Cool fall air and the fragrance of leaves greeted me, trying to reassure me that all was okay. I checked the passenger door and rechecked the driver's side. After all, crime lived a block away.

Two preteen girls walked by as I fiddled with the car. "I heard her say it myself," one said, "he asked her to go out with him."

They seemed unconcerned, even unaware that they approached Wisconsin's worst.

They walked up the street and went right by the prison.

I started toward the entry. The stone 'Walls' enclosed three sides of the complex, towering three times an average person's height. Most of the stones were put in place before the Civil War. Guard stations and gun turrets marked the four corners and the middle of each side. Steel bars on the front, facing the main street, let the public see the ancient buildings of the prison. Chain link fences crowned with razor wire surrounded some of the buildings. No trees grew inside the walls.

I walked down to the entrance in the middle of the block. Ferocious zoo animals were not surrounded like this. What or who lay behind these walls? I was walking into a nightmare.

I heard loud honking overhead. More Canada geese flew in perfect V formation, heading for the marsh. They sailed over me, then over the prison. They honked loudly, mocking all humans, showing how they could fly over *The Walls* with impunity.

I looked up at the guard station on the wall where a man in his mid-forties stood watch. He had graying temples and a little paunch hung over his belt buckle. His eyes stared into the prison yard, but his gaze was miles away. Despite the uniform, despite the clearly visible rifle, there was something paternal about him – the paunch, the short, stocky build. He reminded me of my dad. Maybe he was gazing off to an upcoming fishing trip with his son.

As I neared the main entry, I shook myself back to reality. Guards in uniform, male and female, streamed toward the entrance along with professionals in suits, office workers and secretaries. What was this place? A thousand people came in to watch another thousand people move between the mess hall and their cells.

These people earned their living inside the prison. But why was I here? I began to question myself. My mission – to reform the system by creating writers – faded. Maybe I just wanted to feel good, to tell people, "Hey, aren't I macho? I taught inside *The Walls* today." Maybe I was one of those little boxes in Psychology 101 – 'people who need to help other people.'

Some grade school boys walked up the street. They laughed and jostled each other. One boy ran a stick along the bars facing the street. The boys skittered past me.

Across the street century-old houses faced the prison. Their spacious front porches with lazy furniture spoke of a lifestyle far different than that portrayed by the dirty stone of the prison. A man came out of one house to walk his dog. A woman picked up papers in the yard.

To the neighbors and the school children Waupun Prison was just a part of life. It was what their town did, their industry.

I reached the entrance. My insides trembled. Staff went in one door, visitors another. I was considered a visitor.

In the small waiting room, lockers filled one wall, benches lined the other. The room faced a counter and an electronic surveillance walk-through station.

A mid-thirties woman sat on a bench, her tired head resting on the back wall, a blank stare in her eyes. I guessed she'd taken the bus up from Milwaukee to visit someone. Maybe her husband.

My mind focused on her. She lived separated from her husband now, she in Milwaukee, alone, he in prison, seventy-five miles away from her. How was this prison helping either of them? I wondered. What if I had to live without the people who kept me sane, Kathy, my wife of fifteen years and my two children?

A big guard behind the counter looked me over. He was heavy, maybe two hundred seventy-five pounds with a Santa Claus belly and a round face to match. This was the enemy. I knew enough about prison to know the men hate the guards. I decided I was going to be on the side of the men. As the big guy motioned to a clipboard, his belly hit the counter and a wave rolled up his blue uniform shirt. "Sign in here," he said.

I signed my name, the time and the purpose of my visit. "Oh, yes, the school people said you'd be coming. Your name's Griffin, right? Mine's Wes." He pointed to his name tag. "See, Wesworth."

He looked me over again. "So you came all the way up here from the big city, huh?"

"Yes, officer."

"Wes. You can call me Wes. I hope you're not a Democrat."

The man's charm disarmed me. "Of course I'm a Democrat," I responded. "Aren't you?"

The banter began. In between jokes about how dumb Democrats were, he told me to empty my pockets and put everything in a locker. He gave me a token for the locker. Next he asked for my briefcase. "We don't want you passing out Democratic propaganda in here." After he searched my briefcase, he told me to take off my belt, my shoes, anything with metal. "Okay, now walk through the surveillance machine. It's far more sensitive than the ones in the airport."

It beeped.

"Must be the rivets on your jeans. Stand up there." He directed me to a little platform and he went over my whole body with a hand held detector. "You pass, Griffin. Hold out your left hand."

He pressed a special stamp onto the back of my hand. The ink was invisible, only to be seen with ultra violet light. "You need this stamp to get out of here," he told me. Then he gave me back my shoes and belt.

A man came in to fill the pop and candy machines in the visitors' room. Wes's attention shifted to him. The woman still sat on the bench in the corner, waiting, I supposed, for visiting hours to begin.

"That bench doesn't look very comfortable," I said to her.

"You bet it's not. Dumb asses, I take the bus up to their little shit town and stay overnight so I can see Richard and then they tell me I have to wait. They ever hear of working people? I got to be back in Milwaukee at three this afternoon."

The woman's anger scared me off. I turned and put on my belt. As I did, I looked up. On the other side of a thick glass wall were three convicts in chains, their hands shackled to their sides, their feet chained together, allowing them to take only small steps. All of them had gray hair as I did.

Guards preceded them and followed them. The three shuffled toward the staff door and a waiting prison van. I was horrified - and fascinated. I stared at them as if they were deformed. Why? Did I enjoy seeing people suffer? If this were the Middle Ages, would I be out in the town square watching someone get hanged?

I tried to repress these thoughts. Teaching in prison was supposed to make me feel like a better human being. Instead I felt evil. I was part of the murderous human species this place was built for. I had just been searched up and down, and now chains had been dragged across some suppressed evil in me.

This place was dehumanizing me and I wasn't even through the first door.

Wes turned back to me. I pointed at the departing convicts. "Where are those guys going?"

"Court appearances in Madison," he replied. "And one guy is going to the doctor. He's got cancer."

Wes picked up the phone. "I've got to call for an escort for you. You have to have somebody walk you to the school building. Don't want any loose Democrats in here."

I waited behind the counter with Wes. He talked on the phone, arranged for my escort and then called for the woman's husband to be brought to the visiting area.

While I waited, I looked around. Several cardboard boxes were stacked under the counter. The top box had a small TV, some letters, a few books, some clothes inside. A man's life in a cardboard box. A transfer paper on the outside indicated the owner's name and his location, a medium security prison, also in rural Wisconsin.

A paper on another box stated that the enclosed items (radio, extra socks) were contraband and were to be returned to the sender.

What if I were to be suddenly straight-forward and tell Wes what I thought. "This is terrible, man, calling extra socks 'contraband.' This whole place is inhuman."

But I said nothing and, luckily, the escort appeared on the other side of the thick glass. "Okay, Griffin, you're out of here," said Wes. "Good luck on your class."

In the civil rights movement I learned a song: "Which side are you on?" While many times the issues we face are more complex than picking sides, sometimes life *does* demand a firm stand. How was I going to keep clear that guards were the enemy, if they all acted like Wes?

A glass door, massive enough to crush a person, slid open. The door was controlled by a guard inside a thick glass cage. A small middle-aged woman stood in the doorway. I found out later she was the school secretary. Wes winked at her. "Take this Democrat up to the school, will you, Mary?"

She laughed and stepped back to allow me to go through the thick door.

I swallowed and started into the prison. My knees shook. We passed the guard cage and stopped. The glass door closed behind us. When it was completely shut, the guard in the cage nodded to Mary, and the barred steel and glass door in front of us opened.

We entered a quiet area, almost like a chapel or a reflection room in a hospital. Light streamed in from numerous windows. A man wearing a jacket that said 'Trustee' buffed the floor to a high polish. Fresh 'soothing green' paint covered the walls. A glass case showed items from the history of the prison, old license plates, browning photographs and samples of rope made in the prison factory. Stairs led to a series of offices. A sign said 'Office of the Warden.'

In front of us another control cage blocked the way. It, too, was made of steel and thick glass. Mary gestured to the guard that I was with her. The guard nodded and the door in front of us slowly opened.

"A lot of gates," Mary said.

"Right," I answered. A nightmare from my childhood about going into the forest and never coming back pressed at my mind.

We entered the administration part of the prison. The hall widened with office doors on each side of us. Bright fluorescent lights, green plants. Phones rang, people handed papers to other people, secretaries typed, men in suits strode from office to office carrying papers. A trustee emptied waste baskets, a secretary carried a report across the hall to the chief of security.

"Wait here a minute," Mary told me. "I've got to pick up some papers for the school."

I stepped to a side wall and waited. The door behind me opened. A guard led five chained men into the area. They looked around, confused. The guard handed some papers to a man in a suit. The suit looked the prisoners up and down, complete disdain on his face.

The prisoners went through the next entry, another barred and glassed door. The suit accompanied them. Mary chatted with another secretary.

I leaned against the wall. What was I doing here? Who was I? I was the humanitarian version of the suit. I looked down on the men, too. "I've come to rescue your poor minds from ignorance." Yes, I could hear myself say that. Or more likely, considering my Biblical background, "I've come to lead you out of Egypt into the Promised Land." Delusional Moses.

Come on, Mary. My self esteem dwindled by the second.

Finally she rejoined me and we stepped in front of the door the five prisoners had gone through. Another door. A guard inside opened it and we stepped into a narrow hall with another barred door at the end. Immediately I noticed a difference – high ceiling, sweaty smell, dull lighting, yellowing paint. In a little room off the hall guards strip-searched incoming and outgoing prisoners. The five prisoners stood in there now. I could see a guard with a rubber glove searching up one man's ass. Another man stood naked, his eyes wide with fear.

Mary gently pushed me against one wall of the hallway. "The guard has to see back to the administration section. He has to be sure no other doors are open when he opens one of his. It's the rule."

I waited. One by one the five men, minus their shackles, and with their clothes back on, joined us in the hallway. The guard checked to be sure nothing else was open. Slowly he swung open the last door into the prison. Like the other doors, it was made of steel bars and thick glass. A damp, musty smell came at us. The noise of a thousand men. Dim, unfinished stone walkway. This was it.

As the guard opened the last door into the prison, I caught a fleeting image of myself in the glass. The last door was a mirror. "Who are you?" it asked. "And what are you doing here?"

Ten steps or so and I was through the cold, stone walkway and in the prison courtyard. Everything was gray – the stone walls, the dusty ground, the cell blocks stretching out into the courtyard. Even the sky above matched the dreary walls. September had joined itself with this stone fortress. A chilling breeze reminded me that Waupun was a cold, miserable place.

I consoled myself that I was here to reform this stone-dead place. This was step one.

Everything in the courtyard was mean and dirty – including the men I saw walking through the yard. Men hurried from building to building as if activities had just changed and they had limited time to get to the next program. They were dressed in gray-green pants and gray-green jackets, but somehow each of them managed to look 'bad.' Some men shot me a fleeting glance and then looked away. No welcoming smiles appeared on their faces.

I looked around. Everyone in the courtyard tried to look tough. No one walked, everyone swaggered. Maybe their looks were meant to impress each other, not me.

I can do this, I can do this, I repeated to myself.

Mary pointed to one of the cell blocks. "This is cell block A." Cell block A was right out of late night TV with tiers of cells, one on top of the other. I gaped through the only window, at the end of the tiers. Men filed down the steps on their way somewhere.

I kept staring at the cell block. Men lived in these tiny cages with only gray cement and steel bars to look at. There was no color here, not a yellow chair, not a green forest in a frame. Again I found myself fascinated. The State of Wisconsin had put men in cages. That evil part of me that was mesmerized by violence kept me staring. Finally Mary turned around and said, "Come on."

She strode forward across the yard, ignoring the columns of men. She walked with purpose and I tried to do the same. We approached the school building at the end of the courtyard. "The riot we had a few years ago started here," Mary said. A riot in a school building? How could that be? Weren't schools hopeful places that gave knowledge and wisdom?

Outside the school door a few men stood around smoking, their ashen faces set in permanent scowls. They avoided eye contact with me, but looked me over when they thought I wasn't looking. I guessed at their thoughts. "Here's comes another know-it-all social worker to save us."

The men nodded at Mary and we walked into the building. As she led me upstairs she explained that the first floor contained machine shops. I looked over the railing to a poorly lit hallway. Mary saw where I was looking. "We've had a lot of problems down there." I found out later from the men that guys sometimes got raped in the dark hallway.

At the top of the stairs a guard sat at a table. Mary explained that I was the creative writing teacher. The guard said nothing to me, he simply made a note on a piece of paper. The man looked to be in his fifties. He didn't smile, in fact he looked as if he never smiled. Not a cruel man or an evil one, just very stern.

I didn't know whether I should be reassured that there was a guard in the school or worried that a guard was necessary.

Mary took me to the director of education's office, the man who had interviewed me by phone to teach in prison. He had the big shoulders and bull neck of a bodybuilder, but the hands and easy smile of an educator. He motioned me into his office and, as he shut the door, he pointed to the inmates right outside his office. They were involved in secretarial work. "Can't trust them," he said.

How could a man be an educator, I wondered, if he didn't trust people? As the director talked to me, he revealed that he used to be a university cop. He seemed to be more cop than educator.

"Here's your class list, Ed. Eleven guys, that's good for this place. You've got some bums, but also a few of the bright boys. Watch the bright boys. They'll try to get you to do things for them."

"Like what?"

"Like carrying mail or messages for them outside the prison. Under no circumstances are you to take or receive any mail or messages. Is that clear?"

"Yes."

"You have to understand, Ed, these guys are manipulators."

Long ago I learned that everyone tries to manipulate everyone else. All human beings are manipulators, some more clever than others. How could the director of education call these men manipulators when he belonged to an institution that promoted manipulation on a massive scale?

But this was not the time to raise questions like that.

"I hope you have good eyes," the director said.

"Why?"

"Because there are only a few typewriters in this place and only a few computers. Your students have to turn in handwritten work."

"Can I get some machines donated?"

"Absolutely not. Old typewriters have metal key strokes that can be turned into weapons."

"How about computers?"

"Ahh, this is a maximum place. We don't want to make things too good for these guys. Besides we'd have to disable the communications port."

"I can work with handwriting."

"Okay, any questions, now?"

"No."

"Don't forget to take attendance every class. It's important that we show the warden and the state office that we're running some good programs here and we service a lot of men."

The director took me down a hall toward the classrooms. But first we passed the library and the director invited me in to look it over. Three low shelves housed a scattering of books, and wooden reading tables hosted gang carvings and sketches of women. I asked the civilian librarian if he had *Writer's Market*.

"Heck, I don't know. Let me ask Brian."

A quiet inmate had been following the conversation. He was already on his way down an aisle. He returned with a ten-year-old copy of *Writer's Market* and handed the thick book to me. "Old," I said and handed it back. "Maybe I can get a new copy donated."

The inmate and I exchanged appraising glances. This young man didn't have the appearance of a yard bird.

"There's just no money for books," the director said as he led me out of the library and across the hall to my classroom. Unlike other schools, all the interior walls of the classroom had full length windows in them, so the guard could see into every one. The teacher's desk dominated the front of the room, with the student chairs in five rows of six chairs. Ten men had scattered themselves among the thirty seats.

The director went to the front of the room. "This is Ed Griffin. He's going to teach a course in creative writing. I expect you to show him every courtesy. He's a volunteer." With that he left.

In front of me sat ten bad looking dudes, none of them looking like what I thought of as writers. I had no idea what any of them were in prison for – murder, armed robbery, rape. In the second row two guys stretched out on their desks as if they were napping. At the end of a row a man doodled idly on a piece of paper. In the third row, sitting by himself, was a man who made me nervous. His eyes were watery, his face was soft and fleshy. I could picture him sitting on a park bench waiting for a young victim. As I gazed at him, I realized I was being unfair. But I was the father of a ten-year-old girl.

Behind him four middle-aged men yawned and lounged in their school chairs. In the last row two Native Americans nudged each other and made jokes. Was I to start my great crusade to reform the prison system with these men?

The door opened again and Brian, the inmate librarian from across the hall, came into the class, went to the front row, opened a notebook and looked serious.

Somebody farted loudly. Everyone laughed.

In the next thirty seconds I became a teacher. If I was going to keep control of this class, I had to be good. If I was dull, I'd get a knife in my back. Of course I could always call in the director or the guard, but that would defeat the whole purpose. I came here to give these men a sense of their own worth. But to do that, I had to be entertaining and interesting, yet treat my subject seriously. I had to be one step ahead of everyone all the time.

"Creative writing is a wonderful art that...." I saw eyes glazing over. I stopped and went to the board. "Wanted. Creative Writer." I meant it as a newspaper ad, but the men figured it was a wanted poster.

"Wanted," the doodling man jumped up, "for telling the truth about the assholes who run this place."

"Yeah, right on," the others said.

"Good," I said and wrote on the board — 'telling the truth.' "What's your name?"

"Jerry."

I wrote his name next to his idea. "What else is the creative writer wanted for?"

"For selling love poems to guys to send to their women," one of the men in the back said.

"Great," I said and wrote 'love poems' on the board. I got his name, 'Charlie.'

A big guy in the second row slapped his buddy. "Me and Davey was truck drivers. We got a lot of stories to tell."

I wrote on the board 'telling stories.' "What's your name?"

"Walter."

Brian, in the front row raised his hand. "Writing is something they can't take away from us." I studied Brian again. Maybe here was my first crusader.

I wrote 'can't take away' on the board.

I went on to point out some of the other advantages of creative writing and I told my own story, how I owned a commercial greenhouse and made a lot of money, but I was becoming a vegetable. "Creative writing started me thinking again."

The two native Americans in the back stopped screwing around. I started talking about how to write well. I talked about things like avoiding the verb 'to be,' about using the active voice, about writing honestly. In the front row Brian took notes, the truck drivers listened carefully. "It WAS a dark and stormy night," Jerry called out. "The verb *to be*."

"That's boring," the truck driver, Davey, said.

"Right," Brian said, "nothing is happening."

"It was a fucking dark and stormy night," one of the natives called out.

Everyone laughed, including me. "How could we fix it up?" I asked.

"Lightning crashed through the darkness," Brian said.

"Fucking good," Davey said.

"Right," I said, "that was excellent."

Something was wrong with the way this classroom was set up – rows of desks, with the teacher's desk at the front. The structure of the classroom did not fit what was happening. We were a group. I was there as a resource person, not a god-like teacher.

"Wait," I said. "Let's change this classroom around. Let's make a circle out of the chairs."

"Old fartface Reynolds is gonna be pissed if we change his classroom around," Davey said.

"Yeah," his buddy Walter added, "there has to be five rows of six chairs each or he has a nervous breakdown."

"We can put it all back," I said.

Everybody got up and moved the chairs into a circle so that teacher and student were indistinguishable. Never a fashion horse, I wore jeans and a work shirt, not a whole lot different from what the men wore.

A group of outside contractors began to work on the heating pipes in the ceiling. They ran a reaming device through the pipes right over our heads. It sounded like a hundred plumbers dragging bicycle chains through the pipes. I got up and asked them if they could do their work later. They looked at me strangely and walked away. A few minutes later the director of education came to my classroom. He looked askance at our circled desks. "The contractors told me one of the convicts asked them to be quiet."

The director asked the plumbers to move and my first class continued, now formed into a circle. We went around the room and introduced ourselves and said what kind of writing we were interested in. I was amazed to find out the men did not know each other. They only knew those cons on their own cell block and they told me this was true in all prisons.

I made a mental note. How could a movement happen if the participants didn't even know each other?

We continued with the class, going through all the rules of style, all the slogans that writers carry in their heads. "Show, don't tell," "Write about what you know."

When the class was half over, I asked if anyone had anything to read. Brian raised his hand. "I have an article here." He held up a typed paper. I imagined a report on his trial or an attack on the prison system. I hoped for the latter.

Brian cleared his throat. He started to stand up, then sat back down. He turned to the side and glanced at the guard station out in the hall. No doubt a major indictment of the prison system was coming.

He began to read: "World chess champion before he was thirty, Bobby Fisher…" The article was a short biography of Bobby Fisher and a discussion of his chess strategy. It was not about prison. Why was he nervous before he read it? Then I recalled the first time I read something of my own in class. I could hardly keep my voice steady.

When Brian finished reading, his classmates did not do what the late movies said convicts do – rip their fellows to shreds. They praised him for his work and suggested he try to get the article published.

Nobody else wanted to read anything. I gave a homework assignment. "Writers write. The only way to learn how to write is to write."

The class ended. The scary guy in the second row, now sitting in the circle, still looked scary. Brian came up to me after the class. "Thank you for coming. There is nothing else here. No good courses. Nothing."

I pointed to the classrooms around me. "What about these classes?"

He gave me a look, like I just didn't understand. "Most of the classes here just don't go very deep," he said patiently.

Jerry came up to the front. "Hey, man, thanks for coming."
"My pleasure."

Jerry turned to Brian. "I've been here four years and that's the only class I got anything out of."

"What's wrong with the school program here?" I asked.

"Ahhh, it's adult basic education and it's taught by a bunch of guys who couldn't get jobs anywhere else. Bunch of assholes. One guy was kicked out of another school."

One by one the other men came up and thanked me for coming. They made me feel good.

The men helped me put the classroom back in order. I turned in my class list, used the washroom (making sure I didn't wash off the invisible ink on the back of my hand) and started out of the school building. The courtyard was deserted. Slowly I walked back to the last gate, my eyes taking in this desolate place. No trees brought life to the courtyard and no bushes added color – just massive gray stone walls topped with broken glass. The baseball diamond, the running track and two or three flower beds tried to overcome the ashen color, but they failed. I had never seen a more barren place. No desert could compare with the prison yard at Waupun.

As I walked across the yard I had a strange feeling of completion. I thought back to how I witnessed the first breaths my children took. I knew that somehow I would go on through them. The feeling came back to me in the desolation of the courtyard. I had achieved a life goal. It would be all right if I died now. I had taught in prison. My campaign was launched.

As I waited for the last door to open, I saw myself in the glass part of the door and I wondered again who I was. What kind of strange person would feel he could die in peace after teaching a class in prison?

Chapter 14
Ed
Speechless

October, 1985.Waupun

The next week Wesworth was not on duty at the gate house.
Instead a thin guard with mean eyes greeted me, or rather didn't
greet me.

"You're a volunteer to teach creative writing?"

"Yes, sir."

"Can any of these guys write? I mean, can they even write their
names?"

"Some are very good writers."

"Put the contents of your pockets on this tray. Take off
everything metal and walk through the surveillance machine."

I did and again the machine beeped.

"Step up on this platform."

He checked my back with an electronic wand. "Turn around,"
he said and checked my front. "Get down and put your belt back
on."

I felt like a criminal.

When I put my shoes and belt on and reloaded my pockets, the
guard called the school building for an escort. A few words on the
phone and then he hung up. "You'll have to wait. The director is in
the deputy warden's office and the school secretary's in the
washroom. Step out of the way."

"But my class begins in ten minutes."

"Step out of the way." The guard went back to his crossword
puzzle. I waited a few minutes and then asked him to call again.
"In a few minutes," he said.

A police transport vehicle pulled up. I watched as the guards
led two heavily chained men into the prison. One man stopped

right outside the door and took a look up and down the street. I imagined he was taking his last look at the outside world.

The guard operated the controls that opened and closed the door for this group. "Animals," he muttered as he pulled the lever that shut the door behind them.

"Can you call the school again?" I asked. All week I'd been waiting for this class.

Without answering me, he called the school and this time reached Mary. "She's coming," he said.

When I got to my classroom, the men had already arranged the chairs in a circle. The two Native Americans were not there, but three new men were.

The class began. We talked about openings and endings. I was one hundred percent prepared. I had more material in front of me than I could ever use.

"In regard to openings, you have to get people's attention. Let's try one from a children's book." I picked up *Charlotte's Web* and read the opening lines. *"Where's Papa going with that ax?" said Fern to her mother as they were setting the table for breakfast."*

"That's pretty good," Walter said.

"I read that book to my daughter," one of the new men said. "She loved it."

I picked up Hemingway's *The Old Man and the Sea*. *"He was an old man who fished alone in a skiff in the Gulf Stream and he had gone eighty-four days now without taking a fish."*

"Yeah, yeah, that's good," Davey said. "Keep going."

"The point is," I said, "you have to get the reader interested."

The guy who'd scared me last class raised his hand. "How about, *She had three children – one of each.*"

Everyone laughed. Whether it was original or not, was not the issue. He'd gotten the message.

The class went on. We talked about endings and the use of conflict. The two truck drivers each brought a story and read them out loud. Davey, with only a third grade education, wrote a short piece on lions, printed in large letters in pencil. Walter had used the library's typewriter to relate some of his adventures with women while he was trucking. The article ended with the line, "If you see this truck a-rockin,' don't come a knockin."

Everybody laughed.

I forgot where I was. I was with a group of writers. They struggled to find precisely the right word, just as I did. They started stories that died in the middle, just like some of mine did. They came to class thinking their manuscript was perfect, only to have someone back a pick-up truck through the holes in the story. Hell, my fellow writers often backed eighteen-wheelers through the holes in my stories.

We all polished our work to make it shine. We were writers.

Brian did not want his work read out loud, so I agreed to read it at home. He had two things for me, a short story about a prison guard getting his comeuppance, and an article about why the government shouldn't impose the seat belt law.

The loud clang of the bell surprised me. I was having fun. Brian came up to me after class and thanked me again. He asked me a few questions about my critique of his Bobby Fisher story. The rest of the guys left. Brian glanced at me, hesitated a moment and then asked, "Do you get paid to come here?"

"No."

"Do you care if I ask you why you're here?"

I explained about how I wanted to teach guys to write so they could tell the world about the abomination they lived in.

"You got that right. Thank you. That's what I want to do, write about this place."

Perfect. Here was an intelligent convict who knew how to write.

"I'm in here for murder," he announced, taking me by surprise with this change of subject. "Thanks for not asking."

"Not asking?"

"Sometimes outsiders are too nosy. But you've been respectful, so I want you to know. I'm a lifer and so are four other guys in the class. But you don't have to worry. Wardens will tell you that lifers are a calmer bunch than, say, drug addicts."

I had no idea what to say next, so I said, "Un-huh."

"And guys don't hassle murderers either," he continued, a hint of a smile on his face. "They're afraid of them."

"Ah, that guy behind you?" I asked, trying to find out about the scary guy and giving the lie to Brian's comment that I wasn't 'nosy.'

"Mike? He's a great guy. He's got a college education and he's very intelligent, except when it comes to making a living. He was a jewel thief, twice convicted. This last time he hid his goods in a fake-bottom drawer in his apartment. It's the first place the cops looked."

So much for my ability to 'spot 'em.'

The door to the classroom opened and a guard stepped in. "Inmate Grancorvitz – out. It's time for count."

Brian picked up his books, said goodbye to me, and hurried out. Why couldn't I have more time to talk to him? I left the school building and sauntered across the courtyard, my mind on the class.

"You better cut that out, Mr. Sunshine," a voice behind me said.

I turned. It was Mike, the guy I had so badly misjudged. "Cut what out?" I asked.

"The music. The humming. This ain't no happy place." He gave me a hint of a smile.

"What? Was I humming?"

"Sounded like *Irene, Goodnight.* Maybe you didn't notice, but there ain't no background music here. The screws are against it." We came to his building. "Gotta go, man. See you next week."

I thought about music as I approached the last big door into the prison proper. Music always played in our house, in our car and in our business. Music took the edge off so many situations, it made life enjoyable and led the human soul to the spiritual. Why wasn't it in prison? Why didn't I hear background music in the hallways?

As I walked back to my car, Canada geese flew over the prison. They honked as they sailed over the courtyard as if to call the men to freedom. I knew that if I lived inside those walls, I would watch the geese with longing.

Driving home through the rolling hills of Wisconsin, I played back the entire class in my mind. Hillside after hillside blazed with the colors of fall, reds and yellows, but my mind drifted back to my brief discussion with Brian. He had the intelligence and the writing skill – and the anger at the system – to be the first knight on my crusade.

At home I told my wife about my class and the men in it. She asked me what the men were in prison for and I told her. A worried look came into her eye. "What if there's a riot? What if there's a fight? What if somebody stabs you? What if..."

She made me stop and think. How strange, that I was not afraid. I couldn't explain it to her because I didn't understand it myself. Maybe I thought the guys would protect me, because even in this short time I had made friends there.

I hugged my wife. "Don't worry. I'll be okay."

"I don't know about that."

I thought back to a time when I *did* fear for my life. In the mid-sixties I was a priest in an all-white suburban Cleveland parish. I joined Martin Luther King on his historic march from Selma, Alabama to Montgomery and when I came back my pastor told me there were threats against me and threats to bomb the church. People said they were going to kill that 'nigger-loving priest.' I remember driving into my dark garage late at night, wondering who was hiding there waiting to get me. I sat for ten minutes in a locked car and then crept through the garage to the rectory.

But not prison. I wasn't scared there.

My wife interrupted my reverie. "And anyway, why prison? Why are you so interested in helping people in prison? I mean, there are lots of problems in the world."

I looked at her dumbly. "I don't know. I really don't know."

She did not press me further.

*   *   *

October, 1985. Miilwaukee

The following Monday my writers' group met. A dozen of us got together every other week to critique each other's work.

I waited my turn to say what I was doing. I told the group about the prison and about the men in my class. "One man only has a third grade education, but he's struggling to write. And there's a young man in the class, Brian, who's a really good writer."

I wanted my friends to see that these men were not just criminals, but they were what we all were – writers.

"What's he in for?" a woman asked.

"Murder."

"Yuk," she said.

"It's nice what you're doing, Griffin," a man said, "but I think Wisconsin should have the death penalty. An eye for an eye. If you kill somebody, well that's it."

A clear picture of Brian sitting in the electric chair came to my mind. I shuddered.

"What does he write about?" another woman asked. "Murder and killing?"

"He writes about chess."

"Did you hear three people were shot in the central city last night?" the first woman informed the group. "I think we have to get a lot tougher on criminals."

I had no answer. I was speechless. Brian and the two truck drivers were human beings, trying to better their lives. They were writers. They faced the same problems I did. How could I want one of them dead? How could I wish more lock-up time for them?

But as a society we can't let crime happen. Crime victims are people, too. They have a right to property, to safety and to life. Criminals have to change, each has to face his past, his present and his future. In the few weeks I'd been in prison, I hadn't seen anybody face anything but the chow line.

One woman said she opposed the death penalty. Another mentioned a notorious rape case. A man said criminals used a truck to rob his neighbor's house. "Imagine," he emphasized, "a truck."

"Worst year ever for murder in Milwaukee," another man said.

Tom, my best friend in the group, leaned toward me. "So, Ed," he asked in a gentle voice, "what is the answer?"

I looked down and shook my head. All I knew was that Waupun wasn't helping anybody. Maybe someplace behind the walls, behind all those steel doors, there was an answer. I resolved to start looking for it the following Friday morning.

Chapter 15
Ed
The Visiting Room

The director of education warned me not to get too close to the men. "Especially the smarter ones. Your natural inclination is to favor the ones who do well in your class. They'll tell you that you're the best teacher they ever had. Hell, they say that to every teacher. Once they butter you up, then they'll get you to bring drugs in."

Despite this warning I got close to several of the men through the next few classes. Davey and Walter, the two truck drivers, and I had several laughs together. Davey always wrote about animals, but Walter turned in story after story of law breaking, adventure and romance on the road. In my secret life I wanted to drive an eighteen-wheeler and swagger into a truck stop wearing a lumberjack shirt and a Texas state belt buckle. Walter's stories fed my fantasy.

Brian and I became friends. He paid careful attention in class and when the session ended he and I would talk about prison. He criticized every aspect of it and the ideas behind it. He referenced the history of prisons and quoted state laws establishing them. Here was the first man to write the revolution I had dreamed about. But our conversations were always cut short. The guard would come in and chase him out. After one class I asked him, "How do I go about visiting you here?"

He shrugged, his face set in its usual stern look. "I request that you be put on my visiting list, then Social Service approves or rejects it. Takes a few weeks."

"Social Service can reject me?"

"If you have a criminal record."

"Do you want me to visit you?"

His eyes brightened and he almost smiled. The mask fell away.
"I'd like that very much."

* * *

January, 1986. Waupun

I waited several weeks for permission to visit him. During that
time I observed him carefully in class. He had already served five
years of a life sentence and he followed prison rules carefully. But
on occasion I saw flashes of the anger that must have gotten him
into trouble in the first place. On the way out of the classroom a
black inmate pushed in front of him. In a second Brian dropped his
books and stood ready to fight. Walter, waiting to get out of the
classroom, yelled, "Take it outside, you dumb fuckers," and ended
the fight.

Brian was of average height, clean shaven, with a short haircut.
Up close I noticed that a mean scar slashed across his upper lip.
While Davey and Walter and the others would laugh out loud at
things, Brian did little more than smile. He looked like anything
but a convict, maybe a refrigerator salesman in a department store or
a studious college student.

Brian treated creative writing as serious business.

He presented a great puzzle to me. He told me he had never
finished grade school, but he wrote like a college graduate.

A few weeks later Social Service issued permission for me to
visit him. The following Sunday I drove the seventy-five miles to
the prison, where I went through an experience I will never forget.
Not a riot or a shoot-out, just two hours in the prison visiting room.
It ripped me apart.

* * *

I sat in the small vestibule of the prison, the same place I went
on Friday mornings, where Wesworth greeted me or the other guard
didn't. But today was Sunday. I was part of the visiting public,

mothers and fathers to see their sons, wives to see their husbands, children to see their fathers. On Friday I might assume a little status as a 'volunteer.' Today, it seemed, the brand 'friend of a convict' blazed on my forehead. The guard on duty in the gate house treated all of us as vermin. If we claimed friendship or relation to the disgusting animals in this prison, then we must be animals too. He phoned the cell block for one convict after another, finally coming to me.

"Who are you here to see?"

"Brian Grancorvitz."

He looked up Brian's cell number, just one of a thousand men in this prison. When he found it, he called the guard in the cell block. "Send Inmate Grancorvitz to the visiting room." I noted how he and everyone else on staff in this prison referred to people as 'Inmate' so and so. No one used first names. I couldn't think of any other institution that did that. "Patient Jones, Student Jones, Welfare Recipient Jones, Driver Jones." Only prison reminded the men at every turn that they did not have an identity other than 'inmate.'

The guard ordered me to put the contents of my pockets in a locker, everything except my pocket change. Why the exception? I wondered.

I did as he had instructed and then a guard escorted me and a few others to the visiting area, a windowless room above the area where the men were strip-searched. Fifteen groupings of molded plastic chairs and nicked coffee tables filled the room. At one end of the room a guard watched the whole scene from a platform. Another guard patrolled the groupings of people. The ceiling was low, the paint old, the ventilation poor.

The guard assigned me to a coffee table/chair cluster. "It's going to take a while for us to find your inmate and search him, so you can relax."

Search him? He's been in prison. What was he going to smuggle *out* of prison? License plates?

I sat down and waited. I could hear everything the family in front of me said. The father was the prisoner.

"Dad, can I play with that truck?" The five-year-old boy had his eye on a sturdy, prison-made, wooden truck that another boy played with.

"When the other boy is finished."

"When will that be?"

"You wait. He'll be done soon."

The woman sat back and looked at her husband and son. She looked tired.

After a few minutes the boy saw that the other child had abandoned the toy. He moved to the floor and began to work the truck. The man and woman moved their chairs closer together. They kissed, then broke away from each other. The woman looked as if she'd come alive again. The tough convict appearance of the man softened. He was a lover now. They kissed again, their hands reached out to embrace each other.

Then a tap on the man's shoulder. "Williams, you know the rules about embracing. Visit's over. Say good-bye."

Williams' face changed. He wasn't a lover anymore, he was a convict. Hate filled his eyes.

The woman stood and called the boy to come. He refused to leave the toy truck. His mother pulled him away. He began to scream. The sound filled the low, windowless room. She slapped him and dragged him back to her husband. "Say good-bye to your father," she ordered. The father picked the boy up, but he continued to scream. He tried to push away from his father. Holding the boy with one hand, the father spanked the boy with the other.

While all this screaming, slapping and spanking was going on, the guard stood right behind the father to make sure there was no more embracing.

The woman took the man's hand. Her eyes spoke of longing, of loneliness and of fatigue. She alone had to deal with a screaming child. One minute, two minutes they held hands. I could feel their desire to hug each other. The guard stepped forward. "I said, 'Break it up.' Now get back to your unit, Inmate Williams."

The convict went through the door where I assumed he would be searched again. The woman and child left. I sat and thought.

How could this separation be good? A boy needs a father, a man needs a wife and a woman needs a husband. What kind of system breaks up the family in order to punish and supposedly rehabilitate someone?

I wondered about all that slapping and spanking. Abused children can easily become abusers. As I watched Mr. Williams slap Son Williams, I wondered if I was not looking inside picture within picture? Would Son Williams be in prison someday and spank his boy, who would then – and so on into infinity.

My attention turned to a quiet middle-aged couple. Their son came into the visiting room. He was lean, six feet tall, with an acne-covered face. He didn't *walk* toward his parents – he *swaggered* toward them, his eyes on the other convicts in the room. The woman stood and hugged him. Tears filled her eyes. He let her hug him, but he glanced at neighboring tables to see if anyone witnessed this emotion. He saw me eyeing him and snarled. I looked away.

I'd waited twenty minutes and still no Brian. The prison wasn't that big. You could walk around the whole place in twenty minutes.

I glanced back at the young man. He sat now and his mother talked to him. The father listened, but an intermittent look of incredulity flickered across his face. *How could this have happened to my son?*

Here sat two parents who cared about their son. Why were they seventy-five miles away from him? Why were they not part of his treatment plan? What the hell was this place I was in?

I thought about my own family. It was my family that kept me on the 'straight and narrow.' I may have longed for wild adventure, but ultimately my son and my daughter determined my behavior. *Look after the children* – the message is written on the human heart. This crazy place ripped a man from his family. Yes, a small number of men destroy their families or their families destroy them, but don't the vast majority of convicts belong in the basic unit of our society, the family?

I watched more and more of this family action. I saw fathers come into the visiting room, I saw fathers being told to leave. I saw more emotion than I could handle. Through it all one guard sat at the desk, the other made the rounds and tapped people on the shoulder when it was time to go or when some illegal embracing had occurred. Both of them looked bored.

As I waited, I discovered why the prison allowed people to keep coins. A cola machine and a candy machine occupied a corner of the visiting room. Visitors, unable to bring things into the visiting room, fed many coins into these machines. A promising area for an enterprising reporter to investigate, I thought. What kind of kickback was necessary for the privilege of keeping a machine in this lucrative spot?

After forty-five minutes the door from the prison opened. Brian stood in the doorway and searched for a familiar face. When he saw me, he paced over to me carefully. No emotion showed on his face. He shook my hand and sat down.

"Hey, how's it going?" I asked, the cliché hiding my discomfort.

"Okay."

"This visiting room – it's quite an experience," I said.

"Yes."

"I mean, it shows me how stupid the whole idea of separating families is."

"Two-thirds of convicts end up divorced. This is a system that's supposed to rehabilitate men. It does nothing but tear them down."

I relaxed. Our discussion had begun. Brian had an opinion about everything I asked. "How are the guards in here?"

"Some haven't even graduated from high school. If their father had a job in the system, they get a job. Many of them are in the same economic class as most of us. Many have severe personality disorders. They feed on a job like this."

"No decent guards?"

"You have to understand. There are two systems here, the men and the guards. It's clearly *us* against *them*. This is not a therapeutic atmosphere; this is a war zone."

Therapeutic atmosphere? And this man did not graduate from grade school?

"And the caseworkers and the shrinks?"

"They come in here with preconceived ideas. They're mostly middle-class so they think middle-class is right. The black brothers say the staff tries to make them into little white men."

Preconceived ideas? Something was vaguely disturbing about that. What did he mean?

Our conversation switched to gangs in prison. "I think the warden wants gangs," he said. "If men fight each other in the yard, they don't storm the warden's office. Prison encourages convicts to hate other groups of convicts. It's the old *divide and conquer* strategy."

"How about race?"

"Same story. If the blacks and whites fight, they don't attack the administration. Thursday a fight broke out in the yard. A black against a white. The warden threw them both in the hole and used the fight as an excuse to lock down the institution."

"*Lock down*, what does that mean?"

"Everyone's locked in their cells twenty-four hours a day. The staff gets a breather, an easy day."

I squirmed in the hard plastic chair and there was a pause in the conversation. Brian's brow knitted and he stared at me. I guessed that the silence made him nervous. I tried the line my father always used when he visited me in the seminary: "How's the food?" My dad believed if I was enjoying the food, everything was all right.

"Prison food is nutritious," Brian said, "but it's not individual. I mean one guy likes his toast dark, another light. There's no such thing here. And mealtime is usually a tense time. A lot of fights happen at mealtime. Meals are served when it's convenient for the staff, not when it's good for the men. Most prisons have very early dinners, about 5 PM, because the staff want to get home. Once everyone is locked in their cell for the night, most of the staff can leave. The trouble is we are in our cells from 6 PM at night until 8 AM the next morning. So the institution is run, not for the benefit of the inmates, but for the employees."

We started talking politics and he got enthused. He was well read. News magazines, of course, but also the *Atlantic Monthly*, *the New Republic* and several books, his favorite author being Noam Chomsky.

"Who's Noam Chomsky?" I asked.

He told me that Noam Chomsky was the guru of the left wing. I felt embarrassed because I was supposed to be a left-winger, a liberal Democrat.

The conversation switched to Reagan. Brian tore into Reagan and the Republicans in Wisconsin.

But the real Brian hid under all this criticism. I knew nothing of his background or his family, I didn't know what he thought about me, I didn't even know the details of his crime.

The Catholic Church had familiarized me with 'hiding feelings.' For years I stuffed fear, love, anger and sex behind a Roman collar. Only the slow, gentle work of my wife freed me.

I tried to break the political discussion by a trip to the machines with him. "What would you like?" I asked

For a second he was a kid again. "Peanuts, any candy with peanuts."

I fed quarters into the candy machine. "How about a soda?"

"I don't care. Anything. And another thing about Reagan...."

He backed up every charge he made. When we spoke of Reagan's policies in Nicaragua he said, "The US General Accounting Office has affirmed that much of the aid already sent to the Contras has ended up in the offshore bank accounts of Contra leaders."

I felt inadequate. I wanted to challenge some of his negativity, but I couldn't – he had too much information.

He talked about Indonesia's takeover of East Timor, something I knew nothing about. He discussed the power of the big fruit companies in Latin America and the CIA's murder of Allende in Chile.

As he talked, I tried to think up ways to shift the conversation to the personal, but the guard came by and tapped him on the shoulder.

He stood up immediately. For all his criticism of the system, he followed orders to the letter.

"See you in class on Friday," he said.

"Yeah. Listen, can I come again some Sunday?"

"Sure."

"Next month? First Sunday?"

"Sure. I ain't going anywhere. I've got a life bit."

The guard nudged him toward the door. He complied immediately. As he entered the doorway, he turned and looked at me, a question on his face: *Did you really mean it? The first Sunday?*

I drove home in a reflective mood. It certainly seemed that Brian was a writer who was willing to criticize the system. I had found the first citizen of my new order. What disturbed me, however, was that comment about middle class professionals coming into the prison with preconceived ideas.

Did he mean me?

Chapter 16
Ed
Poor White Boy

February, 1986. Waupun

Be ready for anything – that's what the director of education told me. When one of our classes began, a man in his fifties sat in our circle. I asked him his name. "Arnold," he said, "and I'm innocent. It's the chemicals in the water, that's what done it."

"Welcome to the class, Arnold. We've been going through...."

Arnold jumped up and pointed at every man in the room. His white hair flopped in different directions, his mouth twisted as he accused each man. "Do *you* know about the chemicals? And you? That's what's causing all the trouble. I don't belong here, no, not at all. You there, it's not funny. All the trouble's been caused by the chemicals. They mix them in the water here and you and I drink them and..."

"Shut the fuck up and sit down, asshole," Walter shouted. I could see the paper on his desk. He had a new trucking adventure he wanted to read to us.

Arnold raised his arms to the heavens. "Don't you see? All my life – the pattern – they said I stole a car when I was a kid, but it was the chemicals. And when...."

Arnold ranted on, pointing his finger at one man, then another.

Brian raised his hand. "On the notes you gave us last time, I had a question on page..."

Arnold moved in front of Brian, blocking him out of the circle. "That's not important. Find out what the chemicals are doing to you."

Walter jumped up, shoved his chair out of the way and stood in front of Arnold. "Sit down or I'm gonna knock you down."

Arnold sat down, still muttering. Walter stood by his own chair watching the older man. Suddenly Arnold stood up and pointed right at Walter. "The chemicals have got you. They almost got me. I was polishing stones I got from Lake Michigan and I must have released chemicals from the stones. That's when the cops came and they arrested me for polishing stones."

I wanted people to feel free in this class, but it was obvious I had to do something. Arnold was already violent and Walter was close. I saw the guard sitting in the hall at his desk, but that was the last thing I wanted to do.

"Today we're going to talk about what makes a professional writer. First..."

"... and I said, 'Your Honor, it's the stones,' and then..."

Walter strode across the room in a few angry steps and faced Arnold. But Brian jumped up and got between them. He spoke quietly to Walter, "I'll take care of it," he said. Then he turned to Arnold and pronounced his words in a low, calm voice, "I want you to tell me all about this later, but right now I want you to be quiet."

It worked – sort of. Arnold blinked a few times and started again. Brian stared at him until he sat down, still muttering. He grumbled to himself for the rest of the class, but we managed to discuss what makes a professional writer and we got Walter's story read.

After class Brian came to me. "Listen, I'm sorry about Arnold. He belongs on a psyche ward. I don't know how he got here. He needs help."

I thanked Brian for controlling Arnold, but he changed the subject.

"I....I ...brought you an article about me. From *The La Crosse Tribune*."

I glanced at it – it was about the appeal of his murder conviction.

"I used to have all the articles about me. I wanted you to see them, but they...they..." he paused. Fierce anger blazed in his eyes.

"The pigs ripped my cell to shreds after the last riot. I had all the articles. They – the bastards."

"Would you mind if I got the articles from the paper?"

"No. I'd like you to."

"I meant to ask you a question about when I visited you. What did you mean about people coming into prison with preconceived ideas?"

"You know, it's the magic bullet idea. Conversion to Jesus Christ is going to save us, anger management is going to save us, cognitive skills are going to save us. It's always some magic bullet that the person believes in and they shove it down our throats whether we want it or not."

Hmmm. My crusade to get guys to write about this terrible place – was that a magic bullet? I started to frame a question in my mind. "How about..." But the guard opened the door. "Get back to your cell for count, Inmate Grancorvitz."

I gathered my papers and tried to put this business of magic bullets out of my mind.

As for getting the articles from the paper, I wasn't sure I wanted to know more. What if he'd raped someone or killed an innocent child? Would I still be able to be friends with him?

I debated the issue for a few days in my mind and then I called *The La Crosse Tribune*. This is his story as I pieced it together from the newspaper and from later conversations with him.

* * *

Brian Grancorvitz was born into a Wisconsin family that drifted from farm to small city, never succeeding in either. His parents divorced when he was five and he and his sister stayed with their mother. She remarried and the stepfather drank heavily and frequently beat Brian. Alcohol fed the man's paranoia that the communists had organized a conspiracy against his family. He ordered young Brian to stop watching Sesame Street because it was part of the communist conspiracy.

Brian suffered beating after beating from his stepfather, until he finally revolted. He joined the Marines but went AWOL shortly after boot camp and was discharged from the corps. His life fell apart. An odd job on a farm one day, a warehouse in La Crosse the next and the third day nothing because he was too hung over. He stayed with a different friend every night, only going home when his stepfather wasn't there. Several taverns banned him from their premises for fighting.

For transportation, he stole enough money for a beater of a motorcycle. On his bike he found freedom, riding the rural roads of Wisconsin. Alone on his bike with the beauty of the rolling hills around him, he began to wonder if there wasn't more to life than just 'hanging out.' But he had no direction, no one to point the way for him.

He adopted a late 70's version of hippie culture. He let his hair grow long and smoked the occasional joint. The negative reactions of people in rural Wisconsin satisfied him – he was not a part of this narrow community.

For winter he got an old pick-up truck. On a cold, sunny day in March, 1980 he got into his truck and went for a ride. He had a little grass in his pocket and a knife strapped to his leg in case he ran into his stepfather if he visited his mother.

He drove through the hills around La Crosse overlooking the Mississippi. Life seemed good to him that day, he told me. He was nineteen and he was starting to get some answers. Maybe he would go to Milwaukee and get a job, or follow the advice of his fifth grade teacher and go to college. Old Pops Schneider had told him in the fifth grade that he had real ability. Nobody in his family or among his friends had ever gone to college. Most hadn't finished high school.

The day wore on. The grasses and fields were brown and dead-looking, but there was a promise of spring in the air.

As dark approached he rolled into the small town of Readstown. On the edge of town there was a bar called the Tin Shack. Brian decided a beer would quench his thirst and end a good day. He parked his pick-up and walked into the bar. Country western music wailed on the juke box, smoke drifted near the ceiling. He enjoyed the warmth of the bar after the chill of the evening.

A few patrons sat at tables and two hard-drinking farmers stood at the bar, shot glasses in front of them. Brian went to the bar and ordered a beer. He sat down on a bar stool.

"Hey, look what we got here, a fuckin' hippie," one farmer, call him Logan, said to the other man. Logan was a big man, porky, well known in the area for fighting and drinking. "Fuckin' hippies should stay in Milwaukee," he said for all in the bar to hear.

Brian wasn't from Milwaukee. Currently he was staying with a friend in Gays Mills, another rural town a little further south on the Kickapoo River.

"He's a hippie biker," the other farmer said, pointing to Brian's leather jacket, with a round emblem on the back. "Societies and Sons Motorcycle Club," the emblem said.

"Holy shit, but he has long hair."

"Maybe he's a fag,"

"Fuck off," Brian said.

"We don't like hippie biker fags here," Logan said and swigged down the whiskey in front of him. He slammed his glass on the bar.

Brian snorted his disgust and turned back to his beer. This was the very lifestyle he'd been trying to get away from. He felt trapped in a life that consisted of sleeping, drinking, fighting and fucking, an endless merry-go-round of nothingness.

Logan stepped next to Brian. "What about we arm wrestle for drinks?"

"Fuck off."

Logan stood there, hands on his hips, glaring at Brian

"Quit staring at me," Brian said.

"Hey, hippie, get out."

Brian stood up and faced Logan. All he wanted was to drink his beer in peace.

Logan pushed him. The bar owner said, "The three of you, take your fight outside."

"Yeah," Logan said.

"Yeah," Brian said with more bravado than he felt. Despite their drunken state, it was still two against one.

Outside Logan and his buddy slammed into Brian. The buddy grabbed him and Logan slammed him in the stomach. Brian tried to reach for his knife, but as he did, Logan smashed him in the jaw so hard Brian's teeth went through his upper lip.

Brian finally pulled his knife from his leg sheath and slashed out. As with his father and his drunken stepfather, his anger had no limits. He slashed and slashed, without thinking, not even sure who he knifed.

Suddenly Logan backed away, staggered and fell. Brian saw the dark spots on the man's flannel shirt. *My God, what have I done?* He threw the knife under a car and ran for his pickup. He tore out of the parking lot and headed down Highway 56. A few miles away he saw his buddy, Michael Riley, with his thumb out. He picked him up and did what no hardened criminal would ever do. He admitted to Riley, "Man, I think I just killed a guy."

"You what?"

"At the Tin Shack."

"What are you gonna do?"

"I don't know."

Brian dropped Riley off and started for Milwaukee, then changed direction and headed for Minneapolis. He was confused, caught in a terrible drama he never intended when he drifted into the Tin Shack for a beer.

At midnight he decided to do something that hardly fit the prosecutor's later description of him as vicious and deadly - he went home to La Crosse to see his mother.

At midnight he drove his old truck into the driveway and shut off the ignition. Instantly he was surrounded. The police were waiting for him. Logan had died in the parking lot with thirteen stab wounds. His blood alcohol was 0.29 percent. The legal definition of drunk is 0.10 percent.

Brian was arrested. Since his family had no money, the court assigned a public defender. Brian and the public defender tried to get the trial moved because of extensive local publicity. They failed.

The rural jury declared him guilty of first degree murder and the judge said words that Brian could not even comprehend – life, life in prison.

With hindsight I tried to look at his trial: a bar fight ends up in murder. Planned? Certainly not. Self-defense? It was two against one. Then why the first degree verdict? Brian appealed his verdict twice, but each time the panel of judges split along party lines, the Democratic judges voting to give him a new trial, the Republicans, the majority, affirming his life sentence.

At age twenty this slight young man entered Waupun Prison with the worst of the worst. Within a month he had to fight to stop a homosexual rape on himself and then spend time in the hole for fighting. Five or six times more he fought off would-be rapists, sometimes stopping their attacks, sometimes not.

During the first two years of his sentence he began to read. He read novels, newspapers, history and he read the law. In this last area he soon excelled and became a 'jailhouse lawyer.' He got the sentence of another convict reduced, but was unsuccessful with his own. He learned to play chess and became fascinated with the game. He took every course the prison offered and read his way through the meager prison library.

Five years passed and then he signed up for my creative writing class. I was amazed at how he had changed his life in those five short years. Here was a man who could be a great lawyer or a scientist or a politician. Here was a man of intellectual ability who could make a real contribution to society.

I was impressed with him. I was his teacher, but he had much to teach me. Despite the warning of the director of education, I became his friend.

I gave him the gift of writing. He often thanked me for this gift, but I came to regret giving it to him.

Chapter 17
Ed
There but for the grace of God....

Summer, 1986. Waupun

Every week I breezed through security on my way into the prison. They checked my briefcase and my person for weapons and drugs. I took my belt off and my shoes and I emptied my pockets. But the guards never worried about the most dangerous thing I carried into the prison – an attitude.

This attitude lay deep in my personality and whispered reassuring messages to my consciousness: *You're better than these convicts, you have a lot to teach them, you're not evil like they are. Of course this misguided perspective spoke softly and subtly. You've come into this prison to help these poor guys learn how to write. Once you've helped them with writing, you can guide them to write about prison and then this terrible system will change. Ed, you're a really good guy.*

Academics claim this attitude is present in most people who go into prison to help, to guard, to preach, to educate, to casework or to oversee the whole place.

No machine or special x-ray detects the presence of this attitude and it does far more damage than guns or drugs. It destroys the good work a prison tries to do. Men aren't stupid. They know when someone looks down on them. Prison officials must work hard to root this attitude out of staff. We are all – convicts and prison personnel – weak human beings.

For me the lights came on in class one day. We got off the subject of writing and started discussing crime. "Crime is what lower class people do," Brian said. "Especially lower class, non-white young men. That's crime."

Walter disagreed. "Crime is crime. You break the law, that's crime."

"Crime is what you read about in the paper," Davey said.

Brian began to lecture his classmates. "No, the government says what crime is. And it's not what rich people do, not what the upper classes do. If a car manufacturer designs a car with a faulty gas tank and the resulting explosions kill a lot of drivers, do the owners go to jail? Does anybody?"

"I had a Ford Pinto, but it didn't blow up," Walter said.

"Hold it, you guys," Brian said. "This is serious. How about doctors? If a surgeon performs an unnecessary operation just for the money and the guy dies, does the doctor go to jail? No, he just gets a slap on the wrist. If a man moves his factory to Mexico and hundreds of people lose their livelihood, what happens to the man? Nothing – that's just business. If a factory owner pumps deadly poisons into the atmosphere and people die, like in Bhopal, India, what charges are laid? None."

"Ah, who cares?" Walter said.

"I got a new story about lions," Davey said.

We got back to writing, but an hour later, as I sat in a fast food restaurant having lunch, I thought about what Brian had said. Certainly murder was murder and it was wrong no matter who did it. But did he have a point? Why were some things crimes and others weren't? Did the lawmakers define crime as what poor people did? What about white collar crime and the sins of the middle class? And what about me? Was I a criminal?

Certainly not. I was middle class, I owned property and my wife and I operated a successful small business. I had been a city councilman in Milwaukee. How could I possibly be a criminal when I had studied morality for twelve years in Catholic seminaries? I had heard thousands of confessions and I had preached about honesty and truth.

No, I was the good guy in the white hat. Brian was wrong about crime. But then an incident flashed into my mind. It was thirteen years previous.

Late March, 1972. Milwaukee

Our campaign team celebrated that night. We had just won the primary election in Milwaukee's third district for city council.

The third district had changed radically in the early seventies. The University of Wisconsin-Milwaukee had grown from a small teachers' college to a major urban university of 25,000 students. University professors and students moved into the area. Young, well educated, liberal couples bought the older homes in the district and renovated them. The incumbent alderman reflected the old third district; I stood for the new.

Ten candidates crowded the field for the primary. Everyone knew the incumbent would fall, but I had worked the hardest. In a year's time my wife and I knocked on 10,000 doors. I won the primary and a long time resident of the district came in second. The incumbent finished fourth. The number two man and I would face each other in the general election in April.

Suddenly the campaign was for real. Business leaders probed my attitudes about development and city improvements. Neighborhood citizen groups examined my ideas about university expansion. The Milwaukee Journal interviewed me.

Before the primary our 'new crowd' held raffles and bake sales to raise money. We put up signs and got together for 'stuff-it' parties where we prepared bags of campaign mail. We worked hard, but had fun. Now we had daily strategy sessions. I asked key workers to assume big responsibilities—publicity, door-to-door canvassing, car tops and signs. We faced a tight general election between the old and the new. Older residents of the district backed my opponent. These voters felt a lot of resentment against the university and the changes to the area. Homeowners couldn't park in front of their own homes. Property values went up and so did taxes. Hippies invaded neighborhood parks. The University and the neighboring hospital bought up blocks of houses.

One by one I went to the other candidates who had lost the primary. "Would you back me in the general election?" I asked. Seven of the ten candidates endorsed me – a major coup. The question was: how was I going to get the word out to all the supporters of those seven? I had what today we call *momentum* but I had to let people know about it. I needed a flyer that would go to every home. I checked a direct mail company. The flyer would cost me $1000 printed and delivered.

But our campaign was broke.

A week before the election a bar owner called and asked me to lunch. In Milwaukee in the seventies, the alderman had absolute control over the bars in his district. This particular bar owner, it was rumored, had strong connections to organized crime in Milwaukee.

Nick (not his real name) looked like anything but a mobster. A tailor maybe, or perhaps a wine maker wearing a suit and tie to meet his banker. I shook his hand, a firm, manly grip. His appraising eyes and lively face made you overlook his diminutive stature.

All through lunch he smiled and chatted about old times in the third district. If this was the Mafia, it was a pleasant rendition.

After coffee, talk shifted to my campaign. "I think you're gonna win," he said.

"My opponent has a lot of support. People are upset with all the changes."

"What about the other candidates?"

"Seven of the ten are backing me."

"See, I told you. You're gonna win."

"I hope so," I responded.

He leaned across the table toward me. "You know, it's very important that we local businessmen communicate with our elected officials. I mean, what we're doing now, it's great."

"I intend to be open to everyone," I said.

"I'm talking about *access*. I want to have *access* to my alderman."

"You will, Nick, you will. That's what's wrong with our system, people feel no one is listening. I'm going to change that."

"Yeah, yeah," he said, as if I was talking theory. Then he pulled a fat envelope from his jacket and held it under the table. "Here," he said.

"What?" I asked.

"Here," he repeated impatiently, nodding toward the underside of the table. "I want you to have this."

I took the envelope and stared at the contents – cash. "How much is here, Nick?"

"$900."

It was more cash than I had ever seen, a lot of money in 1972. I held the mailer to the voters in my hand.

"I have to declare this," I said.

"Why?"

"It's the law."

He studied me for a moment. "So declare it."

I looked at my watch. If I hurried, I could get to the direct mail company in time for the flyer to reach the voters three days before the election. There wasn't much time left. "Listen, Nick, I really appreciate your help. Thank you." I left the restaurant, rushed to the company and ordered the flyer.

That night at our campaign meeting I told my manager and treasurer about our good fortune.

My campaign manager, John, looked at me. "You took $900 from that guy?"

"Yeah. I told him we're going to declare it."

"But you're $900 in debt to organized crime."

"It's a campaign contribution, John."

"Give it back."

"Oh, come on, John. I ordered the flyer."

The treasurer, Lou, spoke up. "I agree with John. The guy's a crook."

"So how are we going to pay for the flyer?"

"There are no campaign funds left and no time to raise any," treasurer Lou said.

The flyer was already printed. If I returned the money, the debt would be mine. Even if I won the election, it would take me a year to pay back the $1000.

I argued with John and Lou. Not for a minute did I worry about taking money from Nick. Despite all my upbringing, all my middle class values, all my Catholic morality, I was going to take a $900 'donation' from organized crime because I needed it. Besides, it was only a rumor that Nick was in the mob. Forget what might happen when Nick came to me, his alderman, about a 'matter of importance.'

But John and Lou prevailed. I made an appointment with Nick the next day and went over to his bar. I had nine one hundred dollar bills and a copy of my bank loan in my pocket.

Nick sat at his bar. "Sorry, Ed, no more," were his first words.

"No, Nick, I want to return what you gave me."

"What?" His face scrunched up as if he couldn't hear me. "What did you say?"

I repeated myself.

"Why?" he asked.

But before I could answer he dismissed me. "Doesn't matter." He took the money and shook his head with a look that said I was the most naïve guy in the world. "Good luck to you," he said as I left, his tone clearly implying the opposite.

I won the election by less than 200 votes out of 14,000. I later found out Nick gave my opponent the $900. During my term of office, I had to hold his liquor license in committee twice, once for health and safety violations and once because of criminal activities in the bar. I could never have shut him down if I had taken the money.

"Aw, take it easy, Ed," my inner voice says. "You didn't kill anybody and you didn't hang on to the money. You even told Nick you were going to declare it."

But I *was* going to take it and if it hadn't been for John and Lou, I would have. I had no morality in that case.

My mom and dad taught me that "to whom much is given, much is demanded." I think my action fit on the crime scale with some of the things my students were in for.

Was I different from the men in prison?

No.

There could be no more *I'm better than they are.*

Chapter 18
Ed
Security is King

After a half year of teaching in prison, the walls still stood. Every Friday I got up at 6 AM, drove seventy-five miles to the prison, went through security, walked over to the school building, taught my class, joked with the guys, walked back to the gate, went through security, stopped for a burger and fries and then drove home. I thought my teaching would change things, maybe not tear down the walls, but at least make a dent in them.

But rather than change systems, I realized that all I was doing was bandaging shattered, feeble individuals.

A different solution was to bring more writers from the outside into prison. If I carefully selected sensitive and sympathetic writers, they might themselves write about prison. I organized special 'writers' workshops,' inviting novelists, article writers, screenwriters and especially poets to join me. I discovered that poetry ruled in prison unlike on the outside. Men wrote poetry that told of struggle, loneliness and love. The intensity of their poetry matched the intensity of their surroundings. They valued poetry and they wanted to learn how to do it well.

The men appreciated the new faces, but the workshops involved a tremendous amount of work, for security had to clear each participant. Further I was asking each writer to give up their regular job on that day and to volunteer their time.

The writers who came to prison benefited from their experience, but they were too few and too marginal to the centers of power to bring about major change.

One of the poets saw things I never noticed. Harvey Taylor wore his hair long and played a guitar. In the summer he operated a large crane on the docks in Milwaukee. When the Great Lakes froze in winter, he spent his time writing poetry. Here is what he saw in the prison yard:

Tree Tops

There's no shortage of sunlight
In the hot prison yard.
Shade is another story. . .
just outside the high walls,
beyond the guard-towers,
upper branches sway, and
leaves dance with the wind,
as, a mere bird-swoop away
from that green realm,
down inside the compound,
human beings somehow survive
season after season
with only the memory of
 a miracle so common
it's usually unappreciated:
seeing a tree rise out of the ground.
Imagine a world in which,
you never see anyone's feet,
legs, torso, arms, face –
only fingertips,
and a few wisps of hair.
 Imagine
never looking
a tree in the eye.

Along the Shore, by Harvey Taylor, page 17

The workshops, the poetry and the weekly classes – I enjoyed them all, but I remained restless. The government kept locking up more people and cutting educational programs in prisons. *Enough with the poetry,* I thought, *we need system change.* In the civil rights movement I learned that a person just doesn't go down to the ghetto and pass out Thanksgiving baskets. A person has to ask why there's a ghetto in the first place and why the people living there can't afford their own Thanksgiving baskets.

But I just kept showing up for class every Friday morning. The guys were right. Poetry had a magic about it that was capable of negating the whole sick system. I couldn't rationally explain it, but poetry, like the Canada geese, could fly right over the walls.

On one of those Friday mornings early in 1986 a new man fidgeted in the back row. A white guy in his mid-twenties, he looked very uncomfortable. He said his name was Jim and he wanted to write about some funny things that had happened to him. Walter and Davey said they liked humor, Brian just smiled. I asked Jim if he had something he'd like to read.

"Well, I got this story about how me and some buddies blew up an outhouse."

"All right, let's hear it," Walter said. "Was anybody in it?"

"You betcha."

Jim started to read, tentatively at first, as if he wasn't sure how he would be received, but in a few minutes we were all laughing. His facial muscles relaxed and he stopped fidgeting. The guys gave him a round of applause at the end and then he read a story about how his buddies dared him to jump from a high bridge near Madison.

He sat down and participated in the rest of the class with enthusiasm. I wondered at the dramatic change from nervous squirming to active participation. When class was over, I pulled him aside. "What do you do around here? Your job? Your activities?"

"Nothing. I hate this place."

"I mean what do you do all week?"

"Nothing. I sit in my cell. Sometimes I write."

"You don't leave your cell, even when you can?"

"No."

"Your family, do they come to see you?"

"No."

"Those stories you read – they were great. Ever think of writing about this place?"

Jim sneered. "I hate this place. I can't wait to get out of it. I don't want to even think about it, much less write about it. I write about happy times from my past life."

Writing was important to Jim, but not politics and not prison reform. How did this fit into my crusade?

The guard cleared the classroom and ended our conversation.

Jim came to class every week. At least he got out of his cell for that. He differed from Brian in most respects. Brian approached everything seriously, while Jim loved fun. Brian wrote essays, Jim wrote humor. Brian hid his inner feelings, Jim's were right on the surface.

I started to visit Jim on occasional Sundays. He was soon transferred to a medium security prison and I followed him there for a Sunday visit. This institution provided a lunchroom inside – and a picnic ground outside – for visits. The atmosphere led to more relaxed visits than at the maximum prison at Waupun. My family joined me as well. My son, 14, and my daughter, 12, loved Jim's stories and our visits flew by. I remember one Sunday my daughter was so entranced with Jim's humor that she took out her retainer to eat a candy bar and left the retainer on the table. When we got back to our car, she reported it missing. I dreaded the thought of going back in to the guard house and explaining what had happened, but I did. Luckily the guards on duty understood and I didn't have to sort through too much garbage to find the retainer.

Was it wise to take my children into prison? I don't know, but I know that today they both stand up to the mindless comments one often hears about crime and criminals.

Through my visits I learned a lot about Jim. He, like Brian, came from a home where he was abused. He felt a strong sense of shame about where he was, so much so that I began to suspect it was he who told his family not to visit him there. I think he hated himself, too, and covered it up with his constant joking.

I never asked about his crime and he never volunteered the information, but he did tell me he had a cocaine addiction.

He continued to write humor and I encouraged him. I visited him on a few Sundays for about a year and then one day he was gone, sentence over. Like so many others, I never saw him or heard from him again. But I understood. Jim hated prison and anything to do with it. Unfortunately I was part of that past, a past he wanted to forget.

*   *   *

During the time Jim was in class something happened that taught me a lot about what was really important in prison. On this particular Friday, the director told me I had to shorten my class by half an hour. "There's a group from the state government in Madison coming to inspect the school and it has to be cleared of all inmates. (I wondered why a school should be cleared of its students for an inspection, but I kept my mouth shut.) Instead of two hours, I would only have an hour and a half.

I accepted this change without complaint. At least I had a class that day. Sometimes I drove up to the prison only to find that the place was locked down. The men were confined to their cells and there would be no class. I got the class started quickly and launched into our plan for the day. After forty-five minutes a young security guard opened the door of the classroom, walked in and, without even a nod to me, interrupted what I was saying and told the men to get out.

I have spent a lot of my life in school. From the nuns at St. Ann's to the professors at the University of Wisconsin, everyone held the classroom as inviolate. No one could barge in on a class as this guard had just done. Besides – we had forty-five minutes left.

"There must be some misunderstanding," I said

The guard looked at me for a second and then faced the men. His face tightened and his voice rose. "I said *OUT*."

"We have another forty-five minutes," Walter said.

"The State Inspection Team is due at 10:30," Brian added.

Jim looked worried and began to fidget.

"The director of education…" I began.

The guard cut me off. His whole body tensed. "You men get out of this classroom or you go on report."

Nobody moved. "You got no right," Walter muttered.

"Listen," I said, trying to find a reasonable answer, "why don't you check with the director. He's in his office."

The young guard's face flamed red with anger. "This is your last warning, you men. Get out."

I saw from Walter's face that a confrontation was coming. Another prison riot could start in the school. I tried to calm things down. "Men, I'm going to take this thing right to the top. Not only is this against what the director said, but it's an invasion of the classroom. In my opinion the classroom is sacred. I'm as angry as you, but for now I suggest you comply."

Amid angry mutterings, everyone left. I went to the director immediately. When I explained what had happened, he shrugged. "That's one of the things about teaching in prison. You have to learn that security is top. Just forget it."

But I didn't. On the way out of prison, I stopped at the office and asked to see the head of security. Surprisingly, he admitted me. After I explained the situation again, he said, "That's young Burns, the guy who came into your classroom."

"And?"

"His dad worked here until last year. Had a heart attack."

"Do you think it's right to just barge into a classroom?"

"You come up here all the way from Milwaukee?"

"Yes."

"The director of education tells me you volunteer. Is that right?"

"Yes. Can I get clear the rules for the classroom?"

"You have to understand this is a prison. But what we need are more volunteers like you."

The man was dodging me, not very artfully. "I'm very upset about what happened."

"Yes, I'm sure you are. The Department of Corrections needs good people like you."

"What about the classroom? Can a guard just barge in like that?"

"This is a prison."

What could I say? I had no threat to deliver. If I said I was walking out and would never teach again, his response would have been indifference. After fifteen minutes of listening to him give me public relations, I left, defeated. Security was king.

I was powerless. Funny. That's the word convicts use to describe their situation – *powerless*.

Chapter 19
Ed
Brian's Interlude

I walked into the classroom one day in 1987 to find Brian gone. "Where's Grancorvitz?" I asked the men.

"Gone down to medium," Walter said. "They told him yesterday morning and by night he was gone. He's at Kettle Moraine."

Kettle Moraine. In Wisconsin the words *Kettle Moraine* do not mean a prison, but rather a beautiful part of the state with camel-hump hills and green valleys. Here the glaciers ended and deposited hills of rock rubble, thus the name *Moraine.* The *Kettles* were depressions formed by great blocks of glacial ice. The scenic Ice Age Trail, a National Park, winds through this country.

I visited Brian a few Sundays later at his new prison, a far different place than 'The Walls.' Kettle Moraine was built in the 1960's; Waupun prison was built in the 1860's. Brick cottages and low, modern looking buildings sat on the rolling countryside. A big fence surrounded the prison, but so did the Kettle Moraine. The air smelled of autumn in the woods.

*   *   *

A new Brian greeted me inside the visitors' center. Pants and a fashionable tee shirt replaced the prison-issue pants and jacket. A relaxed smile welcomed me instead of the usual serious demeanor.

He led me to the visiting room which looked like the recreation room in a college dorm. Though the same kind of family separations went on as at the maximum prison, here they seemed less intense.

As soon as we sat down, Brian rushed to tell me about his school. "Man, this is the greatest thing going. I've got English, History, Spanish, Physics and a course in Communications. I had my first quiz this week in History and I got an A+. And every day I get to interact with the PREP staff."

"PREP?"

"Post-Secondary Reentry Education Program. They're all employees of the University of Wisconsin. Not prison staff and they're all volunteers. I think a lot of them have a social conscience."

Enthusiasm filled him. I heard it in his voice and saw it in his eyes. Amazing. The young convict had turned into a student. I remembered that on the outside he hadn't finished elementary school. In prison he had earned his high school diploma and was now in college.

"I entered a writing competition," he said. "The *Milwaukee Journal* Young Writers."

I knew the contest. Writers in their twenties usually won with a clever piece from youth culture. My writer friends called it 'youth fluff.' How could Brian compete with that?

"What did you write about?"

"The inadequacies of the public defender program in Wisconsin."

"Tough subject. Good luck."

We talked about his new life. He had his own room with his own key. He felt like a college student, even though he knew the staff had a master key to his room. "And I'm thinking of becoming a legal researcher and a writer. I can't be a lawyer because of my conviction, but I can do terrific legal investigations."

He paused and laughed at himself. "See that – at Waupun all I was concerned with was staying alive. Now I'm thinking about the future."

"A job, huh?"

"And a woman."

"Whoa, Brian, what's with that?"

He laughed. "No, no one special. This place has just got me thinking about the future for the first time in six years."

I had noticed that, unlike other convicts, he did not crowd around any female speaker I brought into the prison for one of our workshop days. I never thought he was gay, but I wondered at his stand-offish attitude toward women.

"You look surprised," he said.

"Well, I..."

He cut me off. "I have always made a point of holding back. There are female guards and case workers and teachers. A guy in prison has to recognize that he is deprived of normal female contact. I had an art teacher back in Waupun. She was a good teacher and a courteous woman. It would have been easy to misinterpret her courtesy for romantic interest in me. Despite warning myself, I fell in love with her, but luckily I never said anything to her or did anything. Some guys end up in the hole for 'inappropriate behavior' toward female staff."

"What happened with you and the art teacher?"

"Nothing. She moved on to another job."

He paused, a sadder-but-wiser look in his eyes. "You just gotta keep your distance," he resumed. "Anyway, this college program makes you think normal thoughts, normal man thoughts. When I get out, I'll find the right woman."

He switched topics. "Hey, did I tell you, I won my case."

"Your case? Your trial?"

"No, for that case I've lost every appeal so far. The case I'm talking about is the riot. During the riot at Waupun, I was in the school building, but I didn't participate. The guards threw me in the hole anyway and kept me there without a hearing for a month. I took them to court, stating that they had acted illegally and I won. They gave me a cash settlement."

"Great. Who was your lawyer?"

"Me."

"You? You filed all those legal papers?"

"Yes."

My respect for this man grew. Not only did he have to know exactly what prison guards could and couldn't do, he also had to understand legal processes.

"How much cash did they give you?"

"Five hundred dollars. I'm going to buy a new electric typewriter with the money. I wonder if you would sell the old one for me."

Strange, but this stopped me. I traveled one hundred and fifty miles round trip to visit him in prison, but I hated the thought of peddling his used typewriter.

"Ahh, I'm not very good at that."

"I hate to ask you, but there's no one else."

I agreed reluctantly. I sold the typewriter without difficulty and transferred the money into his prison account.

* * *

The next week I got a letter from him. Contrary to my assumption about the young writers' contest, he had won second prize – seven hundred and fifty dollars. The *Milwaukee Journal* published his denunciation of the public defender system in Wisconsin, to the consternation of some in the legal profession.

I wrote to the warden asking him to let Brian go under guard to the awards presentation in Milwaukee. The warden refused. Brian asked one of his other teachers to go in his place, since I was running a writers' workshop at Waupun that day.

When I saw him next he told me he had won another award for writing. The American Humanist Society awarded him a cash prize of two hundred dollars for an essay he wrote on prison. "And you get fifty dollars for being my teacher."

I asked about his grades – all A+s. The man was on a roll.

At this time he told me something hard for me to understand. "I'm changing my name," he said.

"To what?"

"Adrian Lomax."

"You mean, that's what you want people to call you?"

"That's my legal name now. I've already done it – all the legal steps."

"I don't understand. Why?"

He shrugged, as if he didn't want to discuss it. He irritated me with his lack of explanation, but I guessed he wanted a new name to go along with his new identity. Brian Grancorvitz, the hippie biker who'd gotten in a bar fight and killed a man, was dead. Adrian Lomax, thinker, writer, legal scholar, had replaced him.

I started to call him Adrian, though many times I slipped back into "Brian." The prison staff knew he had changed his name legally and if they didn't use his new name, he would have them in court. They began referring to him as: "Adrian Lomax, also known as Brian Grancorvitz." When I went to see him, the officer in the gate house questioned me. "You want to see Adrian Lomax?"

"That's right."

"You mean Inmate Grancorvitz?"

"He changed his name."

"So Adrian Lomax is really Brian Grancorvitz, the criminal?"

I just said, "I'd like to see him, may I?"

Brian – Adrian – whatever his name, fit right in with his Kettle Moraine surroundings. Like the land itself, the *Kettle Moraine*, he emerged from the ice age. The tough kid on a motorcycle had disappeared, as had the young convict fighting to stop prison rapists. He hungered for knowledge, he maintained good grades and he studied the law, often helping his fellow inmates with their cases.

One of the things such a new man does is question the sacred convict code. This code demands that convicts never snitch on each other.

One Sunday I noticed that Adrian looked like he hadn't slept all night. I asked what was the matter.

"Yesterday another guy and I were out working in the garden. This other guy is shorter than me and he's got a bad eye – I think he's blind in that eye – and he's paralyzed on his left side. Anyway, all of a sudden, three black guys walked up and grabbed him. One held him and another hit him five or six times. When he fell to the ground, his assailant kicked him in the head."

"What did you do?"

"Maybe I should've done something, but I didn't know what the situation was. Then the black guys walked back into the housing unit."

"So you were the only witness?"

"Right. Even Ralph – that's the guy that got stomped – didn't know because they got his good eye right away. At least that's what he told the guards."

"Is he okay?"

"No, he's in the hospital. May lose his good eye."

"Damn. Did the guys get in trouble?"

"I was the only one that saw it. The guards questioned me and.....I didn't....I mean I have to live here, too. A snitch is the lowest form of life in all creation. It's the first law of the prison code. And if I said anything, what happened to Ralph, might happen to me."

"Tough spot to be in."

Adrian rubbed his forehead. I had never seen him so upset. "The damn thing is the asshole guy that beat him up is walking around acting smug, his bros crowding around him, telling him, 'You sure fucked that honkie good.' And Ralph may lose his eye."

I thought about this incident all week and I wondered what I would have done. I don't think I would have told the guards anything. If I were a convict, the guards would have been my enemy.

On Friday I got a letter from Adrian:

> *I couldn't sleep Sunday night either. I couldn't bear the thought of that guy getting away with it.*
>
> *What is this prison code anyway? It's a set of values perpetuated by violent inmates for the purpose of allowing them to brutalize with impunity.*
>
> *After a long night of thinking, they questioned me again on Monday. I decided to stand up for what I thought was right and 'take my reward from God,' to quote you, and everyone else be damned.*

I gave a statement telling what I saw. They took the guy to the hole and they're sending him to Portage, the new maximum security joint. Of course, as soon as they took him away, everyone knew that I 'snitched' on him, since I was the only one who saw the event other than the guy's confederates. So now I'm a pariah. No one will have anything to do with me. I can live with that, though.

Even though Adrian had a better life at Kettle Moraine, he didn't let up on his constant legal challenges to those in authority. He named Kettle Moraine's warden in suit after suit. As an example he challenged the warden's decision to make prisoners use the word *prison* on their return addresses instead of the more face-saving *Box #*. State law did not give wardens this authority. (It does now). When mail from his lawyer came to him opened, he sued the warden and the mail room clerks. He documented in writing case after case of staff incompetence and even staff corruption.

I grew nervous. I know bureaucrats – they go after those who challenge their authority. I worried that the prison staff would find a way to punish Adrian. They may have been losing all the battles to him, but they were perfectly capable of winning the war.

I went to Adrian with my concerns. "They're gonna get you."

"Maybe, but this is the way I have to live. I have to hold my head up. I'm a person with rights and responsibilities. I'm not an inmate."

"But why don't you just cool it while you're here, then when you get out, raise all the hell you want?"

"I'm trying to live in the present. Most guys in here would tell you that prison is just something you live through. They live in the future. 'You do your time,' they say. Well, no, not me. I'm living right now. This is what the counselors all tell us – live in the present."

"So write about this stuff now, but wait until you get out to publish it."

"The Department of Corrections has control of me for the rest of my life. If I'm released on parole, they can reprimand me or even lock me up again. Remember, I got a life sentence."

"So, play ball with them. Once you're out and you get some public attention with your writing, they're not going to throw you back in prison."

Adrian looked at me askance. Here was the great prison change agent cautioning one of his students to go along with the administration. Here was the man who wanted prisoners to stand up for their rights, to develop a sense of self worth, telling Adrian to shuffle his feet and say, 'Yes, sir, Mister Charlie.' Here was the strong lecturer against social injustice, the man who came to prison to get inmates to pick up their pens and fight. Yes, here he was urging his first draftee to put the pen down.

It was a key moment for me. I knew I was not a true revolutionary. The true reformer considers only the cause and not the blood to be shed. I feared what the system would do to Adrian and I didn't want somebody else suffering for my cause.

But Adrian ignored me and continued to challenge the system. Without knowing it, however, he had reached the brink of disaster. The ice age was about to return.

Chapter 20
Ed
Harmful Vapors

In the spring of 1988 Adrian told me about a situation in his residence cottage. A guy who liked to do glass paintings had moved into the room next to his. Strong fumes penetrated from the man's room into Adrian's.

"I was getting bad headaches and even feeling dizzy," Adrian said. "I asked to see the bottle of stain. It claimed that the vapors were harmful and should only be used with adequate ventilation."

"Doesn't seem to be something the guy should work with where people sleep," I said.

"Right. I asked the guy if we could make a deal that he would use the stain when I wasn't around. No luck. He said he'd use it when he wanted. So I filed a formal complaint. It went to the warden and he called me in to say that he was having second thoughts about the whole glass painting program. He said the glass could be made into weapons and he was going to ban the whole program."

"The guy next to you is going to be pissed."

"Yes. But he won't know it was me who complained."

As I drove home I thought about how I would have handled the problem. I think I would have cajoled the guy into giving up the stain. If that didn't work, I would have lined up the other men in the unit and tried some power politics. I would not have filed an official complaint.

But this was Adrian. For a convicted criminal, he had a huge respect for the law and for official procedures. He probably wasn't the easiest guy in the world to live next door to, but he was certainly within his rights.

On March 10th the guys who did glass painting went to pick up their supplies. Staff informed them that the program was cancelled. The glass painters complained that the prison was cutting off a legitimate form of art. As Adrian told me later, they next went to Ms. X, the Inmate Complaint Investigator, who listened to their protest. Even though it was against her professional ethics, she named Adrian as the complainant.

Of course, there were threats against Adrian.

That evening the guards came to his room and told him they were locking him up in the segregation unit for his own protection. The next day they put him in a van and transferred him to the Oshkosh Correctional Institution, another medium security prison. 'For your own protection,' the paperwork said.

On March 12th Adrian called me on the phone, collect. He was devastated. He had been yanked out of his classes in the middle of the semester, despite his 4.0 grade average. Oshkosh did not have a college program.

Adrian wrote a long letter to the warden of Kettle Moraine, almost begging to return there. He called me again, pleading for help. "Adrian," I said, "I'll try, but there's little I can do."

This incident stirred me deeply. Here was a man on the way to reform, studying hard, following the rules. The prison system was punishing the victim, not the perpetrators of the threats.

If only I could have talked in person to the authorities, I would have said, "All right, he's a pain in the ass, but he's trying to play by our rules. Show him that our rules are fair and he'll calm down. Work with him, don't punish him."

I organized a letter writing campaign among my writing friends in Milwaukee. I explained the situation to all those writers and poets who had gone to Waupun. All of them wrote angry letters to their state legislators.

Nothing helped. I learned how powerful the system was. Adrian had to start over at Oshkosh, on the waiting list for a cell by himself. The staff assigned him to sweeping floors on his cell block.

Within a few weeks Adrian filed a law suit claiming that the warden of Kettle Moraine had moved him illegally. It took over two years, but he won the case, the judge declaring that the administrators of Kettle Moraine had not shown sufficient cause as to why they had moved him. That victory, however, did not get him back to Kettle Moraine and even if it had, the government had eliminated the college program by then.

At Oshkosh Adrian settled into routine. He swept floors, translated official documents into Spanish for new inmates and – filed lawsuits against prison officials. He created a job for himself helping Spanish-speaking prisoners learn English. He wrote an article suggesting that TV be banned from prisons, claiming that wardens used TV as a control mechanism, a method of drugging people into passivity. After this article his fellow convicts hurled insults and threats at him. Wardens also objected: "TV is good for inmates. It gives them something to do."

After three years he broke a rule – he threatened someone, as he himself had been threatened. He was sent to a new super max prison for several months and then he was returned to his former maximum security prison, Waupun. He wrote to me from there. "I never thought I'd say this, but I was glad to get back to Waupun. The super-max was hell, lock down twenty-three hours a day."

At Waupun Barbara (not her real name), the editor of a small, left-wing newspaper, asked Adrian to write a regular column called *Lockdown*. Though she had never met him, she liked the articles he had been sending her.

An inmate writes about the atrocities of prison. The horns blow and a little chunk of the wall around Jericho crumbles. This was my dream. Adrian had taken the first step.

In one of his columns, he wrote of a man who cried one night for medical help. The guards delayed calling the medics and the man died a few hours later of a brain aneurysm. In another column called *The Gender Gap*, Adrian exposed the conditions of the women's prison in Wisconsin, claiming women were treated more harshly than men. One article mocked prison officials for the dress code they imposed: "Inmates must have their shoes tied, their belts buckled and their shirts buttoned. You are not allowed to wear sunglasses or baseball caps inside."

Adrian sweated over every column, checking his research, struggling to get every word right.

In early January 1993, I opened a hand-written letter from him, unusual because he always typed his letters. Why didn't he have access to his typewriter?

The letter was written on Christmas Day, 1992. Adrian told me once that Christmas was a very hard time for him in prison. I always made sure to write to him in advance. In his letter he said that this was the worst Christmas ever.

He explained that on November 2nd, the day before Clinton was elected, he was finally moved back down to a medium security prison. I smiled. The man measured his life by political events just as I did. In many ways we were very similar. He went on to say that he now felt free to write about a terrible guard he had observed at Waupun Prison. "She is by far the worst prison employee I've ever observed. And that's saying something. She would routinely scream at prisoners right in their faces. Daily she would send men to the hole for minor offenses, such as wearing their stocking caps in the chow line. Never mind that the line extended outside where the wind drove the chill factor below zero. And complaining about prison food. Can you imagine that?"

No, I really couldn't. Men in institutions always complain about the food. We were experts at it in the seminary.

I myself have seen this kind of female guard. They adopt the worst attitudes of the worst males. They are bullies and they dehumanize every inmate they encounter. Thank God they are only a small minority of female guards.

Adrian wrote a column about this guard, which he included in the letter. The column used the guard's real name and detailed how she acted with inmates. Adrian quoted sociologist Kelsey Kauffman, who had developed a typology of guards. Kaufman claimed that most guards avoided being a 'hard ass,' because it was an invitation for a shiv in the back.

Where could I have found a better person than Adrian? Here, right in front of me, in this column, was the thing I had hoped for –

a well written, thoroughly researched criticism of a system I considered uncivilized.

Adrian had highlighted a key section of the article:

Assuming that xxx does not find another line of work or radically change her ways, she will one day be killed by a prisoner.

The same day the column hit the streets, Adrian was thrown into the hole. That was November 18th. Two days before Christmas he was charged with *Lying About Staff, Disrespect, Threats, and Battery*. He was sentenced to 368 days in the hole, the harshest disciplinary sentence allowed by state law.

I didn't see the lies, the threats or the battery in the column. Disrespect, maybe, but that wasn't against the law. No crime in prison would seem to be more important than assaulting a guard. Yet the penalty for that crime was 180 days. The penalty for writing was 368 days.

I wanted to help, but what could I do? I wrote letters and tried unsuccessfully to get newspaper publicity. Only a few writers' magazines, concerned about freedom of speech, published my articles. Adrian himself filed a lawsuit claiming his first amendment rights had been curtailed, but the Wisconsin Court of Appeals ruled against him.

Again I felt a sense of total frustration. A citizen could have zero impact on the prison system.

Instead of putting his pen away, Adrian wrote more columns critical of the prison system for the magazine. Two columns especially angered his keepers. In one he talked of a security director who refused to allow an injured prisoner to receive medical attention. In another he told of a prisoner whose threats of suicide were ignored. The authorities refused to transfer the man to a special control cell, with disastrous results.

The State of Wisconsin increased Adrian's confinement in the hole by one year for each of these columns. He now faced three years in the hole.

After serving almost a year in segregation, the prison authorities relented to the extend of moving him back to a maximum security prison in Green Bay, Wisconsin, where he was allowed to return to the general population.

Despite this experience in solitary, he continued to write his column. The criticism continued, unabated. He was also asked to do a short segment on radio every week about prison.

I heard that a guy I knew from my first class in prison had gotten out early for 'good behavior.' His crime was similar to Adrian's and Adrian was nowhere near getting out. "Why can't you just cool it?" I asked him during one of our phone calls.

"Because it's who I am," he answered.

That was a good answer. Adrian always tried to be true to himself. Maybe that was the way he survived prison.

His next letter admitted that he wrestled with the issue of 'cooling it.' "But," he wrote, "I've rarely felt more sure about prison issues than I do now. And that's because it seems like my efforts are paying off."

He went on to express the hope that the prison system might get tired of him after seventeen years.

Fat chance. Instead they began to play dirty. Barbara, the editor of the small magazine that printed Adrian's column, told me later what happened. A spokesperson for the Department of Corrections contacted her.

"Do you know Adrian Lomax?" the spokesperson asked Barbara.

"Only through correspondence."

"Do you believe the reports he sends you?"

"He always backs up his claims with documentation. Listen, if the Department of Corrections objects to any of the columns Lomax writes, I'd be happy to publish your response."

The spokesperson refused. Instead he offered to send her documents 'that would give her a new perspective on Adrian Lomax.'

Barbara was surprised by what she got in the mail – Adrian Lomax's confidential disciplinary documents. After examining them, she knew they were only minor violations.

My daughter and I visited Adrian at Green Bay. The prison, a very old one, housed mainly young men. Adrian by this time was in his mid-thirties. "What I enjoy doing here is teaching other men," he said. "I get into discussions with other guys and I help them to think, really think, about things."

As always, his demeanor was controlled and disciplined. I, on the other hand, came near to losing it over the way the visiting room guard treated us. She barked out the rules to every group of visitors and indicated her loathing for us in her tone, gestures and words. "Move along now. The State of Wisconsin is giving you the privilege of visiting these lawbreakers. That is, if you can manage to follow our rules."

Only my daughter's cautions kept me from speaking out.

If I couldn't handle this for two hours, how had Adrian managed seventeen years?

During our visit Adrian said nothing about himself – he spoke only about politics and the abuse of authority by prison officials.

Worried that our visit would soon be over, I asked him directly how his life was going.

He shrugged. "I'm never bored. There is always some case to work on. You know, since I've been in prison I've filed close to one hundred law suits. I'm what's known as a serial litigator."

As we left the prison my daughter commented on how he never talked about his own feelings.

A few weeks after our visit, his editor, Barbara, came to see him for the first time in prison. He could not have anticipated what would happen next.

Chapter 21
Ed
The Ultimate Revolution

It's important to pause for a moment and see what kind of a writer Adrian had become.

My days of being his mentor had passed. He had firmly established himself as a writer of consequence. News magazines interviewed him and sought his opinion about prison issues. I would often see his name on the news or in the paper. His article on banning TV in prison got a lot of attention, some of it very negative from prisoners themselves.

Like an elderly parent, all I could do now was sit home and worry.

When people in Wisconsin claimed that prisoners had things too easy and should be put on chain gangs, he wrote an article called *Notes from the Country Club.*

> One morning last fall, I awoke to the sound of water pouring on the floor of my cell at the Green Bay Correctional Institution. The toilet was overflowing, a torrent of effluent gushing out. I leapt from my cot and scurried to gather my belongings from the cell floor, throwing them onto the bed. With no furniture in the cell except the cot and a very small table, I had no place other than the floor to store books, clothing, papers etc.

Water continued to flow from the toilet. And, of course, it wasn't just water. Urine, feces and toilet paper were all part of the mix. There I stood at 6:30 in the morning, barefoot, sloshing in shit-water an inch deep, unable to escape the confines of my locked cell. Prisoners up and down the tier suffered the same fate.

Mentors are proud when their students do well. Despite my worry for his future, I rejoiced in Adrian's writing skills and in his disclosure of the horrors of prison.

Later in the same article, he said:

When I first entered Waupun seventeen years ago, I was young, alone, slight of build — a prime candidate for all the depredations of the sexual jungle swirling in a maximum security prison filled with men who hadn't touched a woman in years. I suffered a baptism-by-fire unimaginable in the sheltered lives of those who now seek to put me on a chain gang. I refuse to accept anyone's assertion that I haven't been punished for my crime.

I felt like a good mechanic who trains an apprentice. The young man learns automotive skills, but of more importance, he cares deeply about cars, just as his teacher did. In a similar fashion Adrian was a good writer, but more, he wanted to do something about the prison system.

The roles of teacher and student were often reversed, however. Adrian explained things about prison no book ever could.

Who are you? – that's the key question Adrian taught me to ask about any convict. Really, it's the question to ask about any person. In prison, there's a shortcut to discovering the answer to the question. Since convicts spend fourteen hours out of every twenty-four in their cells on weekdays and twenty on weekends, find out what they do in their cell.

Adrian listed the activities:

- Watch the soaps. Adrian expressed amazement at the number of hardened criminals who could tell you the intricate secrets of daytime drama.
- Sleep and daydream.
- Get stoned on readily-available drugs.
- Engage in cell-to-cell discussion of romantic-dashing-outlaw-type adventures on the street.
- Play endless games of chess, yelling the moves from cell to cell.
- Enter the world of gang intrigue and carry out complicated plots to gain power in the prison.

Is this what the public is paying for? Criminals watching the soaps?

What did Adrian do in his cell? Study, read, write and think. "When I'm studying philosophy," he says, "wrestling with the concepts of logical positivism and dialectical materialism, the concrete walls fade away and the steel bars cease to exist. In terms of my ability to learn, to grow, and to create, I have defeated my imprisonment. In the world of ideas, I roam as freely as any person on the outside."

But Adrian was blocked in the most vital area of human interaction – friendship. He felt that convicts had to keep a tough exterior to avoid being emotionally injured in this harsh social environment. Further, the attempts by police and prison authorities to get inmates to 'rat' on each other destroyed the bonds of trust. What society ended up with was the exact opposite of what the public wanted – an institution where people learned to be anti-social.

Granted that Adrian wasn't always the easiest guy to get to know, everyone needs friends. "I'll get by with a little help from my friends," The Beatles say – and we all know that to be true. Prison destroys friendship.

We have all heard of great prison friendships, such as those portrayed in *Shawshank Redemption*, but most convicts would say they are the exception. Adrian's experience confirms my own amazement that guys in prison do not even know each other's names.

But the wound of prison goes deeper. Adrian developed a kind of law – the longer a man spends in prison, the weaker the bonds become with the outside. In his own case he told me that during the first few months of his imprisonment family and friends visited and wrote often. Now he hardly hears from them. He uses years, not months, to count the time between visits from some family members. And women – Adrian is eloquent here:

> The result of all this is that I'm a lonely person. Desperately lonely. The emptiness in my life rips at my psyche, so much so that I grasp at straws to fulfill my emotional needs.

> Just the other day I received a letter from a woman I dated before becoming incarcerated, from whom I hadn't heard in several years. This woman kept in touch with me for the first year or so of my imprisonment, then dropped out of sight. I later learned she'd gotten married. In her letter she said things had changed in her life. I know this means she and her husband have split up, especially since she also said she's now living with her sister. She indicated she would like to come and see me.

> I wrote back to the woman and told her I'd be happy to see her. I submitted to the institution the forms necessary to have her name added to my approved visitors list. I know precisely what will happen. She will visit me a few times and keep in touch for a few weeks, maybe months. As soon as she develops a new relationship with a man on the outside or reunites with her husband, she will discard me like a worn-out shoe. I know this

because I've experienced the same process with several other women over the years.

The only use this woman has for me is as a purely temporary means of fulfilling the emptiness in her own life in the absence of a 'real' relationship. The woman is actually insulting me, but I will welcome the insult and be happy for it. I will be thankful for whatever miserable crumbs of affection she throws my way, because those crumbs will be like cool, clear water to a man dying of thirst. I will rejoice in the insult and pray for more.

I am a person existing in grace and harmony on one level, and at the brink of disaster on another. Intellectually I am healthy and strong, ever striving for greater understanding, and continually expanding my horizons. Emotionally I am a critical patient, weak and faltering, dying of starvation. Prison is tearing me apart.

Eloquent, intellectual, observant, sometimes wordy, stand-offish, Adrian was writing exactly the kind of thing I hoped he would write.

One of the people who visited him was his natural father, whom he hadn't seen in several years. When the talk drifted to politics, Adrian's father told him he listened to Rush Limbaugh. "Criminals are ruining the country," his father said. "I carry a gun now, wherever I go. Course I couldn't bring it in here, but the damn criminals are out of control. And these guys on death row, they should just execute them. No more appeals, goddammit."

Adrian was too much of a gentleman to remind his father that if such policies had been in effect in Wisconsin in 1980, his father would be visiting his grave.

* * *

In late 1995 Adrian was transferred to a medium security prison, Fox Lake. I wrote to him and argued for him to tone down his criticism, now that he was in medium security and on the way out. Ed, who had entered prison to blow the horn of freedom, now stroked the quiet harp of submission.

Early in 1996 something happened. Adrian wrote and said, "Finally, I'm going to follow your advice. There's a reason – I have a woman in my life now."

The woman was the editor of the small, left-wing magazine that had printed his work for four years. Adrian told me about her and I later met her.

Barbara, the daughter of a college professor, came to Madison, Wisconsin in 1981 to go to university. She liked the political activism of the city and she stayed on after her degree. She was arrested several times for her protests against nuclear weapons. A thin, wiry woman, I learned a lot about her once when we visited Adrian together. Thirty or so people waited for their visits in the prison gatehouse. Barbara knew almost all the women whose husbands were in prison. She talked to each one, giving a phone number to one for a social agency, telling another of her legal rights and just being a friend to a third. Barbara knew that a prison sentence often affects the wife worse than it does the husband. The wife is left to care for the children without income and without support.

I liked her and I admired her.

Adrian told me that his relationship with Barbara had changed his outlook. "I want to get out of prison in a way I never felt before."

What about his writing? "I pledged to Barbara that I would not again allow myself to be returned to maximum security. I have a whole different set of priorities at this time. When I get an idea now to write a controversial article, my idea gets filtered through a set of priorities that tell me I've put in enough time and that being on the outside with Barbara is more important than writing the article."

In his letters Adrian always commented on the role of the US in the world or he complained about the Republicans in Wisconsin, but he never opened up to say anything about his personal life. In this one letter, however, the real Adrian stood up and said clearly, "I love a woman."

I wrote back and said his experience resembled mine. I used to get up on Sunday mornings and preach about love. But until I left the priesthood and met Kathy, I didn't know what the hell I was talking about.

He wrote again:

> ... As Barbara and I got to know each other, and she became interested in me romantically, she had to peel away layers of emotional deadness on my part in order to get me to open up. It was an interesting process, and we talk about it quite a bit. She visited me at Green Bay for more than a year before we first kissed, if you can imagine that. But it feels very good to be emotionally alive after all those years.

Letters from Adrian still contained lengthy sections dealing with political issues, but a section always began: 'Barbara,' or 'Barbara and I..' Together they weathered an attempt by the State to move Adrian to a for-profit prison in Tennessee. Together they survived a false accusation of violence by another inmate. They were *together* for six years, if you can call *together* the visiting room of the prison.

Adrian struggled to maintain his identity throughout his sentence. By breaking the prison code and by denouncing things like TV, he chose the role of a loner. He has always been a man of principle, but those principles have changed over the years. When Barbara came into his life, he understood the priority of love and adapted accordingly. He is not different than those Catholic priests like myself who have found love to be a stronger force than doctrine.

Revolution? Reform? Those who wish to change systems must give everything, but neither Adrian nor I have been willing to do that. Viewed in another way, however, Adrian has freed his heart from the control of the prison masters. He has performed an act of revolutionary courage – he has fallen in love.

* * *

Early in the new millennium Adrian finally made it to minimum security. While there he worked factory jobs, trying to support himself for the first time in his adult life. He and Barbara broke up during these years, but Adrian didn't change his new ways. He wanted freedom badly. In early August of 2004 he was released from prison after twenty-four years and now lives in Madison, Wisconsin. Even though the romance did not last, I believe it changed Adrian. Once a man has fallen in love, he is changed forever.

As for me, slow to learn, inclined to repeat my mistakes, I next encountered the Canadian prison system.

Book Four

Chapter 22
Mike
How Do You Say *Help* in French?

I went from Spanish-speaking thugs who wanted to watch me squirm in discomfort, to French-speaking convicts who, like their Mexican counterparts, wanted to watch me squirm in discomfort.

The trip from the Mexican prison to the Montreal prison was like a roller coaster ride from obscurity. From hell back up about a thousand lifetimes to earth. After saying goodbye and exchanging phone numbers with whoever was awake, after a quick decision on what clothes to take, the Mexican authorities whisked me off to Mexico City with the brute force of a random kidnapping.

Kidnapped from a dead sleep, I was unable to say goodbye to Jaime and his family, Maria and Roger. Everything felt rushed. I'd spent two years sharing space with those men, their families, and their children. My sudden departure felt slimy and almost abusive. They had helped me change the way I thought about people and life in general. I owed my Mexican friends more than just a quick handshake and a hug goodbye.

Even on the plane ride to Mexico City, the turbulent voyage across the huge country in a plane that wasn't fit for chicken feed transport, I thought about how quickly the years had passed. It felt like only moments ago I was sitting in the courtroom begging for my release. I thought about Nomi and her sudden exit from my life, beyond her control and mine. My presence was a flash in time to most of the people I'd met there, but to me, their existence left an imprint in my mind and in my heart. I'd never forget the time I spent in that prison.

Now I was on to bigger and better things. When we arrived in Mexico City, the pilot, who I might add was completely out of his mind, told me he wanted to do me the biggest favor he could do for anyone who rode in his plane. He introduced his move as a "cowboy" and it consisted of flying the plane up high into the air, then dive bombing for at least ten seconds before pulling it up again and soaring back higher. When he'd had enough, he glanced back at me with a smile.

"You're the first one not to throw up," he said. "Congratulations! You're a cowboy!"

I didn't feel much like a cowboy. I turned to look out the window, to take my mind off of my spinning head and stomach. It was still dark outside. The middle of the night lasted a long time. As we flew over the mountain range that surrounded Mexico City, I saw the most beautiful spectacle possible from the air. The lights of Mexico City at night are unlike anything else. Flying into a big city like Vegas or New York is impressive, but Mexico City is the biggest city in the world, taking twenty minutes to cover it by air. Our crazy pilot flew low to the ground so that we'd see everything. The sights gave me a taste of freedom I hadn't had in a long time. But I was far from being free. I still had eight years to kill.

Three Mexican police officers in a large black SUV met us on the ground. They greeted me with handshakes then shoved me into the back seat of the truck. There I met another Canadian, Lucas, who looked equally as happy to see me as I was him.

"Where are you headed?" he asked me.

"Anywhere but here," I told him. "I'm ready to go home."

The three officers crammed in the truck with us, talking loosely about Mexico and the drugs in the city. Lucas, for some reason, couldn't speak Spanish. He'd been in for nearly two years and hadn't bothered to pick up the language. He said that he had an interpreter the entire time, so speaking to the other cons wasn't necessary. What lessons did he possibly learn from his experience being unable to speak to the people? Lucas hadn't gone through the radical experience that I had. That made me feel good. I was on my way to a better life because I survived any way possible.

A call rattled the police radio, and the cowboy cops in the truck responded with tugs on their seatbelts. The driver yelled something to the back seat that I didn't understand. Mexico City had its own language – city street slang with no chance of sinking into my head The *chilangrians*, people from Mexico City, spoke in a tongue sometimes misunderstood by their own countrymen.

The officer to my right reached behind and snapped a seatbelt across my waist. I watched as the driver placed a red siren on the roof through his window. Without warning, the truck came to a screeching halt, fishtailed around a corner, lights flashing and siren blaring, then raced off into the night, down busy streets, through traffic lights and around stopped vehicles. The passenger up front slipped in a CD and instantly loud dance music erupted from the truck speakers. I knew the group - *The Chemical Brothers*. The music fit the moment, like these cops had been through this a hundred times.

The drive must have been more than ten minutes. My first taste of freedom after two years and I'm already in a high-speed chase, on the way to who knows where, to stop who knows who from doing who knows what. When the truck finally stopped, it was in front of a nightclub. Lights from the club mixed with the truck's red and blues. Scantly dressed Mexican *senoritas* with long brown legs and hiked up skirts cleared a path so the cops could get to a large group of men fighting near the front doors of the establishment. Shirts were ripped off and thrown to the ground. Women screamed and cried out names of men who I couldn't see. I absorbed every second of the melee, amazed by a simple bar brawl as if I'd never seen such a catastrophe in my life, never mind been on the safe side of one. The officers bounced from the truck, guns drawn, instantly beating on the first people they encountered. As if on cue, the Chemical Brothers quit, bringing the sounds of the fight live in stereo.

After ten minutes of crowd settling, the cops got back into the truck, breathing hard and smiling as if they'd just won some sort of championship trophy. They holstered their weapons and turned to the Canadians in the back seat. The driver's eyes were wide with adrenaline. He winked at me.

"Who likes hot dogs?" he asked in Spanish.

He took us to a nearby hot dog vender just around the corner and bought both Lucas and I whatever we wanted. High-speed pursuit, scantly dressed women screaming for their young lives, blood-stained t-shirts and hot dogs. I was beginning to feel a lot closer to home.

* * *

I jolted awake just as the wheels of the plane touched the Toronto tarmac. The two guards on either side of me seemed happier to be home than me, and I was ecstatic. As I looked outside, a warm sense of nostalgia came over me. It was late January in Ontario. Snowstorm.

As miserable as the trek through the airport was, I managed it like I'd made the trip before. Lucas cursed at the Canadian officers for actually making us walk through the terminal, in front of hundreds, if not thousands, of people in handcuffs, a shirt hung over the chain hiding what everyone in the terminal knew was government issue jewelry. I didn't care who looked at me or who whispered to their friends as I passed. They had no idea how good it felt to have my feet on Canadian linoleum.

From Toronto we flew to Montreal, and from there, Lucas and I were sent to a reception center that looked like it fell from the sky and landed in the middle of nowhere, and it was my first taste of real prison in my own country.

As soon as we entered the reception area, we were treated like the biggest pieces of crap I'd ever had the pleasure of being reminded of. Lucas and I were stripped searched together and left in a cell in just our underwear, freezing and hungry, waiting for someone to come and book us in. Neither of us spoke French, and they knew that, so they addressed us in *francios* and scoffed when we couldn't respond.

I was finally moved from the cell and taken to an interview room. The guard left me in the company of an obese and balding correctional officer who had *I hate convicts* written all over his face. He didn't even speak to me, simply nodding to the chair in front of his desk as he wrote in a file.

Without looking up, he muttered a phrase he'd said a hundred times. "Are you affiliated with any motorcycle gangs?"

I smirked. "No. But I wore a pair of chaps once."

His expression said that he wanted to kill me. The province of Quebec had a little problem with their gangs, and I wasn't taking it seriously. One out of every two criminals charged in the province had some sort of affiliation with a motorcycle gang. Whether it was the Hell's Angels or the Rock Machine, if you did crime there, you were linked with them in some way.

He held his composure well for a red faced man. "Answer my question."

I told him that I was affiliated with just myself and wanted to stay that way. He asked me if I had any problems with anyone in the prison, and I felt like saying *him*, but shook my head otherwise. After our quick interview, he told me that I would be going to Unit A until 'further notice'. Further notice was until they beat us or were jumped into a French motorcycle gang. Either way, I had a feeling I wasn't going to leave this place without having to prove my sorry ass again.

* * *

If you've ever gone for a STD examination, it's nothing to really brag about. Chances are, we've all known someone who's had to go for a check up after engaging in foul play with a less than reputable partner. What I didn't know about these inspections was the severe bout of humiliation and demoralization that followed.

As soon as I sat down in the health care chair, a security door at the other side of the room buzzed open. I expected to see a white coat doctor or nurse walk out with a clipboard in hand and my file ready. Instead, out danced a thin man in a fluorescent orange vest, like those worn by a school crosswalk guard, and on the vest, about fifty different buttons all with various sayings or cartoon faces, like his body was in the future but his spirit was puking for mercy at Woodstock. Now when I say dance, I mean he basically did the *sha-na-na* right into the waiting area. His gay aura carried him across the floor, bubbling with a happiness that completely opposed the reception guard. And he wasn't carrying a clipboard. Instead, he had with him two thin vials, and I had a sinking feeling one of them was for me and some portion of my precious bodily fluid.

"Okay," his voice twang like the bottom string on a guitar. "Who's first?"

I didn't want to be the one sitting here and dreading my examination, looking at Lucas's pale face and wondering just how much saliva and urine they drained from him. I stood before Lucas could and followed the nurse into a side washroom. He closed the door behind us and the dreaded awkward silence ensued.

"My name's Pierre," he said and offered me his hand. "Where are you from?"

"Victoria," my eyes on the vial. "I was just in a Mexican jail."

His squeal sounded like my mom winning two dollars on a scratch and win – a little too happy for no real reason. The room shrunk about a square foot.

"I love Mexico," he said. "Went there last year with my boyfriend."

The room shrunk again.

Pierre sighed and sat down on the toilet. He gave me a stern look that meant business. "Now, this may be awkward, but it's mandatory."

He placed the vial on the counter and uncorked it. From a pocket in his shiny vest he produced a single cotton swab on a stick packaged in sanitary wrap. I watched every movement praying that this wasn't what I thought it was.

"Whenever someone comes here from another country, we have to do full tests," he smiled up at me. "Never know what sort of souvenirs you could bring back."

Awkward. Humiliating. Devastating. What more was there to say? I'd never submitted to a STD test in my life, and wasn't about to either. I struggled with formulating a good lie that might get me out of this pickle, but Pierre had heard them all, presumably, and had an answer for everything. After a futile attempt at saving my manhood from getting manhandled, I caved.

After a short debriefing from Pierre of the upcoming process, I debriefed myself by pulling down my pants and underwear. Exposed and unfortunately not in charge of the situation, my face reddened and all traces of dignity escaped from my body. With a watchful eye on Pierre, highly suspicious of his medical practice, I surrendered my manhood to science and allowed the nurse to perform the prickly procedure.

He took my penis in his ambitious little hand, not as a man would in a moment of private intimacy, but like in the moment a man realizes he shouldn't have placed his piece into a meat grinder. It seemed that he wanted to get this situation over with as much as I did, so he moved at a professional pace, holding tight with one hand, and wrestling the sanitized cotton swab out of its package with the other.

The longer the session took, the more nervous I became. When I get antsy, I fidget, I bounce on my toes, I shuffle from side to side, something you should never do when a male nurse has your Johnson in his hand. What could I have possibly picked up from Mexico that I was willing to hide from these people? Who wouldn't disclose a STD to a doctor? Maybe someone who'd been through this humiliating procedure one too many times in their lives and would rather live with the urine of fire than offer himself up to Pierre?

"I'm going in," he said, trying to make light of the moment.

The fidgeting began, and with that nervousness came a bout of shrinkage. I watched my penis move in his hand, retreating back from where it protruded. Pierre caught the motion and cut his eyes up at me, still holding and waiting for the squirming to subside. I tried to breathe normally, like a cowboy would, unfazed by up and down rides in the plane, but the fact of the matter was this situation was not normal and no self-respecting cowboy would let another person lasso his pony in this matter. First day back in my own country, my home in native land, my saving grace, and I was stuck in a washroom with a man named Pierre and my pants down to my knees praying to god that this never got out to anyone I knew.

Pierre inserted the swab.

Then he made the noise. "Duip!" Sounded like a cartoon noise, like something drooping than picking back up. My life was officially over. I could never look at myself in the mirror again.

With a wide smile, Pierre stood and placed the swab into the vial. My pants flew back up and I reached for the door, unaware that a burning sensation was ripping a hole through the side of my penis, and that was only because my burning desire to get to the safety of a French jail cell superceded any other emotion or feeling.

"Now, that wasn't too bad, was it?" he said.

Maybe for him it wasn't.

"One last thing," he said and reached into his never-ending orange vest of humiliation. "I'm going to need a stool sample."

"You've got to be kidding." I said.

He handed me a small plastic jar. "Nope. Please fill it if you can."

"Fill it," I joked. "I've been eating Mexican food for the past two years. Filling it is not my problem."

He scrunched his face in disgust and left me alone. Him, disgusted with me. He had a lot of nerve.

* * *

When a guard escorted Lucas and me into Unit A, we were immediately greeted by a short stocky man with too many tattoos on his body and not enough hair on his head. He pranced up to Lucas and I, the scowl on his face told me he wasn't easily impressed by new fish.

"Where you guys from?" he barked. The guard left us to die in the hall.

"Mexican transfers," I looked at Lucas. He was still rattled from his interaction with Pierre. "Just got off the plane."

Baldy eyed both of us down like we were both suspects in the theft of his missing mane. From out of a door behind him walked a strikingly similar looking man a few inches taller, but not as much beef. They spoke in rapid French, casting curiosity at us, before the second man, who had only a few more shreds of hair on his dome, went back into the room.

"My friend says you look like cops," he folded his arms across his chest. "Are you with the Hell's Angels?"

I said, "I can't even ride a motorbike. But I did wear a pair of chaps once.

He gave me the same nasty smirk as the reception cop. These people did not take lightly to western humor.

He jerked a thumb behind him towards a large row of Plexiglas windows. "That's our room," he said matter-of-factly. "French speaking only."

"Okay," I said. In my head I mouthed the word *psycho.*

He pointed behind Lucas, towards a second room, smaller, and no windows.

"That's the English and other room," the words erupted like vomit. "You watch TV in there."

"Other," I asked. "What's other?"

He didn't answer me, and just as gently as he arrived, walked back through the door he came from. *Fucking weird.* From that moment on, Lucas and I decided to call him Shrimpy.

My cell left me wishing I were back fighting the cockroaches for control of the dark. The cell was a double bunk, with one window stretching from floor to ceiling, no possibility of opening without the aid of a hammer or a hard head, and the room came complete with a French guy who couldn't speak a word of English. Lucas ended up across the hall, alone, which I'm sure he was thankful for.

The only words I knew in French were what I learned in grade school. And the French back then is nothing that a man should even attempt to speak while in Quebec, unless he liked to be beaten in the streets by random strangers. I said hello – *bonjour,* introduced myself – *je m'appelle Michelle,* and hopped on the top bunk.

That began what ended up being one of the longest nights of my life. My roommate, who I just called Fatso because of his inability to fit his baby carriage into the standard government issue T-shirt, spoke to me in French half the night thinking that I could understand him only because I had nodded in agreement one too many times.

On the top bunk, I managed to slip into a semi-coma later that night, with visions of short, bald, tattooed Frenchmen with orange vests filled with cotton swabs singing mariachi around an Air Canada 737. The day seemed like an eternity of procedures.

In the morning, my first morning back in Canada, I went through somewhat of an identity crisis before I had a chance to eat. I rolled over to peek out the window. The evening's snow rested on the yard. As soon as I swung my feet over the edge of the bed, Fatso was in my ear again, telling me his life story at 7:30 in the morning. I complimented him on his food stain over his right nipple and attempted to communicate with him the only way I knew how.

I tried Spanish. "Como se llama?"

His face scrunched. He was perplexed.

Fatso laughed and spoke quickly to me in French, pissing me off immediately. We were in Canada. How could he not speak English?

He held a finger against his chest and spoke.

I sighed and got dressed. He continued to talk. If I didn't know better, I'd have thought Fatso was a raging lunatic.

* * *

"I fucking hate French people more than any other person in the world. And do you know why?"

I sat on the milk carton, which was the chair in the other TV room, watching the black and white television with the 1970s dial channel changer, listening to a brash Brooklyn street thug chirp at me about his bitter feelings towards the French. I quickly realized that Tony was the 'significant other' that Shrimpy spoke so romantically about.

I was scared to ask. "Why are you so angry?"

When Tony spoke, he had one of those authentic New York accents that I'd only heard on TV before that moment. The kind that made your heart shudder with a slight twinge of fear for your life. His eyebrows dug into the bridge of his nose and his turned up lip quivered as he told me his deepest darkest non secret. Everyone could hear him, he made sure of it. That's what Tony was the best at.

"Because dees humps play fuckin volleybahl every time we go to da gym." He turned the channel without thinking. The knob clunked around the dial, reminding me of the days when watching TV was a chore. "Every day, same time, we go to da gym. I wanna play basketbahl, but dees losers always gotta outdo me and put up the volleybahl net before I can get a show ah hands."

"Why don't you get a consensus before you go down?" I asked. *Clunk, clunk, clunk.*

He looked at me as though I'd just insulted his mother. "Consensus? Ain't that when a girl lets you fuck her?"

"I think that's called consensual."

He sneered. "Wha-ever. All I know is dat we bedder play some fuckin hoops one of dees days..." He stood and directed his booming voice across the unit to the French side. "Or we gonna have ta start crackin some skulls!"

He sat with that well rehearsed scowl intact, turned back to the TV, clunked the dial until landing on the *Price is Right*. Finally his face showed a semblance of a smile.

"Hey, I like dis old fuck."

Later that morning, I met the rest of the others. The group consisted of two Mexicans, one Chinese and one Japanese guy who couldn't speak a word of English or French, but he seemed to communicate well with Tony, laughing at everything he said even if it was a direct insult to his race. The others were a tight group of castaways united by necessity rather than preference. The French side of the Unit wanted nothing to do with them, exiling them for being different. Most of the time, the others didn't understand each other, but that seemed to make the room comfortable. After all, if they understood half of the insults Tony hurled at them, there might have been a third TV room for Tony alone.

After two hours of sitting around listening to Tony try to teach the Japanese guy as many swear words as possible, laughing to himself every time he came close to actually pronouncing the word, I left the room to find a quiet spot to sit and think. The others reminded me of my first days in Mexico when I knew no one and the guys taught me how to cuss before anything else. I lay on my bed, staring at the ceiling, smelling the processed air that circulated throughout the entire prison, and thinking about what I was going to say when I finally saw my family again. Two years wasn't a long time, but it felt longer being out of the country. I wondered how they would react to me being home again. How would they feel about what I had done? I never actually spoke to my parents about my trip. They never asked. I was glad of it because I didn't know what to say.

I took my journal out from under my pillow and began writing. I crafted a letter to my mom, explaining how I felt about being away from them. I wrote a letter to my daughter, telling her I was sorry for being so mean to her. That notebook which I had entered my life into helped me prepare what to say before I actually had to say it.

When I wrote in that book, something else happened that I wasn't able to explain. I felt a relief of sorts, emptying my conscience onto the page without even trying, building self-esteem by telling full truths instead of half lies. There was something else that it did, but I wasn't sure of what it was. All I knew was that I had filled two notebooks with poems, short stories and letters, and if I had died right there in Montreal, whoever received those two books would have known every emotion brewing inside of me over the past two years. They would have the portal to my soul in full script form.

I was jolted out of a nap back to consciousness by Tony's loud and abrasive voice at my door. I sat up, attempting to focus on his angry face.

"Hey," he said. "You wanna play basketbahl in da gym?"

"Sure," I mumbled.

"Good. It's me, you, da chink, da jap and da two spics. Dat's enough for a team."

I swung my feet over the side of the bed. "Who are we playing against?"

Tony slammed his fist into his palm. "I don't know, but if dey fuck around and try to stop us, we're gonna show dem how we get down Brooklyn style."

Tony left the room, chest inflated and ego soaring through the clouds.

"Brooklyn style," I said and hopped down from the bed. "Great. I've never even been to Brooklyn."

* * *

After two days in Unit A, I began to miss Mexico. Canadian prisons were messed up. Only half of the inmates conformed to the overbearing rules and codes of conduct, and that was only because the other half, the heavies, made sure that they did. I missed the sincerity of the Mexican people, the traditions and the good manners. Since arriving back in Canada, with my people, living with the *others*, I realized that I'd taken that peaceful time in Mexico for granted. I thought back to all those lonely days, sometimes five or six at a time, when I went stir crazy thinking about how badly I wanted to go home, in the safety of my country's prison, back with the familiarity and back on pace. Boy, was I wrong.

I missed Jaime and Roger, even Carlos and his pitiful attempt at butchering the English language. I wrote them all letters, saying my goodbye via snail mail, hoping they would understand my sudden departure. I thanked them for their friendship and wished their families well. I told them about the new prison and the people around me. The only thing I didn't mention was how miserable I was now that I wasn't lonely any more.

"Hey," said Tony from my open door. "That fucking French Mr. Clean is asking for you out here."

* * *

I walked into the French side TV room and quickly realized why Tony harbored so much animosity towards the French convicts. I understood that I was in French Canada, and that westerners and *others* weren't so revered, but their TV room was a blatant show of disrespect. On the far wall sat a fifty-two-inch wide screen television that blared audio to a French program. Beside it, along the windowsill, fresh donuts and cookies along with a cappuccino machine and decks of cards, board games and books. More so, the room reeked of marijuana smoke. My mouth watered as I entered the room, at first led there by Tony, but he backed away as soon as I crossed the threshold. I had a feeling he'd been warned before about entering the king's chamber.

Shrimpy sat at the back of the room – with him three other men looking equally as mean and just as bald. He waved me over to the table, and as I passed other French men, through the thick cloud of cigarette and hashish smoke, I saw them sneer at me as if I were some leper in the village square. I sat down across from Shrimpy, no idea what new dimension I had just entered.

"You smoke hash?" he asked me, holding out a cigarette towards me.

I took the cigarette. The way they smoked the hash was the same at any end of the country. He placed a chip of hash on top of the burning cigarette and gave me a rolled up piece of paper to suck the smoke through. I inhaled the entire chip, not wanting to show that I was any less of a man by stopping short, wasting smoke, even though half the smoke was tobacco. I nodded and handed the cigarette back. Shrimpy nodded his head and spoke in French to his mates. I hoped that he'd just commended me for taking the biggest toke of hash he'd ever seen a westerner take in his life, singing my praise to his boys, commenting that I must be part French to suck back that much smoke.

Instead, he said. "We are Rock Machine. Have you heard of us?"

The hash hit me square in the center of my brain and flowed outward. I nearly missed his question. My honest answer was *no*. I wasn't up to date with the East Coast biker gang scene. Back home, we had our own problems to worry about, and on the island where I lived, biker gangs were irrelevant in our community. Unlike Quebec, where if you weren't associated with one of the gangs, you were the irrelevant one.

"Of course," I lied. "I've heard a lot about you guys."

Shrimpy leaned forward. A beam of light from the fluorescents above bounced off his bald head and into my eyes.

"What have you heard?" he growled.

Shit.

"Nothing but good things," I told him, remembering the reception cop's comments. "You're a tough gang. You like to fight the Hells Angels."

The men around the table laughed, and that told me that they knew more English than they were letting on. I laughed with them until I noticed Shrimpy wasn't laughing at all.

"We have a rule here," he said. "You're either with us, or you're against us."

Shit. I was definitely no idiot. I'd survived Mexico by placating the villagers, I'd survive this as well. I'm with whoever it takes to get back to BC alive.

I said. "I definitely have nothing against you, if that's what you mean."

Shrimpy flicked the ash off the cigarette and handed me another chip. I smiled, thoroughly enjoying the buzz, my new friends, and my half-assed desperate commitment to their cause.

"Good," said Shrimpy, he nodded to his friends. "We have another player for volleyball this afternoon."

This time, I couldn't hold the smoke in, but I never barfed, because I'm a cowboy. But I did prove to them that I was indeed one hundred percent Anglo-Saxon and I'd walked right into their trap. I'd committed to volleyball. Tony was going to be pissed.

When I returned to the other TV room, I was high and now thanks to my dumb-ass, paranoid. Last night, I'd seen *Brooklyn style* and it consisted of Tony talking ghetto to any random person, shooting the basketball and allowing it to roll into the game of volleyball much to the displeasure of the rest of the unit. I stuck by him, playing a game of horse, under an umbrella of discomfort, every French speaking eye on us, glaring, hating. Brooklyn style was nothing short of being a pest, an immature kid with a bad attitude against anyone outside of Brooklyn. Tony had no sense of diplomacy, and when I arrived in the room, he shot up from the milk carton and shot me his most gnarly snarl.

"Dey tried to convince you to play volleybahl, didn't dey?"

I couldn't lie. "Yeah."

"I know," he said. "Dey tried to make da jap sign on as well. But he stayed strong."

The Japanese guy in the back laughed to himself.

"Don't worry though," Tony said. A slight smile appeared. "I got somethin for their asses. Brooklyn style."

The impending gym class stressed me out, killed my buzz, and made me want to sleep until the BC plane arrived. I'd committed to both sides, and it left me wondering if I could play both sports at once just to appease the entire unit. I'd backed myself into a corner all because I didn't say what I meant, too worried that either side would reject me, cause trouble. My ability to make everyone happy worked in Mexico, where the inmates were easily pleased, but back home, people were far more high strung and complicated.

As I walked back to my cell, a guard with a clipboard stopped me in the hall. "You Oulton?" he asked.

"Unfortunately," I said.

"Pack your shit, we're moving you to Unit B."

With that, he disappeared into the office, too quickly for me to run up and hug him for saving my identity. I stood my ground for a second, thrilled to shit that I wouldn't have to attend gym, which by the way was my best subject all through grade school and secondary.

I packed with a gleeful quickness, which didn't take long due to the fact that I had absolutely nothing to my name. When I arrived at the unit door, before the guard even, I couldn't wait to be free of the place. In three short days, I'd gone from a nobody to a number one draft pick in two separate sports. I'd gone from Mexican mode, to French fashion to Brooklyn style and I hated every moment of it. A lone inmate appeared from the French TV room, saw me standing by the door and walked over.

"Where you going?" he asked in slurred English.

"Unit B," I shrugged. "Guess they need the bed."

His eyes grew wide with dumbstruck awe. "You can't go there!"

There was no way I was going to let anyone talk me into staying with these psychos.

"Why not?" I asked.

"You've been in this unit already," he walked closer. His eyes turned to little balls of squint. "Unit B is where the Hell's Angels are. They won't like the fact that you're coming from this unit. You're basically one of us."

"One of who?" I felt my heart sink a notch.

"A Rock Machine," he said matter-of-factly. "The last guy that changed units ended up in the hospital."

"You've got to be kidding me."

The guard appeared from the office and stomped towards the door. Where was Brooklyn style when I really needed it?

Chapter 23
Mike
My New Drug

On the way to unit B, the guard escorted me to a small room that looked as though it may have been a library at one point. Books collected dust on a series of shelves forced into tight spaces against the far wall. There were chairs set up around a TV on a cart with wheels. The guard ordered me to sit and watch the tape, then knock on the door when I was ready to go. He turned around, and locked me in.

I pushed play on the VCR. The tape whirred to life, picture came on the screen. What appeared was a rules and regulations instructional on how to act in prison. The setting was early 1980's and the message behind the tape was pro-convict. The main actor gave me rules as to how to act around other convicts, not to get into debt, keeping to myself and just do my time. It broke down the rules of the prison and the number of programs available in the system. As I watched the tape, laughing and doubting every word spoken, I wondered if this was a joke.

When I arrived back at the unit, the place swarmed with new faces. I tensed, ready for some sort of confrontation, but none came.

A young guy about thirty years old with red hair and a mustache approached me from the French TV room. He held out his hand and introduced himself.

"Name's Bob," he said. "Where did you come from?"

That question could be answered in so many ways.

"Mexico," I told him. "Did two years there."

Bob smiled. "Really? You're a drug smuggler?"

I nodded. Bob had a twinkle in his eye.

"Done a little of that myself." He began to walk away. "Come on in for a coffee."

I followed Bob into the French TV room and quickly realized that it wasn't just for the French. People walked in and out of the room, coffees in hand, stopping to play cards. The open door told me that the mentality here was nothing like the other.

Bob sat down at a table and I joined him.

"So, you were over in Unit A for a while, huh?"

I thought about lying, but what was the use. If trouble were going to come, it would come whether I was ready or not.

Bob explained that Unit B wasn't as uptight as the Unit A. The men here were mostly *Angels,* but there were plenty of regular guys mixed in. He told me that Unit A was where they put people who couldn't function around others, sort of like a protective custody for gang members who couldn't play nice.

"Are you an *Angel,*" I asked him, using his terminology.

"Nope," he smiled. "Just a regular run-of-the-mill asshole."

But Bob was far from regular. He told me about his life smuggling drugs from Latin America up to Montreal. He shared his plane stories and how he'd been smuggling since his early twenties. He gave me tips on how to get drugs across borders and where to buy cheap drugs without hassles in South America. All his information went in one ear and out the other. My days of smuggling were over.

The men in Unit B were much nicer and more polite. I couldn't believe the complete change in attitude and demeanor than the last unit. In the gym, we switched up sports every day. Volleyball one day, basketball the next, hockey, soccer. With the tension removed from the air, the time went smoothly. Next thing I knew, two months had passed and I'd become immersed into French Canadian prison culture.

Oui! Oui!

* * *

Sitting around in the coffee room one day, Bob entered and slid a business card across the table at me.

"What's this?"

"I wrote a book once," he said. "All about my life as a smuggler. I thought that maybe you'd want to tell someone your story. I have a friend who owns an extreme sports video company. He likes out of the ordinary stories. Maybe you have one of your own."

The name on the card was listed to a production company.

"I told him that there was a guy in here who just spent two years in Mexico and he sounded interested," he said. "Thought you might want to make some money."

I took the card. "I've always liked money."

Bob leaned in closer to me. "Also, I'm a good connection if you're interested."

Just like that. Bob put it all on the table, just as plain as I would have three years ago. I know what he saw. A young man with tons of ambition, taking matters into his own hands by going south to buy and transport drugs into the country. He had no idea about my transformation.

"I don't think so," I said apologetically. "I think I'm a changed man."

Bob laughed. "You're not changed, you're just scared. That's normal when guys come back from doing hard time for smuggling. They get a little shell-shocked. Wait until you get out. Your old thinking will come back to you, don't worry."

I knew that if I decided on selling drugs again, I'd be hurting my family and risking another large sentence. Though the temptation was there, and I figured it always would be, I really hoped for better for myself. The only question, was that possible? I was only two years into ten and the end wasn't even close to appearing in the horizon. These were thoughts for five years down the road.

"I'm getting out tomorrow," he said with a smirk. "When you are released, whenever it is, call me. I'll remember you. My sister's number is on the back."

On the back were ten digits written in pen.

"But give my friend a call. From what you've told me about your trip, you may have a good movie."

I took the card and kept his promise in mind until the day they told me I was headed to BC in the morning. Nothing eventful happened in Unit B. The people treated me kindly and I had plenty of time to write in my journal. But what Quebec did show me was how the remainder of my prison sentence would be. Little did I know, even though I was headed back to my home turf, I was headed to the worst prison in all the country. A place where no amount of orientation videos could make a convict shut up and just do his time.

* * *

April, 2000. Matsqui Penitentiary, Abbotsford, British Columbia.

After one week in Matsqui I realized that convicts in the west would rather be convicts in the east, and convicts who come from the east always talk about how good prisons are back east. But if they were so good, why would they come out west?

That basically summed up every person I met in my first week in Matsqui. When I told them that I'd come from Montreal, they were in awe, asking if I knew so and so, or if I met a guy or if there was a guy...

Every conversation I had revolved around how prisons back east weren't like prisons out west, but when I looked around and saw the fences, the locks and the guards, I felt pretty much like it was all the same.

Upon coming out west, most of the French convicts told me all they could about Matsqui, calling it the most drugs and disease infected prison in all of Canada. They told me that out in Quebec, Matsqui had the nickname *Ratsqui* because of all the informants in the system who hide out there. Needless to say, I was weary about going from the start, but I wanted to be closer to home, and I needed a chance to get out on parole as quick as possible.

When I had the chance to walk around the open prison, I saw what the Quebecois meant. There were packs of young men, strung out and sick looking, spitting and puking in all corners of the institution. The walls of the prison were a pasty hospital green and all along the floor where the wall connected to the ground, cigarette butts and wads of dirt and grime. It seemed that the place hadn't been painted in decades, and nobody cared either way.

I engaged into conversation with numerous strangers, some from BC others from elsewhere in the country, but all drug addicts of some sort. Bad breath, poor hygiene, low self-esteem, pro-convict, the list was endless, and what did the prison officials do about it? Nothing. That was the motto of Matsqui. It was labeled a warehouse for convicts for a reason.

It saddened me to see so many young men ruining their lives with drugs. There were more drugs in that prison than I'd ever seen in my life. I remembered back to Julie, the girl I met in Mexico who was dope sick. There were hundreds of Julies walking around Matsqui, and nobody cared about them, worse of all, they didn't give a damn about themselves.

I heard my name called over a loud speaker one morning. I was told to report to my Internal Parole Officer, sort of like a caseworker. When I arrived, I was met by a woman who directed me to a chair in her office without even looking me in the eyes.

Her office was small and crammed into the corner of another small office and it reeked of an alcoholic hand cleanser. On her desk sat piles of files and folders with convicts' names written on tabs. She turned on her computer as I sat down and we waited in silence until my information came on the screen. after a few minutes of reading, she finally turned to me.

"You must be glad to be back."

The statement came out sounding like an order.

"Yeah..." it was all I could manage.

"'We're going to set you up for some programs," she said. "Everyone does them. It's the only way you'll get out on parole."

She signed me up for cognitive thinking, anger management, and drug and alcohol abuse.

"Wait a minute," I said. "I don't have a drug problem."

I saw a trace of a sarcastic grin on her face.

"You sold drugs and never used them?"

"That's right," I said. "I don't like being high."

I left that office signed up for a slew of programs. My parole officer flat out told me that she didn't believe that I'd never abused drugs and promised if I continued to lie, I'd never get out on parole. When I returned to my cell, I had a feeling that my battle with drugs was far from being over. Somehow they would always be a part of my life whether I was selling them or trying to avoid them. I came to realize that my only real drug problem was trying to keep them out of my life.

I met a few good guys in that first month. There were the groups of athletes and educated convicts who were at the end of a lengthy sentence and had figured out that crime didn't pay in the long run. As much as I tried to make friends, there was always something that would happen that made me back away. I'd meet someone and become friends only to find out that they shot drugs into their arms behind people's backs. I can respect someone who stands behind their drug use and doesn't hide it, but to lie and shoot the shit into your body when no one is looking is too scandalous. For me, that leads to lies, which leads to getting ripped off, which leads to me seriously hurting someone or getting hurt myself. I wasn't there to get make lifelong friends, enemies or get into any trouble. I wanted to go home. That was my mission, and I was sticking to it.

*   *   *

I never realized how much emphasis corrections placed on programs, or should I say, re-programs. My first assignment was Cognitive Thinking. It was supposed to teach convicts to think about consequences before they acted on impulses. The course laid out techniques on how to avoid committing a crime, dealing with negative peers and making good choices for their lives. After seven days in the program, the facilitator called me into her office after class.

"You don't need to be in my class," she told me.

Her words sounded like they came directly from my brain.

"Then why am I here?" I asked.

She sighed and leaned back in her chair. She glanced around the office before answering.

"It's ingrained in our culture," she told me. "We don't let people out of prison until they take these programs. It's a way of telling society that we've at least tried to help you – tried to change your thinking."

"'What's the success rate?" I asked her.

"Very high actually. But half of the people in these programs don't need them. You're one of them."

Now it was my turn to smile. "But in order to get out, I have to take it."

And take it I did. Day after day after day I sat in that class room looking at long sheets of paper hanging from the walls depicting answers to life's little problems. I tuned out most of the days, spending the time instead watching the rest of the class either fall asleep or nod off thanks to government-issued drugs. The entire class was spent emphasizing that there was a better way for us to live, without crime and in confidence. By the end of the program, when I received my certificate of completion, I had only one question lingering on my mind.

If there is a better way to live, why the hell haven't they told me what it is and how to get there?

* * *

I managed to get up early every morning. Usually I'd hit the gym then go to school in the afternoon. One Friday morning, a friend invited me to try a creative writing class. I'd heard famous writer Diana Gabaldon speak a few weeks before, but my interest in the class was low. I'd stopped writing in my journal about a month into my Matsqui time. Something about the atmosphere stole the creative desire to write away from me. I'd enrolled in school in hopes of getting my grade twelve certificate, but half way into the process, lost interest in that as well. I almost said no that day, but by the excited look on my friend's face, and the way he hugged his binder to his chest, I followed. Reluctant and doubtful, but my boredom seemed to be my only motivation.

That's the day I met Ed. The first day in class, I tried to sabotage it. I spoke out of turn, made some pretty funny jokes that went off well with the class and teacher. To my surprise, Ed wasn't like any other teacher I'd tried to rattle in my lifetime. He laughed with us, encouraging my jokes and challenging me to write them down. When he asked me what I wrote, I told him about some short stories and my journal, and I tried to sound enthusiastic, but in reality, my mind was far from writing.

In those few short months back home, I'd failed to get my family to come and see me. I'd been away from two years and when I called, they were less than excited to hear that I was safely back in the country. I tried to get them to talk about my daughter, my siblings, how everyone was feeling about me, but all I received from them was negativity and resentment. After a few phone calls, my emotions couldn't take it any more. I know that I'd put them through a lot of pain, but when would that hurt end? When would they start the long road back to becoming a family? I felt so down about the hurt I'd caused them all, I couldn't even speak to my own daughter when she was visiting my folk's house. I felt embarrassed and weak, not understanding what it was I had to do to get back on level ground with the people I called my blood.

After that first day in class, Ed stopped me and asked about my story. Not my written story, my life story. He seemed like a really nice guy, caring and genuine, which was difficult to find in prison. I spoke as candidly as I could muster, but my natural instinct to lie and make myself sound better than I actually was, took over. Ed believed me, because that was in his nature. He wanted to believe in people and tried hard, almost desperately, to find that good in every convict he encountered. At the end of our first conversation, I left that class promising to be back the next week, but also feeling sick to my stomach. I'd bullshitted a thoughtful old man who'd done nothing to me. I didn't even know why.

* * *

My first piece of writing for Ed was a short story that I'd typed out in less than a day. One page of what I thought would be an entertaining bit of nonsense. In class, the writers brought things they wrote to read out to everyone. Most guys were writing novels, some life stories. I'd shake my head and laugh at some writers because they were so young. How could they even think of writing a life story at the age of twenty-four, twenty-five? When it came my turn, I read my short story. Everyone laughed. For the first time in a while, I felt a sort of accomplishment. The laughter made my heart thump a little quicker. I felt a surge of confidence arise in me. I'd felt that before with writing. Once, in fifth grade, when I was an auburn-headed kid that nobody liked or talked to, I wrote a ten-page story for a class project. I had to read it to the class, and all the kids loved it. They applauded for me, and at the following recess, only two out of the five bullies chased me around the school to beat me up. That day was a victory in my short life. Now as an adult, receiving that same acclaim brought back those good memories.

Ed asked for the story to take home. I gave it to him with a sense of accomplishment. A little conceit lingered in my brain. I only spent a few hours writing it, but he didn't know that. I thought, how amazing that I could just write masterpieces so naturally while these other guys struggled to construct their life stories.

Next Friday, Ed handed me back my story, only this time it was covered in red ink corrections. He had some nerve. I took the editing lightly, and tossed the story away. Since the teacher thought it was garbage, that's where it belonged. That entire weekend I didn't think about writing a single time.

I soon came to realize that was the main problem of the prison. There was nothing to take our minds off of our crime, our victims and our families. The men were forced to sit and watch TV, use drugs and play video games to pass time. I was never forced to comment about my mistake or talk about my time in Mexico, and when I did, people only wanted to hear the horror stories or the parts about the drugs. After a few months, I'd already gotten sick of my time down there even though it was the most enlightening incident in my short life.

That next week in class, I remained behind to speak to Ed one-on-one. I soon found out about his revolution, as he called it, to teach prisoners to write and escape the mental torture chamber we called prison. He filled me in about his life mission as a priest and a politician. This guy was just as lost I was, ending up in a disease-infested prison to sort out where he fit in life.

After a few months in the class, Ed provided me with the best weapon I could have to combat my life troubles. Not only did he teach me how to write, he taught me how to become a writer. I admired him for beginning so late in life. He'd written two books by the time I'd met him, and they were outstanding. Just knowing an actual author gave me encouragement that perhaps I could be one too. Ed convinced me that I didn't need to go to school and study to be a writer, writers just write. Those three words took me from a changed man and turned me into an inspired man.

At Ed's request, I kept at it. He told me that writing will change my life, help me escape prison politics, melt the bars. He promised me that I could create something worthwhile that people would love to read. He said that I, like everyone in the world, have a story in our head that is dying to be put on a page. After weeks of listening to him drill it in my head, and countless hours of writing, editing, red ink marking and reading to the class, I gained a confidence to do something else in my life other than crime and drug smuggling. Mexico had convinced me not to do things that would hurt the people I loved. Ed's creative writing class provided me with the solution on how to avoid it.

* * *

I began studying writing, any writing. Short stories, essays, journalism. I got my hands on style guides and books on sentence structure and even grade twelve English textbooks. Anything that could teach me about the nuances of writing novels. In class, Ed had us write exercises that would force us to use our creativity.

That part was easy for me. It was the science of the process that I wanted to understand. For some reason, in such a short time, writing had become important, so important that I didn't want to do anything else but put these words in my head down on page.

During the course of learning to write, I managed to get a few good jobs in the prison that allowed me to practice writing. The institutional chapel hired me as a clerk, giving me an office and a computer. I'd never used a computer before, so the introduction of the machine both thrilled and overwhelmed me. In those first few weeks of typing and learning my way around the beast, I nearly quit trying to be a writer. I typed at about five words a minute and I lost more data than I saved. The only thing that kept me going was Ed and his brain pounding mantra *Writers write. Writers write.*

In less than a year after joining the class, my entire perspective on life did a one hundred and eighty degree turn. I'd come back from Mexico with a large chip on my shoulder. I was angry at everyone I knew from before - Shelly, Ryan, my family, my friends. I had too many emotions built up inside of me and nowhere to let it all out. I anticipated arguments and fist fights in the future to help lessen the burden of ire that I had pushed to the back of my brain. Now that I was writing, my thinking had slowly changed. Somehow I blocked out all the negative thoughts and only allowed my stories occupy my thoughts from day to day. I'd immerse myself into my work, crafting short stories and I even attempted to write a full-length romance novel, something I never would have attempted three years previous. I had a new idea for the man I was becoming. It didn't involve revenge and *one last try*. It was all about exploring the spark of light that had always been burning in my sub-conscious, this idea that I needed to express myself to satisfy an innate desire to be seen and heard. I never knew what to do before writing came along, and now that it was here, I would never let it go.

After writing the romance novel, aptly named *Breach of the Heart*, I attempted to solicit publishers listed in a book that Ed brought into class one day. He seemed impressed with my attempt at writing and told me I had a commercially viable product and that the next step in becoming an author would be the toughest and the most enlightening. He filled me with so much confidence, I actually felt like an award-winning novelist already.

Like a good teacher, he allowed me to feel the pain that every other writer has felt before - the agony of rejection. I must have sent out fifty query letters only to be awarded fifty rejection slips. They came in all forms. Strict white no thank yous, fluffy let me down easys, bold face I'm sorrys. I tried for six months to peddle that damn book, only to come up feeling less than a writer, but there again came Ed and his coolness. Writers write, he said. They don't stop writing.

Even though I had become a new man, with a new goal and a new perspective, I still had the same bad attitude I'd grown up with. After nearly a year of pushing query letters through the mail and receiving abuse back, I trashed the novel, vowing never to attempt romance again in my life.

* * *

Ed and I developed a strong friendship throughout the coming years. In such a short time, I'd come to trust him as if he were my blood. We spent time after class every Friday, talking about writing at first, then moving on to our lives. He quickly became my best friend on the planet, and I welcomed the relationship. I'd never had a type of friend like Ed before, someone who tried to lead me down the good path instead of the other path that I knew all too well.

Though we shared pretty well exact views on writing, what we didn't share was the opinion of prison. Ed was that liberal type who believed society had to nurture criminals and assist them with life changes. I agreed to a degree, but the conservative side of me believed in the formula of our correctional system. Some people needed to be locked up and forced to deal with their issues. Ed believed in inclusion, I believed in seclusion. Ed wanted to create an island prison where drug dealers, murderers and sex offenders ran together, playing games and holding hands while swimming in a lake filled with chocolate milk. I wanted them to be forced to learn valuable job skills, take programs to address their drug problems, and learn how to treat women with respect.

One day, Ed proposed we write a book on our opposing views. What a concept. The criminal who was for prison, and the outsider who was against it. The insider was trying to get out, the outsider was trying to get in. The idea sounded smart, and I bit. I knew Ed's mission in life - to change people with art and writing - but I wasn't going to let him complete his mission so easily. I strongly believed that prison could change someone for the better, if they allowed the program to work. Ed believed that inmates needed love and attention. I promised him that I'd never see his side of the argument, and we'd create one of the best gimmicks the writing industry has seen in a long time. I wrote non-stop for a year.

A year later everything I wrote contradicting Ed's opinion of the system went into the trash.

Chapter 24
Mike
Howe Sweet Home

You never know what to expect walking into a federal penitentiary for the first time. What we see on TV sometimes creates a false impression about life behind bars. But taking prison lightly will get you hurt. It's a place where assumptions could get you in trouble, more than your ass can handle sometimes.

I never expected to experience half the things I did when I came back to Canada. I thought the Mexican prison would be the hardest test I'd ever have to live through. I thought my own countrymen would welcome me back. I thought it would be like every other time I'd gone to prison, when I knew everybody and they welcomed me with open arms and gifts to get my time going. I was wrong. I assumed too much.

What I learned about my country's prison culture was that though there was respect amongst the cons, everyone was really only out for themselves. Though we all suffered together, most convicts would do anything to make their lives easier, get out sooner. For the few that had principles, they found each other. Like they say in the joint, cream has a way of rising to the top. Though my learning process came with many tests, I found the cream, and it was those people who helped me become a better man.

This section is a chronicle of my lessons learned through being incarcerated.

*　*　*

Cons don't look into the eyes of other cons.

Eye contact – the silent killer. How absurd is avoiding eye contact with another human being just because that person may take it as a threat? In some penitentiaries, eye contact can get you killed. I once knew a dog that would bite anyone who looked it in the eyes. Needless to say, no one went to that dog's house very often to visit his master. Most people in prison walk around with their eyes focused either straight ahead or down at the ground. It's surprising there aren't more head injuries from guys walking into poles, walls, or even each other.

On my first day in the penitentiary, I thought I was tough. I stared another man down until he looked away. Two days later I found out that he had killed two inmates and a prison guard in a prison back east, all on different occasions. When the possibility of murder entered the picture, all of a sudden, my boxer's hands didn't mean a damn thing. I suddenly felt lucky to be breathing.

*   *   *

Cleanliness is next to holiness. If you consider anything holy to be sacred, then a smart inmate would be smart to keep his cell as clean as possible. Most convicts treat other people's property with respect. I've been in some cells where I feel obliged to take off my shoes at the door. I've also been in some cells where a haz-mat suit would come in handy.

When I first walked into Matsqui penitentiary, I thought I had just entered a disaster zone. The intense filthiness of the place screamed out at me, and the smell of unfiltered second-hand smoke lingered everywhere. I saw spit and blood stains on every wall and on the ground around the wall. Garbage occupied dirt-smeared corners of walls, and cigarette butts smoked down to the filter lined the hallway curbs like parking meters. I cringed at the thought of spending the next ten years here. If the hallways were this bad, how would my cell look?

When I walked into my cell for the first time, I couldn't believe that they made people live like that. It was dark as I entered. I searched the walls for a light switch and my fingers danced across something grimy. My shoes stuck to the floor as I walked over to the window – around a desk in the center of the room – and yanked open the blinds. Again, my hand stuck to the cord and left a grimy nicotine slash on my palm. Everything was far from holy.

The afternoon sunlight burst into the room, probably for the first time in a while. The nicotine marks on the baby blue brick walls looked like brown tears falling from the ceiling. Brick upon brick, not a single one clean – not even the one in the far corner under the bed. And the bed? A back problem waiting to happen. Sections of the springs were missing from the middle of the frame. I wondered if the guy before had left with any sort of paralysis in his body. When I flipped the mattress over, a gust of dried urine made me jerk my head back. Both sides of the fireproof mattress contained a deep yellow stain right in the middle. It would have to go. In fact, everything would have to go. I might have committed a crime, but my punishment was incarceration, not degradation.

After hours of scrubbing and deodorising, that cell became my sacred spot. I learned quickly that having a clean place to live was the most important step to getting through a ten year sentence.

* * *

On August 10 of every year in all prisons across Canada there is a traditional day of remembrance for dead cons. The day has been allotted as *Prisoners' Justice Day*. Prisoners take the entire day off to pay homage to convicts who died for the little luxuries we have today. We refrain from eating and refuse to go to any programs or jobs. A common practice for convicts is to go to the kitchen or cafeteria and take their tray of food and dump it in the garbage. If anyone is ever caught eating on this day, they are sent to join the dead convicts via a dirty knife to the throat.

My first PJD made me realise just how crazy we are as convicts. Though I respect the fact that prisoners have died for us in the past, I don't respect the fact that we cause ourselves harm to prove a point to the man. On a day of celebration, which is what I believe

PJD is, we should organise a dinner and take the day off. Besides fasting for a god, I don't know any other culture in the world that starves themselves to give thanks.

* * *

Back in 1995, I answered an advertisement in the newspaper regarding a flag football team in need of some players. I had always been an excellent athlete, football being one of my favorite sports to play.

When I showed up to the field that Friday for practice, I recognised four faces instantly. They were prison guards from the local institution, and they knew me well. Their nervous smiles told me that they were uncomfortable with my presence, but I assured them that my outside life would not affect the team. They shook my hand and told me they were fine with me being on the team.

That practice went better than average. I out-ran and out-played every person on that team. I scored touchdowns, snared flags and gained instant respect from the majority of the team.

All except four members.

Carl, the coach, told to show up at the field for a game the following Sunday. Saturday night, I received a call. It was Carl.

"Mike?" He spoke with a tone of regret. I sensed it instantly. "I'm gonna have to ask you not to come and play for us."

I didn't need to ask why, but I did anyway.

"Some of the guys on the team said that they wouldn't play if you were on the team. They mentioned something about a conflict of interest."

Conflict of interest. More like conflict of insecurity. It was a spineless move and I lost instant respect for those guys. It's not easy living life as a convicted felon. You don't get much respect from society, even when you deserve it.

A convict's natural enemy is the prison guard. Guards are the top predators in any prison and carry with them the ability to mess up a convict's already messed up life. With an unfair swoop of a pen, he can send a convict to the hole, take away his visits or relieve him through fines and charges of the little money he actually possesses. In a sense, the prison guard reserves the ability to be a bully, if he wants to.

I don't understand most guards. They take a job that they know they'll get little respect from, and they expect convicts to just accept them. Who can respect another man locking them in a concrete box every night? And most of these guards come to work with a chip on their shoulder and the intention to mess with a convict's life.

Older cons have told me stories of back in the day when guards never spoke a word to them. The threat of violence was always present in a prison back then. Guards were nasty bullies, armed with batons and bad tempers. Convicts would unite against the system with one whisper of a word. Since everyone was aggressive, cons and guards knew where they stood in each other's minds. Now, the prison guard was more like a social worker armed with a psychology degree and a passive-aggressive nature. They're trained to be more culturally sensitive and are taught to try to help inmates regardless of the crime – but they don't like it and they don't do it. One thing I've learned is that educated assholes are far more dangerous than ignorant ones. I know they hate having to come to work for a wage that just barely gets them by and have to be courteous with people who steal, deal drugs and rob for more money than they see in a year. There's bound to be some animosity involved eventually. I don't blame them for holding a grudge and hating us. I hate them because they're free to do anything with their lives, and they chose to be a prison guard.

I still can't understand why they feel threatened. There has to be a reason for the bitterness. Maybe if guards treated convicts like normal human beings, got to know them as people, earned respect instead of demanding it, they wouldn't feel insecure or threatened in the real world if a convict happened to cross their paths. I wonder how many guards see inmates on the street and turn away just to avoid interaction. What a depressing way to live. What kind of a life is it to avoid people like they would landmines while walking down the street of their own town? When I think back to my football situation, things could have been different. If those guards even knew who I was they wouldn't have feel threatened. I didn't have a desire to hurt them. All I've ever wanted in my life was to live well, play sports. I've always wanted to be someone important that people could relate to. If I wanted to truly be a bad guy, I'd be a monster by now. If I wanted to harm a guard, I would have definitely done that by now. When it came to interacting with prison guards I, like most other convicts, fell victim to assumption, one of the worst discriminations of them all.

* * *

I was thirteen years old when I had my first ride in a sheriff's van.. I remember shrinking into one of the corner back cages reserved for women, children or protective custody cases. Three large adults sat shackled in the front and a woman occupied the cage beside me. The smell of dirty cigarette butts filled the air. Dried brown spit hung from the cage's bars. I was scared to touch the walls. The adult men looked at me with evil eyes, and if it weren't for the presence of the woman next to me, I would have been a victim of their callous words the entire four-hour trip. Instead, all three men decided they needed to talk with the woman in the back. They asked her why she was there. When the answer came back that she was a prostitute, the words and demands became lewder.

"Show us your tits," "Talk dirty to us." I heard it all. My eyes must have been huge when the woman lifted her shirt up over her head and flashed the men her breasts. They all cheered and shook the van side to side.

"How you like them apples, juvy?" the men asked me.

I couldn't say a word. All I remember about the trip was my fear. I wanted to go home. I promised myself I would never make it to the front cage. I didn't want to sit up there with the adults and act like they acted. For the entire ride I choked on second hand cigarette smoke and heard words and requests directed at the female that I'd never heard before in my life.

But I did make it to the front. Many times. And believe me when I tell you that riding in a sheriff's van is the most uncomfortable ride you'll ever have. The seats are made of steel, and all around you is a steel grate fence. They shackle your feet and cuff your hands, and usually, you're crammed in these cages with four to five other men. If you're really unlucky, you'll find yourself in a cage with someone who's dope sick or hasn't had a shower in days, maybe weeks. But there are only two things that you can do once that cage door shuts. Grin and bear it, or beat the shit out of the guy until the sheriffs have to move him to another cage. I've done both, and believe me, I'm not proud of myself.

* * *

Once, I went on a sheriff's trip from Victoria to Vancouver. The trip entailed driving in the secured van, boarding a sheriff plane, and travelling throughout the entire Lower Mainland in a different van. When I left the first prison, they strip-searched me. When I arrived at the airport on the other side, they strip-searched me. What they thought I could have picked up along the way and hidden with my hands bound together still boggles my mind. When I arrived at my destination, they strip-searched me again. When I asked why I'd been strip-searched three times in one day, the guards responded as if they thought I had something to hide.

Strip-searches are one of the worst parts about being in jail. I always wonder what it must be like for the guards that have to come in and do it. How embarrassing for them to have to look at dozens of naked grown men and ask them to bend over and touch their toes while they look inside their asses

I've gotten used to being strip-searched. Most of the time, I remove my clothes even before they get the chance to tell me to. I think they get a little disturbed that I'm so willing to get naked for them.

Once, two guards escorted me into a room to be strip-searched. They were engaged in a conversation about baseball. They ignored me as I stripped down to nothing. I stood there naked in front of them for a whole minute before either one acknowledged me.

"Hey," I said. "Are we doing this, or what?"

One of them waved me away and said we were done. I put my clothes back on and left. The whole experience led me to believe that even the guards don't want to be involved in the strip search process.

It's embarrassing for a heterosexual man to have to look at another naked man for a living, even though they choose to do it by working here. But what they fail to see is the long-term emotional impact strip searches have on a man. Both guards and inmates have issues around sexuality that may be aggravated during a search. There are so many inmates who have been victims of sexual assault in their lives. They've been forced to strip and do things to people of authority. Some of these things may be why they're in jail in the first place. The government tries to secure the integrity of the jail by strip searching prisoners, but they can also crush the confidence of a human being. Convicts understand that it happens for the safety of all people involved in the system, but it's done with such cruelty that it does more damage psychologically in the long run. Look at me. I dance naked for them. If that isn't a mental problem, I don't know what is.

The first time I was strip-searched? I was twelve. At twelve years old, a juvy guard told me to take off my clothes. I refused and backed up into the corner of the small holding cell. He took a step towards me and told me it was part of the induction process into the juvenile center and if I didn't do it on my own, he would remove my clothes for me by force. Those were frightful words to hear at twelve years old. I'd never been a victim of any sexual assault, but just the thought of a grown man ripping my clothes from my body scared me to death. I fell to the floor in the corner of the cell and cried. I had no idea what else to do. The guard locked me in, and in minutes, returned with a counselor who talked me into submitting to the search. It was hard enough for a twelve-year-old to comply with that once in his life.

By the time I turned fifteen, I'd probably been strip-searched at least fifty times.

Once I was arrested in the United States. I was sent to a prison, which at first glance looked like an office building in the center of town. The sheriff's car drove into an underground parking lot and into a confined area. The police officer led me into a small waiting room adjacent to the garage and sat me down on a bench. He removed my handcuffs and disappeared through a side door. About ten minutes later, a voice echoed over a small speaker in the wall and told me to walk through the door. The door opened with a hiss and I passed through. The next room was tiled from top to bottom. I saw shower nozzles three feet apart all around the room.

"Take off all your clothes and put them in the drawer."

"What drawer?"

Suddenly a drawer slid out from the wall. I walked over to it and looked inside. I stripped all my clothes off and placed them in the drawer. It closed as soon as I stepped away from it. I glanced around the room. It was as bare as I was, except for the shower nozzles and a large tinted window that I hadn't noticed seconds earlier.

"Close your eyes and mouth and shower under the delouser."

"The what?" I asked. I had no idea where I was supposed to talk. I just called out into mid-air.

Suddenly the nozzles gurgled. I closed my mouth and eyes and waited. Warm white liquid shot out from every nozzle. I took a deep breath and slid directly under one of them. The liquid had an alcohol smell to it and felt like watered down hair gel. I rubbed it into my hair and pubic region because I thought that's what I had to do.

"Okay, you can shower now."

I opened my eyes and saw that the drawer had opened again. inside was a small towel and a bar of soap. I washed the chemical spray off, then took a minute or two to just feel the warm water on my face. The water shut off with a jolt. A second door hissed open.

"Go through the door and wait on the bench."

Beyond the door was a long hallway. Men and women walked casually around. One man had a mop and was hard at work dragging it across the linoleum.

I was confused. I walked out into the hallway, practically naked and dripping water from under the tiny towel. The door hissed closed behind me. I tiptoed over to a bench at the side of the hallway and sat down. People walked by me, pretending to ignore the fact that the towel was barely covering my private parts. I watched the man down at the other end of the hall with the mop in his hand. Back and forth across the width of the hall he swung his instrument. Slowly he made his way closer and closer to me. I began to feel cold. I didn't know what was worse, sitting out in the hallway naked and cold, or showering in a delouser with who knows how many twisted people watching me behind a tinted window. I felt like a lab experiment.

Eventually the janitor reached me. By that time, I was almost dry. He was an older man, about fifty or sixty. He had on an orange jump-suit with the name of the prison on his back. When he got to where I sat, he stopped mopping. He lifted his eyes from the floor up to mine. He let out a snort of disapproval and shook his head. I gave him a smile and lifted my bare feet so that he could mop. His face wrinkled into a smile as the mop swept underneath the bench and past where I sat.

"Damn strip searches," he said without looking back at me.

I couldn't have agreed more.

* * *

There are all types of drugs in prison. Heroin, cocaine, marijuana, pills. There are drugs that are offered by the prisons themselves. Methadone, sleeping pills, Valium. I know guys who drink bottles of cough syrup to get high. Drugs are everywhere. Without drugs, it wouldn't be prison. It would be like Paris without museums or Mexico without the beach.

If it weren't for drugs, there would be more people dying in prison. If prison was drug free, people would get mad over anything and fighting would be the biggest problem. Violent criminals would exercise and become stronger and probably end up bullying the younger and weaker. Drugs are the ultimate equalizer in the game of survival of the fittest.

Drugs dictate how we live in here. How I live, even though I don't do them. If people are high, I'm relatively safe just because of the fact that nobody is going to come after me when they're high, happy and helpless.

Drugs even keep hope alive for some guys, reducing the amount of stress, helping them focus on remaining non-violent and getting back out on the street. In that case, drugs give people a brief opportunity to look at themselves and get their lives together.

The one thing that most tax paying citizens don't know is that criminals come in totally clean, and leave as junkies. It happens to 80% of the people who walk through prison's doors. The hope of the government is that those same people return on a parole violation hooked on drugs, realise how messed up they are, then lean on the system to carry them the rest of their lives. And the system does it without complaint. Drug abusers are cash cows to the highest degree.

Even though I'm thankful for drugs quelling my prison, plain and simple, drugs ruin lives. In all my years of dope dealing I've never seen how they can help people. I've broken millionaires and respectable doctors and lawyers with cocaine, and I've watched athletes and good men and women crumble into nobodies. And it all began the same way. Once in a while, weekends and vacations. Eventually, drugs become a 24/7 commitment.

I don't even take aspirin. I have no idea what it's like to be a junkie, nor do I know what it's like to go on drug binges. My experience with drugs is only in the second person – the pusher. I've grown up around drug use my whole life. I've had many friends who've been addicts. I think the one thing that qualifies me to give my perspective on drugs is that I've actually had the nerve to sit down with junkies and ask them difficult questions about their so-called 'problem.' I never ask because I want to help. I ask because I want to know:

How did I contribute to this person's loss of life?

Why do you really think people do drugs in prison? Boredom, loss of hope, fear. Peer pressure and pain are some other ones. When I look into the face of an institutional junkie, I see a scared human being. A lost soul. Deadened eyes. I think these guys can't handle what's going on around them and want a way out. I wonder why they just don't kill themselves. That seems like a sure way to go instead of using dope for years on end. The thing is they don't want to die, they just want to get away. Most junkies want to numb the pain of everyday prison life. Killing themselves takes away their chances of receiving help, which they're afraid to ask for but want deep inside beyond that shell of insecurity. This is where prison steps in and pretends to help, but they don't really want to solve the problem. Drugs cost money and create money on all levels. Government or black market.

Drug addicted convicts never have a chance to be officially rehabilitated. A desire to have a better life comes from an innate feeling deep inside. Drugs take away that ability to want something better for yourself, and when you're spending time locked up, that depressing feeling only amplifies. As long as taxpayers continue to pay into the system, they'll never become part of the solution. Their choice to just look away and believe that the government is doing a good job only elevates the problem. We'll never get rid of the drug dealing/using mentality unless we take interest in the system.

This system that relies on guys like me to help it sustain life. When I sell drugs to people, create new drug-addicted criminals, I fuel the system's fire. I encourage addicts to commit stupid crimes and I send these people back to prison. Because of my greed and neglect, the system maintains a healthy glow and these prison authorities get a chance to use their pointless psychotherapy on drug users.

When I condone drug dealing, I aid this system to breathe. I give it life every time I sell a gram of dope or a kilo of cocaine. By my statement as to how good drugs are to the system, I'm denying every convict an opportunity to make a positive change. Now that comment sounds really off base.

Instead of worrying about punishing prisoners for their drug use they have to think about ways of discouraging these users from taking the drugs. Sometimes that means heavier security, and other times it means putting the con in a place where he has no access to other human beings, but most of the time all it takes is a little compassion and the will to help. The only way to stop them from coming in is to emotionally change the person bringing the drugs in – but emotional change for most convicts would be like a frontal lobotomy. Besides, like I said, the government likes us living this way. They hope everyone in prison gets involved in using drugs. If you use drugs, you have an identifiable disease. The government loves disease. Diseases create higher spending and bigger budgets. They love it when a prisoner crawls to them for help. This is where the programs and other courses come in. Once a convict is in touch with his emotions, he can accomplish almost anything. And if everyone could accomplish anything, there would be no need for social funding.

There are hundreds of guys like me who continue to believe in the system. They believe that drugs are an important aspect of their lives and they continue to sell the shit, grasping for that dream of becoming rich and powerful. But like anyone inside for big drug crimes will tell you, pursuing a career in the business will end up costing you a decade of your life inside – guaranteed.

I don't sit around with my eyes shut and my brain turned off. I know drug addicts and I know they don't want to fight for anything they believe in, besides dope. They'll never take the steps to change their lives. If they did, that means they'd have to sit in their dirty cell and face their brutal reality through sober eyes. That's way too painful and could create ambition for violence, and the government knows this. So they let drugs come in.

Many years ago the government tried to promote a drug that would help heroin addicts quit. After deliberating on various methods, and probably getting a huge payoff by the manufacturer, they settled on a miracle drug called methadone.

Methadone was touted as the saviour of all heroin addicts. Taken as a pain reliever for junkies coming off the drug, the plan was to take gradually shrinking doses as the desire to use heroin diminished. Most addicts would start at 100 millilitres and work their way down to zero.

Junkies see methadone as free drugs. The government has just stepped up the methadone program so that anyone, I mean anyone, can walk down to the nurse's station and get free methadone. I know people who are on more than one hundred and fifty millilitres a day. They walk around comatose, more so than on heroin. I see people swallow their methadone, then puke it back up into a cup and sell it for heroin. This is what the government supports. It's the access card to the correctional system's revolving door.

As for the rest of us. The ones who don't use dope. The pushers. We sit and wait. We wait for the day we're told we can go. There's no methadone clogging our brains. There's no heroin addiction to help keep us calm. When we walk out the door, we're met with scowls and looks of resentment – it's all part of the game. We're free thinking people with a lot of potential to succeed, but most of us choose to do the dirty work of the system. Unofficially they love us drug dealers, and believe me, they only wish that we would break down and become addicts and fall into the cycle of never ending recidivism.

Drugs will never help solve problems. It'll never solve the pain inside. Drugs act as a pacifier, numbing people's emotions and feelings. Drug users and dealers are two different people. Users are predictable. They'll always struggle with their problem. And when one kicks the habit, another one is created by me – the pusher – so addicts are never in short supply. When dealers finally see the effects of drug use, they go one of two ways. They either quit selling, or they don't. They feel compassion or they see the dollar signs. Either way, the system gets some blood from them. If they quit selling, prison is free from them for good, but that's not what this place really wants. They want guys like us to come back. They give us information that will change our lives, but we constantly fail to internalise it – and that's what keeps them in a job. The true knockout punch would come the day they legalise drugs. Then the only dealers on earth would be the government themselves.

* * *

One afternoon in the spring of 2001, a man named David moved into the cell beside mine. David and I knew of each other from our hometown and due to the fact that we were so alike, we instantly became friends.

David was a charismatic guy. Intellectual, articulate, charming – every envious quality a guy could have. He was thirty years old but had a presence of a much wiser man. People looked up to him and valued his opinion.

On the street, we were businessmen. Prison allowed us to get to know each other in a more personal way. He became the older brother I never had.

David was a well-known drug dealer, hated equally by police and other dealers. The police felt threatened because of his ability to elude them, and other drug dealers felt threatened by his ability to put them out of business. It was hard not to respect that.

He had more going for him personality and capability wise than most convicts, but the way he dealt with people was slightly arrogant. He couldn't see that men in prison were emotionally bankrupt and bitter, and instead of treating them like an equal, he looked down on most of the cons. It wasn't his fault though. He just couldn't let go of his individuality; it was the only identity he knew. He failed to realise that not everybody had experienced success like we had.

Soon, other convicts began to question David's sincerity when he spoke to them. The character he paraded on the surface drowned the real person underneath. No one in the prison had any intentions of getting to know the real human being inside, they just wanted to hate the person they knew on the ground level.

One morning about four months after David arrived, he fell victim to the worst kind of emotion in prison – jealousy. Sounds of screams and fighting next door woke me up. Then, David's door slammed shut.

I rushed out of my room and looked through the small window next door into his cell. Two masked men were beating David with a lead pipe. I did the first thing I could think of to save his life. I walked back to my intercom and pressed the button.

"Yeah," said the guard on the other end.

"Can you open my neighbour's door, please? His buzzer isn't working," I said. I was anxious to get in there, but I remained calm.

As soon as the door opened, I rushed in and tackled the two men to the bed. David regained his stance and together we fought off the assailants. The noise and commotion in the hall must have alerted the guards because twenty of them came running down the hall a minute later.

They stopped in the middle of the hallway in shock. David was naked, covered in blood and nearly in full shock. One of the men stood breathing heavily in the hall. I held the other one down on the bed with rage in my eyes. I wanted to choke him to death.

I ripped off his mask so I could see his face. His eyes were red and wide with fear. His face changed color as he lost the remainder of his breath. I felt his neck tighten under my grip. I wanted to teach him a lesson for being such a coward and jumping a sleeping man. All other sounds and shouts from out in the hallway disappeared as I stared into his eyes.

"I'm sorry," he gasped.

His pleas for mercy brought me back to reality. A guard ordered me to back off, and I stood up and let the assassin breathe.

When the ordeal ended, the guards took David to the hole along with the masked men. They were all shipped to different prisons. They took me to the segregation unit and questioned me about the assault. I told them nothing. The warden of the prison came to me while I was in the hole and told me they wanted to send me somewhere else because they thought my life would be in danger if I returned to the general population. I told him my life would be in danger if I *didn't* go back. People would automatically assume that I went into protective custody and I wasn't prepared to defend myself against a false accusation for the rest of my life. Protective custody was a place where convicts went when they couldn't handle doing time in general population. It was for weak and scared people, not for me. He made me promise I wouldn't retaliate against anyone. I told him I had no desire to cause any trouble again.

When I returned from the segregation unit to the general population, some of the prison blasted me for interfering in an assassination plot. The rest of the prison commended me for risking my neck for my friend. I found out later that the inside community had shunned other convicts in the past for not backing their friends up in an unfair fight. Half the place loved me, the other half wanted me dead.

Still, few convicts spoke to me. Behind closed doors I was a walking dead man. I knew who they were because there was anger in their eyes as I passed them in the hallways. Out of nowhere a rumor started that I'd run out of my cell and yelled for the guards. I ended the rumor by confronting anyone who mentioned it. Other guys on my range stood up for me and said I didn't yell a word to the guards, but the stress of walking down the hallway every day wondering if someone was going to leap out of a cell and stab me made every day feel like I was in a war.

I was plotted against and almost attacked by an individual in the prison, but an unknown lifer stepped up and vouched for me. That time was the most fearful of my life. I slept with a knife and a steel pipe by my bed every night for three months. It was also the loneliest time of my life since returning from Mexico.

I didn't regret helping a friend.

Chapter 25
Ed
Canada

In 1988 our family moved to Western Canada. My wife and I longed for adventure in our older years. We had tired of suburban America and Reagan Republicans.

I said goodbye to Waupun prison. The big walls still stood, families were still separated, the State of Wisconsin had imprisoned hundreds more people in the time I had been there and my crusade to create another generation of Papillons had failed miserably.

I had marched into prison with the words of Isaiah clearly in front of me:

> I have appointed you
> to open the eyes of the blind,
> to free captives from prison
> and those who live in darkness from the dungeon.
> (Chapter 42, verse 6)

I wanted to be like little David, hurling a stone at the giant prison system. Instead it was Goliath 15 – Ed 0.

But maybe I could succeed in Canada. A few months after arrival, I called the prison system. "I'd like to volunteer to teach creative writing in prison."

"Thank you, sir, but we have a full college program at our Matsqui Institution. Part of our program is creative writing."

Good. The program already existed. There was no need for my services. Yet this made me sad because teaching in prison put me in touch with the realities of life and kept me devoted to the value of my craft.

A few years later I picked up the paper one morning and saw that the college program at Matsqui prison had been cancelled. "Why should convicts get a free college education," the Canadian right wing asked, "when we have to pay for it?" Forgetting the fact that education prevents recidivism, the Canadian government had imitated its southern neighbor.

I called the prison system and volunteered again. This time they took me up. The director of education invited me for a preliminary visit.

* * *

I drove forty-five minutes from the metropolitan Vancouver area, out into the Fraser Valley. On a rural road I came over a rise and saw the prison. I had to stop the car, the view was so striking. It was a Russian Orthodox triptych turned on its side. In the foreground, down a slight depression from the road, a field of broccoli grew. The deep green color of the plants made the base of the triptych. Behind the field and above it the prison spread out, razor-wire-topped fences and an ugly, squat building reaching out in four directions, its barred windows proclaiming its identity. Then above the prison – it appeared to be right on top – was Mount Baker, its snow-covered peak presiding over the activities of human beings in this valley as it had for centuries. What a contrast. The living green field, the dull concrete and steel prison and then the snowy majesty of Mount Baker. Emotion filled me. This was the vision – to bring life and beauty and majesty to the prison, to integrate prison back into the world of nature.

I drove on – the vision had reminded me why I came here.

Matsqui Institution, like many Canadian prisons, is located in a rural area. In that way Canadian prisons are no different from American prisons. They are not placed where most of the inmates come from – the big cities – thus making it hard for families to visit. In Wisconsin most of the prisons were located within fifty miles of each other in the rural center of the state. Here in British Columbia many prisons are situated in the Fraser valley, a job relief program for depressed rural areas.

But in many other ways Canadian prisons are different. I found one difference right away in Matsqui Institution. I met the director of education who took me to the school building and introduced me to a group of writers. These men met weekly, led by an inmate named Tom Elton. "Ed Griffin has offered to teach a course here," the director said. "You men can decide if you'd like him to do that."

Whoa. What was this? Democracy? Choice in a prison? Despite the fact that I had to go through another layer of decision, I was impressed. I described my course to the men and they readily agreed to have me teach there. As I left I expressed my admiration to the director.

"Well," he said, "these guys don't own much, but they do own their creative writing program."

The director found a way to give me a little honorarium. It was only a fifth of what the former university professors received, but it was the first time I'd been paid to teach in prison.

Tom Elton, a man who had spent most of his life incarcerated, spread the word that the new creative writing teacher was okay. In my experience the word that circulates around a prison will make or break a staff person. The reputation of a teacher, social worker or administrative person will determine the effectiveness of that person's program before it even begins.

Tom was a wiry man in his late thirties, with most of his body covered by tattoos. In his teens he served time in an old maximum security penitentiary on the banks of the Fraser River, a prison no longer in use. As part of a prison gang, he participated in the killing of another inmate and his short sentence became a long one. According to his prison record he caused a lot of trouble – that is, until he found creative writing. First poetry, then short stories. Writing changed him, gave him an art, a craft.

I moved easily into the writing class thanks to Tom. Week after week I went to prison – it was almost like a retreat for me. I drove out there early on Friday morning, tired from my own writing and from trying to make a few dollars. By the time I left the prison, I felt renewed, charged up to write. The detached observer of human behavior would say I needed prison more than prison needed me. But I knew with certainty that what I was doing was worthwhile.

It was not the starkness of the surroundings. It was not the smoke-filled classroom nor the bad coffee. It was the joy of witnessing new life. The men found a whole new part of themselves, their writer selves.

Writing also led the men to start thinking about their lives. In the words of Aristotle: "Art releases unconscious tensions and purges the soul."

One man neatly summarized my teaching style after attending a few classes. Vern, a large black man with a lot of intelligence, sat in the back of the class and eyed me with a look of sheer skepticism. After a few sessions he felt comfortable enough to read his own work. I praised it at the end. He looked at me with that suspicious eye and asked, "Griffin, are you trying to shove sunshine up my ass?"

* * *

I noticed small things about Matsqui prison. One day I saw an old, fat, gray striped alley cat selecting choice bits of meat from several papier-mâché bowls. A convict standing outside the kitchen area saw me looking. "Them bowls are for Stinky. I'm the only one that can feed him."

"Where does he live?"

"In them bushes over there," he said, pointing to some low-growing evergreens near the sick bay. "He comes out at meal time and I feed him." Then he pointed beneath the kitchen steps, where I saw a box with a cushion in it. "This is where he sleeps at night."

"What's he doing here?"

The convict blinked and gave me a deadpan look. "Life. He's doing life. Killed a rat."

I laughed and he went on to tell me that Stinky was the only inmate who could crawl under the main gate of the prison and chase birds. "I seen him there yesterday. He musta got a pass."

The next week as I walked by the kitchen, I saw another guy standing there. Again bowls littered the area on the other side of the fence. I pointed to the bowls. "Stinky?"

"Yeah. I'm the only one that can feed him."

A few weeks later a third prisoner stood outside the kitchen. I asked about Stinky and he informed me that *he* was the only one who could feed him.

Clearly, Stinky had it made.

Stinky made me wonder why prisoners couldn't have pets. Psychologists have found that pets are good for most people. Yes, there would be some problems in prison if everyone had a pet, but reasonable people can come to reasonable solutions. The therapy value would be worth the hassle.

More noticeable than one cat were the murder of crows that flew back and forth over the razor wire fences. "Caw, caw," the crows screeched as I walked through the gate after my class. They seemed to be laughing at me. "He doesn't know the answers. He thinks he's solving the problem of crime, but all he's doing is putting Band-Aids on a few tortured souls."

At Matsqui prison there were two dining rooms, one for the staff and one for the inmates. I suppose this is common to all prisons, indeed to most institutions. But there's something wrong with this practice. How could staff ever help these men if they made themselves different from them? Why not break down that wall between 'us and them'?

People moved from building to building at Matsqui through chain-link fenced walkways. I couldn't help noticing the way men walked. When other inmates were looking, thy moved like wrestlers. Their chests were out, they strutted through the corridors like upside down triangles with legs. When people were not looking, men shuffled along with their heads down.

Adrian had made me sensitive to the issue of identity in prison. I suppose there are countless identities to choose from. You can be the macho dude who tries to scare everyone else off. You can be the compliant, contrite, perfect prisoner. Or you can be a proud individual who sets his own course in life. This last is what Adrian strove for.

Two people at Matsqui showed me examples of the struggle to have an identity in a place where everyone wore a green jacket.

As I was walking along the corridor between buildings one day, I was surprised to see a woman prisoner coming toward me. She had the same green jacket as the men, but she carried herself in a totally feminine way. She had long hair and wore make-up, lipstick and earrings. As is my custom with all the inmates, I said, "Good morning." She responded in a high pitched voice.

When I got to the school, I asked one of the teaching assistants (educated inmates who assist the teachers), "Since when did Matsqui start taking female prisoners?"

"Fooled you, did she?"

"What?"

"You must have seen Joan. She was in the process of becoming a woman when she was arrested."

My mind immediately pictured what kind of hell this woman would have to go through in a male prison. "Must be pretty hard for her."

The teaching assistant shook his head. "No, Joan's got a lot of friends. She's outgoing and most guys just let her be. She doesn't belong to anyone."

Again the late night prison movies were all wrong. In the movies this woman would have been raped repeatedly or possessed by some hairy ape.

I asked some of the female staff about the woman. One of them told me that the female guards and teachers took pity on Joan and brought her female undergarments and cosmetics.

I saw Joan many times in the corridor, though I never stopped and talked to her. I'm sorry I didn't. I admired her courage. I had no idea what her crime was, but I admired the fact that she knew who she was. She did not consider herself a lesser human being. She was not an inmate, she was a woman.

*   *   *

The other case of a person with a strong identity was a young black man from New York. His name was Deltonia R. Cook, D. R. Cook, which was abbreviated to Dr. Cook. He was in prison for murder. Dr. Cook maintained an aura about himself that said, "I am a free man." Unlike some of his fellows he did not look 'guilty.' He held his head high, he walked through the prison and through life with a vital sense about him. The man was alive, despite being in prison.

I learned the details of his crime at his retrial.

Dr. Cook was a Gulf war veteran, a US Marine. He came from a strict Muslim family with a mother who cared deeply about her children. He was a small man, but wiry and tough, hardened, I thought, by Marine training, but he told me later that prison was what had really made him tough.

As a Marine, Cook spent time in Vancouver while stationed at Whitby Island in nearby Washington State. On May 19, 1992 Cook and a sailor from Whitby Island, a large black man, took a cab from Marine Drive in Vancouver to the apartment of some women in New Westminster. The cab driver was held up and murdered. The association of cab drivers hounded the police to solve the crime. After a seven month investigation, the RCMP asked American authorities to hold Cook. In the interim Cook had been discharged from the service and had moved to New Orleans. The RCMP had waited past the time they could legally extradite him, but with the cooperation of the Americans they spirited him back to Canada, illegally, on a commercial flight.

The sailor claimed Cook had done it

Like many black Americans, Dr. Cook was poor. Canadian legal aid supplied him with a lawyer that Cook felt to be inadequate. At his trial no hard evidence came forward, no fingerprints and no gun but several cab drivers sat very visibly in the court. Cook was convicted of second degree murder and sentenced to life in prison with no hope of parole for fifteen years.

A lot of questions remained about the trial, however, and a
second trial was ordered. The sailor refused to cooperate with
Canadian police at the re-trial. The RCMP arranged free transportation
and accommodations, but the man did not show up. The police did
not seek to extradite him from the US.

The second trial ended in a reaffirmation of Cook's sentence,
but he has always maintained his innocence. He claimed that the
sailor threatened him and forced him to take the rap. The sailor was
much bigger than Cook.

One day Cook let me look at a copy of his prison file. Prison
psychologist Pierre J. Ouellet had interviewed Dr. Cook for four
hours. "The interview failed to reveal the presence of any
narcissistic or antisocial traits, which was a first in this writer's
experience.... I cannot identify criminogenic factors or treatment
needs... This is a very interesting and unusual case."

Dr. Cook was the chairperson of the lifers' group at Matsqui.
On one occasion he put up signs about a meeting of this group.
The sign said that prisoners had to stick together to defend their
rights.

Cook told me the warden was upset with the sign and called
him into his office.

"I want you to take those signs down. They promote violence."

"The lifer's group doesn't promote violence.   Men need a
group to help them figure out how to handle a life bit."

"Young man, you talk in your flyer about defending your rights.
You would get a lot more benefits for the lifers' group if you'd
learn to go along with the administration."

"We have the right to hold meetings and to advertise those
meetings."

"I'll close you down in a minute, if I think you're promoting
violence."

"According to the mission statement of the Correctional Service
of Canada, yes, we do lose the right to go where we please and we
lose the freedom to drink alcohol, but all other rights and freedoms
we still have."

"Don't quote the law to me, young man."

"About the signs...."

"You can leave them up, but if I ever hear any talk about promoting violence..."

To us on the outside it is not unusual to confront authority, but in prison, it just isn't done. Most prisoners would have sat sullenly through a lecture by the warden. Then, when excused, they would have torn the signs down, cursing the warden with every sign.

Not Dr. Cook. Externally he was locked up in jail; inside he was a free man. He knew he had rights and he stood up for them.

* * *

Cook joined our writing class and that's where he became known as *Doctor* Cook. He fulfilled the requirements of our writing class four times over. To gain a diploma, he had to get 60 credits – Cook got 242. At larger gatherings of prisoners, he spoke of the benefits of creative writing. His voice carried with it the resonances of Martin Luther King and a number of men signed up for class. "Creative writing has changed my life," he said. "I just wanted to share my discovery with others." In 1998, the Surrey Writers Conference honored him with their Special Achievement Award. This award is only given to those who have made a significant contribution to their writing community. Under guard, prison authorities allowed Doctor Cook to attend the award ceremony and the assembled writers, four hundred strong, gave him a standing ovation.

* * *

I made a bad mistake with Dr. Cook one day in class. In teaching dialogue I pointed out that each person speaks in a distinctive way with a vocabulary different from other people. And a person should speak consistently with their nature. Cook had given me permission to read his trial summary so, as an example, I quoted a line from his trial that the sailor reported Cook had said. Everyone in the class knew Cook and knew his non-violent nature. The sailor had reported

Cook as saying: "Give me your money or I'll kill you." Everybody in the class knew Cook would never say anything like that.

Dead silence in the room. And then some uncomfortable squirming.

I tried to go on. "There are several mistakes to avoid when writing dialogue. The first is…"

I looked up. Something had changed radically in the classroom. It had to be cleared up.

"Hey, what's going on?" I asked.

Cook took the lead. "I'm sorry, Ed, but we never talk about a guy's case. See, everybody worries about informants. It's happened before. A man is just talking in prison and then all of a sudden he finds out that a guy he thought was his friend is an informant. The informant misquotes him and says he said this or that."

Others in the class added their comments, such as, "You know, the cops promise a guy a year off or even more if he will testify against another con. You got to be real careful, man."

I felt terrible and apologized profusely.

Cook accepted my apology. But I apologized again.

"Hey, come on, Ed. It's okay. Nobody else around here apologizes for anything. Now let's get back to learning about dialogue."

* * *

Dr. Cook was quite the writer. Here's a poem he wrote.

During the Crackling of early morn the Angel of death spoke to me in my cell
he said "Go right back to the pain if you want to heal it"

so for so many years.......
I have waged war against the demons
who drug me through hell on my back by my hair

I have learned to defeat the raciest demon
    who called me a nigger
the police demon
    who lied on me at my trial
the thief demon
    who stole food from my cell
I have learned to defeat the prisoner demon
    who tried to stab me in the back
the guard demon
    who beat me when my hands were cuffed
the priest demon
    who tried to force me to practice his religion
I have learned to defeat the love demon
    who left me after my conviction
the survival demon
    who made me fight when I didn't want to
the humiliation demon
    who humiliated me by stripping me naked after
visit with my best friend

I have learned to defeat all the demons all but one
the one inside me the one Called Grudge

if I do not learn to forgive
when the other demons reappear
He will be stronger and I will have defeated myself

Victory through forgiveness

*   *   *

Doctor Cook wrote articles about the plight of North American blacks. Yes, he saw the need for prison reform, but it wasn't his first concern. The main thing he claimed for writing was personal. "Writing can make you a free man," he would tell the audience at our annual graduation ceremony for the writers who had completed the program. "Writing can heal your soul."

One day I came to class and he was gone. "Sent down to lower security," the guys told me. Another soldier lost to my grand scheme. But things were changing. In the time I knew him, I did not form him into a soldier of prison reform. In fact, I didn't even try. I just stood back and marveled at his strong personality. Instead of teaching him, I came to admire and respect him.

Chapter 26
Ed
The Mirror Image

For years I had driven down 152nd Street into White Rock, B.C. to teach my creative writing class to adults. One day, only an hour after I had driven down the street, a young woman, fifteen or sixteen years old, disappeared. The authorities found her body later that day in the bushes near the street. She had been raped and murdered.

Every week as I drove past the spot, I saw fresh bunches of flowers. What a sad event. The young woman had been on her way to see her boyfriend when someone pulled her off this busy, main street in broad daylight.

The family had just moved to British Columbia from Ontario. The parents could hardly talk to the media. Here was the other side of crime and I grieved over this young woman's death. Three months later a thirty-one year old ex-con walked into a police station and gave himself up. He confessed to murdering the young woman and was sentenced to life in prison.

Why had this tragedy happened? What kind of person did this? Such a person is a threat to society. He needs to be locked up until the shrinks are sure he's cured. Granted that wardens and prison experts say only twenty-five percent of those in prison need to be there, this man was one of the twenty-five percent. The saying 'the best prison reform is the bulldozer' was wrong.

What if this man shows up in my writing class someday? Will I be as sympathetic to him as I am to other men whose victims I have never heard of? Will I talk about the hard life this man has lived, about his lack of social skills?

Let no one ever say that my response to crime is, "Oh, don't worry about it." I think society should get a lot tougher on crime.

The warehouses men go to now – what we call prisons – are actually easy. I call for a program where men have to face what they have done. Real change is hard work. The restorative justice people offer creative answers to 'restore' the victim, the convict and society. Social and psychological scientists could certainly devise programs that would truly and permanently change behavior. Yes, I will admit that nothing's going to work for a very minor percentage of convicts. This ten or fifteen percent must be incarcerated.

*   *   *

Like the crows, I crossed into the prison every week, they going over the razor wire and I, under. But they seemed to fly with clear goals, while I was filled with conflict and questions.

I had to park far from the gate house so every week I had a long, reflective walk on my way in. I noted how the crows flew together, in a murder, but I worked alone. Why hadn't I joined with others who were working for positive change? The John Howard Society performed worthwhile services such as sponsoring halfway houses. I could easily have become an 'expert,' someone the media called on whenever there was a news story about prisons. Or I could have been a 'gadfly,' a persistent, irritating critic who followed prison authorities around and commented on everything they did.

I did help men find jobs, but alcohol and drugs often negated my efforts. One man lost a job as quickly as I found one for him. There's a prison saying, "Once a druggie, always a druggie."

Out of desperation to make a difference I put one of my ideas on paper. Prison reform would only come when convicts rose up themselves to protest their conditions, like the people of India, like union workers, like American blacks, and like North American women. I suggested that convicts organize. The warden may say he's against racial gangs, but as long as the blacks, the whites, and the Hispanics are fighting each other in the yard, they are not in his office demanding change.

I showed this paper to a friend who is working toward his Ph.D. in criminal justice. He praised the good parts of my essay but pointed out several illogical points. For example, I claim to be non-violent, but I recommended that union members 'deal severely' with snitches and those who break solidarity.

Union participation leads to a sense of involvement and responsibility, but two big problems lie in the way of prisoners building a union movement. Drug use makes many men totally unreliable and second, police and prosecutors dangle reduced sentences in front of people if they turn others in.

The union movement, however, is a constructive answer to the problem of prisons. Convicts would take charge of their own lives and negotiate the terms of their existence. This is the definition of democracy – and rehabilitation.

Prisons do not need more social workers and shrinks, but rather some tough union organizers (and very patient wardens).

*   *   *

The Ph.D, call him John, and a fellow parole officer, Frank, forever ruined my clear-cut division between the good guys and the bad guys.

Prison work doesn't always attract the brightest of the professions. I've met some prison shrinks and social workers who needed a lot of help themselves. But John was an exception. He worked in a protective custody prison, helping men plan their releases. He had a national reputation as an expert, giving conferences and advising other officers how to help men get ready for the world again. His scientific approach to prison problems impressed me. Talking to him, I felt like a freshman addressing the professor.

Frank, the parole officer, was everything I said parole officers weren't. Frank cared about the men. He respected them. I watched how he dealt with one writer I knew. He honored this man's ability as a writer. Instead of stressing the man's problems with the law, he encouraged his potential as a writer. And he did this in the face of a big failure on the writer's part when first released on parole. The writer re-offended, but Frank continued to work with him, accepting him not as an inmate, but almost as a brother.

The more time I spent in prison, the less I knew for sure. I didn't even have my own certainties to fall back on.

* * *

If I was confused when I walked into prison, I knew that everybody around me was, too. This prison bureaucracy took confusion and ineptitude to a new level. This was a bureaucracy with a difference – they could screw up all they wanted as long as the convicts didn't escape. The clients served by this bureaucracy were lawbreakers with zero status in our society.

Right-wing politicians attack the soft life inmates supposedly enjoy, but the mother lode of public rip-off lies in the waste and ineptitude of the prison bureaucracy.

A few examples show the problems I faced while trying to accomplish simple things. Multiply that by one thousand if it's a convict trying to get his possessions after a transfer or trying to take the required programs so he can get out of prison.

I needed a badge to get into prison, a badge which was kept in the gate house. Every week I entered the gate house, signed in and traded my driver's license for the badge. One Friday it was gone. "Somebody from security came down and threw away all the out-of-date badges," the guard said.

"My badge was out of date?"

"Apparently."

"Nobody told me."

The guard shrugged.

"I've got to get to my class," I said. "I'll see about getting a new badge afterwards."

"Hold it. I can't let you in without a badge."

It took a half hour for the guard to find someone from the education office who could identify me. Then it took two months for me to get a new badge. I had to have a paper from the school stating that I was a teacher. Security had to sign the paper and then

I had to set up a meeting with the photographer. And every week I was held up in the gate house until somebody could identify me.

Another example – getting a room for a meeting. At one point the warden decided the prison needed more evening activities. I cooperated and arranged to have a writing group consisting of prisoners and outsiders meet in the evening. The director of education assigned us to meet in a hall-like room in which a loud fan whirled overhead.

"Can we turn off the fan?" I asked.

"Sure. Let me show you how."

The director took me to a utility area. "Here's a timer switch. You turn it past 10 and the fan will shut off. Watch."

Nothing happened.

"Oh, I know," he said. "There's a switch inside the control room. Somebody must have turned it off. Just a second." He reached for the control room door. It was locked. "Don't worry. I'll get that switch set properly before your meeting."

A dozen prisoners and half a dozen outsiders showed up for the writers' group. The fan rotated on and no switch would turn it off. I asked a guard if we could use a side room. I explained all about the fan and the noise. "I'll go get a key," he said, but he had that look about him that said, "You'll never see me again."

When the guard did not come back with the key, we dragged chairs outside to the walkway. It was a warm summer evening. Another guard came by. "What are you doing here?"

I explained again about the writers and the meeting and the fan and the guard who went to get a key.

"Nobody cleared this meeting with me and I'm in charge of meeting space. And how come all your people are wearing Visitor tags?"

I shrugged. "They gave them tags when we came in."

"Well, they shouldn't have. You are the only one with enhanced clearance. The other people have to be escorted."

I blinked at this dubious honor and said nothing.

"I'll have to talk to the people up front," the guard concluded and turned to go.

"Ah, about that guard who was going to get us a key to the side room. I was wondering ..."

"Did he say he would get the key?"

"Yes, but..."

"If he said he would get the key, that's it. Now everybody back inside."

"How can I get a better room?"

"You call me in the daytime at extension 354."

The rest of the evening we competed with the big fan and the next day I called Extension 354. "Try 356," I was told. When I reached 356, I was told to try extension 358. At 358 I left a message which was never returned.

* * *

The only thing that was not confusing about prison was my class. I got to know the men in this class and we got along very well. One Friday morning, a hefty man with a salt and pepper beard walked in, nodded to me and sat down. A presence had entered the room.

He was about my height and weight – 6 foot and 190 pounds. I was 58 then and he looked to be a few years younger. His name, he said, was Davi Harpine and he was a convict. "I'm not an inmate. Inmates are what the guards call us. I'm a convict." He turned to the man next to him. "What page are we on?"

"Page 21."

He looked around the room. It was clear to everyone, including me, that we were all going to work on page 21.

Davi was there to learn, to work, but he was not without humor. He turned in manuscript after manuscript for me to critique and I marked up his work with my red pen. He wrote an imaginative piece called *The Slasher*, in which I was portrayed as a dangerous criminal wielding my red pen.

After class one day he and I talked. He said he was an American. "Oh, yeah? That's where I come from, too."

He went on. "I'm one of those hippie flower children from the sixties,"

I laughed. "I guess that's what I was, if you can call a straight Catholic priest on the picket line a flower child."

"I was at the Democratic convention in Chicago in '68 and I was in Selma."

"Selma?" He had my full attention. I marched in Selma with Dr. King. It was one of the turning points of my life. "You were there, Davi, on the march to Montgomery?"

"Yeah."

"So was I."

Here was a man, roughly my own age, who had shared the ideals of my youth and was willing to march for them. I was looking into a mirror.

"Five minutes to count," blared the public address system. He handed me a poem. He left for count and I read the poem on my way out of prison. I know little about poetry, but his words filled me with their music and their power.

IMAGES

Migrant workers,
farm labour camps
Low life existence,
singing the blues
Money makes you wise,
poor man, the fool
Doing the devil's dance
Doing the white trash boogie.

Foster home, juvenile court,
reform school
Demeaning, brutal,
structured process
Democracy at its best
Doing the devil's dance

Dystopia

Doing the puberty boogie

Menial labour, minimum wage
A father's shame, a child's future
Drone, prisoner of society
Doing the devil's dance
Doing the wage slave boogie

Choices lost, dreams shattered
intelligent thought scattered
Perpetual prisoner of the state
Doing time, learning to hate
Doing the devil's dance
Doing the convict boogie

Word of honor, blade of steel
Emotions submerged
forgot how to feel
Walls close in, mind won't heal
Doing the devil's dance
Doing a man's boogie

Tattooed veins, lackluster gaze
Floating in a mindless maze
Overdose, death, a fix away
Doing the devil's dance
Doing a junkie's boogie

Oppressive, archaic,
machine government
Counter culture movement
revolution in the air
Anarchy springs from
a hidden lair
Doing the devil's dance
Doing the anarchist's boogie

> Revolution, game called change
> Played, middle against the high
> Low supports the pyramid
> Doing the devil's dance
> Doing society's boogie.

When I finished the poem, I wondered why this thoughtful man was in prison.

At the beginning of class the next week, I called for the homework. Every week I gave a short assignment. That way the men had to write at least one thing a week. When Davi alone passed in a paper, he glared around the room. "What's the matter with you guys? We're in this class to learn. When Ed says there's homework, we do homework. Is that clear?"

Nobody said anything.

But he was a gentle man. Nobody was kinder to a new writer than Davi. Outside of class time he read countless manuscripts for the men. In class his suggestions were always preceded by words of praise.

Even though he called me 'The Slasher,' he stood up at our writing program graduation and paid me a supreme compliment. He said I had brought laughter back into a prison.

I was touched by his statement. To make people laugh, in my opinion, is a great gift. And laughter, like writing, leads to a more spiritual self.

I hoped Davi's words would mark my grave: *Here lies Ed, who brought laughter back into a prison.*

If Davi and I had our similarities, we also had our differences. His maternal grandmother was a full blooded Choctaw. She married a white man and left the reservation in the early 1900's. His grandparents sharecropped land near Stillwater, Oklahoma until the Great Depression. In 1933 the family lost its land and migrated to California, where they worked as migrant farm workers. Davi grew up in poverty and learned the ways of the street. Born into an Irish Catholic family, I was raised in a safe, middle class neighborhood in

Cleveland Heights, Ohio. Davi was bounced from foster home to foster home and finally into reform school. I had a college education, post graduate work in theology and a masters in social work. I had a chance in life, Davi had almost none. I often wondered whether our roles would be reversed if our childhoods had been exchanged.

On October 29, 1991 Davi entered Canada. He was being hunted by the US Marshall's Fugitive Squad who had a *shoot on sight* warrant. He was wanted on a charge of manufacturing and distributing methamphetamine, which in the United States carries a mandatory life sentence. At a small border crossing in the mountains of British Columbia, Davi was pulled over for a secondary customs inspection. He feared the authorities would deny him entry into Canada and would turn him over to US authorities. He commandeered the customs post at gun point and when arrested, pleaded guilty right away to unlawful confinement so that he would be sent to a Canadian prison.

He hoped to apply for refugee status in Canada. Canada refused to give him a hearing.

How could this gentle man, this man of intelligence and art, manufacture drugs and hold people at gun point? If there was a way to change his behavior, I knew it was not through locking him in a cage. It was through giving him a stake in the very system he opposed and through intelligent discussion of the role of law in society.

What had happened to two men who had marched in Selma with Martin Luther King? Why did I follow the laws and he didn't?

These were more questions for the crows to mock me with. The crows were sure of their flight path. I wandered in the dark, sure of very little.

Later Davi told me about his last days in Canada.

After four years, his appeals were exhausted. In the spring of 1996 Davi's aged mother traveled from the States along with Davi's fifteen year old son for a visit. When the visit was over, Davi hugged his mother and son and watched them leave the visiting area. As Davi walked back to the prison proper, he was suddenly surrounded by guards. They put him in handcuffs and leg irons. "We're getting you ready to be deported. You're going back to a maximum security facility."

"Okay. I understand, but can you wait until my mother and my son clear the prison? I don't want them to see me chained up like this. My mother's not in the best of health."

"The schedule is the schedule. The officers are waiting."

"Just five minutes. Give them time to clear the gate house."

"You're going through now."

In full view of his mother and son, Davi was brought into the gate house. His mother cried. His son looked at his father and could not understand why they were treating him like an animal.

Davi was returned to the States. Prosecutors offered him a deal if he would name his accomplices. Davi would have none of it. He was tried in Oregon and sentenced to fifty years. For a fifty year old man, that's a life sentence. He spent four years in the Federal prison in Atlanta, where my wife and I were his only visitors. And then to a prison in Lompoc, California where he was diagnosed with a severe case of diabetes. He is writing a book on how people in prison can adjust their diets to meet the challenges of this disease. He writes on, he says, with no joy in his heart, but still he writes on.

I fear the winter will come before this strong, productive tree can bear fruit for society. Davi is an intelligent, artistic person who is confined to a warehouse for the rest of his life. Granted that he has failed society, society has certainly failed him.

As I prepare this book for publication, thirteen years after Davi came to my class, he still sits in an American prison. He's survived diabetes, severe back pain and other ailments common to men our ages. He's lived through gang wars and prison riots in some of the worst federal penitentiaries. He works whenever he can in prison industries so he will have enough money to pay for phone calls and letters to his family and friends.

Sometimes when I look in the mirror, I'm bothered that I haven't done more for my mirror image.

Book Five

Chapter 27
· Ed
The Exclamation Point

In October of every year famous novelist Diana Gabaldon comes to the Surrey Writers' Conference. She volunteers her time to drive out to the prison and spend the morning with the creative writing class. She talks with the guys, answers their questions and always leaves behind a lot of writing books for their library.

A few weeks after her visit in October of 2000, class had already started when the door to the classroom shook with pounding.

I stepped over to the door, continuing my instruction as I went. "The exclamation point – it's just not needed. It calls attention to itself. If your writing is strong, you won't need an exclamation point."

I peered through the thick glass and opened the door. It wasn't even locked. Massive shoulders, bulging arms and a square face confronted me. "Is this the creative writing class?" he asked. "My name's Mike and I'd like to join."

No matter who he was, I would have said 'welcome,' but something straight and honest flickered behind the big, smiling face. "Come on in, Mike," I said. He gave me an appraising look for an instant and then said, "All right."

He didn't come in, he stepped past me and then *slid* to the center of the classroom as if the floor was a hockey arena. "Relax everyone, Mike's here," he reassured the class. "The boxer is becoming a writer. I've heard about this class and it's excellent." Suddenly he stopped dead still, his arms out in front of him. In a voice louder than anything I had ever heard – so loud that I saw people outside the closed door of the classroom stop and turn – in this deep, dramatic voice, Mike started, "To be or not to be, that is the question."

He sank to his knees in front of everyone. The same booming voice. "To be an entertainer, that's what I want. I'm here to learn." He sprang to a crouching position and then plunged backwards, the flip chart crashing down, hit by his solid shoulder. He was flat on his back. "I want to knock them dead. My writing has to be *dynamite*." People again turned in the hall outside the classroom, no doubt wondering why the word *dynamite* bellowed from the floor.

Then the show was over. He got up and sat down in our circle. The big face smiled, reassuring me. "Sorry, Ed," he said. "I love drama."

I laughed. He wasn't challenging my authority, he was coming at creative writing with his own fresh approach.

Where was I? Oh yes, the exclamation point. I was wrong to oppose it. The exclamation point had just entered the classroom.

* * *

Mike came every week. He started to write, mainly short stories. Many of his stories featured a colorful boxing promoter called Langston Law. Through his stories I learned things about Mike, that he had been in a Mexican jail and that he used to be a boxer. He told me that he had heard Diana Gabaldon talk and he asked after her lecture if he could make any money writing.

"If you're good," she responded.

It's all Mike needed to hear.

He came to class with his friend, Jacob. The two of them had great plans to develop and produce a TV show aimed at young adults. Together they generated enthusiasm and interest in our class. We were alive with ideas and writing projects.

Often I would ask Mike or Jacob to teach a class and they did so with zip and solid material. We became a community of writers. We were not teacher and students; we were fellow writers involved in our craft. It was almost like the writing retreats you hear about, where writers go away for the summer and sit down to write. Prison became a writing retreat. Each Friday we would get together and discuss manuscripts.

And in the process we had a lot of fun.

One day in class I started talking about romance writing and I said that many romances were written by men using female pen names. My own creative writing instructor had written one. I said that while this market was lucrative, it demanded good writing.

A few weeks later Mike showed up in class with the first chapter of his romance novel, *Breach of the Heart*. He read the first chapter. When he was finished, I knew he had the craft of romance writing down.

"Hey, that was pretty good," Mac said. "Howdja do it?"

"Research, man, research. I read several romances and I read one of the writing books Diana Gabaldon gave us."

"Yeah, but how did you figure out what that chick in your story was thinking?"

"You just have to get in touch with the female part of yourself, that's all."

Only Mike could say something like that in prison and get away with it. Anybody who might want to laugh at him had just to take a second look at him and decide not to be pulverized.

With Mike the stage curtain was always open. He could turn a dull class into tremendous fun. He loved to act and he illustrated points in creative writing with mini dramas of his own invention.

But as I got to know him, I discovered a very deep person. One week he would amuse us with the exploits of Langston Law, the next week he would make us all think about loneliness with the story of a man and his pet wolf, and the next week we would each see our own foibles in the story of a loser out on a blind date.

Mike was like knowledge – you go through one door, and then you discover there's another door and another, on to infinity. This business of writing a romance, it could have been because I had said it was a good way to make money, but as I got to know Mike I found out he really was sensitive to the needs of women. It wasn't just an act. In fact, strange to say, *nothing* was an act for this man who was always acting.

Mike talked to me about prison and crime and about how men changed their lives. The secret for Mike was straightforward honesty. He had decided there would be no more lies in his life – about anything. "See, I'm very careful about what I eat and I keep myself in shape. Just like I don't want any pollutants in my body, I don't want any more lies in my heart."

We talked more and more after class. He told me one day that he really appreciated my course, because now he saw for the first time in his life that he could make money at something besides crime. I think he meant more than just writing – he also told me that he had figured out his life goal and that was to entertain people. Writing was only one way to do that.

When he said that to me, he made me feel very good.

*   *   *

Mike reminds me of a scene from *Grapes of Wrath*. Ma Joad worries that prison has changed her son, Tommy (Henry Fonda). She asks, "Did they hurt you an' make you mean-mad?"

Tommy reassures her, "No, Ma. I was at first, but not no more."

Still she probes more, "Sometimes they do somethin' to you. They hurt you and you get mad, and then you get mean and they hurt you again and you get meaner and meaner—till you ain't no boy nor man any more—just a ole walkin' chunk a mean-mad. Did they hurt you that way, son?"

Like Tommy Joad, Mike is one of the few people who have survived prison. (But I hold with Ma Joad – I don't want no chunks of mean-mad walking the streets after their sentences.)

In fact, I'm surprised Mike isn't 'mean-mad.' One of the steps for his release was a visit to a parole psychologist. He told me about this interview.

The psychologist, a man small in stature, thirty-something, an employee of the prison system, called Mike into his office.

"How are your plans for release coming, Inmate Oulton?"

"Fine. I'd like to be a writer eventually and I know…"

"Hold it. That's a totally unrealistic goal. Writing is a hobby."

"I know I won't make money at the beginning, that's why I'm learning how to be a physical fitness trainer. As a former boxer…"

"This is ridiculous. You have to pay for food and lodging. Maybe you can spend your time in here writing stories, but outside you have to work. You have to get realistic, young man. I'll have a report on you ready in a week or so."

When Mike read the report, he saw that he had 'unrealistic goals and faulty planning for the future.'

When he told me about this, I was so angry that I went to the Director of Education and complained about this psychologist. "He's cutting the very heart out of what I'm trying to do," I said. "I'm trying to teach these guys a skill they can use in later life."

I'm still waiting to hear the response to my complaint.

Chapter 28
Ed
Steps to Freedom

May 13, 2004. Mike's parole hearing.

Here he would ask for day parole, living in a halfway house at night and being free in the daytime.

It was a time of promise and excitement. Tulips opened fully to the sun and rosebuds promised great things with just a little more daylight. Rhododendrons blossomed and people planted petunias and marigolds in their gardens. Inmate horticulturists had planted wax begonias along the walkways of Matsqui prison.

I took a day off school to appear in support of Mike. As I walked past the rows of wax begonias, I realized they rested against the wall of the hearing room. Would the outside reflect the inside? I'd know in a few hours.

Inside the building, Mike, his parole officer, and the Catholic chaplain, a nun, waited. Sister came up to me. "Only one extra person is allowed to testify," she said. "And I'm going to speak on Mike's behalf."

"Sister," I replied, "I took a morning off work and drove forty-five minutes out here and I'll be damned if I don't testify."

Sister nodded agreement and sat down.

After an hour of waiting, we were called into the hearing room where two members of the parole board and a staff person waited. First the staff person laid out the case, Mike's crime and the issue before the board – should Mike be allowed to live in a halfway house on Vancouver Island?

His internal parole officer reported positively about his time in prison but mentioned that he had used marijuana once.

Then the probing began, the two members of the parole board firing question after question at Mike, one man playing good cop, the other, bad cop. Why did you take marijuana? What is your relationship with your daughter? Your mother and stepfather have agreed to take you in and your stepfather has offered you a job. Tell us about the difficulties you've had with your stepfather. Why did you use marijuana?

They tried to get Mike into verbal traps, contradicting himself. This went on for *two hours*. Finally, the committee took a break. Mike's internal parole officer came up to me. "Don't you just love these kinds of things? I think they're great."

I could hardly believe my ears. I assumed she had taken courses in how to deal with human beings. You don't beat people up for two hours and then call it wonderful.

Mike and I went outside along the walkway with the begonias. Sister stood with us. A former warden walked by and Mike greeted him by his first name. "Hi ya, Jerry," he called out. "How's it going?"

This was Mike's way. Friendly, on a first name basis with the entire world.

The warden, a wise and kindly man, responded "Hi, Mike." The two chatted for a few minutes until the hearing resumed.

In the hearing, the good cop said, "I'm going to give you a tape of this interview, Mike, so you can hear how you spent two hours talking about yourself. That's the problem. It's all about you."

For God's sake. Mike had spent the time answering their questions about himself.

Next the parole officers called on Sister for a statement and then it was my turn. "Excuse me, gentlemen, but I'm not letting go of this man." I leaned in and tapped the table for emphasis. "He's a talented man. He's got a career in writing, in entertainment ahead of him. I'm going to stay with him, fight for him, help him."

The parole officials thanked me and we all left the room. A half hour later we were called back in. They granted Mike parole, but warned him that one violation, one marijuana cigarette, one drink would void his parole and he'd be back in prison.

The next day I wrote to Mike:

It is rare in life that one experiences a high, at least
a natural one. I had such a moment yesterday and it
stayed with me all day, through the long hours of
teaching and it's still with me.

Mike got out and went to a halfway house in Victoria on
Vancouver Island. My first trip over was to give him an old computer
that Lee, my principal, had donated for him. We installed it in his
room at the halfway house and then went out into Victoria to buy
some connecting cables.

Going shopping with Mike was an experience. He stopped in
front of a candy store. In the window a woman worked with a
machine that stretched and twisted caramel candy. Mike stood out
in front of the window and began to imitate her motions – not in a
way that insulted her, but in a manner that made her laugh. A crowd
gathered and Mike started a huckster line about going in and tasting
the delicious candy. One-on-one he would talk to people, win their
confidence and invite them into the store.

It worked. Several people from the sidewalk crowd went in and
bought candy. Mike was the state fair huckster, the entertainer, the
master of street theater.

He had no connection with the owners of the shop, no
commission to bring people in. This was Mike's street theater and it
was for free.

I laughed harder than I had in a long time.

But there was one minor incident that came back to haunt me.
We went into a store on our search for computer goods. The prices
stood at the high end, while staff helpfulness rated at the low end.

"Do you want USB or parallel port cables?" the clerk asked in
an imperious tone.

I looked at him blankly.

"Which?" he demanded.

"I don't know."

"Well, you'll just have to bring the printer in," he said and
turned to the next customer.

As we left, Mike 'accidentally' tipped over a minor display and was about to do the same to a whole table of goods when I stopped him. He seemed unduly angry. Yes, the clerk was a horse's ass, but there are a lot of them in the world.

I went back to Victoria a few weeks later to get him a virus checker. Afterwards he treated me to a sandwich and then we walked around downtown. Since it was the height of the tourist season, restaurants were packed with people from the States, from Germany and from many Asian countries.

We came to one restaurant that had sidewalk tables. Mike told me to wait a minute and then he walked up to a table. An elderly couple were having coffee.

"Did you folks enjoy your dinner?"

"Yes, thank you. It was delicious. You have a wonderful city here."

"We appreciate folks like you visiting us."

Mike Oulton, chamber of commerce.

He turned to a table where two young women picked at their salad dinners.

"Ah, ladies, is the dinner all right?"

"Yes, fine, thank you."

"You do our restaurant proud. Such beauty at our front door."

Mike Oulton, suave maitre d'.

All I did during this street theater was stand there in amazement. It was totally beyond me to walk up to strangers. I motioned to him, *Come on.*

Instead he pulled me over to another table where a man his age sat quietly drinking his coffee. "Look, Ed, here's how you relax. This man's worked hard all day and he's letting the tension escape from him. I'm sorry to bother you, sir. I just wanted my friend to understand the art of calm reflection."

The man at the table smiled.

Mike Oulton, guru.

It was a wonderful evening, full of laughter and life. I felt lucky to have him for a friend.

During the days he worked for his stepfather, painting houses. It was money, he said, but nothing he wanted to spend his life at. He told me that he had spent a few evenings with his daughter, age eleven, and that she had really enjoyed being with him. I could readily imagine that. The thing that worried me was how the girl's mother would feel. All of a sudden this tremendously entertaining man is released from prison and takes the daughter out for exciting evenings, while mother has spent years nursing colds and buying school supplies.

Visiting with his daughter was the most important thing he could do. I knew from our conversations that she was the one person who mattered the most in his life. Over and over he said to me, "I have got to make her proud of me."

In August my wife and son accompanied me and we took Mike out to dinner. It's hard to entertain people, as everyone knows. It takes effort and it's not a subject taught in prison. But once again Mike showed his natural ability. He correctly assumed that we didn't need to do the town. Instead he took us to Ogden Point along Victoria's seawall and out to a pier jutting into the Strait of Juan de Fuca.

Again, he had us all laughing the entire evening.

By this time Mike was on e-mail at the library and he gave me a sense of what it was like to get out of prison. He was the kid in the chocolate factory, the stranger in a strange land.

> Ed,
>
> This e-mail shit is driving me crazy. It took six days to get the first one off and I just figured out how to respond to your reply. Of course, I won't ask for help. I hate it when these young kids come and whip off an e-mail without a problem. I go to the library to send mail. I only get a half an hour at a time to write and send mail. What sucks is that it takes me that long just to get into my mailbox. Slow and steady - right?
>
> Life outside the walls is fantastic. I'm meeting people and getting rejected by women every day.

When I walk down the street, I say Hi to everyone
I meet. I must have the strangest smile on my face
because most of them cringe away from me. I'm
just trying to be friendly, but maybe I should stop
talking to complete strangers. Next thing I know,
I'll have a warrant out for my arrest. I can't help it.
These people don't know what it's like to be free.
It's like moving to a new country. You want to know
everything about the place, the people, the culture.

Mike went on in the email to tell me about his troubles with
various government agencies. ICBC (the Provincial car insurance
people) wanted $3000, family maintenance wanted $40,000, his
credit card company wanted $4,000 and he had a $700 medical bill.

I just skimmed over this last statement and thought no more
about it. Why didn't I see the financial pressure he was under?
Why was I so blind?

Chapter 29
Mike
Tsunami

June, 2004. Freedom at last.

Imagine that you're trapped on a deserted island for a decade. On this island you have all the food you need, you sleep in a comfortable hammock between two sturdy palm trees, and your only primal contact is with small monkeys who live in the trees above you. Everyday you follow a certain routine to survive. Certain work needs to be done in order to keep your mind busy and your heart strong. Even though you watch the monkeys lounge around all day, eating bananas and having sex with each other, you're not jealous because you know that the work you're doing is for your survival. Staying alive is your passion. Preventing yourself from going insane on the island is your twenty-four hour a day job.

Now imagine being rescued from the island – no more struggling to stay alive each day and cleaning up after the lazy monkeys – and you're dropped into the middle of society. A city, town. Wherever there is community. Far from the environment filled with monkeys. Imagine that you have nothing upon returning from the island. Your home, car, clothing, family, money, even that picture frame with your kid's picture in it, gone. Now get moving and, *Good Luck*!

Imagine the feelings involved with that first day off the island. In a matter of twenty-four hours your life goes from lonely, destitute, fearful, tragic, cautious, angry, sorrowful – to a life that's lonely, destitute, fearful, tragic, cautious, angry and sorrowful, only now you don't have the free time to feel that way any more. There are new obstacles to conquer, and if you don't get over these obstacles, your community is going to eat you alive and you'll wish that you were back on the island.

That's what it's like getting out of prison.

In my second week out, I began to really miss the monkeys.

The first thing I did after spending six years in prison was go on-line for the first time. I wanted to get mainstream as fast as I could and the only way I knew how was to explore the Internet.

I'd never used computer lingo in my life. In fact, I'd never been online before that moment, but if I could survive a prison in a third world country, I could figure out how to get in cyber-touch with the rest of the world. After four hours on a library computer, I realized that I could potentially waste my entire life online. I'd just come from spending every minute of my day in line, so I decided the Internet would be a working relationship.

My first night out of prison felt like I had just run the *Boston City Marathon.* My heart pounded with excitement thinking about what the next day would bring. I wanted to jam the past six years into one day. I lay in that bed in the halfway house, shocked that just a night before I was locked in a cell. I wanted to do so much. I had a million projects and only one objective – create the best life I could. Survive on a new island.

I went to a community halfway house. A halfway point between prison and independent living. The house was a beautiful Victorian home. On the front door was a brass plate signifying the house as an historic artifact. The front of the house overlooked the Straight of Juan de Fuca and the docks where cruise ships frequented night and day. With the cool sea air behind me, I entered the first phase of my new freedom.

The staff members at the house were excellent. They showed me my room, introduced me to the other guys and gave me a clear explanation of the house rules.

They placed me in a doublewide bedroom with a walk-in closet and a patio overlooking the front yard. The room itself had high ceilings and was big enough to fit two single beds. The odd part of the room was the makeshift wall my roommate had constructed out of dressers and TV stands. It ran from one side to the other, separating my half from his. I felt as though I'd moved into a furniture warehouse.

My roommate was an older gentleman, who kept to himself and disliked everyone in the house. I told him I was used to dealing with people who liked to be left alone. He sneered at me and instantly my thoughts reverted back to the lazy monkeys.

When he left for work the next day, I snooped on the other side of the great wall to see how he lived. What shocked me was the amount of space he had compared to my side. I had more than ten feet of floor space compared to his five. He had managed to fit his single bed right against the back wall of the room. The dressers that constructed the great wall faced his bed and I assumed he used them to store his belongings. He had a TV at the foot of his bed, and the entranceway into his little compartment was no bigger than a doorway. It hit me. *His side of the room was laid out similar to a prison cell.*

* * *

As I walked downtown for the first time, I felt more alone than any time on the island. I spent half the day down by the inner harbor, watching the boats and the people, but mostly trying to understand where exactly I was, and who I was. I walked out of prison with a debt sheet longer than my criminal record. I had outstanding bills with an insurance company, child maintenance and a credit card company. None of them wanted to hear my side of the story. All they wanted was their money, and if I wouldn't (or couldn't) pay, then I could look forward to a day in court. It seemed that my life wasn't truly complete without a court hearing sometime in my future.

So to be a proactive member of my society, fit in and be somebody who was welcome, I needed to square away the people who were after me, face responsibility and deal with outstanding matters. If I wanted to truly be free, I needed to free myself from all restraints.

When I tried to get my driver's license, I was denied because of outstanding child support payments. The lady at the DMV gave me a number to call. When I tried to access money from my bank account, the woman at the bank told me that my accounts were frozen. She too gave me the same number to call – Child Maintenance Enforcement Program. My body was out of prison, but my credit was serving an undetermined sentence in Child Maintenance hell. I'd officially gone from deadbeat to deadbeat dad.

When I called the maintenance people, they were shocked to hear from me. I was directed to a caseworker who seemed surprised to actually hear my voice. When the caseworker told me I owed them $40,000, I actually laughed. It wasn't funny or a joke, I just didn't know what else to do.

The rigorous life of a mental patient continued.

As for the rest of the financial world, I owed the insurance company $20,000 in unpaid tickets, insurance claims and late fees. My credit card debt was $4,000, and the money in my account was gone – that was another $2,000. Fresh off the island and into a debt pool of $66,000. Every program they'd forced me to attend in prison never once dealt with this problem.

I went to court to fight the $40,000 debt to child maintenance. It seemed like lynching rather than litigation. I decided that I didn't need a lawyer for such a simple matter. The judge suggested that I should have one, but I refused. I'd been through worse, and I figured that since the worst they could do was throw me back in prison, I had nothing to worry about.

In front of a packed courtroom, they told me how shameful I was and critiqued my role as a father. I was ordered to make payments on the outstanding debt until I could prove that I had been in prison. When I left the courtroom, I was so mad that I broke the front door of the courthouse by slamming it against the wall. If the judge saw the broken glass on the sidewalk, she would have her proof quite quickly that I wasn't concerned about being locked up.

The sad part was that all this occurred before I even saw my daughter for the first time.

Everything I needed to feel complete was taken hostage, and offered back to me at a price. The more time I spent alone thinking about fighting for my life back, the more I rejected it and ignored it.

When the mother of my daughter threatened to keep my daughter away from me, I wanted to give up on becoming a father too. An emotional tsunami was about to destroy all portions of my confidence, creating an unnatural disaster that would make my life a living hell.

* * *

September, 2004 – Still free

I did some great things that summer. I got involved with different acting projects. I did some Shakespearean theatre and acted in a small movie. I also worked a few different jobs – one with my father at his painting company, but I soon quit when I realized I was miserable. I got a job with an alarm company that had its salesmen travel door-to-door soliciting their deals, but I quit that when it became too sleazy. Finding a job was easy for me, but keeping it proved to be a challenge. Everyday I wrestled with the notion that I should be doing more with my life. I struggled with the fact that I had wasted almost my entire life in prison. I felt that every job was just a time-filling routine. I worried that I wasn't going anywhere, and that I might get stuck doing something I hated for the rest of my life just to keep up with the heavy debt I was in. Quitting, starting – it was all the same. One was as easy as the other.

* * *

December, 2004 – Freedom pays a price

The week I was arrested, I had a great job at a sports company. I enjoyed the work because I set my own hours, traveled to speak with customers and cold-called stores in an attempt to get the gear on the shelves. I'm a natural salesman. The job actually made me feel good about my life.

But everything else outside of that office was killing me.

The pressure of the debts robbed me of my good nature. I was resentful towards the people around me – my family, my daughter, and the staff at the halfway house. I concealed my emotions from people around me. I didn't want to have to explain myself a hundred times a day and *no*, I didn't feel like talking about it.

I'd managed to convince my parole officer that I had life figured out. We were making plans to move out of the halfway house and into my own apartment. They thought that I was saving money from my work, but I wasn't. I was foolishly spending my money with no regards to the future I was supposed to be creating for myself. In an act of rebellion, I decided not to give Child Maintenance the monthly payments ordered by the court. Instead, I tried to give the money directly to my daughter's mom. My new caseworker threatened to seize my accounts again and take away my driver's license if I didn't follow their rules. I told him to stick his rules up his ass. They suspended my license that day.

The pressure of being a half-decent father consumed my every thought. When I was with my little girl, she got anything she wanted. I spent most of my money on her, taking her shopping, to movies, to dinner. She was my only friend at that time. I enjoyed being with her, but I hated everything about my life.

I managed to stay away from my old crowd. I tried to make friends with people in the "straight" world, but I had nothing in common with them. The people from my theatre group had never seen a man with his throat cut or fought for his life against an armed assailant. People I met while playing sports had the morals of a ground snail. They whistled at fifteen-year-old girls and made degrading comments to women that made my blood boil. Making friends proved to be more difficult than dealing with my loneliness.

I met a woman at one of my acting jobs. She was a good girl, from a good family. We managed to build a good relationship before I purposely tried to ruin it. She gave me a good fight. She tried to help me as much as possible, but she wanted me more than I wanted her. She became a victim of my cruelty and didn't even know it. I resented her for her life and her kindness, and although she never felt a thing, I hurt her more than she could ever know. And I felt nothing.

My family put on a brave face when I was around. They, like many other families, were the kind to forget and never talk about how we all felt. They never once asked about my time in prison, nor did they mention a reason why they never came to visit. Neither did I, but I'm sure I was the only one who was aware of it. These people were my community support group. They were the people I was supposed to lean on when things began to feel weird, but unfortunately, and to no fault of theirs, they were the ones who felt weird to me.

I had turned into a scared man. The burden of living every day weighed heavy on me. That was the first time in my life I had contemplated suicide – freedom suicide. I wanted out of this world that forced me to be part of the three-ring circus called life. I wanted to go back to the island and deal with the monkeys and the structured days. Every moment on the street felt like a demand. *I had to do this. I needed to do that.* Everyone had great advice but no one had solutions.

My parole officer ordered me to see a shrink. Every week I told her that things were great. She believed it and we had a great relationship built on the mutual understanding that neither one of us gave a shit about the other. I couldn't, and I wouldn't tell her a damn thing about how I felt.

How was I feeling? I felt like crying for no reason at all, and I felt like that every day. When I woke up in the halfway house, I wanted to go back to sleep. I knew that as soon as I got up, I would begin to worry about where my life was. My job, my relationship with my family, my finances. I thought about the bills I had to pay at the end of the month and where I was going to get the money – legally. I thought about the program I would have to attend and the theatre practice I'd have to show up for that night. Socializing with people I didn't understand, or to be honest, even like. The brave facemask I'd have to wear, when underneath, I just wanted to cry.

I'd never lived with stress in my life before. Inside prison, the island, my life was structured and predictable. Outside, every day was a new challenge. The stuff they taught me in programs didn't solve one single issue that I had in society. The only time those teachings every came to mind was the moment I decided to take another shot at crime. I was sick of suffering for no reason. Why was I holding back emotions like a sucker just to please everyone around me? I decided to give up trying to cope with life, and take on the role I felt most comfortable in. I was tired of working to no end, for little respect and zero credit.

I felt let down by the system that released me. When I sat in that parole meeting and told the board about my plans, they suggested to me that I was going to fail, but released me anyway. When I told my parole officer about my daily routine, she chastised me for not showing up for my programs, but ignored the fact that I had committed to doing positive activities with my free time. Everything seemed so focused on what they wanted, I lost track as to what I wanted for myself.

I'm not blaming the system on my failure, but I will blame them for not preparing me for the barrage of stress I endured on parole.

I know what I did was wrong. I walk around with my head up and my eyes open. I know that I should have confided in my family and friends. I should have used Ed more. I should have concentrated on one thing at a time. A job. One leisure activity instead of four. I should have been more honest with my girlfriend and developed a meaningful relationship with her. I should have dealt with every situation on its own, instead of throwing it on the pile of stress with the other problems in my life. This is evident to me now that I'm back in a cell, but why didn't I have the answers then? Why was life so hard to figure out when you're in the midst of it, and so easy when you're segregated away from it?

The answer is clear: because I care too much about life to let it just happen. I'm not in prison because I want to be, I'm here because I lack the ability to make good of the moment. I'm ashamed to say that I can't cook, balance a checkbook, fill out a tax form, save money, hold a relationship, make friends with squares, play recreational sports without hurting someone, or keep appointments. I've either never cared about these things or been too self-absorbed to even try. Now, these simple tasks I've ignored my entire life, are the things that I care the most about. Mixed with the strain of having to please everyone around me, there were times when I was out that I wished I were back on the island with the monkey.

At least the shit they were throwing at me didn't hurt so much.

Chapter 30
Ed
Back on the Island

Mike kept sending funny emails all through the fall. Occasionally he called me from his office. He was now doing phone sales for a sports company. And then in November there was nothing for a long time.

One day Sister called me from Matsqui. "Mike's been arrested in Victoria. He got in a fight in a store with a security guard. It was over a purchase."

Things flashed through my mind. The computer store, the $40,000 family maintenance bill, Christmas coming and no money. Pressure, pressure, pressure and no friends. Certainly his attack was not justified, but I knew where he was coming from.

I wrote to him right away and told him to forgive himself. Not to wallow in self-recrimination. But I began to ask questions myself. Why does the prison system make a guy go through all kinds of programs while he's in jail and then send him out the door with almost no help? Who was around to help Mike handle pressure? Who was there to give him financial advice?

And the worst question – where was I? Did I deliberately ignore his bills?

When things jumble in my mind, when I feel great emotion, I have to write poetry – my own kind of poetry. It only happens once or twice a year.

Michael

Prison – you devil – you have grabbed him again.
    Your naysayers said this would happen.

Your shrinks and your guards and your young college grads
rejoice.
He's back. More work for you.

Damn you. Bloodsuckers. You have won this round.
He's yours again for now. He blames himself, but I blame
you.
Your pious advice, and your half-assed programs.
What he really needed was love and support.

The terrible truth – I let him down, too.
I am a distant part of that prison devil.
Oh God, cleanse me.

There is a light in him – art: writing, movies, entertainment,
laughter.
The light will burn inside him and fill his body.
We, his friends, will feed that light.
He will beat you, Prison devil.
Art and love are stronger than concrete and steel.

One day in January, I went out to Matsqui to teach my creative
writing class and he was there. He strode in during a class, walked
up to me and hugged me. I began to cry, but quickly hid it.

Mike went through a period of depression. He kicked himself
for his failure to make it. He felt he had let his mother down and
especially his daughter.

Friends wrote to me. One man sympathized with Mike but said,
"My wife had a more practical reaction. She said there should be
counseling and guidance for newly released people in Mike's
position. NOT group therapy, just help in terms of financial advice
— how to declare bankruptcy, deal with creditors, handle child
support, etc.

How else is a person who's been on the shelf for all those years
supposed to adjust to all those outside pressures?

"I guess the lack of such support is a big piece of what sets people up to fall... again."

A parole officer in another prison, a friend of mine, gave me advice – and hope. "I see guys come in and out of prison all the time. What is important is that Mike does not lose faith and his focus. The ones defeated by being brought back give up on everything. The odd one, the rare one, uses this 'defeat' to re-energize himself. I think he could do this with help from people like you."

Mike and I started talking again after class. I was full of advice and gave it, until I am sure he was ready to walk away from me. But he stayed with me and I eventually shut up and just stood by him. I wanted him to know I was there for him.

His mood improved and he began to write again. Soon he was his old self, but now there was a maturity about him. A new determination to succeed replaced an undisciplined past. Realistic plans took the place of ignoring the unpleasant realities of ordinary life.

In 2005 he turned thirty and he told me it affected him deeply. "Where am I going?" he asked. "What have I done with my life?"

As others at the age of thirty, he began to think about the words of the song:

> Take your place on the great Mandela
> As it moves through your brief moment of time
> Win or lose now, you must choose now
> And if you lose, you're only losing your life.

He was thirty and ready to go, but the prison door wouldn't open.

Chapter 31
Ed
The Jail before the Jail

Fall, 2003. Surrey PreTrial

I needed money. New thermal windows for the house, a glassed in porch for our senior years and some help for the kids – that sort of thing.

I saw an ad to teach English to adults who had not graduated from high school. I applied and the principal, Lee, called me in for an interview.

Lee is a short, wiry man. His office does not befit his rank – a small office in a temporary building, looking out on a sidewalk between two other temporary buildings. The floors creak in these old buildings and the smell of books competes with the musty odor of old wood.

I'd never met the man though I had heard of him by reputation. "Lee is the guy who comes up with creative programs," – that's what people said. "He's the most creative guy in the whole system."

We chatted for a few minutes. Like me, Lee was a former American. "My roots are in the Jewish community of New York City," he told me.

It seemed Lee believed the same things I did – the war in Iraq was terrible, prisons were places of brutality and degradation and George W. Bush was a hell of a poor president.

In one way Lee and I were different – he worked within the system and tried to accomplish as much change as he could, whereas I had always told myself I was a rebel outside the system.

We got down to business. I made my pitch. "I'm a writer and I know English literature and I know grammar. I'll do a good job for you."

He waved his hand, brushing aside my pitch. "Oh, I've got people who can teach English. I don't want you for that."

I started to get up.

"Hold on. I've got another job for you." He told me about a new provincial program to teach the GED in the local pretrial center. "You've done great work in prisons, Ed, and this would be a perfect job for you."

To be honest, I wasn't even sure what the GED was. I've since learned it's a high school equivalency test, helpful for getting a job.

His phone rang. There was an emergency someplace on the big campus of temporary buildings. He was gone.

That was the last I heard from him for a few weeks. In early October he called and told me to get clearance from the PreTrial Centre, even though I already had clearance from Matsqui. Sometimes I think it's harder to get into prison than it is to get out.

A week later, another call. "You start on Thursday night, October 23. Good luck." That was it. No forms, no detailed instructions, no nothing. "Go and start the program."

I did. It was Thursday, October 23, 2003.

Surrey PreTrial is maximum security. I had to wear a badge and I had to put an alarm gizmo on my belt. If I pushed the big red button on the gizmo, guards would come running. They had offered me one of these at Matsqui, but I turned them down. Here there was no choice.

Every door – I mean every door – in PreTrial was opened by someone in a control room on the first floor. To get to the library from the entrance, I had to stop at three doors, press a button, wait for a response, state who I was and then wait for the door to buzz open.

Class was to be held in the library. Across from the library was a bathroom labeled Staff. I asked for a key – bathrooms are important for men in their sixties. Nothing doing. No key to the executive washroom for me. To use the toilet, I had to buzz through three doors and go to the staff room.

Control monitored every hallway with a camera. This place was indeed maximum security.

I entered the library and looked around. Good. No camera. While I planned nothing out of the ordinary, I wanted the men – and myself – to be relaxed, out of the camera's view for at least a short time.

At Surrey PreTrial there are six different living units for men and now six for women. When I started, the women had not yet come to the building. Each unit has some individual cells and some two-person cells, plus a small common living area. A unit holds from twelve to thirty people. The prison does not allow any mixing of units because co-accused might get together and agree on their story. The authorities strictly enforce this separation.

The same rules applied to school. Never mind if I could gather men who needed basic help from the different units. I was not to mix units under any circumstances. I understood the reason for this rule and I supported it, although it made my job a lot harder. When a unit came down to school I might have beginning learners mixed with high school grads and in a few cases, college grads.

What were we going to study – trigonometry or the multiplication table?

I took a deep breath and called the first unit down.

The door to the library – as all doors there – was heavy steel with a double window of unbreakable glass. A few minutes later seven men in red suits stood at the door.

I began to sweat. Why? I'd worked in a max place in the States. Every week I went into Matsqui. What was so scary about these guys?

Maybe all the steel doors had me spooked, maybe it was that they all wore red suits. I don't know.

The door buzzed open and in they came, excited, man-sweat smell. They all looked pale – not enough sun. Lots of handshaking and "My name is Tom," and "We got a school here – finally. Shaun's the name." And so forth.

I made coffee for the men and gave them pens and pencils. Other prisons pay men a nominal amount to attend class, but there was nothing like an incentive here, so I determined to at least save them the canteen cost for pens, pencils and paper.

We talked about the GED as a high school equivalent. I told them I was a writer and we talked about that. Then I registered them one by one.

Tom had been in PreTrial for six years.

"Six years?" I couldn't believe it. As a kid in school I remember learning that Americans had a right to a speedy trial. Maybe Canada was different.

"It's an immigration thing. Another country wants me."

Shaun didn't tell me anything about his crime. "I only made it to Grade 8. I'm 35 now and I'm getting too old for this crime game. I want out."

A perfect person for school.

David had a clean-cut look about him. If I had seen him on the street, I would have assumed he was in college. "I've got a high school education and a year of college," he said. "I just came down here to look around the library."

"Can't you come down to the library when you want?"

He gave me a cynical snark, as if I had just asked him if he'd like to go with me for a drink at an area pub.

"This place is the pits," he said. "There's nothing to do. Thank God you've started this school. We have AA once a week and NA (Narcotics Anonymous) and nothing else. Twenty-three hours a day we're on the unit, one hour in a cement courtyard surrounded by concrete walls."

"You mean you spend the whole day on your unit?"

"Yeah. And for a lot of that time, we're locked up. Staff break. Staff dinner. Count. We're in our cells."

What could I say? I had no nostrum to give.

Shaun got up. "Anyway, thanks for coming. I'm going to look around the library now."

The next guy was Spencer. Maybe in his forties. A couple of fingers missing. "I want school," he said. "My son is in Grade 4 and my daughter is in Grade 6. I want to be able to help them."

And then Jack. Age twenty-one. "Listen, teach," he said. "I've spent most of my life in jail. Juvie and provincial jail. Man, I'm sick of it. I want to get my school, but I screw up as soon as I get out. Drugs. They put me in a halfway house and then they start laying religion on me. I walk out the door, steal a car and get some dope."

I was to hear that over and over in the coming months.

I registered the other two. Similar stories. I've changed the names and the stories slightly, but these were the men in PreTrial.

I gave them an assignment to write about a safe place they knew as a kid and the program was off the ground.

On the next Thursday I was surprised to get some stories back. "I had a fort in some thick bushes and when my old man got liquored, he start whaling on me and, I'd go to those bushes and hide." "We had some woods at the end of our street and me and my buddies made a club house from some lumber we stole. That's where we went when we skipped school. But one guy's dad found the shack and told the other parents and they tore it down."

Lots of stories, but common to many of them was parental drinking and abuse. The old rule was proving true – bad parents, bad kids.

Week after week I went back, every Thursday night. The numbers increased. I had less and less time with each student, but slowly I learned about PreTrial, the true and the false, the good and the bad.

PreTrial, Remand and *Jail* are all the same thing

PreTrial is a short-term place where people are held while they wait for trial. Tell that to Tom who's been there for six years. Canadian justice moves slowly, a good thing, I think. Fewer mistakes. But six years?

PreTrial is not a place to be sick. First of all it's hard for the men to get to medical care. Unit staff, guards, are the first problem. "You're just faking," and comments like that. The next problem is the nurses. Some are good and competent, others less so. Working in a jail is not a prestigious item on your resume and the pay is less than adequate. Often the nurses have limited English or have not updated their medical knowledge. After I had been there awhile, I was amazed to have people come to the library and ask for information on the drugs they were given. "This stuff is addictive? I didn't know that." I heard that more than once. And, "I've got enough trouble with drugs without taking on a new one."

The jail pharmacist did not give out an information page on prescribed drugs. When I go to my neighborhood pharmacy, I always get an information page on a new drug.

People can die under this care – and they have. One doctor, however, is the exception. Everyone says he is a good and caring man.

I learned a lot about the guards who worked there. Since I was teaching the GED, one guard asked me how a friend of his could get his GED out in the community. Just talking to the guard, I knew this was really for him. A few weeks later, he gave me his opinion of the men in PreTrial. "They're all scumbags. They can't learn a thing and you're wasting your time here."

One night I buzzed control and said, "Five men to return to Hotel unit." I had given them supplies, a cup of coffee and I had checked up on their study progress. I couldn't do much more, because I had to see six units in one evening.

Control answered. "You mean five *inmates*."

No, I didn't mean five inmates. First of all these men were not convicted. They were all awaiting trial. They were not *convicts*. But more important, I hate that word with a passion. I hear it at Matsqui. "Inmate Jones, report to health care." Day in, day out, men hear their names called out in this fashion. Not *Mr. Jones*, but *Inmate Jones*. What other institution does that? What is the long-term effect of reminding someone over and over that they are an inmate?

I repeated myself. "Five *men* to return to Hotel unit."

Control's tone rose. "Five INMATES."

I said nothing. The door did not buzz open.

Time passed. A minute. I was involved in a war of wills – one I was going to lose. If I wanted to get the next unit down for school,

I had to give in. But I thought up a compromise. "I have five to return to Hotel unit," I said.

There was a long silence and then the door buzzed open.

Despite the negativity of most guards, I met a few with souls. One man was always cheerful to me and polite to the men. He called me aside one night. "You know, if I were running this place," he said, "no one would ever leave here without a high school diploma and full job training."

And one supervisor showed great understanding that this jail thing wasn't working. He apologized for some of the more stupid regulations as he shrugged and said, "What are you gonna do?"

In general supervisors seemed wiser and more humane than the guards.

No universal statements apply to PreTrial. There are good guards and bad guards, good health care workers and bad health care workers, good residents and bad ones, too.

What is true of PreTrial, as is true of all prisons, is that there is an *Us* and a *Them*. This is a poisonous atmosphere. No true help can ever be accomplished in such a setting.

Jail is a place to dry out or to come down from terrible addictions. One man opposed my negative comments about jail. "Thank God for this place," he said. "Without it, I'd be dead." I tried to make distinctions, but he wasn't having any.

Jail is a place to meet old friends. Time and again the conversation drifted off to who knew who, who did time with whom in juvie. For some of these guys, jail wasn't a punishment – it was old home week.

Jail is a place to get hit in the head with a coffeepot by another guy who didn't know how to control his anger. Time and again the public address system would call out "Code yellow." The guards would run to whatever unit the code yellow was and quell the disturbance. Then the PA system would call out, "Stand down, code yellow," like some pretend military camp. Sometimes people who were just minding their own business got caught in the middle of a fight. Actually, I'm surprised there weren't more fights. Put twenty to thirty men on unit, men who had very little control over their emotions, keep them on the unit for twenty-three hours a day, lock them up for long periods, treat them like animals, make it hard for them to contact their families, have them endure the tension of long hours in a trial and you are going to have fights.

What was the institution's response to fights – counseling? take the pressure off? play some music? No. Their response was to put the instigators in segregation. No TV. In the cell twenty-three hours. No phone. No school. No privileges. No contact with others.

Jail was a place to watch some good TV, the universal baby sitter of prisoners. I sympathized with men who enjoyed TV shows, but in another way it made me angry. The authorities were encouraging a generation of couch potatoes.

Jail was a place to return to over and over, until one day the person woke up and said, "Enough." But time and again I saw a man leave, his buddies would give him high fives and two weeks later he'd be back. One man told me that he and his buddies made bets on how long someone would be out and when they would come back. It was a sub-cultural ritual.

* * *

2004

I worked through November and December. Lee suggested I have school during Christmas week and I agreed with him. School for the men at pretrial was a break from a terrible routine, a place where they were respected as individuals. The New Year came, new people came into jail, others left or were sentenced, and some came back. It hurt when they came back.

Spring came and then summer. I told Lee that the program was working too well. It was wearing me out. Every Thursday more and more guys were coming down to class. I had to stay later and later to get everyone in and then I had to correct homework and do the paperwork on weekends. Meanwhile an area-wide jail reorganization had occurred and six units of women were added to Surrey PreTrial. Lee hired a female teacher – his idea being that we would work

together, teaching the women on Tuesday nights and the men on
Thursday. "It's important that you work together," he told me. "A
team."

I met Janey (not her real name) at a coffee shop before she
started. She was a big woman, not overweight, but with the shoulders
of a guard on a football team. A kindly expression soothed her
tough-looking face.

She had worked on Vancouver Island in a prison as a teacher's
aide and Lee felt she would be perfect for the job. While I was
strong on writing, she was good at school subjects, math and English.

Lee prided himself on picking the right people for the job.

She started work. I, who had always worked alone, gave myself
a lecture or two about working with others, about being
accommodating. I noticed Janey liked to sit behind the desk, while
I preferred to walk around, lean against things, even sit on the table
once in awhile. She worked well with both the men and the women,
though her approach was different than mine. She helped people
feel good about school, while I was encouraging them to write and
to figure themselves out.

At least from those aspects we made a good team.

Part of the job was bringing supplies into the prison, pens, paper,
books, coffee supplies and so forth. When I worked alone, I brought
everything in. But now we were a team, so I asked Janey for help.
She told me she had no money to buy things. "No problem," I
explained, "the school system will reimburse you."

"I don't even have enough money to front for anything."

"Well, then get the office to open a charge for you."

She said she would. Meanwhile I continued to bring in all the
supplies. This meant stops during the week at three different stores.

Time went by and Janey never went to the office to get a charge
account. All the shopping and carrying was up to me. Irritating, but
maybe I could find a way to get her to share the workload.

One night Janey was busy talking to someone and I noticed a
woman looking desperately for a book. "Let me help you," I said.

"I'm looking for a book called *James Bond*."

I helped her look and soon spotted it. "Here," I said as I pulled the book off the shelf. As I did a paper fell out, an obvious note from someone.

I read the note. I can't recall the exact words, but it was a love note written in modern lingo. "I miss you, baby. I can't wait to see the new pimping shoes you bought." Comments like that.

She was excited. "It's from my boyfriend. He's in here, too." She reached for the letter.

"No way," I said. "You can't do this. You can't use the library as a message center." The prison authorities had impressed on me that co-accused were to be kept apart. This note was just a love note, but the principle was important and I respected it.

"If it happens again," I said, "you won't be allowed to attend school."

"Okay," she said, without much enthusiasm.

I showed the letter to Janey and told her what I had told the young woman.

"We have to tell the authorities," Janey said.

"Why?"

"Because they broke the rules."

"We're not cops. The letter isn't about crime, it's about love. What if I warn the young man that one more letter and he doesn't come to school anymore?"

Janey seemed to agree and the matter ended. She was different from me. She had worked for several years in the other prison and I felt that she identified with staff more than she did with those in prison. While I was polite and formal with staff, she was downright friendly. But with the prisoners, the roles reversed.

When the young man came down, I warned him about the same thing. "No more letters in books. One more and you're out."

He agreed and I was satisfied. I thought I had solved the problem without getting either of them in trouble. Truth be told, I found the incident rather romantic, but I maintained strong official opposition to it.

When we came into the prison the next week, the young man was gone. I was shocked. He had been moved to a different remand center. I suggested to Janey that we should make it clear to the young woman that we had nothing to do with him being moved.

Janey said nothing. I repeated myself. No response.

I thought her behavior strange, and the more I thought about it, I wondered if she hadn't told the authorities without consulting me. We had previously agreed to be forthright with each other, very necessary in a setting such as this.

The next time we were to go into PreTrial, I asked to speak with her for a few minutes before class. We arranged to meet outside the building. Open communication was essential when we both taught the same class and we were in a dangerous environment.

"Janey, I have to ask you – did you turn in those two young people?"

She got very angry and her face reddened. "You have no right to ask me that question, Ed."

I thought I had every right to ask her. So I repeated the question.

"Listen, Ed, you can just do this job by yourself." She walked away, got in her car and left.

I stood there with my mouth open. Obviously, she had turned the young people in. I had hoped that my direct question would be the chance to open up some real dialogue, but it clearly hadn't.

I went into the prison and told the program coordinator that the female teacher was called away to a family emergency and there would be no school for the women that evening. I knew the women would be disappointed, but I had made a rule for myself that I would never be alone with the women without another teacher being present.

The next day Lee called me and reported that Janey had called him and said that I was abusive to her.

For the second time in two days, I was agape in absolute amazement. I know myself. I've had sixty-eight years of practice and I know that I didn't even raise my voice. I just asked a question.

I was surprised at Lee and a little disappointed. The man was a mentor for me, a hero of the good fight in the middle of a bureaucracy. Didn't he know me? Didn't he talk to his colleagues about me? I had worked with five or six of his colleagues. Any one of them would have laughed at the charge that I was abusive to a woman.

A few weeks went by. I worked alone with the men and Janey worked with the women. I didn't see her or talk to her directly. She used supplies that I brought in, but never replenished them.

Lee called me in and asked if I would allow a mediator to solve the problem between us, but I did not want to work with her again. After saying I was abusive, I could never trust her again. I told Lee he could fire me if he wanted to, but I was through working with her.

For me, the big danger at PreTrial was not the inmates, it was another teacher.

* * *

Fall 2006

I went on vacation for a few weeks that summer and I told relatives the story of the dangerous teacher. They all told me to quit. When I got back from vacation Lee called me in again. "I can't let this go on," he said. "I want a team in PreTrial. So what about it?"

"Well," I said, "everyone, including my wife, tells me to quit this job, but the problem is the guys I've been working with. I can't walk out on them. They won't leave me alone. I wake up in the middle of the night and I'm thinking about them."

"Okay," he said – and nothing more.

Two weeks went by. "What happened to the female teacher?" a guard asked me. "She hasn't been here in two weeks."

I shrugged. "I don't know." But I guessed that Lee had let her go or had offered her another job.

After a month, Lee called me. "I've hired a new teacher. She'll meet you this Thursday."

Thursday came and as I got out of my car a slight woman got out of her car and called over. "Ed? Are you Ed?"

We met. She said her name was Barbara (her real name) and Lee had hired her to work with me. She had black curly hair and an air of uncertainty about her, perfectly understandable when walking into an environment like PreTrial.

She pointed to the two big bags of paper, books and pens I was carrying. "Listen, I'd like to take over doing some of the shopping."

Great. She wasn't even in the door and she had done more than the last teacher to make it a team.

But in the month since the last teacher, I'd reexamined myself. Maybe it was me that had to change. The very thing we accuse others of, we are often guilty of ourselves. Janey believed in *My Way or the Highway*. Maybe I did, too.

We walked in the front door and started to work together. Politically, we were both in the same place – on the left. We were strangers in the PreTrial center, not part of the staff, two people teaching the men and women and advocating for them as much as we could. We had fun together, but we worked hard and we both cared deeply about the students.

What is missing in jail is respect, respect for the residents, respect for the guards, respect for the people who work there. How could we preach respect if the two teachers didn't respect each other?

* * *

Who are the people in jail? Over the months Barbara and I came to know many of them. Some were sad people who sobered up, got out, re-offended and then appeared back in jail. Others were trying to make a change in their lives. Jail was the bottom and they had hit it.

However, it's true that we never saw the worst of jail – the ones who didn't come down to class, the ones who heard the word *school* and stuck up their middle finger.

One of our students was Jack. Barbara and I never found out what he was in for, but what an un-criminal he was. Even in his red prison suit, he looked like a young businessman. During class if the men got rowdy, Jack would politely tell them to cool it – and they did. He sat at the end of the table with his fellows in a row along the side, establishing himself as an authority figure.

When his court case came up, I wrote a letter for him, as we do for all our students, informing the court what the person had been up to while in jail. Most letters are routine – worked on his own for X hours, etc. But for Jack I said:

An unusual man. A man who buys a calculator so another man can learn some basic mathematics. This happens in prison, where funds are scarce. A man who turns down the chance to make a few dollars as a tutor in prison, so another man can earn the money. And still, this man tutors others – for free.

> Jack knows how to fit in, yet he stands apart from others. I don't know the nature of his crime, but it seems to me that it's just a hiatus – a youthful mistake – in a promising future. I have talked to Jack about further education, even if it's night school and I hope the court will support me in this. The man has ability, brains and common sense.

> Where should he be in the near future? I can see him working, I can see him attending university night courses, I can see him as a happy family man and a father. The one place I *can't* see him is in jail.

The court released him and I never heard from him again. Maybe someday I'll see him on the street. I hope the best for him.

* * *

Another of our students was Rob Osborne (his real name). He'd been in the news for stealing a lot of cars. One of the last cars he stole was a bait car and the camera in the car caught him in a drug-induced frenzy. High on crystal meth, driving at excessive speeds, he smashed into a parked car, shouted obscenities and tried to fire a gun out the window. The video from this incident was shown all over North America.

Jail sobered Rob up and he showed up for school. We gave everyone a pad of paper and a journal book. We told them to write every day in their journal. "Writing helps you figure out your life," we said, "and it also helps you with your English."

Rob took two journal books and the next week he asked for two more. He let us read his journal. The man poured out his soul in those books: prayers for his mother who had disappeared a short time after his arrest, touching love poems to his girlfriend, stories from his childhood, and things that happened to him in jail.

Rob wrote with a great sense of drama. His English grammar and construction were poor but the man had a sense of drama that some work a lifetime to develop. He could build a story and then hit you with a dramatic conclusion.

Once he wrote about a long day in the back of a sheriff's van. The van went from jail to jail picking up people before it delivered Rob to court. Rob wrote about pulling into a juvie facility where he'd been before. In the yard he saw a guard he knew and the man had gotten older. Rob reflected on what was happening to his own life – guards got older and he was still in and out of jail.

Rob was self-aware and intelligent. He was not the animal the media made him out to be. But because the media had painted him as a wild man, guards treated him unfairly and he spent a lot of time in the hole. When the local papers ran a story of the disappearance of his mother, they headlined it *Mother of Car Thief Missing*. Rob objected, writing to the paper and reminding them a woman was missing, not who her son was. Rob himself got a picture of his mother and made up his own poster, an amazing task in a jail where people had no office supplies. He asked us to distribute the poster in Surrey, which we did.

The journals he wrote told Rob's real story – an alcoholic mother who loved him, but often made mistakes in raising him. He told how he loved her, he wrote his prayers for her and – the most important thing – he made a personal vow to end his drug addiction in her honor.

After a year in jail, Rob pleaded guilty. He was tired of PreTrial, visits with his girlfriend, she on one side of glass, he on the other, a phone their only connection. The judge sentenced Rob to four years and he went to Matsqui and joined my writing class and – he's one hell of a writer.

I watched him often at Matsqui. He was an honest man, open, straightforward. I watched guards – one in particular – try to get him to explode. This guard, a woman, put silly regulations on him and then sat back and waited for the explosion. Could he go to health care? No, he couldn't. He didn't apply yesterday. Could he go into the school for his creative writing class? No, he couldn't. He didn't have the right institutional-issued shirt on.

While at Matsqui, Rob learned that his mother had been found dead. Rob felt that addiction had taken her life and it reinforced his promise that addiction would take no more people from his family.

One morning, as I walked into the prison, I felt sad and depressed. Once again, prison authorities were objecting to the newsletter my class was working on. My head was down as I passed through the last door into the prison proper. I took a few steps more and then suddenly Rob jumped out of a side hallway at me.

I jumped back and then began to laugh, laugh so hard I cried.

"I didn't jump too fast," Rob said. "I didn't want you to have a heart attack on the spot."

My depression disappeared. Rob trusted me enough to play a joke on me.

A few months later Rob got out of prison and is doing well. His life has changed – he's living the promise he made to the memory of his mother – no more drugs. He's got a job, a girlfriend and he's well on the way to writing his own story.

*   *   *

At PreTrial, when we were working with the women, it was very sad for me to hear the women talking about their children. "My kid's in grade seven and she's learning a little Algebra. I want to learn it myself so I can help her." "I call my son every night and he says, 'Mommy, when are you coming home?'"

Women were in prison for many of the same reasons the men were there – selling drugs, robbery to support a drug habit, violence and, on occasion, murder. No matter what their crime, Barbara treated them with kindness and civility. It hurt her when a woman came back to jail. Every week she went around to every man and every woman who came down to school and asked them how they were doing. She recorded the number of hours they had worked on their own and she let each person know that what they did was important.

One night Barbara brought a unit down and ten young Chinese women accompanied the other women. They spoke not a word of English. I tried to teach them some basic English, but there was little I could do in twenty minutes once a week.

I felt very sorry for these young women. I don't know why they were there and they couldn't tell me. But their attitude, their bearing, their laughter among themselves all spoke loudly that they were not criminals. Young girls to be sold as prostitutes? Slave laborers smuggled in, on their way to the States? I knew nothing. One of them took me to our world map and pointed to the city of Fuzhou on the southern coast of China, near Taiwan.

Barbara discovered that the women were not going to regular court, but to immigration hearings. I tried to teach them court words – lawyer, judge, appeal – but it was very difficult.

And then suddenly – like so many others of our students – they were gone. That is, all but one of them. I don't know the reason why this one woman was kept behind, but she couldn't talk to anyone. It was solitary confinement without the cell. Every time she came down, she looked worse than the week before. The other women on the unit told me she wasn't eating and she cried a lot. I wrote a letter to the director of the prison, but the women on the unit told me that nothing happened. And then one week, she was just gone.

Barbara and I got involved with the lives of our students and it was hard for us to just have them leave without explanation.

On another occasion a guard went to the director of the prison and reported that a woman had collected a number of red pens from her fellow students. She emptied the red ink from the pens and dyed her hair. When Barbara and I heard about this, we both laughed. But the authorities didn't laugh – they stopped us from giving out red pens.

* * *

One night a big man lumbered into the library for school. He was six foot and way over two hundred pounds. His presence filled the small library.

"I hope to God there are no PCs down here. I hate the fucking PCs."

PCs – Protective Custody – are men whom other inmates might harm. People who have been in a fight, former cops, sex offenders, people with severe mental problems. Inmates in all prisons know that society dumps on them so they have to find somebody to dump on. Thus the hatred of PCs.

"My name is Mohammed Omar," he said, "and I take no shit from anybody."

Barbara and I looked at each other. This guy was going to be trouble.

We gave him a cup of coffee.

"That's the only reason I came down here. I heard you guys serve real coffee, not like that shit they give us here."

"Have a seat, Mr. Omar," I said. "Do you want a GED book to study from?"

"I might as well take one as long as I'm down here. I need a thick book to hide my tobacco stash. (Smoking was banned at this facility.)

Mohammed returned to his unit.

"Oh, boy," I said to Barbara when the door closed behind him.

"A real winner," she said.

Mr. Omar came down every week after that – every week that he wasn't in the hole. He spent a lot of time there for smoking, fighting, and disobeying guards. Over the months, however, Barbara and I noticed a change – the man was actually studying. Despite all the talk, he was learning what a compound sentence was and how the Canadian government functioned.

At the risk of getting hit in the face, I took him on over his attitude toward PCs. "I love it, Omar. The authorities have you fooled completely. They are glad you hate PCs. 'Let him rant,' they say. 'Then he's not bothering us.' Omar, you've fallen for the oldest trick in the book. This works really well in American prisons, where the warden subtly encourages the fights between Blacks and Whites and Latinos."

"Fuckin' PCs," was all he said.

I was serious. I liked a lot of the people in PC. They were human beings. Their interests were no different than Omar's.

Lee arranged for the GED test to be given right there in the prison. Mr. Omar took the test, which took two days. He did well on science, literature, social studies and writing, but not so well on math. During this last test, the invigilator and a guard began to chat together. "Will you shut the fuck up," Omar exclaimed, frustrated with the math.

Any other time, Omar would have been thrown in the hole, but the guard couldn't respond that way with the invigilator, the exam watcher, there. After all, Omar was right – there should have been no talking.

Every week thereafter Omar blustered into the library, but he always brought with him new recruits for school. We had a tutor program at Surrey PreTrial, whereby people could earn a dollar an hour for helping others with their schoolwork. A dollar an hour wasn't much, but it was the going rate in the jail. Omar asked to become a tutor.

Barbara showed me her record book – despite all the bluster, the man had turned in every single homework assignment. We agreed and Mohammed Omar, the *fuckin' this and fuckin' that* swaggering tough guy became one of our best tutors. He worked with other guys for well over two hundred hours.

And he passed the math test the next time around.

* * *

Months passed and change came. They installed a camera in the library, which made no difference, and Lee Weinstein suddenly left the job, which made a lot of difference.

Lee was a creative educator who built the largest adult school in Surrey. Even though his accomplishments were big, his focus was always on the individual learner. Lee designed programs for all kinds of people – for jockeys, stable workers, sex trade workers, single moms, at risk youth and people in prison.

I remember a conversation I had one night at PreTrial with an intimidating young man. Call him Kelly.

"Hey, teacher," he said, muscles bulging, massive shoulders blocking my escape route. "I want a fuckin' book."

Lee always told us, "When a guy asks for a book, it's a great moment. Honor it. Get him the book."

"What book is that, Kelly?"

"*A Short History of Nearly Everything,*" he said. "It's by a guy named Bryson. It's a science book. I started reading it on the outside."

Kelly looked like maybe he beat people up for the mob. A science book?

"So, what got you into reading, Kelly?"

"Ah, this teacher guy. Actually, he was the principal. I got sent to the office for… Never mind. But this principal – Weinstein was his name – he sits me down and we start to talk and I tell him I never read a book in my life, so the damn guy goes out and buys me a book and gives it to me the next week. I read that whole book and I still have it at home. It was about this rich dude and a guy in prison. *A Man in Full* it was called."

I got the science book, charged it to the school account and gave it to Kelly. When he was finished, I glanced at it, then went out and bought a copy.

But that's just one example. Lee paid for cookies and little treats for the people in prison at Christmas time. When we asked for more time to teach, he fought for us with the school administration.

Perhaps his greatest accomplishment was to put out an amazing book, called *Prison Voices*, a collection of some of the best inmate writing in Canada.

A new principal took over from Lee and immediately killed our book budget. School was not about learning, it was about money. And this happened even though we knew the program brought in far more money to the school district than they had to spend. We did not teach in a school building, but in the jail, therefore there were no building costs, no heat, light, insurance or janitorial costs.

The bad news, however, was offset by some good news. The old guard at PreTrial retired and new, progressive management took over. They promoted the good guards and left the bad ones to keep on locking and unlocking doors. The director of programs came to us and said, "How about a booklet featuring the inmates' art and writing?" This was an idea we had proposed to the old crowd and got a quick, "No."

Previously teachers had just been tolerated, but now we were valued.

* * *

For the residents, the tragedy of Surrey PreTrial lay in the fact that it *was* a family. Here were old friends from juvie days. Here were people who understood what you had just gone through when you were arrested. The people in jail were your family. They supported you when you had trouble with the guards. They were not like the television image of prisoners, snarling, hate-filled men and women who would cut you as soon as look at you. These people were your family.

And that's a tragedy. The *them* – the doctors, nurses, teachers, ministers, shrinks and guards – are excluded from this family

Why can't society provide a caring institution for people awaiting trial? A place where the *us and them* of jail gets broken down. A place of competent, caring professionals. A place where guards are paid well and trained well. A place where respect rules, a place where people get individual attention, a family of guards, teachers, professionals and residents who welcome a person and who help them.

I never forgot the tribute one woman wrote about a guard in the first jail she was in. She called this guard an angel, a woman who greeted her, who told her that she was now among friends and reassured her that help was waiting for her.

That's what jail should be.

*   *   *

September, 2007

Four years after I started the program, the School District did not renew my contract. They said that all teachers had to have a teaching certificate (necessary for those who teach children and teens, but hardly needed for those who teach adults). I have a masters' degree, but I don't have a teaching certificate

It looked for awhile that I could retain my job by the school board getting me a letter of permission. But another teacher with no experience in prison, but with a teaching certificate, took advantage of the situation and took my job. My twenty-two years of work in prisons meant nothing.

Bureaucracies don't make much sense sometimes.

The day I cleared out my teaching materials and said goodbye, I had trouble holding back tears. I used to moan and complain about what a hard job it was and how tiring, but I didn't really know myself. I loved this work and I was very sad to leave all the men and women I had come to know, both staff and inmates.

I went home and my wife saw how sad I was and she hugged me.

Chapter 32
Ed
Trying to Get Out

In February of 2006 Mike was transferred to minimum-security, Ferndale Prison. This facility sits in the rugged foothills of the Cascade Mountains. The famous Westminster Abbey sits on a nearby peak, overlooking the Fraser River. From the prison you can see a luxury home high on a hill, rumored to belong to a rock star, although no one ever provided a name. All around the beauty of the mountains takes your breath away. New cottages house the men and not even a small fence surrounds the place.

But it's still a prison as Mike was soon to find out.

He had spent about fifteen months back at Matsqui medium-security prison after his arrest on his first parole. At Matsqui Mike served on the inmate committee and helped defuse several tense situations. He had a successful escorted pass where a guard in civilian clothes took him to a writers' conference. Everybody knew Mike at this prison and they were used to his ways. While not everyone appreciated him, those in charge of the prison knew that the man was not a convict in his soul and that he approached most things with good common sense.

The word is, however, that it's easier to get parole from a minimum prison, thus Mike asked to be moved to Ferndale.

Almost from the start things did not go well. The atmosphere is very quiet at Ferndale. You don't hear loud talking and laughter and you don't hear the slamming of prison doors. Everyone is sort of retired at Ferndale. The convicts have learned to hide all their boisterous rule-breaking while the guards and staff laze about. They sit around and reminisce about the old tough days at the max prison. They're all experts at solitaire.

Into this quiet atmosphere roars exuberant Mike Oulton, like a muffler-less chopper into Pleasantville. He came into the prison just as he roared into my class – loud, funny, testing everybody with his jokes and stories.

The people at Ferndale didn't like him. Prisoners weren't supposed to talk and laugh with guards. But Mike did – people were people. Prisoners were supposed to be submissive and quiet when they talked to caseworkers. Not Mike. He talked to staff as if they were human beings, asking questions such as, "How do you feel today in this great sunshine?" He treated them as people and assumed the same from them.

But no. Ferndale is a prison and the old "us and them" goes on there, too. Us good guys against 'them' bad guys.

He had two months to go before his parole date. When people tried to put him into programs or into jobs, he knew it was only for a short time, so he joked around with them. When they asked him what job he wanted, he answered, "Robot." When he took a job sweeping the floor in the prison factory, he sang at the top of his lungs, irritating some, entertaining others.

Ferndale was new to him and Mike would admit he was nervous. He overdoes things when he's nervous, when he's on new ground. A new prison, a new class, a new relationship – like all of us, Mike gets nervous. If the people around him relax and enjoy him, everything works out fine. But if people are uptight, it's a disaster. I remember a teacher who did not get along with him because she saw him as a threat to her authority.

This is the problem – uptight staff, nervous about their authority and in walks this troubadour, this wandering minstrel of life and love and laughter.

The French social scientist, Michel Foucault, claims that society identifies and punishes people who don't follow the rules laid down by the rich and powerful. These are the people to be feared. They are not afraid to break the rules. So the rich and powerful call them criminals and brand them for life so they can't upset the dominant classes. The staff at Ferndale heated the branding iron and waited for their moment.

It all happened over a cellular phone. Of course, cell-phones are not allowed in prison. The prison authorities can't regulate them and telephone companies can't reap the huge profits they make from prison phone systems. Yes, inmates can arrange drug deals, or order an execution on any phone, official or not official. They can also use a phone to talk to their children, to their wife or to their AA counselor.

Mike's roommate got a cell-phone. Mike didn't know where the man got it and it made him nervous – Mike only had a short time to go before parole.

One morning, a week before Mike's parole hearing, the guards came into his cottage to do a search. They found the cell phone hidden in a sock in Mike's part of the room.

"Is this your cell phone?" the guard asked.

"It's not even my sock."

"If it's not your phone, then whose is it?"

"Look, officer," Mike said, "if I don't tell you, you guys will slap my wrist. If I do tell you, I am liable to get a knife in my throat."

Without any more investigation, Mike was put in handcuffs and leg irons and returned to Matsqui. His parole officers at Matsqui and at Ferndale reversed their support for his day parole. No one sought a warrant to check the records of the cell phone. No one knew who paid the bill, who made all the calls.

Mike's scheduled parole hearing went forward as planned on April 20 at Ferndale. Mike asked me to be his citizen spokesperson. I got a substitute for my morning class and sat down in the hearing room. Mike was brought to Ferndale in chains and appeared in the hearing room with leg irons and handcuffs, but he was able to convince the guards to remove his handcuffs. "I talk with my hands," he said.

The Parole Board consisted of two older white men. Every parole hearing I've been to, one man plays good cop and the other, bad cop. I don't know what they would do if they disagreed. Maybe they never do.

They began by hearing from the parole officers. The woman from Ferndale said she no longer supported Mike for day parole. Behind her voice, I heard all those other retired people who work at Ferndale. Then the parole officer from Matsqui spoke up. This young woman also reversed her support and said that Mike had probably gone back into the drug trade.

You've got to be kidding, I thought.

An unusual thing happened next. A woman named Deb McKay was also at the hearing. I knew her from Matsqui, where she had worked for years. I knew she had been Mike's parole officer until recently when she was advanced to an administrative position.

The bad cop called on her. "It's most unusual to have three parole officers here, Ms. McKay. What did you want to say?"

"With all due respect to my colleagues," she said, "I want to speak for Mike. In my opinion he's ready to return to the community. He's done a lot of good at Matsqui and I know he wants to get out and start on his writing career. I'm asking the board to grant him day parole."

It's one thing to stand up for your opinion and it's another thing to stand up when two of your colleagues are lined up against you.

Next the Parole Board began to question Mike. Parole Boards do not go over the good things a man has done – they rehash all his mistakes. So there was no mention of the fact that the administration at Matsqui had often asked Mike to step into tough situations, no praise for his work getting the lifers their own kitchen, no pat on the back for writing twenty-three screenplays.

Mike did fine – personable, polite, direct and honest.

"Now about this cell-phone, Mr. Oulton," the bad cop said. "I must say I don't have much respect for the low-life who owns the phone. He didn't step forward and admit it was his. But my question to you is – did you ever *use* the cell-phone?"

"I did – once," Mike replied. "My teacher, my friend, Ed," he gestured toward me, "was very sick and I couldn't reach him. I found out later he went into the hospital the next day. All day I called on the regular phone here, collect calls, and Ed's answering machine kept rejecting the calls. Finally, in desperation, I used the cell-phone and then I reached him."

The negativity went on for the better part of an hour. Mike is narcissistic. Mike is violent. Mike failed before on day parole; he's going to fail again. Mike thinks like a convict.

Then came my turn. I've learned by sad experience that the Parole Board only values their own. The first time I appeared before the board for another man, they asked me if I was a lawyer. When I said I wasn't, they stopped paying attention. So now I tell them everything: ex Catholic priest, city councilman in Milwaukee, Wisconsin, Masters in Social Work, business man, teacher and writer.

I was sitting next to Mike and all the time he talked, my eyes were on that chain that held his feet. After I introduced myself, I let some emotion show. "I don't know if it's appropriate," I said, "but these chains on Mike go right through me. Long ago he stopped being my student. This man is my brother, my friend. I hate these chains on him."

When I said that, Mike started crying.

I went on to say how much community support Mike had and how I planned to be right there for him every step of the way, particularly when he dealt with financial matters. I gave them four letters from writers and friends. One was from a TV producer who said she was working with Mike on a TV series.

The Parole Board sent us all out of the room. Mike was locked in a cell. Deb McKay and I went outside for awhile.

"Hey, Deb," I said, "that was great. I really admire what you did. An act of courage. What do you think his chances are?"

She shrugged. "I can't say. They suspect the cell-phone wasn't his."

A short time later we were called in and the Parole Board told Mike that he was denied day parole, but that he could apply again in a few months. "Bring something new back to us," one board member said. "Take a program."

Mike has always offered to take any program the prison wants him to take, but every time he signs up, the program director screens him out. "Doesn't need it," gets stamped on his application.

I am sure Mike was upset and disappointed, but I was angry – partly at myself. I should have concentrated on the cell-phone. The parole officers had changed their recommendation based on suspicion, not on fact. Innocent until proven guilty and all that. I should have hinted that there were legal questions here for the parole officers, assuming guilt without getting a warrant to check the records.

All day I was angry and I remained so until I talked to Mike the next day after class. He seemed in better shape than I was. He forgave the guy who didn't stand up and say the cell-phone was his, he analyzed his own behavior at Ferndale, and he determined to play the prison game until his next shot at parole. Truly, I was the one who should have been lectured by the Parole Board. I wasn't violent, but I was angry as hell.

The staff at Ferndale was vindictive. Mike refused to play their game and they got him for it. This is the way all prisons work.

* * *

After Mike's positive first reaction, he entered a period of deep depression. "Hell with it, Ed," he said to me one day after class. "I'm just gonna wait for my statutory release date. I'm tired of jumping through hoops for these jerks around here."

He waved his hand in the direction of his parole officer's small cubicle.

His depression wasn't helped by the news that the cell-phone owner got parole a short time after the incident at Ferndale.

"When is your release date?" I asked.

"January, 2008."

"Over a year away? No. Absolutely no. You're not wasting another year here." I had no right to say that – this was his decision and his life, but I just couldn't see him sitting in this warehouse another year. "Tell you what, Mike. I'm going to start a letter-writing, publicity campaign to get you out. You know, something with escalating steps."

"No, wait. Let me try the parole way one more time."

"Who will be your parole agent?" I remembered the experienced parole officer, Deb McKay, who supported him despite the opposition of her two colleagues.

"The woman who turned me down last time."

"Get out of here," I said. "The one who claimed that you were using YOUR cell phone to get back into the drug trade, when you were really trying to reach me in the hospital? That one?"

"Yes."

"You're a better man than me, Mike Oulton."

"I've got no choice. I can't pick and choose parole officers."

Mike went to her. She said, "You have to give the parole board something new, something to show you that they've changed. Why don't you take an anger management course?"

I know Mike had to resist the urge to make a joke about bringing them something new – "You mean like new money?" But he said nothing and went to the anger management instructor.

She talked to Mike for awhile and finally said, "You don't need this program, Mike. And by taking a spot in the program, you take the place of someone else who might really need it."

Mike returned to his parole officer and reported what the woman had said. The parole officer repeated her words from before. "You have to give the parole board something new."

So Mike went back to the program instructor and signed up for the course. "I'm sorry," he said. "If I want to get out, I have to take this course."

*   *   *

"Mr. Baldwin clearly understands the significant relationship between his emotional reactions and his thinking."

Mr. Baldwin? When Mike was arrested in Mexico in 1997, he gave his name as *James Baldwin.* So during his entire time in prison in Canada, he was referred to as "James Baldwin," even though everyone – and I mean everyone – knew his real name was Mike Oulton. The PA system would bark out, "Inmate Baldwin, report to the first floor bubble," or wherever. In informal moments, everyone called him 'Mike,' including the warden. I always felt that the official use of 'James Baldwin' was another way to remind Mike that he was a low-life criminal.

In any case, Mike aced the anger management course. "Mr. Baldwin is capable of communicating in an assertive manner as well as problem solve without resorting to conflict. In his relapse prevention plan, Mr. Baldwin was able to identify and demonstrate the appropriate assertive communication skills."

Assertive communication skills? How can you be assertive with people who have total power over you?

*   *   *

The struggle continued. When would Mike get parole? Mike fought depression and wrote a well thought out parole package. I swallowed my anger and composed a polite and caring letter to the parole board. I got five or six other people to write in. Mike took his package to his parole officer. She examined it and said, "Well, Mike, looks like everything's here, ready for your parole. Just one more thing – we need to get an update on your psychological profile."

"What?" Mike almost shouted. "That's gonna take months."

"Well.........Anyway, we need it."

Mike knew the assessment would be little different than previous ones. The psychologist would come out and tell him he was narcissistic, the latest shrink buzz word.

Mike told me about this new delay and I fired off another useless letter to the warden.

The psychologist finally came and interviewed Mike. Good, I thought, now he'll get out. But no. His caseworker decided to combine two reports she had to do, so he would have to stay until she finished the one report. *Out in May* turned into *Out in July*. I felt powerless, much like these men often feel. Mike had spent an extra fifteen months in jail because his roommate had a cell phone. And now the roommate was long gone on parole.

And the reports from psychologists – what a travesty on the profession of psychology. Bombastic, negative, digging out every incident from his past life and magnifying it into a major problem. I thought the profession of psychologist was to help people. Yet in Mike's report, there was not one helpful note. No "Here's a good trick when you get angry." No, "Here's how to handle your emotions." Just a collection of bad stuff from the sociopath handbook.

Over the years a lot of guys have let me read their prison reports. In only one case, that of Dr. Cook, did the person I read about correspond with the real person. Most of these reports are just 'ass covering,' reports written with the sole purpose of proving to the public that when so-and-so reoffends, "we told you so."

How sad that the men and women in prison know that what they say will be used against them, so they decide ahead of time to hide certain truths. What happened to confidentiality between therapist and patient?

These professionals are in the employ of the prison industrial complex. Like doctors who work on death row, they contradict the values of their profession.

Internal parole officers, caseworkers and other officials imitate their more 'educated' peers and talk about 'criminogenic factors' and the like.

* * *

On July 11, 2007 Mike finally has his parole hearing.

It's 8:30 in the morning on a very hot day. Mike is perky, confident. As I wait for the hearing to begin, I wonder if this parole hearing will be like all the others I've attended – a feast of negativity and an attempt by the parole board to provoke Mike.

I imagine the parole board paraphrasing Shakespeare:

I come to bury Mike Oulton, not to praise him.

The evil that men do lives on;

The good is oft interrèd in their prison cells.

I'm sure the parole board's motivation is the best. They want to assure the public that the man will not revert to crime when things go bad. But is this how we evaluate people, by provoking them? In our everyday world we get to know people by talking to them and by finding out what they have done, both bad and good. The parole board never spends anytime on the good a man has done.

The hearing starts. First Mike's parole officer speaks. Fifteen months ago she was the woman who said he was using a cell phone to make drug deals, when he was really trying to reach me in the hospital. She's the one who kept piling requirements on him, keeping him in prison and costing taxpayers $50,000. I found out later she used to be a prison guard, but had advanced herself to become an internal parole officer.

I'm not expecting the best from her. I know that behind all the psych words, all institutional members work to keep the machine going.

She speaks in a quiet voice. "I'm recommending that Mike get day parole. He's completed programs I've asked him to take and, with the exception of some minor incidents, he's complied with institution policy."

Wow. Good start. But will she hold up if they drag up every bit of dirt in Mike's life?

The female parole board member starts the attack. She's a middle-aged woman, kindly appearance, maybe like somebody's mom. "Let's review the initial offense when you were arrested in Mexico."

She grills Mike about the arrest. "Why were you using a fake name? Is James Baldwin a real person? How much money did you hope to make?"

Mike answers all the questions directly. This line of questioning goes on for about ten minutes.

I glance at Mister Parole Board member. He's following the discussion. I can't decide if he's scholarly or hostile. He interrupts his colleague and in a few minutes I know what he's like – compared to him the woman is the good cop.

"Let's talk about the incident that happened when you were last on parole," he says. "You were arrested with drugs and with cell phones."

"Yes, I was."

"You have said that this was a sudden thing, that all of a sudden you decided to sell some heroin."

"That's right. I needed money for Christmas. I wanted to buy my daughter something nice. I was under a lot of financial pressure at the time. Child maintenance was after me, the car insurance people wanted me and so forth. I sort of had a nervous breakdown that morning. I just couldn't take the pressure and so—

"Wait a minute. I don't believe this *nervous breakdown* thing. There's another interpretation – that you had been selling for months and this morning you just got caught."

Mister parole board member glances at Mike's parole officer and then at me. He's scored a point and he wants the audience to nod in approval. He takes a satisfying sip of his water bottle. I don't respond and I can't see the officer's face. Will she stand up to this sort of pressure?

Mike responds, "No, that's not what happened."

Again and again Mister bad cop tries to catch Mike in contradictions. He's got Mike's psych report open in front of him, several sections highlighted. It's the same report I read and didn't find one positive word in the whole thing.

Deadly. On and on. He makes a point – a glance to the right and the left and then another small sip.

"You smoked marijuana just a few months ago in prison."

"I was terribly bored and depressed at all the delays in getting out on parole."

"That's no excuse. Is that what you're going to do when you're out?" Glance, glance, sip.

"You say you love your daughter, but what kind of a father have you been?" Glance, glance, sip.

This goes on for an hour and a half. Mr. Bad Cop stars in this show. Finally the board turns to the parole officer and once again asks her opinion. *Here we go*, I think. *She will cave.*

I think back to another one of Mike's parole officers who said she really loved this parole-board-hearing theater.

But this parole officer doesn't cave in. She repeats her earlier support.

The board calls on me.

"Every Friday for four and a half years, I have spent forty-five minutes after creative writing class with Mike Oulton. I think I know him better than anyone. He started as my student but now he's my friend. He's an amazingly talented guy and I hope you will give him a chance to prove it.

"You have said that Mike failed the last time he was out. I failed also. I just ignored an email he sent me, telling me of the financial pressure he was under. This time I'm going to be right there with him. He and I are going to meet every week. Mike has a reporting sheet he's developed for these meetings."

Mike handed the board members a two page check-list of his goals and the necessary steps to reach them.

The female board member thanked us and asked us to leave. "We'll call you back when we've reached a decision."

The parole officer, Mike and I go out to the waiting area outside the hearing room. Mike and I sit together and the parole officer sits opposite us. In a quiet voice Mike tells me he didn't do his best. Under my breath, I respond, "No, you did fine. Straight, direct, honest."

This isn't going to work. We can't talk openly here. The woman who has kept Mike in jail for fifteen months sits right across from us. How can either of us say anything honest? So the three of us chat: how to overcome the heat, her visit to India, my garden peas, the show on TV last night.

She's a nice woman, polite, intelligent. Yes, her world is limited to her family and to her work, which is prison, but a lot of people live in small worlds. Maybe even me. I sit back and look at her. Why is my world so full of muted colors? Other people have clear black and white visions of the world, good guys and bad guys, truth and falsehood, right and wrong. This parole officer is bad and she's good, uncaring and caring, right and wrong. The hearing we just went through was good and it was bad.

In the end, the truth is multicolored. There is no black and white.

After an hour the board calls us back in. The board grants Mike day parole and cautions him to stay close to me and to avoid association with those involved in crime.

We thank the board and leave the room. It's almost time for count so there's no time to discuss the hearing. Mike gives me a big bear hug as he usually does. He's happy and I'm happy. I know it's the end of his time in prison.

A few days later, on July 16, two days before his 32nd birthday, Mike Oulton walked out of prison for the last time.

Chapter 33
Ed
Dear Reader

Dear reader,

My views on prison? The sound-bite answers are:

- We've been tough on crime, now let's get smart on crime
- Prison is a warehouse
- Prison is a crime school
- Prison is a taxpayer rip-off. We're not getting much bang for our buck.
- We need more prison employees, not fewer. But let's train them to help people change, rather than train them how to warehouse people. And yes, they need to be paid much better. Now it's an occupation of last resort.
- The media are voyeurs. "Are you satisfied with the sentence given the offender?" The humanitarian, the religious person concentrates on restorative justice, not on punishment. The media ask the grieving family about closure. Seeing the criminal reform would be closure, but what resolution comes from putting someone in a warehouse for years?
- Let no one say I'm soft on crime. I call for a system that demands of criminals real change. Right now convicts don't have to alter their behavior, they just have to do their time. Boring, but easy. I call for wardens and experts to devise correctional facilities that really correct, that demand socially acceptable behavior and the personality structure to support it.

- Democracy works. Involve the inmate in the process of change. "What programs would you like to take?"
- Art works. Offer a range of arts, painting, music, acting, writing, stained glass. Programs say, "There's something wrong with you and we're going to fix it." Arts say, "There's hidden talent in you and we're going to help you bring it out."
- Education works. It's the way out of crime. It costs at least $100 a day to keep a man in prison. You can do a lot of education for $100 a day.
- Personal attention works. An ombudsman, a social worker, someone to follow up on everyone. Small caseload. Reporting to someone outside the prison.
- Success works – or should work. The prison staff that sends people out and keeps them out should make the most money. Deep in the subconscious of every present day prison employee lurks the thought, "Will there be work next year?"
- And then there's Mike Oulton——

The more Mike came to class, something strange started happening to me. Despite all the friendly – friendly stuff, despite "blowing sunshine up a lot of asses," (in the words of a former student,) I am distant from these guys. I know the plan – welcome them to the class, work with them, be friendly, appreciate what they do, even write a letter for them if they need it, sympathize with the stupidities of prison and never judge them. The plan works, it's worked for over twenty years, but it's all distant from me. I go home at night and sleep well.

I'm sure this goes back to my priesthood training. That's exactly the approach the Catholic Church wanted me to have as a priest. I call it the "I am a rock" stance. Only with my family, do the walls come down. The rest of the world sees a friendly guy, but never gets to know the real him. The rock.

Class ended one Friday and Mike and I sat alone in the classroom. "I've got a problem, Mike," I said.

"Yeah?"

"It's hard to talk about. I'm scared."

He did something I could never do – he stood up, pulled me out of my chair and hugged me. "Come on, Ed. You're okay. You're a gutsy guy. What's going on?"

I sat down. "You know—I mean, you know I have prostate cancer?"

"Yeah, I know."

""My cancer," I muttered, "it's way up."

"Your PSA?"

"Yeah. In June it was under Point 1. Now it's 14."

"Shit."

"It means the cancer is active again. I'm going to the Doc next week."

"You're a fighter, Ed. You know, that stuff you wrote."

Mike had read the articles I wrote for the newspaper when I got prostate cancer. I wrote and wrote, edited and edited until I had crafted a new person on paper, a guy who could stand up to cancer, a guy who could go on with his life despite cancer.

"I know," I said.

There was a long moment of silence between us. Then he got up again and put my head in an arm lock, which deteriorated to his arm around my shoulder, which deteriorated to another hug. "You're a fighter, Ed," he repeated. "Fight."

"Yeah," I said and felt much better.

What the hell was going on? I was supposed to be the man in control, the guy with the answers.

I look back now and I know the rock had acquired a friend.

* * *

What is friendship? It is certainly magic. Mike Oulton is good for me. He makes me laugh and laughter heals the soul. He gives me hope. Let me explain. Everything I've ever tried in my life, I succeeded at. I wanted to be a Catholic priest and I became one. When I left the priesthood, I wanted to get a master's degree so I would have the 'ticket' necessary to get a good job. In a year and a half, I got my masters. Then I wanted to get involved in politics, so I campaigned for another year and a half. My wife and I knocked on 12,000 doors in our district and I was elected to city council in Milwaukee, Wisconsin. Another success. When my term was up, my wife and I did something absolutely crazy. We opened a business we knew nothing about, a commercial greenhouse. We studied and worked hard and we made it, building a successful business over thirteen years. Then another wild change – we wanted to leave Ronald Reagan's conservative America and immigrate to Canada – and we did. Success.

But one accomplishment has eluded me – getting commercially published. I've done everything the books recommend – sent out hundreds of queries, entered contests, gone to conferences, and joined writing groups. No luck. I've published my books by Print On Demand.

In one way it doesn't matter – writing restores my spirit, but in another way writing doesn't pay any bills. So here's the hope part.

It's eleven o'clock and the other guys have left the classroom. Mike and I have twenty minutes before he has to go for count.

"I finished your book, Ed," he says. "*Prisoners of the Williwaw.* I really liked it."

"Great," I replied. Like most authors who have had their books published by Print On Demand, I'm used to friends and relatives telling me they enjoyed the book. It's the damn agents and editors who don't say that.

"No, I mean it," Mike said. "It's very visual. It would make a great movie."

"Yeah, a friend of mine and I turned it into a screenplay a few years ago and HBO optioned it for a year, but they didn't renew the option."

"Can I see the screenplay?" Mike asked.

I gave it to him the next week and two weeks after that, he had a new version of the screenplay written. "I've added a dog," he said.

"A dog?"

"Yeah. Everybody likes dogs."

I laughed. This was typical Mike – human, real, funny, alive. He was right – the dog added a lot to the screenplay and was even a symbol of the whole situation.

But the hope part. "Listen, Ed," Mike said, "I'm going to promise you this – I'm not sure how and when, but I am going to see this film made."

The thing is – I believe Mike. He's far different from me in this area. Mike is not afraid to approach people, to do wild and crazy things to get publicity, to give the media the excitement they crave. I'm too conservative to do all that. Someday Mike will get my book turned into a movie.

*   *   *

A thing that is very hard for Mike to do is to call someone collect. It's a pride thing, but I insist that he call me and he does. He's come far in his life. I know his history – the foster homes, the parental neglect and the early introduction into the life of crime. I have no illusions that if my background had been as hard as his, our roles might well be reversed. Not only has Mike given up crime, but he's purged his mind of 'the criminal way of life.'

Every week he walks me to the prison gate after class.

I point ahead to the prison gate house. "Son-of-a-bitch guard," I say, "gave me grief over my badge. 'Out of date,' the asshole said."

"The guy with the little goatee?" Mike asks.

"The same. Jerk."

"Go easy, Ed. He's not the greatest of guards, but his wife's undergoing cancer treatment. He's not sure if she's going to make it."

I look at Mike. How in the hell did he know that? The only way Mike could have gotten that information was to have had a honest-to-goodness conversation with the guard, the kind a convict does not have with a guard, nor a guard with a convict. Somehow Mike had been able to cross the line and treat this man as a human being and the man had responded in kind. Although he was critical of many guards, the convict/guard division was more in my head than it was in his.

What kind of a crazy mix-up was this? It seemed that everything was reversed in my relationship with Mike. I was older, but he was often wiser. He was told to take an anger management class, but I was the one who needed it. I was supposed to be the great humanitarian, but he was often more humane.

I came into prison to cause a revolution and what I found was a friend. Working in prison has cut me off from many people, but it has also opened me up to new worlds of friendship.

* * *

In many ways Mike is my opposite. He's young, I'm old. He's an actor and a publicist, I'm shy of the spotlight. He frightens some people with his wild humor, I scare them off with a wheelbarrow load of earnestness. Mike is orange, while I'm blue. Mike is not going to step forward and join my crusade to reform prisons. This is where I have come full circle. Instead of coming into prison with my own agenda, I have met Mike where he is.

Mike is somebody. This loud, creative boxer-writer-actor has hammered this message into my head, not by preaching but by being himself. Like Adrian and Dr. Cook and Davi, Mike *is* somebody. I've learned from him – he treats everyone he meets as a person.

Every few months I bought three dozen donuts and brought them into the guys in the writing class. But I changed after meeting Mike. I bought an additional box of donuts for the guards in the gatehouse.

* * *

You are somebody. How different that is from, "You must join my crusade or my religion or my anger management program."

You are somebody. Those are the secret words, the words of power that lie hidden in the gray corners of the prison. If a guard or a staffer or a convict listens carefully he or she will hear those words and a soul change will happen.

The words come from Jesse Jackson: Such simple words, but so concealed in prison.

You are somebody. Those words are in the chapel of every denomination, they are implicit in most systems of philosophy and they are enshrined in the UN. These words hide in the guards' locker room, in the staff lounge and in the corner of every cell. You have to be looking to find them.

Structural reform will happen if the public and their legislators accept the fact that prisons are full of somebodies.

If prisoners believe they are somebody, then drugs won't be necessary. If staff believe, they will stop doing things that demean prisoners.

If a guard believes that he or she is somebody, they might just remember that prisoners are somebody, too. And, of course, vice-versa.

If prisoners believe in themselves, then victim talk will end. If staff believe that prisoners are people, then talk of prisoners being *sick* will end.

If prisoners believe they are somebody, then the negativity associated with prisons will end. Shows like *Oz* will go off the air.

* * *

Mike and I began to write this book together. He believes in me and I believe in him. He has changed and so have I. Twenty years ago the gods gave me the gift of writing and now I have given it to him. Seventeen years ago I would have tried to line him up for my crusade; ten years ago he might have tried to sell me drugs.

I went into prison shouting the words of change: *reform, inhumanity, racism.* Now I listen carefully every week for those silent words: *You are somebody.* I have to start with myself. I have to respect every convict I meet and every staff person.

You are somebody.

Chapter 34
Mike
Dear Reader

Dear Reader,

I've always been an ambitious person. It's just that most of it was directed at criminal activity that usually ended up with me in prison. I've struggled with my identity my entire life, and it wasn't until I met Ed Griffin that I figured out who I was.

Throughout this novel, I've somewhat danced around the point that I've been trying to make. I apologize. I've taken the long route to get you to the end of a journey that originally started out as two men, one young old man and the other an old young man voicing their opinions of the Correctional System of Canada. I wanted my story to show the differences of both prison systems, plus provide you with a clear cut vision of how I went from self-absorbed to self-aware over the period of eight years. I hope you were entertained as well as enlightened.

When Ed and I first began this writing journey, we had completely different views on this system. We started out as opposites, he with the opinion that prison doesn't help men change, and I with the opinion that prison is the answer to change. Somehow, we both ended up wrong.

Writing has proven to be the greatest accomplishment I have ever made. Because of the creative writing class at Matsqui, I've learned that finally there's something in this world that I can depend on to make my life worth living other than the pursuit of money. I've learned about the impact words have on people. Every week in class, I read a chapter of this book to other convicts. People enjoy the stories of my time in Mexico and look forward to the next chapter. They go off and write their own stories, inspired to do something with themselves because of my own life turnaround. I became a *Griffinist* and didn't even know it.

Ed came into the prison looking to change men, make them revolt against the government and their rules, sabotage every ideal associated with the system. He failed miserably at his own hand. What he never intended to find was a group of people who desperately depended on the system to give them the answers they needed to be free men. What he never imagined was the profound impact he'd make on one man who was on the verge of self-destruction.

The common denominator here is writing. Writing and art changes lives. It gives people an outlet to express themselves in ways that a system won't provide. When the prison sits a group of convicts down in a classroom and proceeds to tell them how to think or act, it only makes them angrier. Art allows the man to think on his own terms, express himself in any way he feels is right. There's no right or wrong with art. It's like good medicine. It just works.

Prison is a relentless emotional struggle. Convicts struggle with the pain they've inflicted on their families, their victims, and themselves every day. Most politicians would like for the public to believe that we're all callous human beings without a trace of empathy, and that we need to be analyzed, scrutinized and ostracized for there to be any form of justice. I used to believe that prison could do a man some good if he needed time out from life to think about his role in our community, but what good is that time out if he isn't given a new path to travel down? During my time in prison, the only program or class I've seen that actually works is Creative Writing. Whether it's the activity that allows the men to vent, or it's Ed and his relentless reassurance, there's something there that's working. The prison system should look at it for some answers.

These days, Ed's become the bitter one. He deals with my hardships regarding prison worse than I do. I've learned that things take time, and parole hearings aren't for the better of society, but more so in the interest of job security (something I never would have admitted five years ago). Because of my experience, Ed's learned that the system, as backwards as it is, will never change. They'll just sit and listen to you cry and moan, then wait for you to tire or die. There's nothing in the world that will make prison change the way they handle criminals. I think Ed and I have both learned that the real fight comes at an individual level. The convict will change if he wants to, and if he wants to, he'll find that way.

The actual writing I produce isn't what changed my life. The fact that someone actually took the time to show me did. Ed's kindness and dedication to this craft made me see that I don't need a lot of money and fame to be a man, what I needed was a piece of mind that I'm doing something positive for myself, and in the future, everyone around me.

I'm going to go on and write movies and television shows and do what I can so Ed and I can sell some books. I've developed a talent for script writing and I'm not going to stop until I win an Oscar. I know that those are high expectations, but if I didn't have ambition, you wouldn't even know who I was.

ISBN 1425150039